CANALETTO & ENGLAND

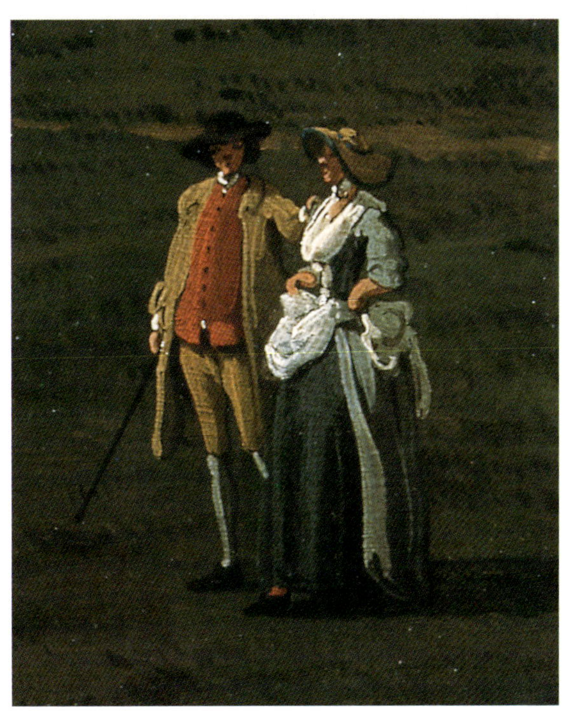

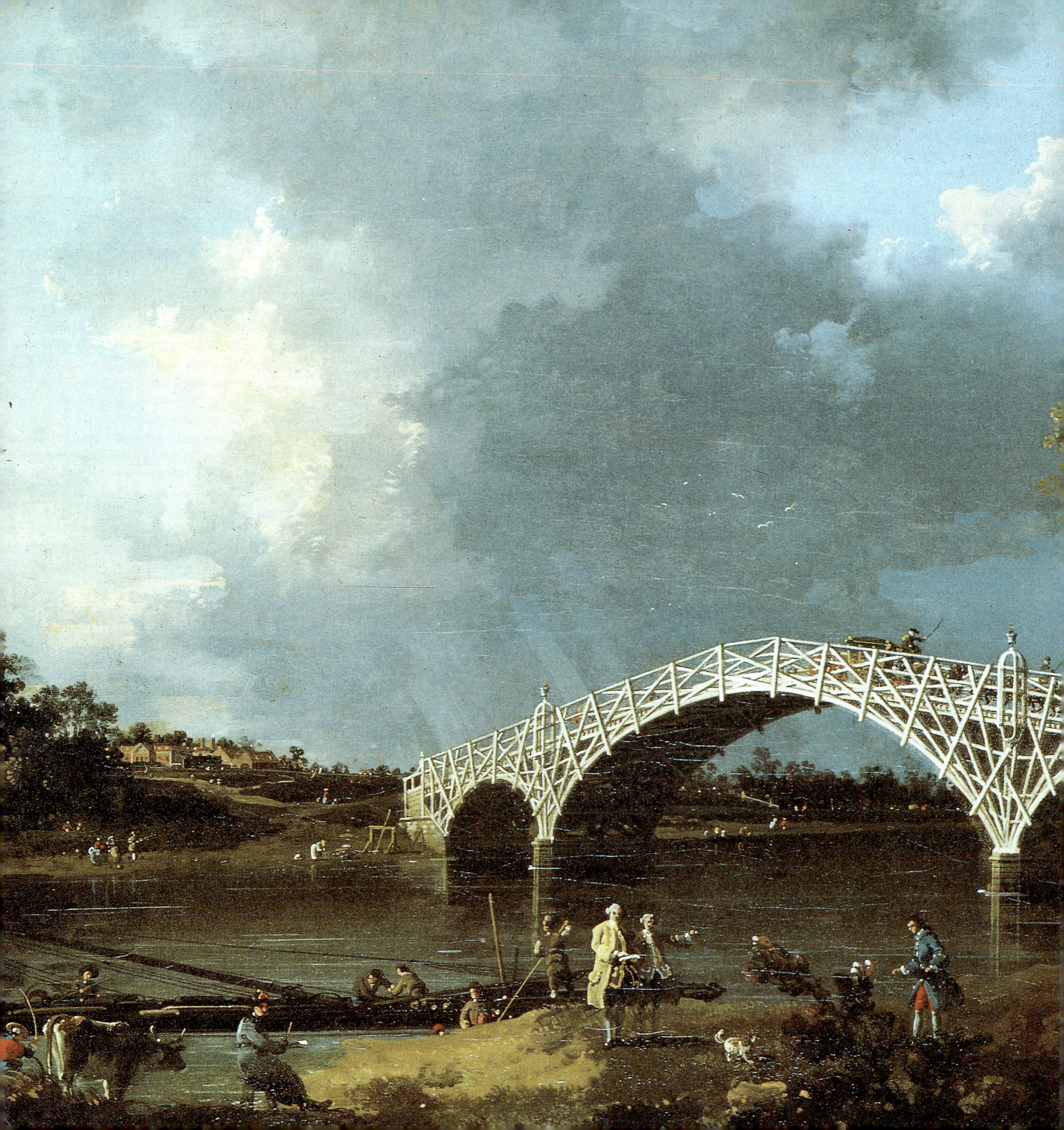

CANALETTO & ENGLAND

edited by Michael Liversidge and Jane Farrington

Birmingham Museums & Art Gallery

in association with

MERRELL HOLBERTON
PUBLISHERS LONDON

SPONSORED BY BRITISH GAS

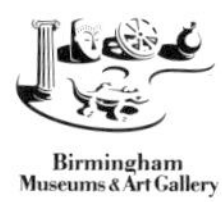 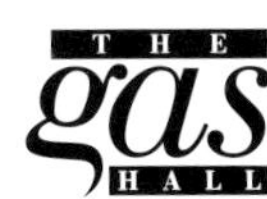

The catalogue accompanies the exhibition held at
Birmingham Gas Hall Exhibition Gallery 14 October 1993 –
9 January 1994

Copyright © 1993 Birmingham Museums and Art Gallery and
the authors of the essays and catalogue

First published in 1993
by Merrell Holberton Publishers Ltd
Axe & Bottle Court, 70 Newcomen Street, London SE1 1YT

All rights reserved

ISBN 1 85894 001 X [paperback]
ISBN 1 85894 002 8 [hardback]

Produced by Merrell Holberton
Designed by Roger Davies
Typeset by August Filmsetting, St Helens
Printed and bound by Graphicom, Vicenza, Italy

FRONT COVER ILLUSTRATION
Canaletto, *Warwick Castle: the east front from the outer court*
[cat. no. 23] (detail), Birmingham Museums and Art Gallery

BACK COVER ILLUSTRATION
J.M.W. Turner, *Warwick Castle and Bridge* [cat. no. 111],
Whitworth Art Gallery, University of Manchester

ENDPAPER
Canaletto, *Old Walton Bridge* (detail), pen and ink with grey
wash, 13 × 32 ins (33 × 81.2 cm), Yale Center for British Art
(Paul Mellon Collection), New Haven

FRONTISPIECE
Canaletto, *Old Walton Bridge* [cat. no. 35] (detail), Dulwich
Picture Gallery

PHOTOGRAPHIC CREDITS

All drawings from the Royal Library, Windsor Castle, are
Copyright 1993 Her Majesty The Queen
Photographs have been supplied by the Lenders. In addition there
are the following acknowledgements:
Lewis Photo Ltd. (cat. no. 43, Joseph Nickolls)
Paul Mellon Centre for British Studies, London (figs. 12, 28, 29,
Thomas Gainsborough, Samuel Wale, Edward Haytley)
Richard Green (fig. 11, Francesco Zuccarelli)
John Webb (figs. 4, 5, Canaletto; cat. no. 45, Scott)

CONTENTS

SPONSOR'S FOREWORD

British Gas is delighted to sponsor the *Canaletto & England* exhibition. The company has long believed in the importance of supporting the Arts. This exhibition gives the public the opportunity to see the best of Canaletto's English work and that of his contemporaries brought together under one roof for the first time. We hope that all those who visit this exhibition will find it an enlightening and enriching experience.

Canaletto & England is a significant sponsorship for British Gas. Many of our customers live in the West Midlands, where the exhibition is based, and we have many links with communities in the Region. We are pleased therefore to be making this contribution to the cultural life of the Region by sponsoring this exhibition – the opening event in the recently refurbished Gas Hall Exhibition Gallery.

There can be no doubt that the Gallery is destined to become a major source of pleasure to people from within and beyond the West Midlands. We have readily taken the opportunity to show our support through our sponsorship of this exciting exhibition.

CEDRIC BROWN FEng
Chief Executive, British Gas plc

DIRECTOR'S FOREWORD AND ACKNOWLEDGEMENTS

Canaletto & England is the first exhibition in Birmingham's new Gas Hall Exhibition Gallery. It opens just over a hundred years after the first Art Gallery in Chamberlain Square. The exhibitions held in the 1890s sought to give inspiration and enjoyment and those aims remain as important today for the Gas Hall's exhibition programme. It is a happy coincidence that the first Art Gallery was funded by the Gas Department. Now in 1993, British Gas plc has generously sponsored the opening exhibition in the grand interior of its former Gas Rates Hall.

The opening exhibition on Canaletto and his English paintings reveals another historic link with the Midlands and its past. In the mid eighteenth century, Canaletto travelled to Warwick to paint five views of the great fortified medieval castle – a building that he was to depict more times than any other in England. Two of those views are now part of the permanent collection of Birmingham Museums and Art Gallery and form a centrepiece in this exhibition.

We are greatly indebted to the many public and private lenders who have made this exhibition possible. Canaletto was in England for less than ten years. An exhibition which focuses on a comparatively small part of his achievement must rely heavily on the generosity of a few key lenders. I would particularly like to thank the Duke of Richmond and Gordon and the Trustees of Goodwood House, the Duke of Northumberland and the Trustees of Northumberland Estates, Viscount Coke and the Trustees of the Holkham Estate, the Dean and Chapter of Westminster, the Sir Andrew Lloyd Webber Art Foundation, the Governors of Dulwich Picture Gallery, and the Thyssen-Bornemisza Collection, Madrid. The exhibition has been selected in close collaboration with the art historian Michael Liversidge and we are greatly indebted to his scholarship and vision in bringing the project to completion. I would like to acknowledge the help and advice of J.G. Links and also thank the catalogue contributors and the publishers Hugh Merrell and Paul Holberton. The exhibition installation has been designed by Stanton Williams architects, who also have been responsible for the design of the Gas Hall itself. Wingate and Johnston Ltd have sponsored part of the transport costs and the Museums and Galleries Commission have put much time and effort into arranging insurance cover through the Government Indemnity Scheme. On my own staff, I would like to thank Jane Farrington, exhibition organizer and co-selector, Stephen Wildman, Lee Handley, Carl Turner, Ann Parker-Moule, David Buttery, Elizabeth Smallwood, Caroline Gant, Evelyn Silber, Lorraine Flanagan, Mik Barton and Rebecca Burkill. Finally, I would like to acknowledge the generous sponsorship of British Gas plc without which the exhibition would not have taken place.

MICHAEL DIAMOND
Director, Birmingham Museums and Art Gallery

THE GAS HALL EXHIBITION GALLERY DEVELOPMENT APPEAL

PATRON
The Rt Hon
The Earl of Aylesford

CHAIRMAN
Patrick Welch

VICE-CHAIRMAN
Sidney Roberts

FOUNDING PATRONS
Sir Anthony Beaumont-Dark
Sir Michael Bishop CBE
Kevin Butler
Sir Adrian Cadbury
Michael Cadbury DL
George Carter
The Viscountess Cobham DL
Michael Corbett

Lady Day
Ed Doolan
John Douglas OBE
Mark Fisher MP
Francis Graves OBE DL
Derek Inman
Simon Livingstone
Harish Patel

CORPORATE PATRONAGE
OF THE GAS HALL

GAS HALL PATRONS
British Gas plc
Grimmitt Holdings Ltd

GAS HALL ASSOCIATES
Canon (UK) Ltd
Hi-Lo Manufacturing Ltd

CORPORATE MEMBERS
BT
Kleinwort Benson Group plc
PowerGen plc
Tilbury Douglas Plc

The Gas Hall Appeal is indebted to the many organisations and individuals who have contributed so generously to the Exhibition Gallery Development, including:

Birmingham City Council □ European Regional Development Fund
Friends of Birmingham Museums and Art Gallery
Museums & Galleries Commission Capital Grants Scheme
Museums & Galleries Improvement Fund

Lord Austin Trust □ Bank of England □ Barrow & Geraldine S Cadbury Trust □ Birmingham Common Good Trust □ Sir Michael Bishop CBE
Conrad and Celia Blakey □ British Gas plc □ The Bryant Trust □ BT □ C L Cadbury Charitable Trust □ J and L A Cadbury Trust
Robin and Jayne Cadbury □ William A Cadbury Charitable Trust □ Cadbury Schweppes plc □ Canon (UK) Ltd
The George Henry Collins Charity □ Baron Davenport's Charity Trust □ Sir Graham and Lady Day □ The John Ellerman Foundation
Mr and Mrs William Ellis □ The Esmée Fairbairn Charitable Trust □ The John Feeney Charitable Trust □ Forest Investments Limited □ Forte Plc
The Charles Henry Foyle Trust □ The Sir Robert Gooch Charitable Trust □ Grimley Charity □ Grimmitt Holdings Ltd
Walter Higgs Charitable Trust □ Hi-Lo Manufacturing Ltd □ Hortons' Estate Limited □ Mrs Thelma Justham □ Charles and Tessa King-Farlow
Kleinwort Benson Group plc □ KPMG Peat Marwick □ The Laird Group Plc □ LJC Fund Limited □ S & D Lloyd Charity
The Henry Moore Foundation □ Oakdale Trust □ Ove Arup & Partners □ Bernard Piggott Trust □ The Pilgrim Trust □ PowerGen Plc
The Ratcliff Foundation □ Mr and Mrs Sidney Roberts □ C A Rookes Charitable Trust □ The Roughley Charitable Trust
The Royal Bank of Scotland plc □ Salamander Charitable Trust □ Stanley Smith Memorial Fund □ Councillor Renée Spector and Mr Cyril Spector
Mrs Hazel Stevens No. 2 Settlement □ Monica D. Sturge □ Sir John Sumner's Trust □ Tarmac PLC □ C B & H H Taylor Trust □ Tilbury Douglas Plc
Douglas Turner Trust □ The Eric W Vincent Trust Fund □ W E D Charitable Trust □ Wakefield Trust □ Mr and Mrs P W Welch
Welcodix Equipment Co Ltd □ Welconstruct Trust □ Wesleyan Assurance Society □ The Workman Trust
The Appeal is grateful also to its many other supporters, including anonymous donors. JULY 1993

The City of Birmingham Museums and Art Gallery Development Trust (Gas Hall Appeal Fund): Registered Charity No. 701785

LENDERS

Her Majesty The Queen [cat. nos. 7, 15, 16, 17, 59, 62, 63, 64]

The Visitors of the Ashmolean Museum, Oxford [cat. nos. 39, 80]
A.H. Baldwin & Sons Ltd [cat. no. 104]
The Governor and Company of the Bank of England [cat. no. 42]
Bath, Victoria Art Gallery [cat. nos. 92, 93, 94]
Bedford, Cecil Higgins Art Gallery [cat. no. 99]
Birmingham Museums and Art Gallery [cat. nos. 1, 23, 24, 60, 67, 68, 77, 81, 82, 87, 90, 96, 100, 102, 103, 106, 120, 126]
Bolton Museum and Art Gallery [cat. no. 98]
Bristol Museums and Art Gallery [cat. nos. 40, 47]
Cardiff, National Museum of Wales [cat. no. 70]
Viscount Coke and the Trustees of the Holkham Estate [cat. nos. 2, 3]
Dublin, National Gallery of Ireland [cat. no. 114]
The Governors of Dulwich Picture Gallery [cat. no. 35]
The Provost and Fellows of Eton College [cat. nos. 61, 121, 122]
The Fishmongers' Company [cat. no. 49]
The Syndics of the Fitzwilliam Museum, Cambridge [cat. no. 89]
Sir Brinsley Ford, CBE, Hon FRA, FSA [cat. nos. 55, 56, 65, 66]
Gloucester City Museums [cat. no. 84]
Trustees of Goodwood House [cat. nos. 9, 12]
Harari & Johns Ltd [cat. no. 41]
Liverpool, Trustees of the National Museums & Galleries on Merseyside (Walker Art Gallery) [cat. nos. 85, 86]
London, the Trustees of the British Museum [cat. nos. 8, 20, 26, 32, 33, 34, 54, 88, 108, 109, 117]
London, the Guildhall Art Gallery [cat. nos. 46, 71, 75]
London, the Museum of London [cat. nos. 50, 74]
London, the Trustees of the National Gallery [cat. no. 36]
London, the National Maritime Museum, Greenwich [cat. no. 30]
London, the Trustees of the Tate Gallery [cat. nos. 48, 76, 115, 116, 124]
London, the Trustees of the Victoria & Albert Museum [cat. nos. 58, 78, 95, 118]
Midland Bank plc [cat. no. 51]
The National Trust, Tatton Park (The Egerton Collection) [cat. nos. 4, 5]
National Westminster Bank Collection [cat. no. 43]
New York, The Metropolitan Museum of Art [cat. nos. 25, 44]
The Duke of Northumberland [cat. no. 6]
City of Nottingham Museums: Castle Museum [cat. nos. 83, 125]
Plymouth City Museum and Art Gallery [cat. no. 69]
Private Collections [cat. nos. 10, 11, 13, 14, 21, 28, 29, 31, 45, 105, 110, 123]
Sheffield City Art Galleries [cat. no. 119]
The Thyssen-Bornemisza Collection, Madrid [cat. no. 22]
Truro, The Royal Institution of Cornwall, The Royal Cornwall Museum [cat. no. 97]
Rafael Valls Ltd [cat. no. 57]
Washington, the National Gallery of Art [cat. nos. 37, 38]
Sir Andrew Lloyd Webber Art Foundation [cat. no. 19]
The Dean and Chapter of Westminster [cat. no. 27]
The Whitworth Art Gallery, University of Manchester [cat. nos. 53, 79, 111, 112, 113]
Worcester City Museum & Art Gallery [cat. no. 72]
Yale Center for British Art, Paul Mellon Collection [cat. nos. 18, 73, 91, 101, 107, 127]

Canaletto and England

M.J.H. LIVERSIDGE

For the history of eighteenth-century English painting the notebooks in which the engraver George Vertue assiduously chronicled the affairs of London's art world and recorded his own observations over a period of some forty years from 1713 until 1754 are an indispensable source of information, anecdote and critical comment.[1] In the early summer of 1746 Vertue noted that:

Latter end of May. came to London from Venice the Famous Painter of Views Cannalletti […] of Venice. the Multitude of his works done abroad for English noblemen & Gentlemen has proc-urd him great reputation & his great merrit & excellence in that way, he is much esteemed and no doubt but what Views and works He doth here, will give the same satisfaction — tho' many persons already have so many of his paintings.[2]

In another entry he made a few months later Vertue adds some more information about what may have prompted Canaletto's arrival in England:

Signor Canaletti (a sober man turnd of 50) a Venetian painter of Views came to London — as he had done at Venice many nay multi-tudes of paintings for English Noble & Gentlemen and great num-bers bought by dealers & sold here gave him a desire to come to England. being persuaded to it by Sig[nor] Amiconi History painter at his return to Venice coud best acquainted him with his success here. and also of the prospects he might make of Views on the Thames at London. of them he has begun some views. its said he has already made himself easy in his fortune and likewise that had brought most part to putt into the Stocks here for better security. or better interest than abroad — or that of late few persons travel to Italy from hence during the wars.[3]

Whether or not Canaletto actually brought with him money to invest in London remains unknown: certainly, however, he had been a successful painter since the early 1720s, enjoying a lucrative business supplying views of Venice to a clientele that included a high proportion of British patrons, and there is some evidence to suggest that he was financially shrewd in his deal-ings with agents and collectors who bought his paintings. In the 1740s, though, the market for Canaletto's Venetian scenes was much less buoyant than it had been. There were fewer foreign visitors to Venice after 1742 when the War of the Austrian Succession spilled over into Italy and the English Grand Tourists who had been so important to Canaletto's success mostly avoided the region. At the same time Canaletto's business was adversely affected by the consequences of his own success. The competition from imitators, copyists and rival view-painters which he had encouraged by his example was one factor; another was Canaletto's own previous exploitation of the market so that his customers already had as many of his Venetian subjects as they wanted. For these reasons Canaletto had already turned to new subjects and to making etchings in the 1740s in an endeavour to restore his fortunes.[4] It is in this context, too, that his move to London in 1746 can be explained.

The "Signor Amiconi" who, George Vertue suggests, persuaded Canaletto to leave for England because he knew of his reputation there and told him about the prospects (in both senses, perhaps) which London offered a view-painter was the painter Jacopo Amigoni. He had worked for ten years in England, from 1729 until 1739, decorating the interiors of London and country houses with histories and mythologies done in the Venetian rococo manner and also painting portraits. Before Amigoni there had been other Venetians doing similar work in England: Giovanni Antonio Pellegrini during the years 1708–13, Marco Ricci (1708–16) and his uncle Sebastiano Ricci (1712–16), and Antonio Bellucci (1716–22). Canaletto's view-paintings are, of course, completely different to anything these earlier visitors had done in England, but their experience may have encouraged him to believe that as another Venetian painter he would find new patrons among those who were familiar with his compatriots' work. He must also have been aware that landscape paintings by Marco Ricci and another artist working in Venice, Francesco Zuccarelli, appealed to English collectors.[5] It is very likely as well that Canaletto knew Antonio Joli who had established himself in London soon after leaving Venice where he had worked from 1735 until 1742. Joli painted scenery for the theatre, but he was also a view-painter whose style imitates Canaletto's. After leaving Venice he worked briefly in Germany before coming to London where he stayed until 1749. He was the scene-painter at the King's Theatre in the Haymarket from 1744 to 1748 and also painted many London views [see cat. nos. 41 and 42].[6]

There were, therefore, strong links between English patrons and Venetian painters. Canaletto himself had been working for the English — visitors to Venice and agents acting on behalf of

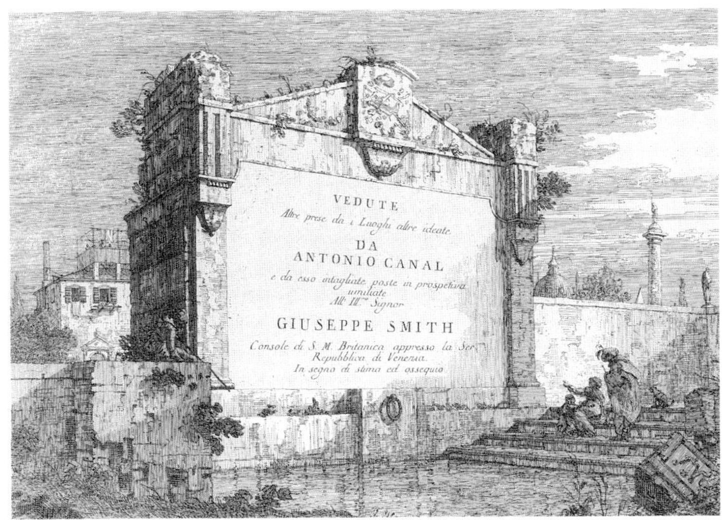

Fig. 1 Canaletto, frontispiece to the album *VEDUTE Altre prese da i Luoghi altre ideate da Antonio Canal* (Views taken from actual sites and others from the imagination), etching, $4\frac{3}{8} \times 6\frac{3}{8}$ ins (11.1 × 16.1 cm)

collectors in England — for twenty years before departing for London in 1746. The earliest record of an English patron of Canaletto's occurs in a letter written from Venice on 8 March 1726 by an Irishman, Owen McSwiney, to the second Duke of Richmond about two *capricci* of imaginary landscapes and architecture with allegorical tombs commemorating British worthies, for which Canaletto painted the "perspective and landscape" in collaboration with another artist, Giovanni Battista Cimaroli; in each picture the figures were contributed by a third painter, in one by Giovanni Battista Piazzetta [cat. no. 1] and in the other by Giovanni Battista Pittoni.[7]

Owen McSwiney is one of the more colourful characters among Canaletto's British contacts. He had been forced to leave London for the Continent in 1711 to escape his creditors after failing as a theatrical impresario (earlier he had been an actor and had also written plays). By 1721 he had recovered sufficiently to set himself up in business again and was procuring Italian singers and operas for the London stage and had also diversified into the art world, acting as a dealer and agent for British collectors for whom he bought and commissioned pictures. It may have been his connections with the theatre that first brought him into contact with the young Canaletto, whose father Bernardo Canal was a scenery painter and had

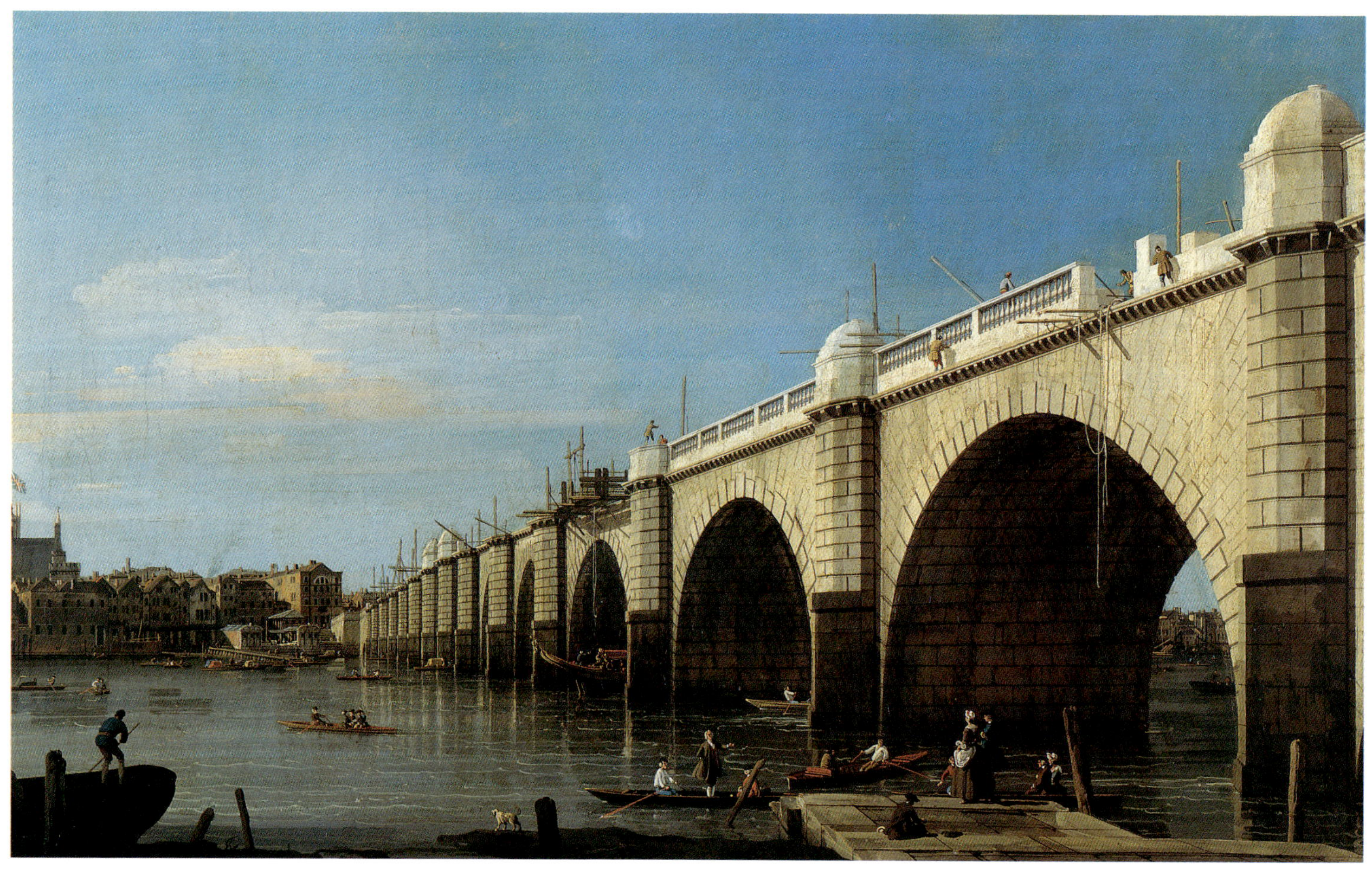

Fig. 2 Canaletto, *Westminster Bridge under construction, from the south-east*, oil on canvas, 23 × 37½ ins (58.5 × 95 cm), Collection of the Duke of Northumberland

devised the settings for operas by Vivaldi in Venice and Alessandro Scarlatti in Rome. Antonio Canal, who became known by the diminutive Canaletto to distinguish him from his father, is recorded professionally for the first time in Rome in 1720 where he was Bernardo's assistant in designing the scenery for productions of two of Scarlatti's operas. Something of Canaletto's early association with the theatre can be detected in the fanciful architecture of the two tomb *capricci* mentioned in McSwiney's letter to the Duke of Richmond in 1726. However the initial contact was made, it was McSwiney's patronage that established the close connection between Canaletto and England which lasted for almost the whole of his working life.

By 1725 Canaletto was already acknowledged as the lead-ing exponent of view-painting in Venice. A flourishing tradition of specialist *vedute* or view paintings had developed there, as in other Italian cities, over the previous twenty to thirty years. Very little is known about his emergence as a topographical artist in the early 1720s, but the quality of his work – especially his brilliantly original way of suggesting light – quickly established his supremacy and transformed the genre. As a contemporary put it in a letter written in 1725, Canaletto's paintings were far superior to those of Luca Carlevaris (the originator of Venetian *vedute* and until the 1720s the principal practitioner), and were astonishing everyone who saw them because in each picture "you can see the sun shining in it". The same writer added that Canaletto is "a remarkable landscape painter, whose works are in great demand here and in London … with a style very much of his own and a very perfected manner".[8] The letter suggests that Canaletto may already have supplied view-paintings to English buyers: if that is so, they would probably have been ordered through Owen McSwiney. Certainly he was responsible for obtaining from the painter the first of his Venetian scenes to enter an English collection for which there is surviving documentation. In a letter to the Duke of Richmond dated 28 November 1727 McSwiney reports on the progress made on some of the allegorical tomb pictures and goes on to discuss four view-paintings by Canaletto which he was supplying; the letter also mentions two more views previously obtained for another English client:

The pieces which Mr. Southwell has, (of Canals painting) were done for me, and they cost me 70 sequeens. The fellow is whimsical and vary's his prices every day: and he that has a mind to have any of his work, must not seem to be too fond of it, for he'l be ye worse treated for it, both in the price and in the painting too. He has more work than he can doe, in any reasonable time, and well: but by the assistance of a particular friend of his, I get once in two months a piece sketch'd out and a little time after finished, by force of bribery.

I send yr Grace by Captain Robinson […] who sails from hence tomorrow, Two of the Finest pieces, I think he ever painted and of the same size with Mr. Southwell's little ones (which is a size he

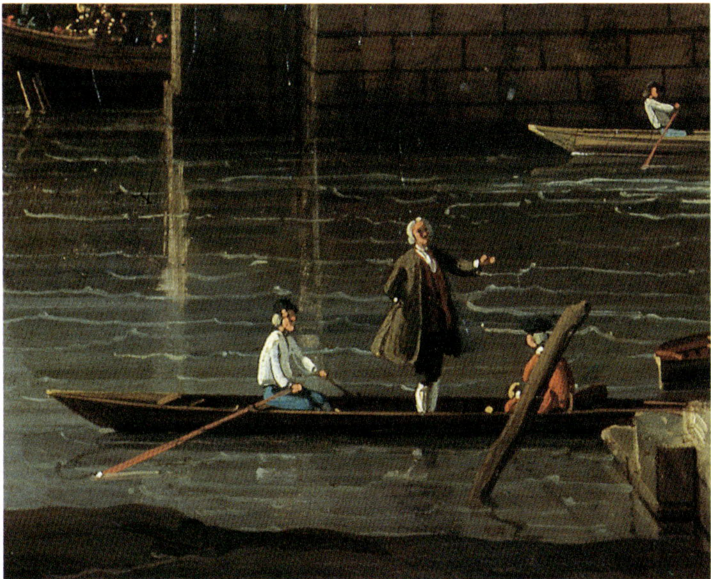

excells in) and are done upon copper plates: They cost me two and twenty sequeens each. They'l be delivered to yr Grace by Mr. John Smith, as soon as they arrive in London.

I shall have a view of the Rialto Bridge, done by Canal in twenty days, and I have bespoke another view of Venice for the by and by, his Excellence lyes in painting things which fall immediately under his eye.[9]

McSwiney's letter vividly reveals his entrepreneurial role as an agent handling Canaletto's paintings, more or less placing a standing order for pictures which he then sold on to clients; at the same time he was probably also acting as an intermediary between the artist and British buyers, both visitors to Venice and other collectors at home.

Something of Canaletto's personality comes across, too, in McSwiney's correspondence. With his paintings so much in demand he could be difficult to deal with, and with so many orders to fulfil his pictures could sometimes seem mechanically repetitious. McSwiney says as much in a letter to John Conduitt in 1730:

I'm glad you have given ye commission to Mr. Smith for yr pictures of Canaletto, & I hope you'l like 'em when they are done; I am, it may be, a little too delicate in my choice, for of Twenty pieces I see of him, I don't like eighteen & I have seen several, sent to London yt I wou'd not give house room to […] He's a covetous, greedy fellow & as he's in reputation people are glad to get anything at his own price.

In the same letter he mentions six Canalettos supplied by himself (the Richmond and Southwell pairs, and two views bought for Sir William Morice) which, he says, "… are in his buon gusto – nay, compare these with any other you know & you'l soon discern ye difference".[10] These letters are generally cited as evidence of Canaletto's capricious temperament and commercial instinct for making money to the detriment of his art. While there is no doubt some truth in all this, McSwiney may have had another purpose in cultivating the impression he gives of the artist: by encouraging the belief that Canaletto was difficult to handle and could not always be trusted to do his best work for a patron without recourse to an agent such as himself he might keep more of what was becoming a profitable business in his own hands. Trading as he was in cultural commodities between Venice and London, capital cities with two of the most vibrant mercantile econo-

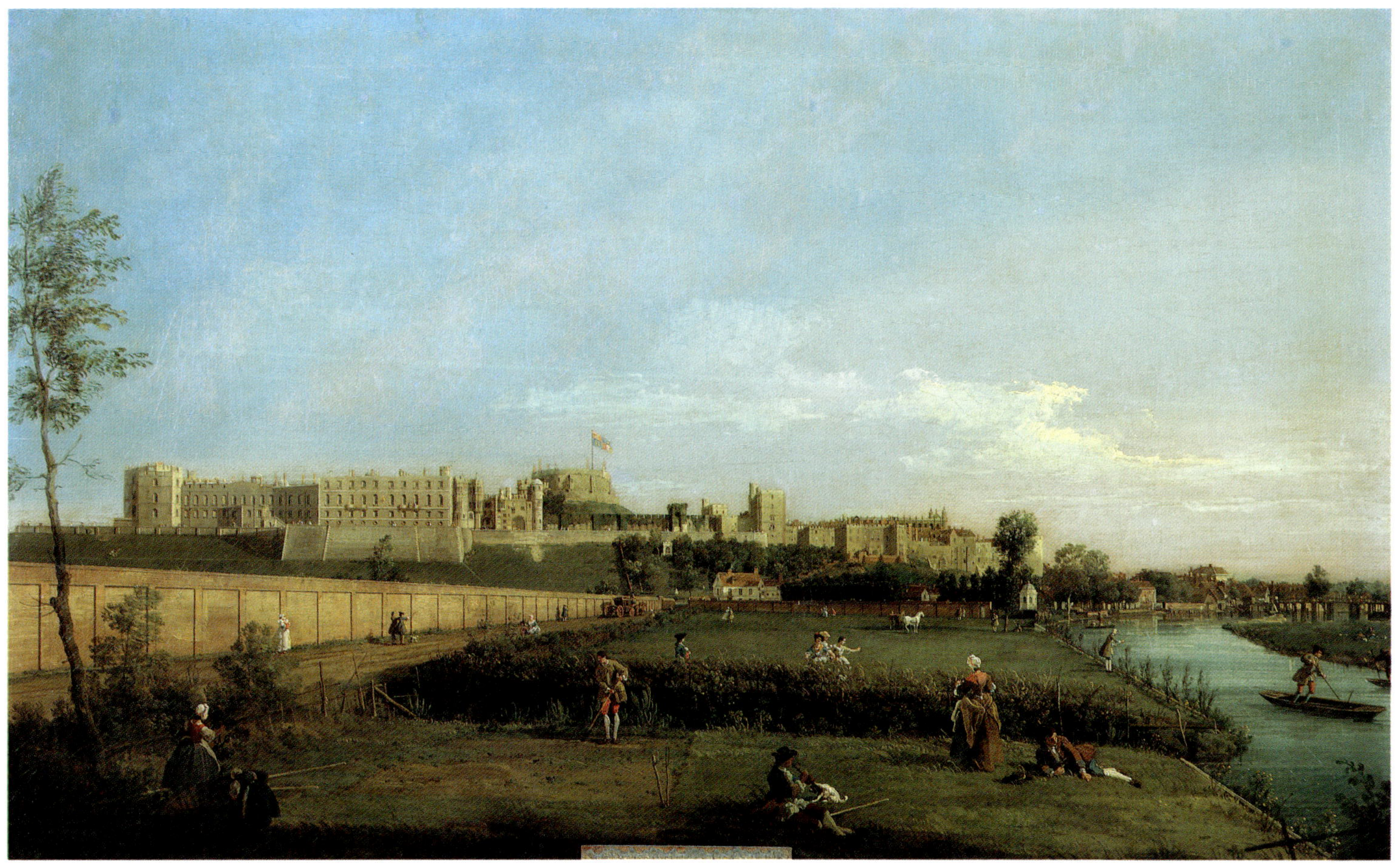

Fig. 3 Canaletto, *Windsor Castle*, oil on canvas, 33 × 54 ins (84 × 137 cm),
Collection of the Duke of Northumberland

mies in eighteenth-century Europe, he clearly knew how to exploit the market forces of supply and demand.

McSwiney was not the only British resident in Venice with a commercial interest in Canaletto's work. References in his letters to John Smith in London and John's brother Joseph Smith in Venice show that he was closely involved with other prominent figures among the merchants engaged in Anglo-Venetian trade. Joseph Smith in particular was to become not only the most important agent supplying Canaletto paintings to the English from the early 1730s but also the most prolific and constant personal collector of the artist's work. Over a period of some thirty years he acquired an unrivalled collection of his paintings, drawings and etchings which eventually, in 1762, he sold (along with many more fine eighteenth-century Venetian pictures and a number of earlier works as well) to George III. Altogether there were fifty-two paintings (more than half of Venice, but including five of architectural antiquities in Rome, two magisterial London scenes, and a number of picturesque *capricci* of which thirteen are from a set of twenty-four overdoors), over one hundred and forty drawings, and forty-six etchings which included the set of thirty-one plates comprising the *Vedute Altre prese da i Luoghi altre ideate* (Views taken from actual sites and others from imagination) dedicated on the title sheet to Joseph Smith [fig. 1] which were issued as a collection just before Canaletto left for England in 1746.[11]

Joseph Smith very likely became the principal point of contact between English collectors and Canaletto at least from 1733 when McSwiney left Venice (he went initially to Dublin, and was back in London by 1737) and possibly earlier. Smith had settled in Venice at the beginning of the 1700s and by 1709 was well established as a merchant; his business, which included financial dealings, flourished and he lived in considerable style, leasing and eventually buying a substantial palace on the Grand Canal as well as owning a smart villa at Mogliano on the mainland. He became an avid collector of contemporary Venetian paintings, but he had many other interests besides: opera and the theatre (Goldoni dedicated one of his plays to him), antiquarian studies, collecting books and also publishing. He was certainly acting as an agent securing Canaletto paintings for English clients by 1730, and had acquired his first works by the artist for himself shortly before then. Probably it was through McSwiney that the association began since the Irishman was living in Smith's household in the 1720s. At any rate, in 1730 Smith was writing to Samuel Hill of Sherstone Park in Staffordshire that:

At last I've got Canal under articles to finish your 2 peices within a twelvemonth; he's so much follow'd and all are so ready to pay him his own price for his work [...] that he would be thought in this to have much obliged me, nor is it the first time I have been glad to submitt to a painter's impertinence to serve myself and friends, for besides that resentment is lost upon them, a rupture with such as are excellent in their profession resolves 'em either not to work for you at all, or which is worse, one gets from them only slight and labour'd productions [...].[12]

The two pieces are now at Tatton Park [cat. nos. 4 and 5]. In the same year Smith supplied two more Canalettos to another client in Ireland.[13] What was to become one of the most productive artist-agent and painter-patron relationships of the eighteenth century with profound consequences for the development of English topographical painting had begun its course. Over the next few years Joseph Smith undoubtedly used every opportunity to find buyers to commission views through him: his phrase "to serve myself" is a very apt one. Although the extent of Smith's 'exploitation' of Canaletto has been questioned in the absence of extensive documentary evidence, contemporaries certainly believed that he was a major buyer and supplier of the artist's work. Thus, in 1736 Count Tessin from Stockholm wrote after a visit to Venice of Canaletto "having been engaged for four years exclusively for an English merchant called Smith", and Horace Walpole (who met him in Venice in 1741) noted that "Mr Smith engaged him to work for him for many years at a very low price & sold his works to the English at much higher rates".[14] Since almost every English Grand Tourist of quality who went to Venice seems to have visited Smith's house it seems perfectly natural to assume that they would have arranged to buy their souvenir views through the one Englishman resident there who was in close and constant contact with the painter. His own collection of Canaletto's pictures may well have served as an encouragement to place orders, not least because it demonstrated the quality of work that could be obtained through Smith. Furthermore, since Canaletto was apparently inundated with work throughout the 1730s it probably needed a reliable local agent to negotiate orders, oversee the completion of commissions, process payments and handle shipping arrangements; alternatively, Smith may have carried a selection of pictures he had bought for resale and thus provided a more convenient way to purchase paintings. Since by the 1730s copies and imitations of Canaletto were beginning to proliferate in Venice, buying through Smith also offered a guarantee of authenticity.

The volume of business that Canaletto received from British patrons in the 1730s was impressive. A measure of the scale of his output for the English is provided by two remarkable sets of paintings: twenty-four for the fourth Duke of Bedford, probably ordered in 1731 when the patron was touring Italy (now at Woburn Abbey, but originally hung in Bedford House, London); and another twenty-two paintings which probably the statesman George Grenville first bought and which subsequently descended to the Harveys of Langley Park.[15] Other English collectors had smaller numbers of Canaletto pictures. The fourth Duke of Leeds reportedly bought four through Smith (and possibly more, if he was the original purchaser of all eleven sold from the Leeds collection in 1920). The Countess of Essex commissioned six of which four are referred to by Smith in a letter to Lord Essex in 1734: "By the force of a Constant reminding Canal of his engagement to serve Lady Essex I have made him sett aside some other work ... of much less Importance to me and apply all his skill to finish the four Peices she Commission'd me to procure for her and att last I have gott them and they are gone by a ship sail'd this week for London ...."[16]

There must have been many more which cannot any longer be connected directly with Smith. In 1735 he published a collection of engravings by another Venetian artist, Antonio Visentini, reproducing twelve of the Grand Canal pictures he owned. The series, entitled *Prospectus Magni Canalis Venetiarum*, served to advertise Canaletto's work more widely and attracted orders for painted versions of the views reproduced in the plates; and the sale of the prints individually or in sets was presumably itself another means of profiting from Canaletto's work.[17] The venture was evidently successful: not only is there a large number of painted versions, but a new enlarged edition with thirty-eight plates was published in 1742 and reissued in 1751. All the additional prints are of paintings that had been through Smith's hands, but whereas the original fourteen pictures were still in his collection when it was sold only one of the twenty-four newly illustrated works passed to George III in 1762.

The 1742 and 1751 editions of the *Prospectus* (the later reissue being re-titled *Urbis Venetiarum Prospectus Celebriores ex Antonii Canal Tabulis*) were probably published to make up for the decline in orders that followed the outbreak of war on the Continent. Fewer English tourists coupled to the fact that there were so many Canalettos already in England meant that both artist and agent-patron were encouraged to explore new possibilities. One result of this interlude was the set of thirty-one vividly spontaneous and picturesquely expressive etchings which Canaletto produced in the 1740s and which were published as a set with the title-page bearing a dedication to "Signor GIUSEPPE SMITH Console di S.M. Britanica" [fig. 1].[18] Since Joseph Smith was not appointed British Consul in Venice until June 1744 it is generally assumed that the etchings were issued shortly before Canaletto's departure for London in 1746. The dedication might signify more than the esteem and gratitude the artist owed his patron: Smith may have sponsored the project financially, perhaps hoping to profit from the market in original prints which was rapidly expanding in both Venice and London. Certainly he continued to support Canaletto by commissioning paintings for his own collection in the 1740s; as well as some more Venetian views, he ordered a group of five large Roman scenes, and a set of decorative architectural caprices showing famous buildings in Venice "elegantly Historiz'd with Figures and Adjacencys to the Painter's Fancy".[19] At the same time he was also buying drawings.

It was Joseph Smith, too, who arranged for Canaletto's introduction to English patrons on his arrival in London in 1746. Their old associate Owen McSwiney was pressed into service again, this time to bring him to the notice once more of the same Duke of Richmond who had been the first English client known to buy anything by Canaletto. On 20 May 1746 the Duke's former tutor Thomas Hill wrote to him after meeting McSwiney:

The only news I know to send to you, is what I had this day from Swiney at the Duke of Montagu's, where we dined, & he, I think, got almost drunk. Canales, alias Canaletti, is come over with a letter of recommendation from our old acquaintance the Consul of Venice to Mac in order to [effect] his introduction to your Grace, as a patron of the politer parts, or what the Italians understand by the name of *virtu*. I told him I thought the best service I thought you could do him w[d] be to let him draw a view of the river from y[r] dining room, which in my opinion would give him as much reputation as any of his Venetian prospects.[20]

In due course, but not until 1747, Canaletto painted two views from Richmond House in Whitehall for the Duke (*The Thames and the City of London* and *Whitehall and the Privy Garden* [cat. nos. 12 and 9]). They are masterpieces of topographical painting, unsurpassed in Canaletto's œuvre. As Ellis Waterhouse has written of them, he "never painted better pictures in his life. The enchantment of the Venetian sunshine was still upon him, the weather when he was painting them must have been fine, and the two most sparkling views of London that have ever been achieved were produced, sprinkled with little figures as alive and full of London character as his Venetian figures had been alive with *genius loci*."[21] They are paintings in which Canaletto has responded to the refreshing stimulus of a new subject, applying to his representation of the London scene the same qualities of precise observation and luminous brilliance that he had perfected in his earlier views of Venice. Their clear light, crisp drawing and enlivening detail are without precedent in England.

Before he painted the Duke of Richmond's pair Canaletto had already completed several London views. They are all river scenes which with one exception include the new Westminster Bridge which was nearing completion in 1746 and would have opened in 1747 had not one of the piers settled, making it necessary to dismantle and rebuild two of the arches

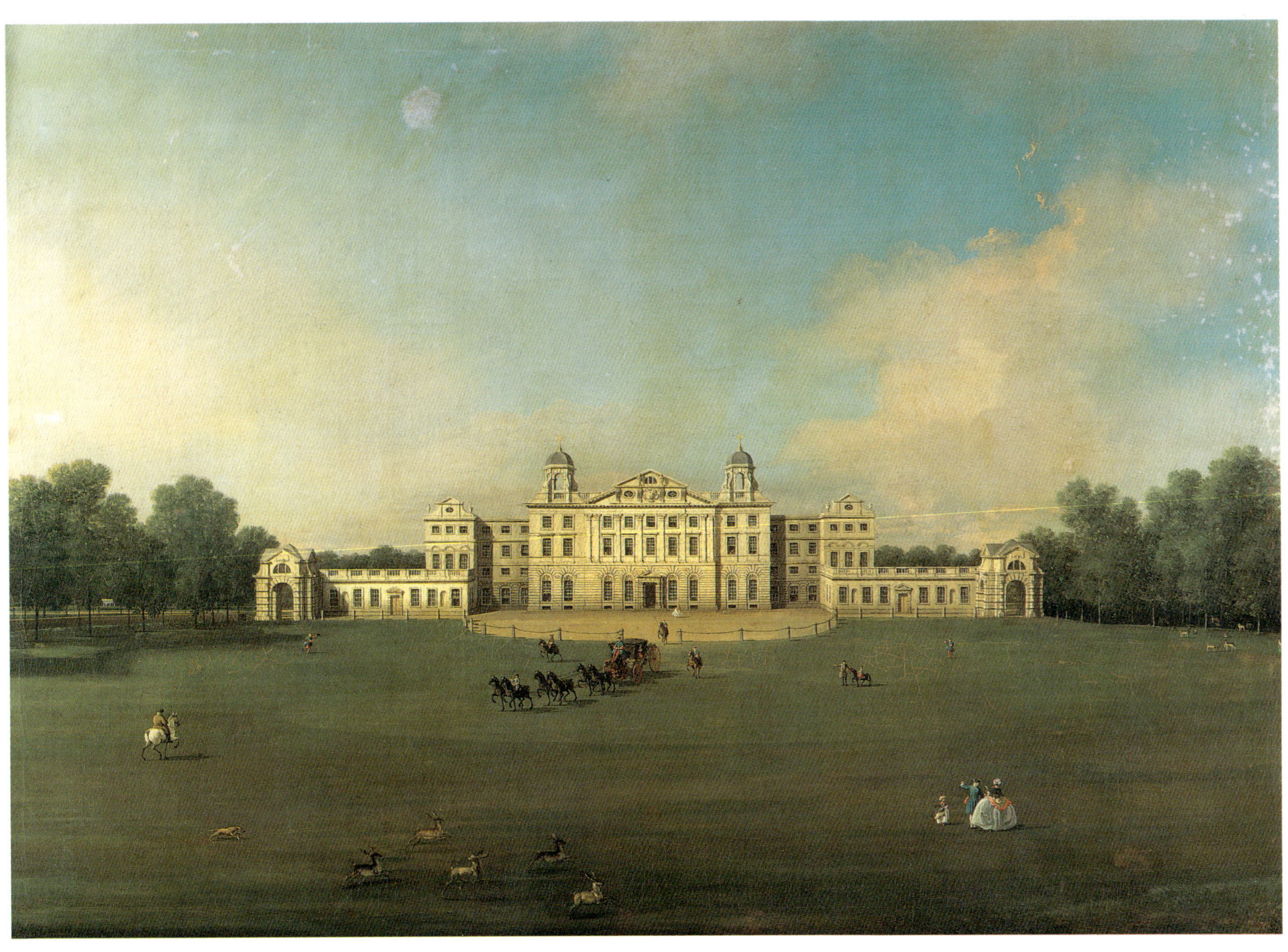

Fig. 4 Canaletto, *Badminton House from the park*, oil on canvas, $33\frac{3}{4} \times 48$ ins (85.7×122 cm),
Collection of the Duke of Beaufort

so that the project was not finished until 1750. The two most striking of Canaletto's first London pictures, both done in 1746–47, were painted for Sir Hugh Smithson, one of the Commissioners responsible for the scheme. One shows *London seen through an arch of Westminster Bridge* [cat. no. 6], the view of the Thames towards the City dramatically framed by the arc of wooden centring; the other, of *Westminster Bridge under construction from the south-east* [fig. 2], is no less powerful as an image with the brightly illuminated stonework of the bridge shown sharply foreshortened into the picture.[22] Both pictures were very influential, introducing a novel pictorial approach which later English painters made use of: the view through the arch of a bridge is a device found from Samuel Scott in the 1740s onwards through to the nineteenth century, and the acute recession of the other composition recurs from William Marlow to J.M.W. Turner and beyond. The arch motif would have been well known at least from 1747 when an engraving of Canaletto's painting was published, but the qualities of light and clarity which characterize both pictures were transmitted directly to Samuel Scott and his pupil William Marlow who both worked for Smithson and would have known the originals. The 1747 engraving of *London seen through an arch of Westminster Bridge* [fig. 14] bore a dedication to Sir Hugh Smithson which must have promoted Canaletto's reputation with potential patrons. Smithson had married Lady Elizabeth Seymour who was heiress to the Percy estates and in 1750 he succeeded to the Earldom of Northumberland when her father, the seventh Duke of Somerset, died; in 1766 he was created Duke of Northumberland. First as Sir Hugh Smithson and then as Earl of Northumberland he was one of Canaletto's major patrons in England, eventually owning six paintings: the two Westminster Bridge pictures, a *View of Windsor Castle* (1747) [fig. 3], and views of three of his properties, *Syon House, Middlesex* (1749), *Alnwick Castle, Northumberland* (1752) [fig. 7], and *Northumberland House, London* (1752 or 1753) [fig. 8], all still in the Northumberland collection.

For the first two years he was in England Canaletto painted and drew almost exclusively London views for which evidently there was a ready market. Before 1748 there is only one view done further afield, of Windsor Castle for Sir Hugh Smithson [fig. 3]. In 1748 he began to paint a new type of picture which corresponds to a category of topographical subject, the 'country house portrait' or estate view, which was well estab-

lished in contemporary English painting. The Duke of Beaufort commissioned two canvases of his Gloucestershire seat, *Badminton House from the park* and *Badminton Park from the house* [figs. 4 and 5], which are usually dated 1748, and for Lord Brooke (Lady Smithson's cousin) Canaletto painted two views of *Warwick Castle: the south front* [cat. no. 22] which were paid for in July 1748 and a third of the same subject for which payment was made in March 1749.[23] These have the even, luminous tonality that is typical of Canaletto's English pictures, with bright accents of local colour supplied by the figures which add life to the scene. The view of Badminton Park is remarkable for the wide expanse of its relatively featureless prospect. At Badminton there had been recent improvements carried out to the house and park, and at Warwick Lord Brooke was engaged in alterations and landscaping work: the patrons presumably commissioned these views to display their status as well as their taste, and their concern was more with accurate delineation than pictorial effect.

It is not always easy to be certain precisely when Canaletto's English paintings and drawings were done, but between his arrival in 1746 and the summer of 1749 something like eighteen paintings were produced of which twelve are London views. Two Westminster Bridge paintings had been engraved, both in 1747. Drawings are more difficult to calculate: perhaps a few were made for sale, but there is no reliable evidence except in the case of one of the south front of Warwick Castle for which Canaletto received 10 guineas in 1748. The prices of only three paintings from this period are known: two Warwick Castle pictures cost £58 in July 1748, the third 30 guineas (£31–10–0) in March 1749. Not all the paintings can have been so cheap: a pair of very large London views each nearly eight feet wide bought by a visiting Bohemian nobleman, Prince Lobkowicz, would have brought much more (a similarly sized painting by Canaletto was estimated at £60–£70 by George Vertue in 1751), but even so total sales cannot have amounted to a great deal.

A rather curious but very revealing entry in Vertue's notebook for June 1749 explains why Canaletto was not attracting as much business after three years as might be expected. Apparently some of London's art dealers were putting it about that his English pictures were less accomplished than his Venetian views and were even insinuating that not everything which came from his studio was entirely from his own hand. It

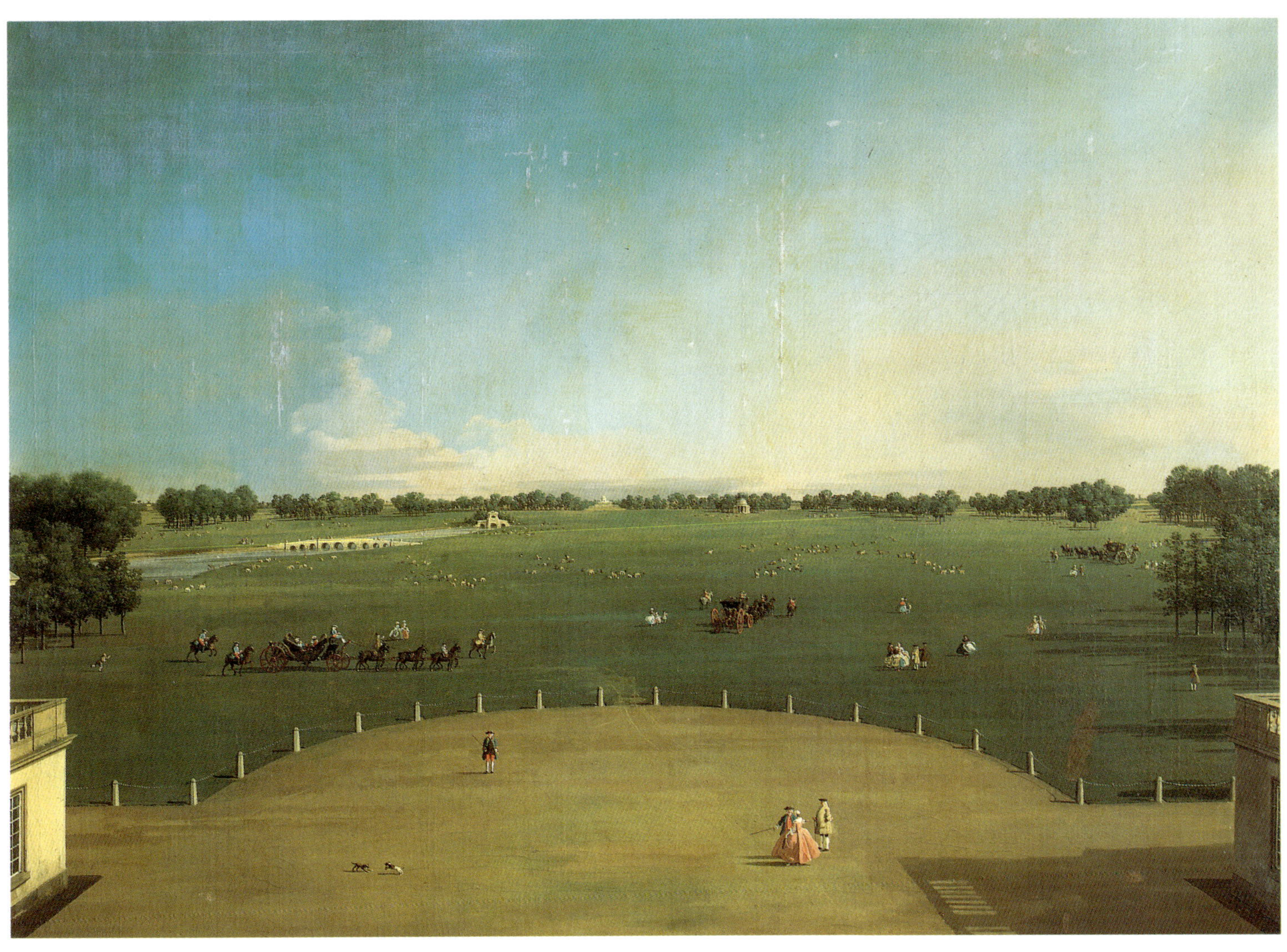

Fig. 5 Canaletto, *Badminton Park from the house*, oil on canvas, $33\frac{1}{2} \times 48$ ins (85.1×122 cm),
Collection of the Duke of Beaufort

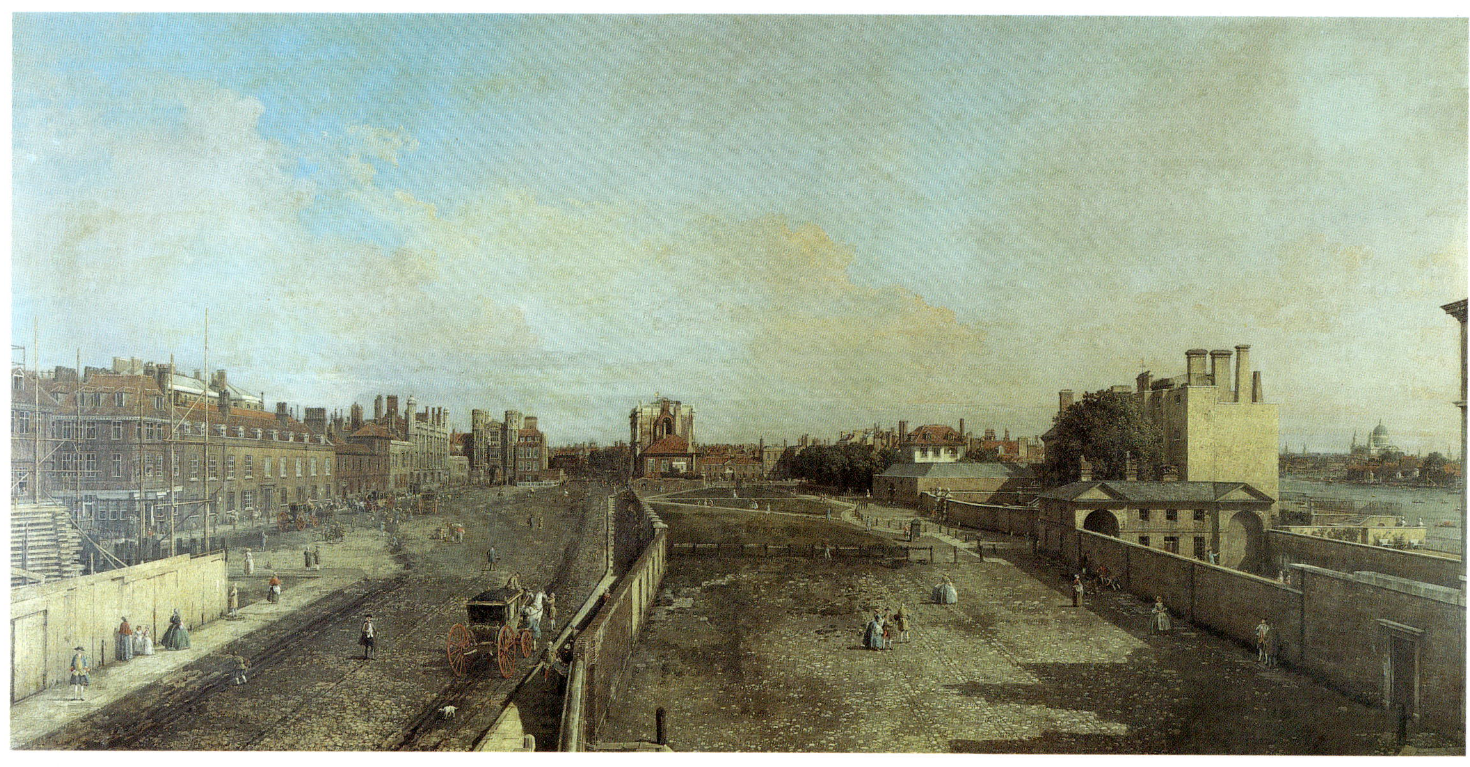

Fig. 6 Canaletto, *Whitehall and the Privy Garden, London, looking north*, oil on canvas, $46\frac{1}{2} \times 107\frac{7}{16}$ ins
(118×273 cm), Collection of the Duke of Buccleuch

is true that Canaletto's English pictures sometimes lack the subtlety and vivacious brilliance of his best Venetian scenes, but compared to what else was available in England at the time and to most contemporary topographical works his paintings are greatly superior. Brian Allen has argued that because topography was considered a relatively inferior category of painting it had a limited appeal at the time, and whereas Venetian prospects (like other Italian subjects) connoted elegance and education because they evoked the Grand Tour the same was not the case with London scenes.[24] The criticism and rumours Vertue reports seem to have been circulated by some of London's art dealers who were finding their own lucrative trade in copies and imitations of Canaletto's pictures diminished by his presence, and they may also have struck a chord with English painters who at the time, led by William Hogarth, were vigorously promoting the cause of a national school and encouraging patrons to support local rather than foreign artists. Vertue writes:

[...] he does not produce works so well done as those of Venice or other parts of Italy [...] done by him there. especially his figures in his works done here, are apparently much inferior to those done abroad. which are surprizeingly well done & with great freedom & variety — his water and his skys at no time excellent or with natural freedom. & what he has done here his prospects of Trees woods or handling or pencilling of that part not various nor so skillful as might be expected. above all he is remarkable for reservedness & shyness in being seen at work, at any Time, or anywhere. which has much strengthened a conjecture that he is not the veritable Canalletti of Venice [...] or that privately there, he has some unknown assistant in making or filling up his [pieces] of works with figures —[25]

Significantly, the next passage Vertue wrote concerns the success of foreign artists in England at the expense of native talent ("it has been an old observation in England — that ye Arts of painting & sculpture wants encouragement — and that none but foreianers have excelled in any branch of those politer Arts …"), and since he was closely associated with Hogarth and his circle the opinions he cites about Canaletto's work may very well reflect contemporary artistic hostility to the Italian in some more nationalistic quarters.

The rumours were evidently damaging, and in 1749 when commissions were not coming in Canaletto apparently resorted to painting pictures for which he hoped to find buyers independently. This would explain the advertisement he placed in the *Daily Advertiser* on 25 July 1749:

SIGNOR CANALETO hereby invites any Gentleman that will be pleased to come to his House, to see a Picture done by him, being *A View of St James's Park*, which he hopes may in some Measure deserve their Approbation. The said View may be seen from Nine in the Morning till Three in the Afternoon, and from Four till Seven in the Evening, for the Space of fifteen Days from the Publication of this Advertizement. He lodges at Mr Richard Wiggan's, Cabinet-Maker, in Silver-Street, Golden Square.[26]

The painting advertised is almost certainly either the imposingly spacious view of *The Old Horse Guards from St James's Park* (Sir Andrew Lloyd Webber Art Foundation) [cat. no. 19] measuring more than eight feet across which was bought by Lord Radnor or, less likely, a smaller picture of the same subject showing it from a different angle with more of the park in the foreground and elegant company parading.[27] Demolition of the Old Horse Guards began in late 1749 so the date of the advertisement coincides well with the subject of the pictures.

Only four paintings can be assigned to 1749, but in 1750 the demand for London river views seems to have revived considerably. Whether Canaletto was working to order is not known, and he may have returned to the subject anticipating that he could sell speculatively painted pictures of it more easily than anything else. It was not until 1750 that he produced the first versions of what were to prove his most enduringly influential London scenes, the two majestic prospects of the Thames from the terrace of Somerset House, one looking towards St Paul's and the City [see cat. no. 14] and the other to Westminster Abbey and the new bridge which had finally been completed in 1750 [see cat. no. 15]. A third composition of *Westminster Bridge from the north: the Master of the Goldsmiths' Company's Procession* showing the bridge extending right across

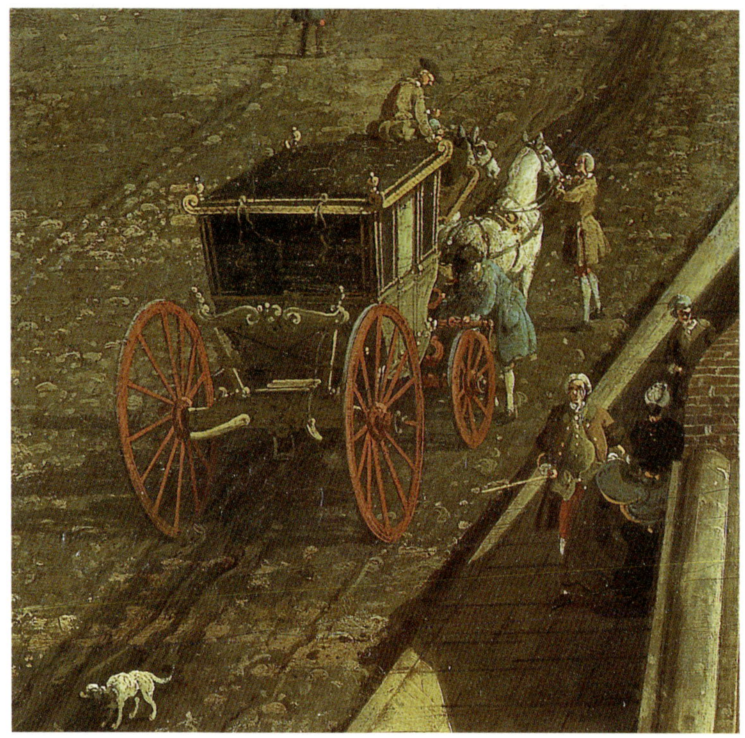

the foreground and the river festively alive with livery company barges and a profusion of smaller boats also dates from this year [cat. no. 13]. There are two paintings of each subject which can be dated 1750, as well as finished drawings. An engraving of one of the paintings, *The Thames from the terrace of Somerset House, the City in the distance*, was published on 1 August 1750.[28] The views from Somerset House in particular are two of Canaletto's most accomplished English compositions. Like his Grand Canal scenes they are dominated by the broad sweep of water in the foreground and enlivened by details of boats and spirited figures leading the eye into a carefully calculated and balanced composition in which the whole scene is unified and brought to life by the play of light and atmospheric effect. The two largest versions of each, the pair now in the Royal Collection,[29] may not, however, have been painted in England but for Consul Smith in Venice when Canaletto returned there for a visit which lasted from late 1750 until about mid–1751.

Joseph Smith bought six finely finished London drawings

from Canaletto which are now with the rest of his collection in the Royal Collection. Two of them are of prospects taken from Somerset House terrace [cat. no. 15]; the others are all of Westminster Bridge [cat. nos. 7, 16, 17].[30] The two huge paintings are Canaletto's most meticulously elaborated London pictures and come closest in grandeur of conception as well as careful delineation to his Venetian views; evidently, as he was working for his most generous and demanding English patron, he gave them special attention, but perhaps because of their size and painstaking execution they can seem rather mechanical in some passages compared with other works actually painted in England.

Canaletto was back in London around the middle of 1751, and by July had finished another of his demonstration pieces intended to attract custom. On 31 July he placed another advertisement in the press announcing that "Signor CANALLETTO ... has painted the Representation of Chelsea-College [the Royal Chelsea Hospital], Ranelagh House, and the River Thames" and inviting those who might be "pleas'd to favour him with seeing the same" to view it at his lodgings. The painting itself is not very inspired, but the subject is interesting in that it showed Ranelagh Gardens which had been developed as a place of fashionable recreation in the 1740s in competition with Vauxhall Gardens over the river [see cat. nos. 28 and 29].[31] By depicting a popular social resort Canaletto was presumably hoping to appeal to a wider audience, especially since those who frequented such places would have included the monied classes and picture-buying public. If George Vertue's estimate of its price is accurate it was an expensive picture: he reports in August or September that "Lately ... Canaletti. painter has [been] painting a large picture ... of Chelsea College. Ranelagh Gardens &c. and parts adjacent. with barges & boats figures ... being a work lately done to shew his skill – this valud at 60 or 70 pounds ... it is thot that this view is not so well as some works of Canaletti formerly brought into England. nor does it appear to be better than some painters in England can do."[32] At about the same time he did another equally large view (more than 90 inches across) of *Whitehall and the Privy Garden looking north* (Duke of Buccleuch) [fig. 6] which gives a more extended and expansive treatment to the same scene he had earlier painted for the Duke of Richmond.[33] Like the *Chelsea Hospital with Ranelagh House* picture this was painted as a speculation, but it did not sell until

it was bought from Canaletto in Venice in 1760 by John Crewe. The Chelsea painting may have been difficult to shift, too: certainly it had been cut in half before 1802 when the right-hand part alone is first recorded in a sale, which rather suggests it might not have found a buyer in 1751.

Canaletto is not mentioned again by Vertue. He remained in England from 1751 until 1755 (there is no convincing evidence whatsoever for a conjectural return visit to Venice in 1753), essentially painting much the same kinds of view that he had done before. One previous patron, the Earl of Northumberland (Sir Hugh Smithson before he succeeded to the title in 1750), employed him to paint his newly inherited properties, the picturesquely romantic *Alnwick Castle, Northumberland* ([fig. 7]; probably 1751, as there is a copy by Samuel Scott dated 1752) and the newly refashioned palatial *Northumberland House, Charing Cross* in London ([fig. 8]; 1752, engraved in 1753).[34] The Alnwick view is particularly interesting because it is the painting in which Canaletto comes closest to the conventions of English picturesque landscape and topography which were still very much in their formative stage of development in the 1750s. However, the painting looks as though it has been done not from reality (unlike the Warwick views which are so much more convincing and preserve the scale of figures relative to architecture) but from a drawing or print by an English topographer, and this might explain why it comes so near to works by English painters. It was also copied both by Samuel Scott and (at least twice) by William Marlow, so it was one of Canaletto's paintings which exerted a not inconsiderable influence on those who carried his example forward into the mainstream of English view painting. The *Northumberland House* painting was no less significant, since through the engraving of it and numerous painted copies by various hands it became a key work in the development of the urban street scene in English topography – its impact can be felt from Scott and Marlow through to the watercolourists of the end of the century like Malton, Dayes, Girtin and the young Turner.

Also in 1752 Canaletto painted two more pictures for Lord Brooke of *Warwick Castle: the east front from the outer court* and *Warwick Castle: the east front from the inner court* [cat. nos. 23 and 24]. For these he received payments of 32 guineas (24 March 1752) and £50 (27 July 1752).[35] In these the light playing on the architecture and vivid touches of colour supplied by the figures deftly painted in the liveliest of rococo accents render

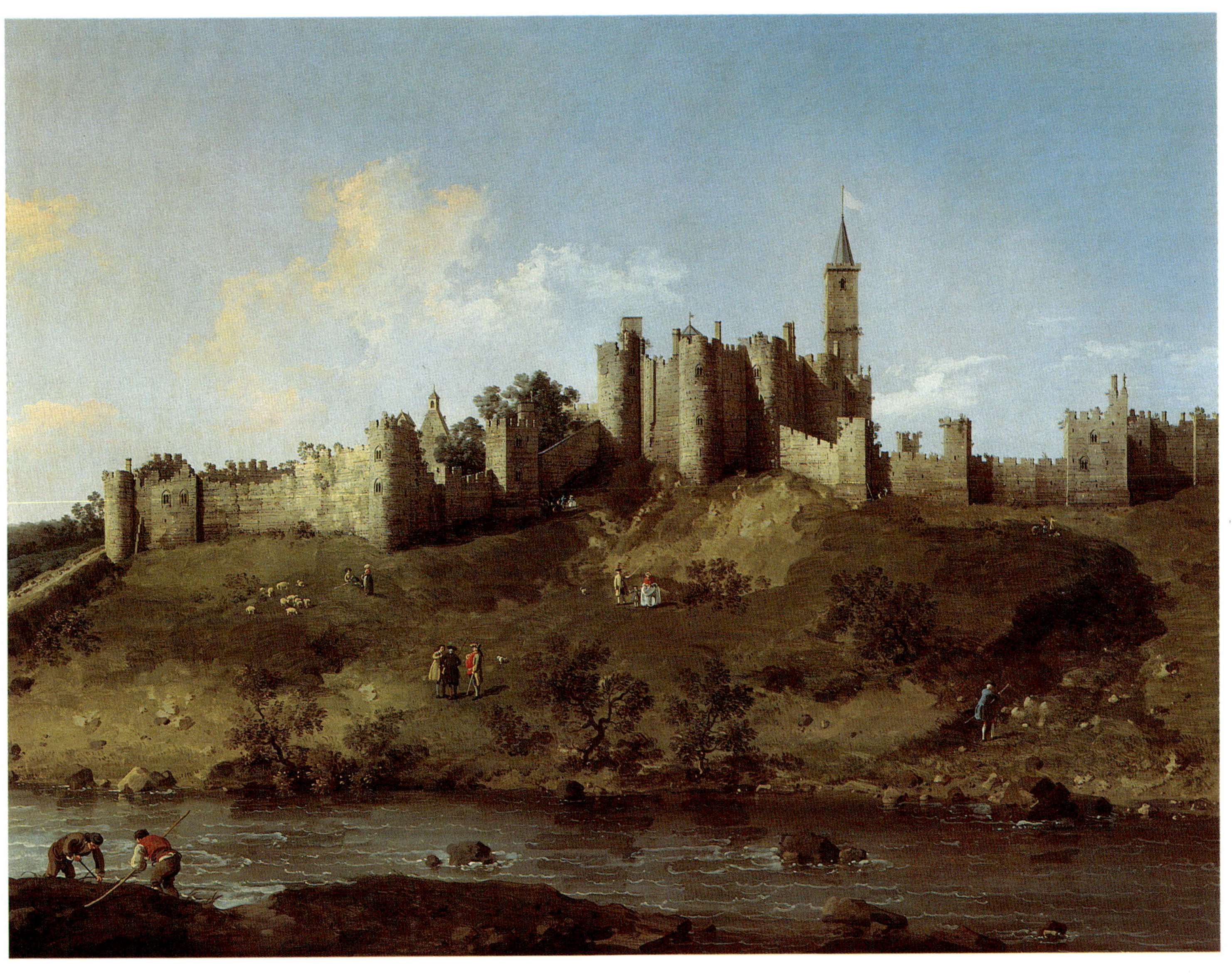

Fig. 7 Canaletto, *Alnwick Castle*, oil on canvas, $44\frac{3}{4} \times 55$ ins (113.7×139.7 cm),
Collection of the Duke of Northumberland

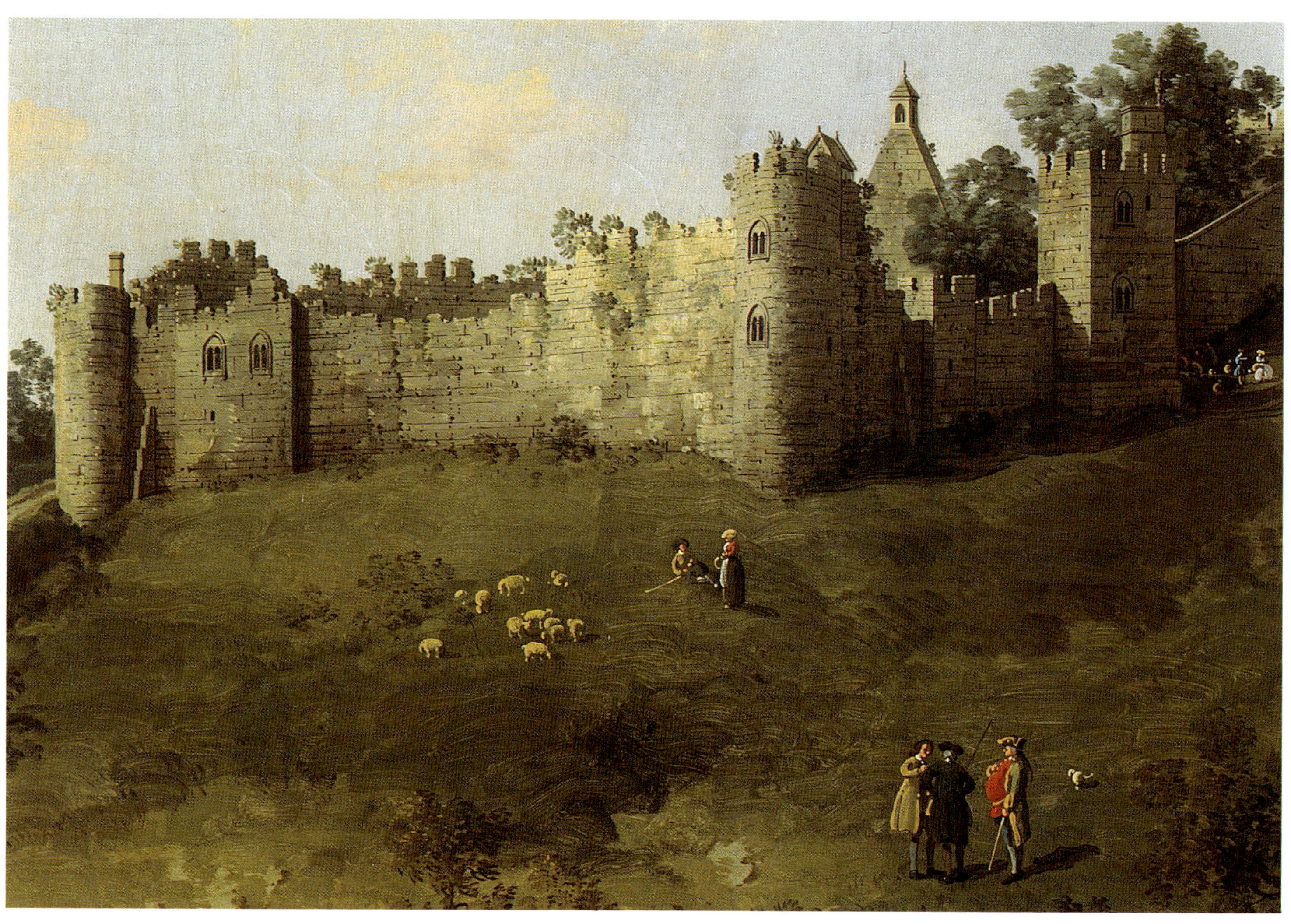

Detail of figure 7

the scenes two of his most radiant and picturesquely conceived English pictures. The later, larger payment may also have covered the two superb pen and wash drawings from which the paintings were developed [cat. no. 25]: these were later owned by Paul Sandby who may have been given them by Charles Greville, Lord Brooke's son.[36] Both the paintings and the related drawings communicate a sense of light and exacting draughtsmanship which Sandby emulates in many of his own views of Windsor Castle done for George III, and his treatment of figures to add interest to his scenes also owes much to Canaletto's example in these works.

Between 1751 and 1753 Canaletto was assiduously cultivating new sources of patronage. There were new subjects to paint, like the New Horse Guards of which there are two paintings.[37] The splendid gleaming Palladian stone building by John Vardy, finished in 1753, was an impressive addition to London's public architecture proclaiming the classical virtues and imperial civic culture which mid-Georgian England asserted. Such major new buildings aroused national pride and public interest beyond London, so were a potentially profitable subject for engravings. Two were issued after Canaletto drawings by the print publisher Robert Sayer, one dated 2 November 1752 showing the New Horse Guards not yet completed and another on 2 November 1753 with everything finished.[38] Selling drawings to be engraved evidently became an important source of income to Canaletto, especially immediately after he returned from Venice in 1751 – presumably because painting commissions and sales were scarce. Of six pictures which can be dated 1751 only one was certainly a commission (Lord Northumberland's *Alnwick Castle*), and only three paintings (all for old patrons) can be firmly assigned to 1752 (*Northumberland House* and the two Warwick Castle subjects for Lord Brooke). If the painting business was fairly dormant producing drawings for the print publishers was an alternative and it had the additional commercial attraction of serving as a means of advertising to potential new patrons from a wide social spectrum.

That this was Canaletto's strategy seems to be confirmed by the range of prints reproducing his drawings which appeared in 1751. Ten were issued altogether. They include an unusual (for Canaletto) panoramic *View of London from Pentonville* [cat. no. 33] apparently first printed in 1751 and republished in 1753, three prints of Ranelagh Gardens, one of St James's Park showing polite company indulging in the fashionable 'parade' which was an important aspect of London's social life, and four of Vauxhall Gardens [fig. 22]. In other words, in response to the specific requirements of the print publishers Canaletto was concentrating more on themes that would have a wider general appeal. Orders may have resulted from them: the paintings of *The Grand Walk in Vauxhall Gardens* and *The interior of the Rotunda at Ranelagh* [cat. nos. 28 and 29] were probably painted after the engravings had appeared.[39]

Canaletto returned to Venice at some point in 1755. The last twelve to eighteen months of his time in England were, as far as paintings are concerned, a particularly productive period for him. Two new patrons appeared who each ordered six pictures from him. One was Thomas Hollis, a rich but rather reclusive man with radical sympathies and a supporter of the American colonists (he was a benefactor to Harvard University) who had met Consul Smith in Venice in 1750 or 1751 and thereafter remained a friend and correspondent of his. It may have been Smith who prompted Hollis to order six pictures from Canaletto. From inscriptions copied from the backs of three of the original canvases it is known that they were painted in 1754 and 1755, but as a group they are a puzzling collection.

There are three smaller paintings, all the same size, of *The Capitol in Rome, St Paul's Cathedral*, and a *capriccio* of *Buildings in Whitehall* showing the Banqueting House by Inigo Jones with the statue of Charles I taken from Charing Cross and other transplanted buildings. The choice of subject is surely not purely arbitrary: perhaps the intention was to represent London as the heir to the legacy of ancient Rome and Renaissance Italy. The other three pictures were all larger: one was of *The interior of the Rotunda at Ranelagh* (a different view to the earlier painting, seen from the other side of the huge domed space), another showed *Old Walton Bridge* [cat. no. 35], and the third (which cannot now be traced) was described in the 1884 sale at which they were all dispersed as a "View of Westminster, during the building of the Bridge".[40] The Ranelagh and Walton Bridge pictures were both similarly inscribed in Italian on the back and dated 1754; of the smaller pictures a similar inscription is recorded only for the Capitol view which is dated 1755.[41]

Of all the series, the *Old Walton Bridge* painting is artistically by far the most interesting since in it Canaletto's sense of atmosphere and locality reveal a sensibility for the English landscape which goes beyond purely topographical concerns. As Nicholas Ross has observed, it is "a rare and charming landscape" in which "for the first time Canaletto appears to have painted an English landscape in an English way."[42] Its picturesque effect is reinforced by the pastoral scenery and presence of the watering cow, elements which perhaps reflect similar features in English painting of the time. They are also reminiscent of landscapes by Francesco Zuccarelli who had arrived in England in 1752. A second, more extensive and even more picturesquely contrived view of Old Walton Bridge was painted in 1755 for Samuel Dicker M.P., who paid for the bridge (erected in 1750) and whose house is seen amongst the trees to the left across the river. This was engraved [fig. 15] from a drawing Canaletto made and inscribed as having been taken from the picture ("Disegnato … appresso il mio Quadro Dippinto in Londra 1755 …") [endpaper] and through the print it had some impact on English artists.[43] Another of Canaletto's scenes in which his assimilation of English taste is apparent is the drawing of *Hampton Court Bridge* [cat. no. 34], of which an engraving was published by Robert Sayer in 1754. Its curiously rustic-Chinese character made it a popular picturesque subject for English artists, and the number of imitations and

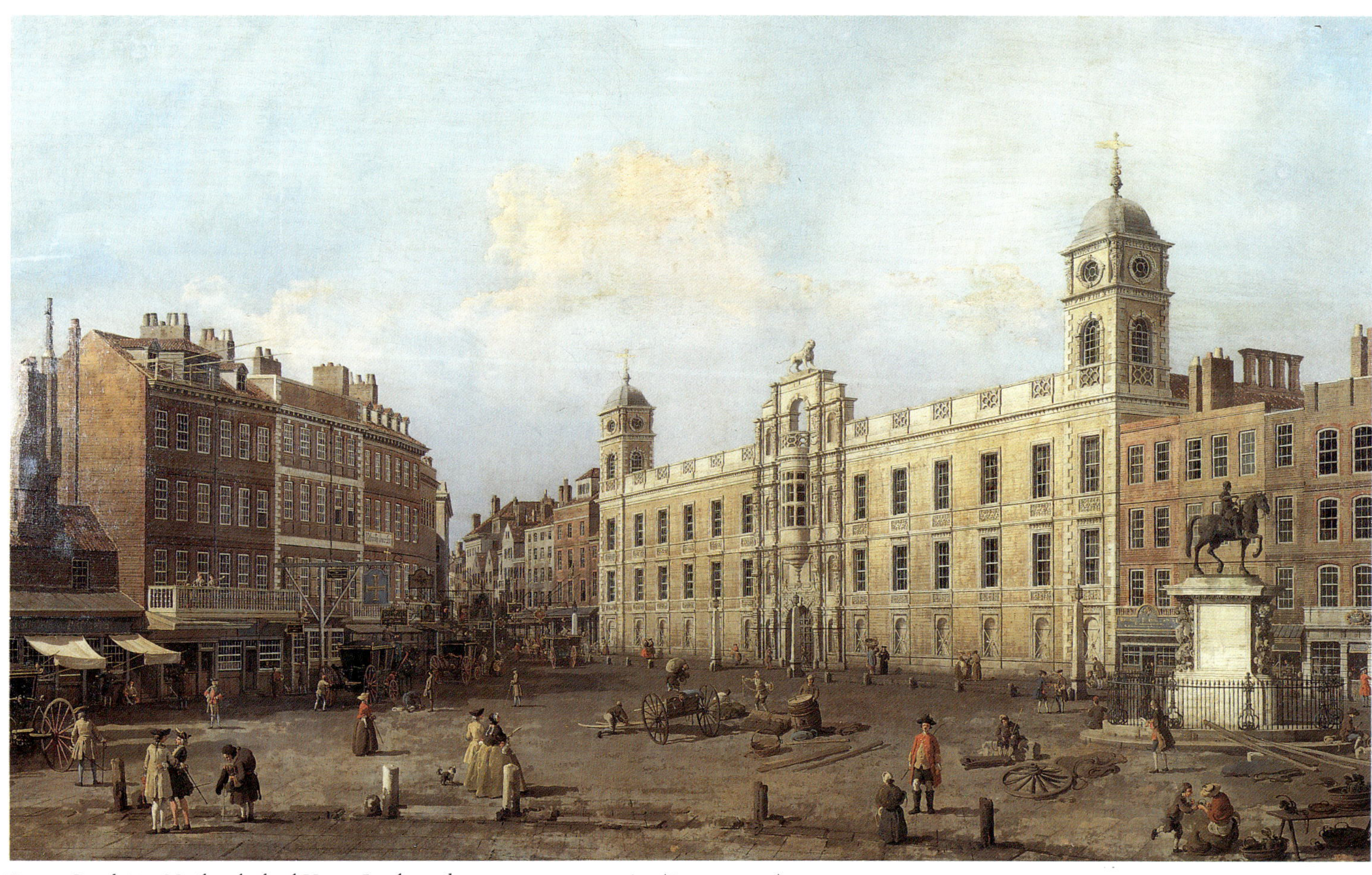

Fig. 8 Canaletto, *Northumberland House, London*, oil on canvas, 33 × 54 ins (84 × 137 cm),
Collection of the Duke of Northumberland

reinterpretations of Canaletto's treatment of the view are indicative of how his influence was felt by painters and draughtsmen in England.[44] One more painting might be considered with this group because it too conveys a similarly picturesque feeling. This is the famous 'view' of *Eton College Chapel* in the National Gallery, London [cat. no. 36], a picture in which Canaletto has rearranged the buildings and invented others.[45] The almost *capriccio* treatment of the view (which may be based on drawings and reminiscences from a much earlier visit to Windsor in 1747) accords well with Canaletto's style around 1754–55 and both the landscape element and marvellously summarised figures which give the foreground an elegantly sanitised rustic charm correspond to similar qualities in the Walton Bridge pictures.

The other set of pictures painted in England are strikingly different to the rest of Canaletto's work there, but they again show his preoccupation with the *'stile pittoresco'*. They are a group of *capricci* which descended in the same collection until 1937 when they were sold by the Earl of Lovelace. From their provenance it is thought that they were originally commissioned by either the third or the fourth Baron King; one of the series, a very picturesquely composed *Sluice on a river with a 'reminiscence' of Eton College*, is signed and dated "A.C./1754". The most interesting are two upright compositions, *A river landscape with a ruin and reminiscences of England* and *A river landscape with a column, ruined Roman arch and reminiscences of England* [cat. nos. 37 and 38]. In these Canaletto artfully disposed a variety of ingredients — English landscape scenery,

'Roman' remains, Renaissance-style buildings that recall Palladio and others in the eighteenth-century manner of England's neo-Palladian classical revival architects, Italianate country architecture and church spires that belong to the English countryside. As fantasies they are richly imaginative. They also arouse curiosity: what were they for, and do they have any meaning? Decorative paintings of picturesque antiquities and ancient Roman remains imaginatively combined were popular at the time, and a good many of the kind were brought back to England from Rome where Giovanni Paolo Pannini had a healthy business supplying them to Grand Tourists. They evoked both culture and nostalgia, reminding viewers of the classical past on which so much in eighteenth-century England was modelled. Canaletto's *capricci* served a similar purpose.[46] They might also be connected to another contemporary context, the eighteenth-century English landscaped gardens in which nature, artifice and architecture invoke pleasurable contemplation in scenes informed by referential meaning. Landscapes like those created at Stowe, Rousham, Chiswick, Stourhead and many other country houses were, in a sense, *capricci*: Canaletto's paintings are part of the same intellectual world.

No record of Canaletto in England exists later than the 1755 date inscribed on the second painting of Old Walton Bridge and its related drawing. No other English subjects can be dated that late, and Canaletto must have left to go back to Venice that year. Between 1755 and his death in 1766 there is little information about him, but the documented sale to an English visitor in 1760 of the large view of *Whitehall and the Privy Garden* suggests that there were still from time to time buyers for his work from England.

It is sometimes said that Canaletto's time in London was not especially successful or productive. Allowing for the eight months he was away in Venice, between May 1746 and his departure in 1755 he was in residence for just over eight years during which he produced about sixty paintings (some of them very large topographical prospects); nearly two dozen engravings were published after his work (the majority from drawings), and he made a fair number of finished drawings for sale. J.G. Links may be right in calculating his income for the period at around £3,000, but if that is so it probably compares quite favourably with not a few English artists at the same time, at any rate with all but the most successful portrait painters who

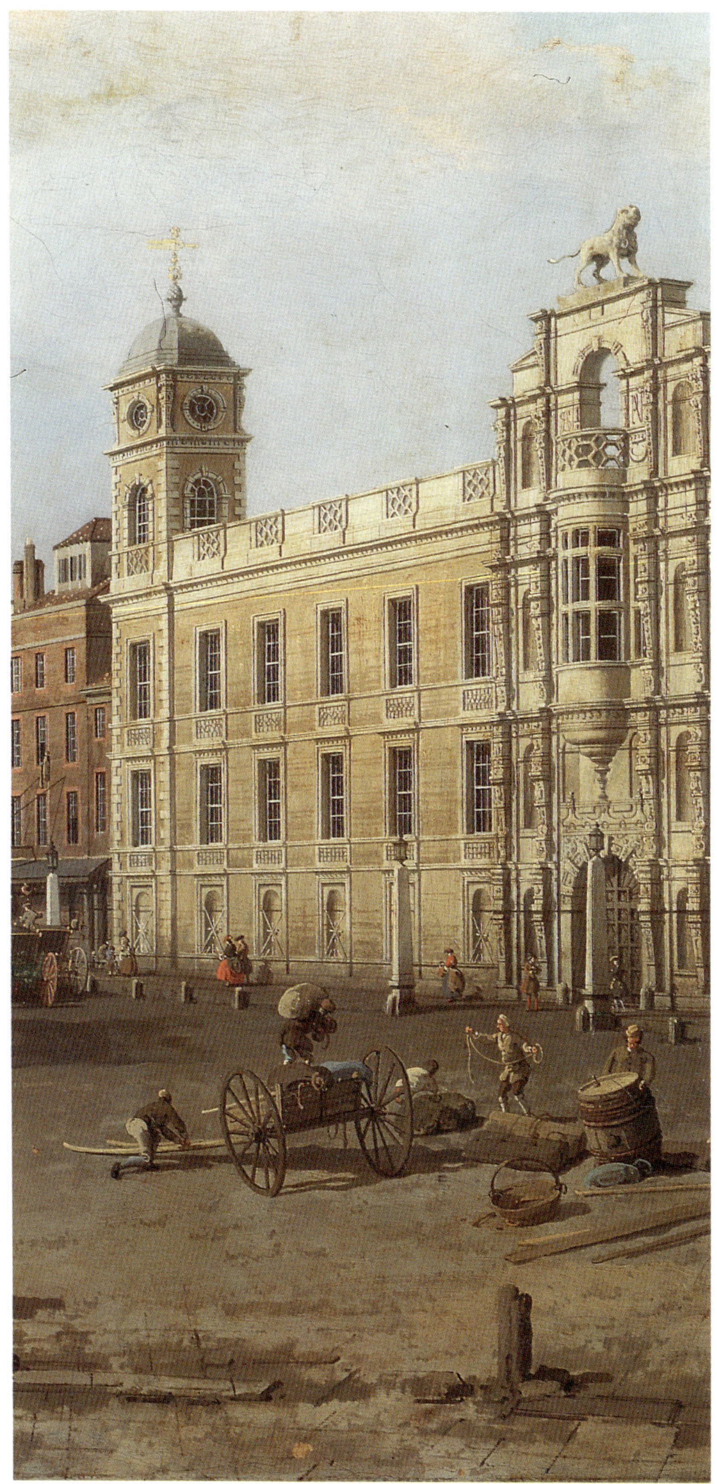

had a steadier demand anyway by the very nature of their profession.[47] It is worth remembering that in 1755 William Hogarth was paid £525 for the largest painting contract of the time, the three huge canvases which made up the vast altarpiece for St Mary Redcliffe in Bristol. Various reasons have been advanced as possible causes of his departure in 1755 but not the one which is perhaps the most likely: Zuccarelli was more in vogue for decorative landscapes, and for view-painting there was more competition from English practitioners like Samuel Scott who had adopted his manner in response to the taste in topography which Canaletto had helped to create.

Canaletto left behind him a body of work which constitutes the most complete visual survey of mid-Georgian London by any one artist. His pictures do not only provide a record of what the city physically looked like; they also depict its commercial and social intercourse, their figurative detail adding a narrative element and presenting a fascinating microcosm of London life, manners and the composition of its urban community. And beyond the capital city Canaletto's views of his patrons' country seats offer occasional glimpses of a different world which gives an impression of how the privileged élite for whom he worked perceived their place in the social and cultural fabric of eighteenth-century England. He also left behind an artistic legacy which exerted an enduring formative influence on topographical conventions in English view-painting.

NOTES

1. George Vertue Note Books, *Walpole Society* XVIII, XX, XXII, XXIV, XXVI, XXIX (Index), XXX, 1930–1950.

2. *Walpole Society* XXII (Vertue Note Books III), 1934, p.130.

3. Entry dated October 1746; *Walpole Society* XXII (Vertue Note Books III), 1934, p.132.

4. For a discussion of Canaletto's development of new themes in the 1740s, see J.G. Links, *Canaletto and his patrons*, London, 1977, chapters 9 and 10.

5. Francesco Zuccarelli settled in Venice ca. 1730; one of his patrons there was Canaletto's principal English patron, Consul Joseph Smith, who encouraged him to move to England in 1752. Zuccarelli stayed in England 1752–62 and again 1765–71 (in 1768 he was nominated a foundation member of the Royal Academy). Smith also owned paintings by Sebastiano and Marco Ricci, including several landscapes by the latter.

6. For Joli, see the catalogue by Harley Preston, *London and the Thames: Paintings of Three Centuries*, London, National Maritime Museum (at Somerset House), 1977, nos. 16–21.

7. Altogether between 1721 and 1730 McSwiney commissioned twenty-four tomb paintings; ten (including the two pictures from the series on which Canaletto worked) were sold to the 2nd Duke of Richmond for Goodwood House, the rest to Sir William Morice. The Richmond set were engraved and published in London in 1741 (*Tombeaux des Princes, Grands Capitaines et Autres Hommes Illustres Qui ont fleuri dans la Grande-Bretagne vers la fin du XVII et le commencement du XVIII Siècle*). See W.G. Constable (revised J.G. Links), *Canaletto*, 2 vols, Oxford 1976, II, nos. 516, 517; Francis Haskell, *Patrons and Painters: A Study in the Relations Between Italian Art and Society in the Age of the Baroque*, London 1963, pp. 287–291, gives an account of the whole project.

8. The writer was a painter, Alessandro Marchesini, advising a Lucca merchant and collector Stefano Conti about the purchase of view-paintings and recommending Canaletto rather than Carlevaris. See Francis Haskell, 'Stefano Conti, patron of Canaletto and others', *Burlington Magazine* XCVIII, 1956, pp.296–300; and Haskell, *Patrons and Painters*, 1963, pp.227–28.

9. Quoted from Constable (revised Links), *Canaletto*, 1976, I, p.174. A sequeen (*zecchino*) was worth approximately half of one pound (ten shillings).

10. Quoted from Links, *Canaletto and his patrons*, 1977, p.28.

11. On Joseph Smith's Canalettos see K.T. Parker, *Canaletto Drawings at Windsor Castle*, London 1948; Michael Levey, *The Later Italian Pictures in the Collection of H.M. The Queen*, London 1964; Michael Levey, *Canaletto Paintings in the Royal Collection*, London 1964; *Canaletto Paintings and Drawings*, exhibition catalogue, London, The Queen's Gallery (Buckingham Palace), 1980. For Smith generally, see F. Vivian, *Il Console Smith mercante e collezionista*, Vicenza 1971; and Haskell, *Patrons and Painters*, 1963, pp.299–310.

12. Quoted from W.H. Chaloner, 'The Egertons in Italy and the Netherlands 1729–34', *Bulletin of the John Rylands Library, Manchester* XXXII, no. 2, 1949–50, p.164.

13. Constable (revised Links), *Canaletto*, 1976, I, pp.18–19, and II, nos. 166, 220; Links, *Canaletto and his patrons*, 1977, p.33.

14. Constable (revised Links), *Canaletto*, 1976, I, pp.21–24.

15. Constable (revised Links), *Canaletto*, 1976, I, pp.110–12, and II, nos. 4 (for Woburn series), 188 (for Harvey series, dispersed in 1957).

16. Quoted from *Canaletto: Paintings and Drawings*, 1980, p.16 (note 15).

17. Constable (revised Links), *Canaletto*, 1976, II, Appendix E, pp.662–72; Links, *Canaletto and his patrons*, 1977, pp.39–40.

18. For Canaletto's etchings, see Ruth Bromberg, *Canaletto's Etchings*, revised edition, San Francisco 1993.

19. Manuscript catalogue of Smith's collection (Royal Library, Windsor), quoted from Constable (revised Links), *Canaletto*, 1976, II, no. 451.

20. Earl of March, *A Duke and his Friends: The Life and letters of the Second Duke of Richmond*, 1911, II, p.602.

21. E.K. Waterhouse, *Painting in Britain, 1530–1790*, Harmondsworth 1962, p.157.

22. Both paintings are in the collection of the Duke of Northumberland: Constable (revised Links), *Canaletto*, 1976, II, nos. 412, 434.

23. The Badminton pictures are in the collection of the Duke of Beaufort: Constable (revised Links), *Canaletto*, 1976, II, nos. 409, 410; for the Warwick Castle pictures, see David Buttery, *Canaletto and Warwick Castle*, Chichester 1992.

24. Brian Allen, 'Topography or Art: Canaletto and London in the mid-eighteenth century', in Malcolm Warner (ed.), *The Image of London: Views by Travellers and Emigrés, 1550–1920*, London (Barbican Art Gallery), 1987.

25. *Walpole Society* XXII (Vertue Note Books III), 1934, p.149.

26. From the copy cited by Hilda F. Finberg, 'Canaletto in England', *Walpole Society* IX, 1921, p.34. George Vertue also records the advertisement (July 1749) and adds a note explaining that the rumour about the "unknown assistant" arose because of confusion with Bernardo Bellotto, Canaletto's nephew and another view-painter who was also known as Canaletto (Vertue Note Books III, p.151).

27. Constable (revised Links), *Canaletto*, 1976, II, nos. 415, 416. There is also a carefully finished drawing in the British Museum which corresponds very closely to the larger picture (*ibid.*, no. 734) [cat. no. 20].

28. Constable (revised Links), *Canaletto*, 1976, II, nos. 428a, b (*Thames from the terrace of Somerset House, the City in the distance*), 429a and 430 (*Thames from the terrace of Somerset House, Westminster Bridge in the distance*), 436 and 436a (*Westminster Bridge from the north, Lambeth Palace in the distance*).

29. *Ibid.*, nos. 428, 429.

30. *Ibid.*, nos. 732, 745, 746, 749, 750, 751.

31. *Ibid.*, no. 413; the advertisement is reproduced in Links, *Canaletto and his patrons*, 1977, p.73.

32. *Walpole Society* XXII (Vertue Note Books III), 1934, p.138.

33. Constable (revised Links), *Canaletto*, 1976, II, no. 439.

34. *Ibid.*, nos. 408 (Alnwick) and 419 (Northumberland House); both Duke of Northumberland collection.

35. *Ibid.*, nos. 446, 447; see also Buttery, *Canaletto and Warwick Castle*, 1992, p.42.

36. Constable (revised Links), *Canaletto*, 1976, II, nos. 759, 760.

37. *Ibid.*, nos. 417, 418.

38. *Ibid.*, no. 737 for the original drawing for one of the prints; the engravings, both by Thomas Bowles, are catalogued in Appendix E, p.682.

39. *Ibid.*, nos. 421 (Ranelagh) and 431 (Vauxhall). These two paintings must be a pair: they are the same size and, in the absence of any evidence of provenance to the contrary, it can be assumed that they have remained together since they were painted.

40. *Ibid.*, nos. 396 (Capitol, Rome), 420 (Ranelagh), 422 (St Paul's), 437.

37. *Ibid.*, nos. 417, 418.

38. *Ibid.*, no 737 for the original drawing for one of the prints; the engravings, both by Thomas Bowles, are catalogued in Appendix E, p.682.

39. *Ibid.*, nos. 421 (Ranelagh) and 431 (Vauxhall). These two paintings must be a pair: they are the same size and, in the absence of any evidence of provenance to the contrary, it can be assumed that they have remained together since they were painted.

40. *Ibid.*, nos. 396 (Capitol, Rome), 420 (Ranelagh), 422 (St Paul's), 437b (Westminster), 441 (Walton Bridge), 472 (Whitehall *capriccio*).

41. The inscriptions on the Ranelagh and Walton pictures read: "Fatto nel anno 1754 in Londra per la prima ed ultima volta con ogni maggior attentzione ad instanza del Signior Cavaliere Hollis padrone mio stimatiss[im]o. Antonio Canal detto il Canaletto." The fact that he describes the Ranelagh picture as done "for the first and only time" has caused some problems of interpretation in view of the existence of the earlier version [cat. no. 29], but since the Hollis painting reverses that composition Canaletto's inscription is strictly speaking accurate.

42. N. Ross, *Canaletto*, London 1993, p.124.

43. Both painting and drawing are in the Yale Center for British Art (Paul Mellon Collection); see Constable (revised Links), *Canaletto*, 1976, II, nos. 442, 755, and Appendix E for the engraving by Anthony Walker.

44. *Ibid.*, no. 730, and Appendix E for the engraving by James Hulett.

45. *Ibid.*, no. 450.

46. *Ibid.*, nos. 367, 473, 474, 475, 478, 504 for the whole series.

47. Links, *Canaletto and his patrons*, 1977, p.78.

Venetian Painters in England in the earlier Eighteenth Century

BRIAN ALLEN

By the beginning of the eighteenth century Venetian art, especially of the Renaissance, had long been known beyond the borders of Italy. During the seventeenth century Venetian pictures were collected widely throughout Europe, including England. When in the 1620s the Gonzaga Dukes of Mantua sold their collections to King Charles I, London could begin to rival Madrid in its holdings of North Italian art and Venetian art was given especial prominence in the collections of Lord Arundel and the Duke of Buckingham. The court painter Anthony Van Dyck owned magnificent examples of Venetian art such as Titian's *Vendramin family*, now in the National Gallery, London.

Relations between England and Venice have always been unusually friendly. Although by the end of the seventeenth century Venice had long been in decline as an economic and maritime power the English recognised a potential similarity in political and economic affairs and there existed a widespread admiration for the efficiency and stability of Venetian government. It was to the Republic that England first sent a Resident Ambassador. It might even be argued that in the aftermath of the Glorious Revolution the monarchy in England, with little more than nominal power and controlled by a powerful, almost feudal aristocracy, had come to resemble the position of the Doge in relation to the Venetian oligarchy. However, unlike their Venetian counterparts those men of power in England were acutely aware that their country was entering a period of unparalleled influence and wealth. Nevertheless for some time Venice had come to typify in the English mind all of Italy and had provided English writers from Shakespeare onwards with an unfailing source of subject matter.

By the late seventeenth century Venetian painters regularly travelled, not only all over central and northern Italy but also across the Alps into Austria and the German states where innumerable small palaces were springing up, offering rich opportunities for the decorative painters. Further afield, Venetian painters were welcomed in Spain, the Netherlands, France and, early in the eighteenth century, England. The pursuit of grand-scale public and private patronage which led to the arrival in England of the first wave of Venetian decorative painters had even earlier provided the impetus for Antonio Verrio (1639?–1707), with the encouragement of the Duke of Montagu, to make the journey to England from his native South Italy in 1672. Montagu's cousin, Charles Montagu,

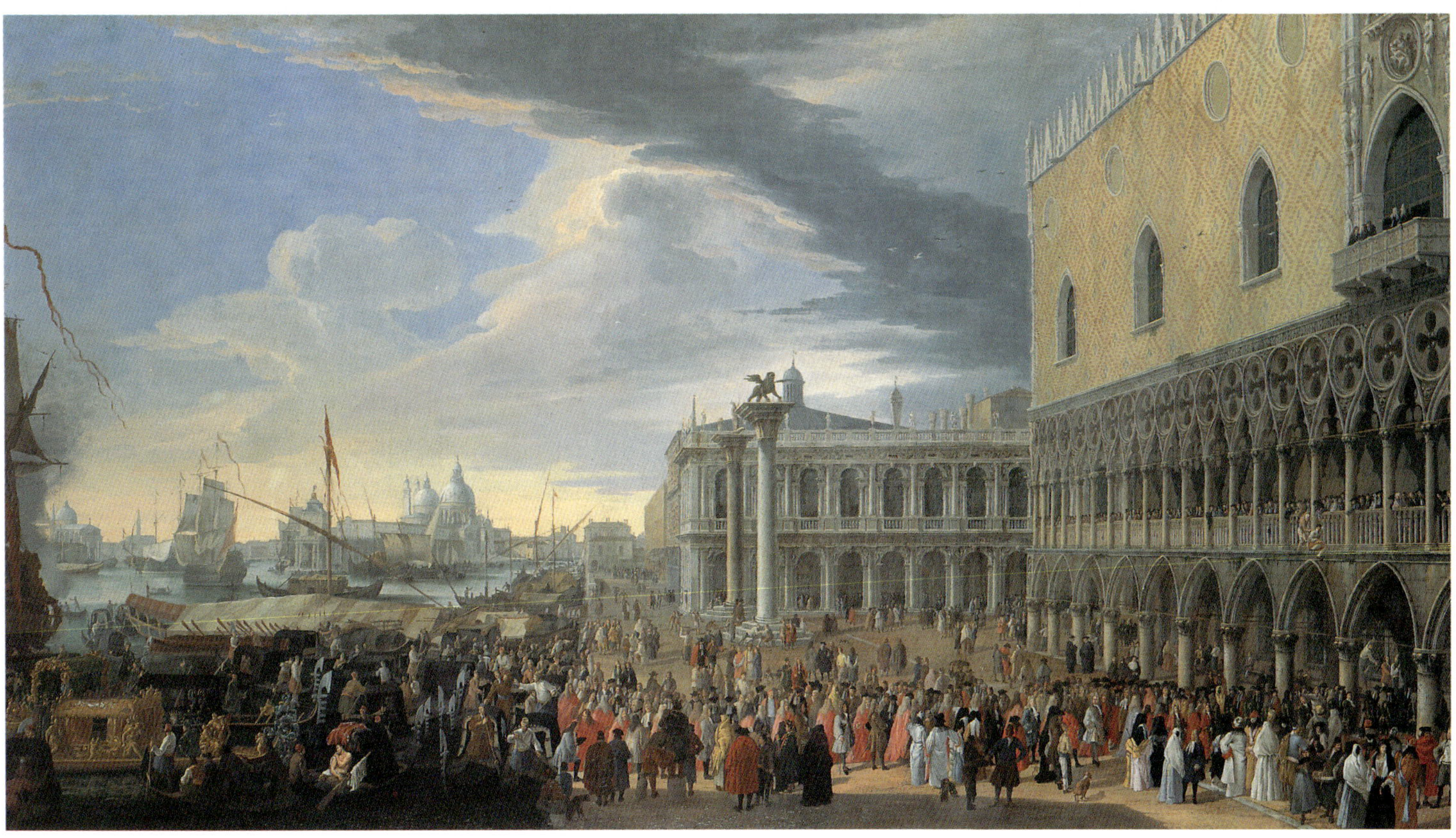

Fig. 9 Luca Carlevaris, *The arrival of the fourth Earl of Manchester in Venice in 1707*,
oil on canvas, 52 × 104 ins (132.1 × 264.2 cm), Birmingham Museums and Art Gallery

fourth Earl and later first Duke of Manchester (1660?–1722), had been sent in 1707 by Queen Anne as Ambassador Extraordinary to Venice with a view to his securing the support of the Republic in the Grand Alliance against Louis XIV. He had previously visited Venice in the winter of 1697–98 in an apparently unsuccessful attempt to gain the release of some English seamen detained in the galleys of the Republic. On that occasion he was entertained with great ceremony and would no doubt have had the opportunity to see the best of contemporary Venetian painting. He was a prominent and cultivated member of that group of Whig aristocrats who consolidated themselves after the Glorious Revolution of 1688. By the time of his second visit to Venice he was having his house, Kimbolton Castle in Huntingdonshire, remodelled by the architect John Vanbrugh, who was also employed by his friends the Duke of Marlborough and the Earl of Carlisle. Apart from a passion for opera, he seems to have had a good eye for painting and quickly commissioned works from several of the leading artists in Venice. From Luca Carlevaris (1663–1730), by then already established as the leading view-painter in the city, he commissioned a large picture showing his landing at the Piazzetta [fig. 9], and his counterpart Alvise Pisani, one of the two Venetian Ambassadors who had visited London a few months earlier, commissioned a similar view showing their arrival at Tower Stairs (Staatsgalerie Schloss Schleissheim, Munich).

On his return to England at the end of 1708 Lord Manchester persuaded Antonio Pellegrini (1675–1741) and Marco Ricci (1676–1729/30) to accompany him, presumably with the promise of work at both Kimbolton and his town house in

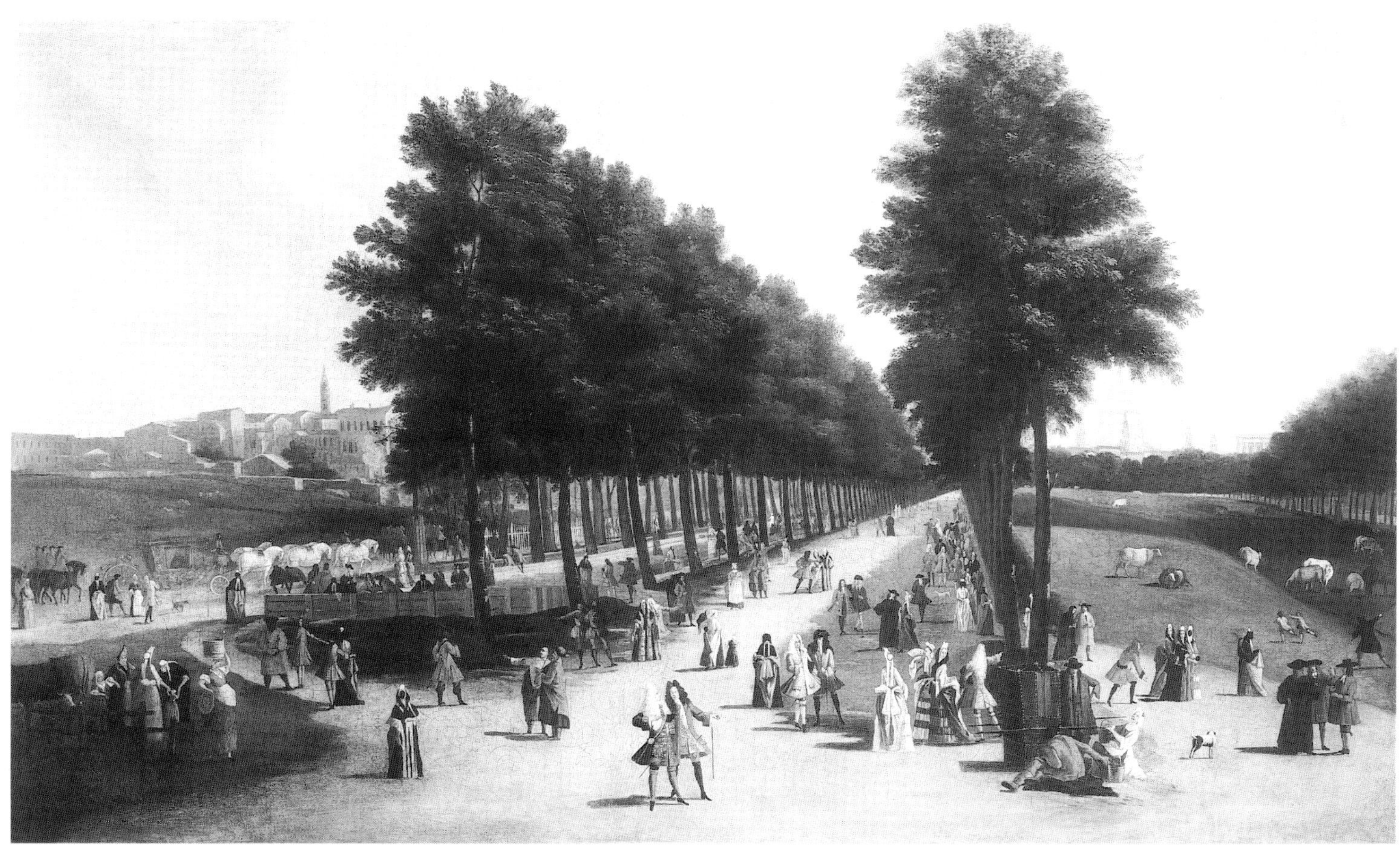

Fig. 10 Marco Ricci, *A view of the Mall from St James's Park, London*,
oil on canvas, 45 × 76⅞ ins (114.1 × 195.2 cm), National Gallery of Art (Ailsa Mellon Bruce Collection), Washington

Arlington Street, as well as the potential patronage of his noble friends. With much of Pellegrini's work for Lord Carlisle at Castle Howard – his most extensive scheme – destroyed in the disastrous fire of 1940, the wall and ceiling paintings at Kimbolton, despite some clumsy nineteenth-century repainting, remain as his outstanding achievement in England. They give the frequently dull medium of oil on plaster something of the sparkle of his native technique of *fresco secco*. With his range of pastel colours and his lively calligraphic brushwork, Pellegrini can be seen as a link between the late seventeenth-century master Luca Giordano and Canaletto's contemporaries the Guardi brothers. On the walls of the staircase at Kimbolton a Roman Emperor, probably meant to represent William III, rides in triumph whilst on the ceiling the theme is continued with

Minerva pointing to a portrait of the young William. The most brilliantly vivacious section is the musicians' balcony on the wall where a flautist, an hautboy player and a silk-clad trumpeter sound a triumphant fanfare, while another figure leans over the balcony to toy playfully with a dog. Although some of his contemporaries disparaged his apparently slapdash technique, Pellegrini played an important role in accustoming an English audience, used to the comparatively clumsy garishness of the recently deceased Verrio, to a more spacious and elegant kind of composition.

Marco Ricci, the other artist to return with Lord Manchester, was best known as a landscape painter. He executed a number of overdoors and overmantels at Castle Howard when Pellegrini was working there, including a remarkable view of the Mall from St James's Park [fig. 10]. How interesting it is that one of the first attempts before Canaletto to paint a social spectacle with courtiers and townsfolk promenading in a park should have been executed by a Venetian. Indeed the kind of witty observation displayed by Ricci in other works of this kind, like his half-caricatured musical groups, must have been of interest to the young Hogarth.

Although he had collaborated with Pellegrini in designing and painting stage scenery, Marco Ricci seems to have fallen out with his compatriot and returned to Venice to fetch his uncle Sebastiano with a view to putting Pellegrini out of business. Arguably, however, a more important reason for his return to London early in 1712 had presented itself — the decoration of the cupola of the dome of Wren's St Paul's Cathedral which was now virtually complete. This is not the place even to outline the complex story of the commission to decorate the dome of St Paul's but suffice it to say that virtually all the decorative painters of note coveted what was seen, alongside the great dining hall at the Royal Naval Hospital at Greenwich, as the greatest prize of the day. John Talman writing from Rome to his friend Henry Newton on 18 November 1711 noted, somewhat optimistically as it transpired, that Ricci was "setting out for England to paint the cupola of St Paul". In the event neither of the Ricci, nor Pellegrini (who came closest), managed to wrest the commission from James Thornhill who undoubtedly benefited from the kind of attitude demonstrated by one of the Trustees of St Paul's, Archbishop Tenison, who apparently exclaimed: "I am no judge of painting, but on two articles I think I may insist: first that the painter employed be a Protestant; and secondly that he be an Englishman". The commission, probably from King George I, for the *Resurrection* in the chapel of the Chelsea Hospital, possibly a memorial to Queen Anne who had died on 1 August 1714, would have been some consolation for the loss of St Paul's and the Prince of Wales's Bedchamber at Hampton Court, which also went to Thornhill. However, Sebastiano continued to enjoy considerable private patronage from Lord Burlington and William III's great favourite the Duke of Portland, whose chapel at Bulstrode in Buckinghamshire he painted in 1713–14. Although it was destroyed in the mid nineteenth century we have some idea what the walls of Bulstrode's chapel might have looked like from several vigorous oil sketches relating to it by Ricci.

The two Riccis' departure for Paris in 1716 coincided with the arrival of another adopted Venetian, Antonio Bellucci (1654–1726). Bellucci had already had a modestly successful career in Venice, Austria and Germany and in England he found employment mainly through James Brydges, first Duke of Chandos, at whose house, Canons at Edgware in Middlesex, he would have encountered one of the few households in England that, at its peak in the early 1720s, with its orchestra and choir headed by Dr Pepusch and then by Handel, approached the splendour of the courts of baroque Germany. Bellucci's decorations in the chapel at Canons — *The Nativity*, *The Descent from the Cross* and *The Ascension* plus many smaller canvases set into the ceiling — survived the untimely demolition of that great house in 1747 and through the perspicacity of Thomas, second Lord Foley, were re-erected in the parish church of Great Witley, Worcestershire, which unexpectedly acquired one of the most exotic interiors of its kind in England. So for about a decade or so before Canaletto emerged as a painter in Venice in the 1720s a group of powerful arbiters of taste in England gave considerable support to these emigré Venetian history painters. Although the next generation of English patrons no longer so readily held the artist captive as part of their household Canaletto and many other foreign artists in the mid eighteenth century still clearly looked to London as potentially the most lucrative market-place in Europe.

With the exceptions of Antonio Joli [see cat. nos 41 and 42] and of Francesco Zuccarelli (1701–1788), whose first lengthy stay began in 1752 [fig. 11], Canaletto was the last of the great Venetian painters to visit England in the eighteenth century. When he returned to Venice in 1755 after nine years working mostly in London the artists of the increasingly prosperous metropolis had begun to organize themselves along more professional lines, and the establishment in 1768 of the Royal Academy had, within little over a decade after Canaletto's departure, set the seal of establishment approval on their increasingly varied activities. Unlike other foreign artists, such as the Swiss-born George Michael Moser (1706–1783), who had settled in London many years earlier and played an active role in the politics of the art world, eventually becoming the first Keeper of the Royal Academy, Canaletto seems to have been remarkably uninvolved in the issues that concerned those avantgarde artists who gravitated around Hogarth's St Martin's Lane Academy in mid-eighteenth-century London. It is as if Canaletto's only reason for travelling to England was a commercial one. Secure in his status as one of Europe's most celebrated artists, albeit in the lesser genre of topographical landscape painting, Canaletto can hardly have felt the need to concern himself with the minor professional concerns of the artists of his adopted country. Indeed, this view is to some extent supported by that great chronicler of the art world George Vertue, who tells us that Canaletto came to England "to putt [his fortune] into the Stocks here for better Security. or better interest than abroad", for in the mid eighteenth century London was indeed the fastest growing commercial centre in Europe. Canaletto's compatriot Jacopo Amigoni (ca. 1685–1752), who spent a decade in England between 1729 and 1739, so Vertue tells us, had left England a wealthy man, taking £4,000 or £5,000 with him on his return to Italy. If Vertue is to be believed, Amigoni was eventually instrumental in persuading Canaletto to make the journey north.

Languishing in Venice in 1746 with an ever diminishing supply of Grand Tourists reaching his studio because the War of the Austrian Succession had made travel to Italy increasingly difficult, Canaletto had attempted to diversify by offering alternatives to his conventional views of Venice in the form of Roman subjects, *capricci* and etchings. A visit to England must have seemed an increasingly realistic solution to his dilemma, especially if, as is very likely, Amigoni had been able to give him an accurate impression of the burgeoning London art market. Amigoni had himself shown considerable resourcefulness in adapting to the changing artistic climate in London, which had dramatically affected his practice as a decorative painter. The overwhelming dominance of the new Palladian style of architecture by the mid–1730s created considerable problems for those decorative painters schooled like Amigoni in filling cavernous walls and ceilings with illusionistic splendour. The tendency in Palladian interiors towards the creation of plaster compartments on walls and ceilings severely curtailed the activities of the decorative painters who, since Verrio's arrival from Italy half a century earlier, had enjoyed unprecedented patronage decorating the numerous new country and town houses built in the aftermath of the Glorious Revolution of 1688. Reluctantly, but with a considerable degree of success, Amigoni turned instead towards portraiture and printmaking, and despite apparently never having painted portraits before, by the mid–1730s Amigoni was in demand by

the Royal Family and many of King George II's court and was able to charge, so Vertue tells us, as much as 60 guineas for a full-length picture.

Although Vertue says he had very little reputation for striking a good likeness, in any case not a trait that unduly concerned most English sitters at this date, Horace Walpole writing later in the century is perhaps unduly harsh in dismissing Amigoni's female portraits as "mere chalk, as if he had only painted from ladies who paint themselves". We know of about forty or so portraits executed by Amigoni in London in the 1730s, and he had with some shrewdness also begun to exploit the market for prints which Hogarth, amongst others, had exposed earlier in that decade. Returning from a trip to France in 1736 Amigoni brought back with him the engraver Nicolas Edelinck (1681–1767) so that there were now four printmakers in his studio, if we include himself, his daughter Carlotta and Josef Wagner who had joined him from Bologna in 1732. Vertue reminds us that Amigoni's involvement in printmaking continued right up to and even beyond his departure from London at which time "he was about publishing a Sett of prints of Views from pictures of Canalletti's", and he apparently intended "to sett up a print shop in Venice".

Amigoni would also have had other tales to tell Canaletto about what he might expect should he depart for London since at the peak of his fame in the mid–1730s he had been a victim of an orchestrated although ultimately rather absurd campaign that exposed the most overtly xenophobic insecurities of the Hogarth circle. Since January 1731 James Ralph (1705?–1752) had been editing a pro-ministerial newspaper called the *Weekly Register* in which he set about reforming the taste of the age. Within a short time Ralph began singling out the work of his friend the "ingenious Mr Hogarth". In October 1733 he began publishing a series of twenty essays entitled "A Critical Review of the Publick Buildings, Statues and Ornaments, in and about London and Westminster" in which he defends Palladianism but also ridicules the work of foreign painters, particularly Amigoni, who were decorating those buildings. On 4 May 1734, ironically the day the English decorative painter Sir James Thornhill died, Ralph launched a vitriolic attack on Amigoni and those British patrons who preferred the work of foreigners. Amigoni's paintings, according to Ralph, were "only calculated to please at a Glance by the artful Mixture of a Variety of gay Colours, but have no solidity in them". This was

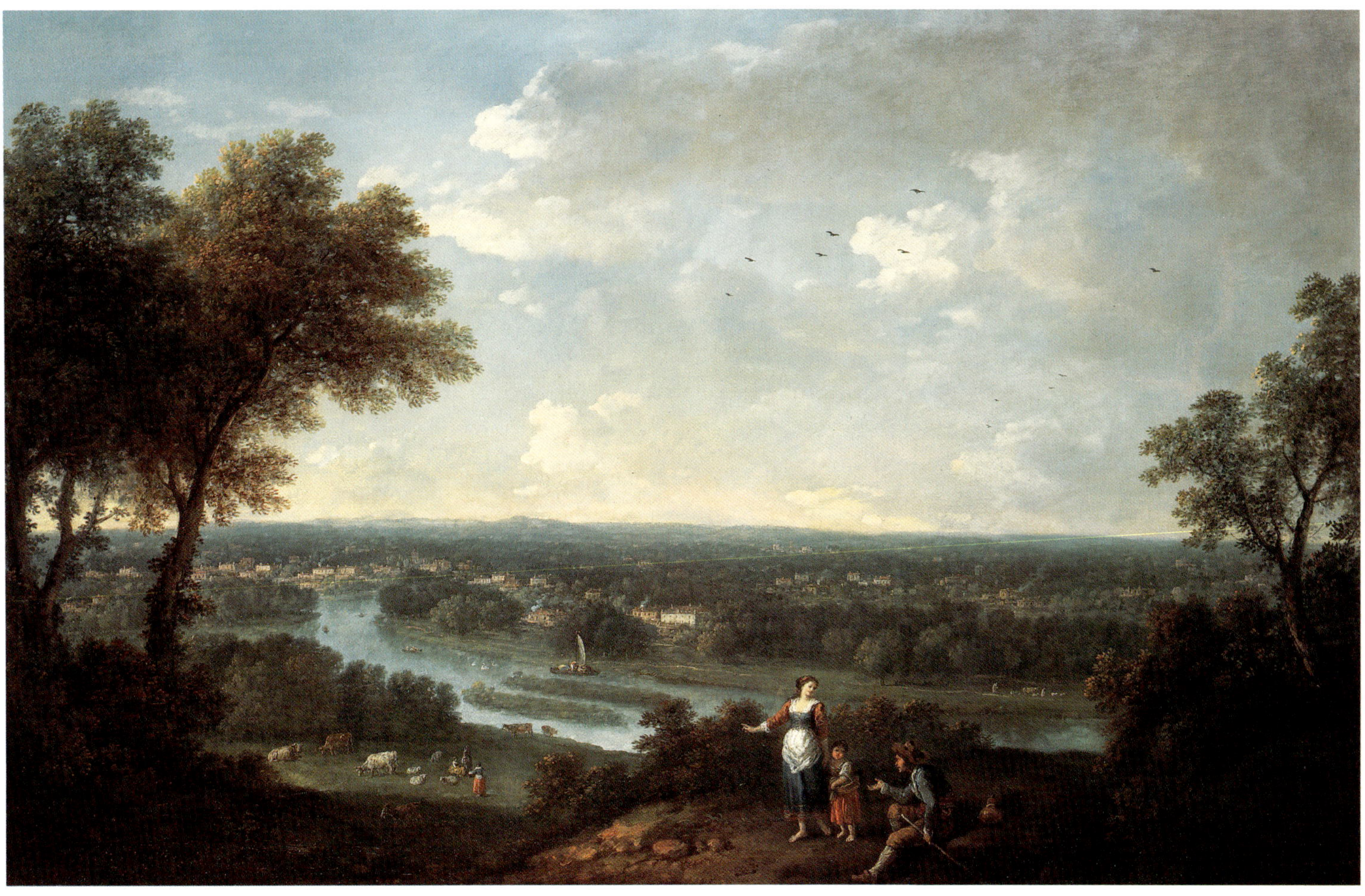

Fig. 11 Francesco Zuccarelli, *A view from Richmond Hill along the River Thames towards Twickenham*, oil on canvas, $33\frac{1}{2} \times 49\frac{3}{4}$ ins (82.5 × 126.5 cm), London art market (courtesy Richard Green)

of course all part of Ralph's defence of English painters such as Hogarth and Francis Hayman who were desperate for opportunities to establish their credentials as history painters. There may have been a more personal element in Hogarth's position – a desire to usurp Amigoni and thereby take revenge for the humiliation his father-in-law Thornhill had suffered at Moor Park in Hertfordshire. There Amigoni had recently been commissioned by the owner Benjamin Styles to paint a series of canvases which replaced others by Thornhill which Styles had been forced to pay for as a consequence of two law suits arising from a dispute over the artist's charges.

When Hogarth discovered early in 1734 that Amigoni was

negotiating with the governors of St Bartholomew's Hospital for the decoration of the new building's staircase he moved quickly to pre-empt him by offering to decorate the stairway for nothing, thereby throwing down the gauntlet to the foreign history painters. The resulting paintings, *The Pool of Bethesda* and *The Good Samaritan*, represent an extraordinary leap in scale and ambition for Hogarth, who hitherto had produced mostly small-scale group portraits, and we can only speculate about what Amigoni might have produced.

A few years later Hogarth was able to exercise much greater control over the decoration of another charitable institution in London, the Foundling Hospital. There can never have been

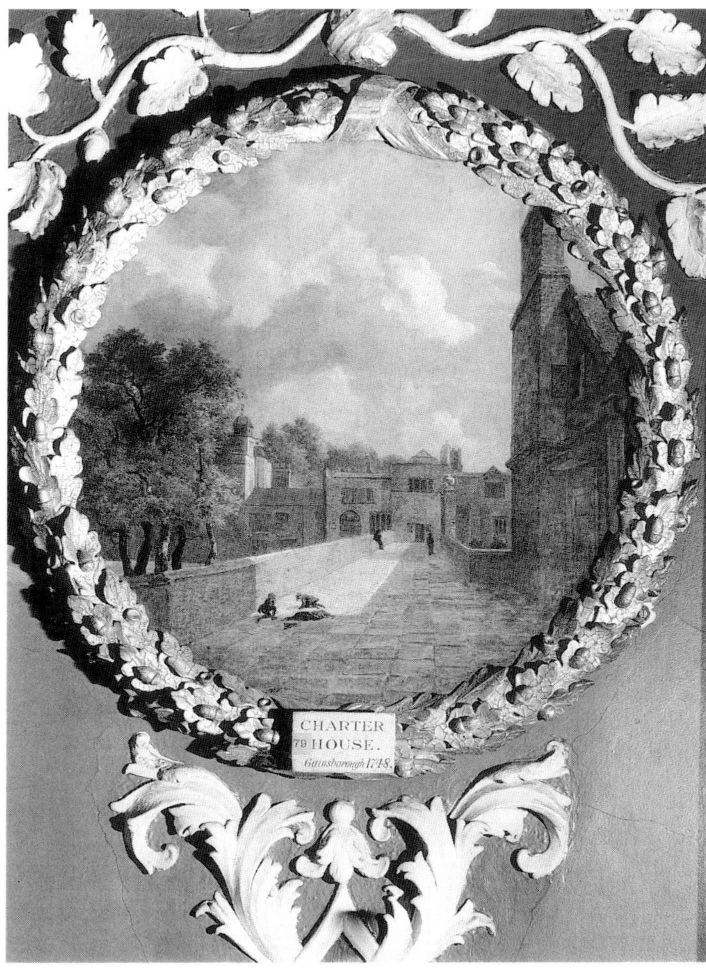

Fig. 12 Thomas Gainsborough, *Charterhouse*, oil on canvas, diameter 22 ins (56 cm), Thomas Coram Foundation for Children, London

the remotest possibility in the later 1740s of Canaletto being invited to contribute one of the decorative roundel landscapes that sit alongside the four large history paintings in the Court Room there, although those works presented by Samuel Wale [fig. 28], Edward Haytley [fig. 29] and even Richard Wilson and Thomas Gainsborough [fig. 12] certainly suggest an awareness of Canaletto's style. In fact there was a long established tradition in Britain for landscapes of identifiable places, whether in the form of engraved views of London or other towns popularised by Wenceslaus Hollar in the seventeenth century and continued by the Bucks, or the fashionable country house 'portraits' of Knyff, Siberechts, Tillemans or Wootton. Until the 1720s this kind of painting had been almost exclusively in the hands of visiting foreign painters, usually of Dutch or Flemish extraction, but by the 1740s British artists like George Lambert and Joseph Nickolls [see cat. no. 43] had made their mark.

What is so particularly mystifying to modern writers on Canaletto is that those comments that survive by his contemporaries in London seem to suggest that his work was not seen as any better than that of the native talent. "On the whole of him something is obscure and strange", wrote Vertue in June 1749, "he does not produce works so well done as those of Venice or other parts of Italy which are in Collections here and done by him there". It can of course be argued that a British audience was increasingly discriminating in its attitude towards landscape painting by the mid—1740s. Not only were good quality landscape paintings by the great Rome-based seventeenth-century painters like Claude, Poussin, Gaspard Dughet and Salvator Rosa arriving in England but so, too, were outstanding examples by the great Dutch landscape painters like Ruisdael and Hobbema. This more sophisticated taste encouraged the relegation of the kind of topographical landscape practised by Canaletto, no matter how well done, into the kind of work that Jonathan Richardson described in his essay *The Connoisseur* of 1719 as being unable to "Improve the Mind" or "excite Noble Sentiment". Richardson's former pupil Joshua Reynolds was still echoing these sentiments just after Canaletto's return to Venice in the second of his *Idler* essays, published in 1759, when he criticized those painters who merely "imitated" nature. This resulted in painting "no longer being considered a liberal art, and sister to Poetry; this imitation being merely mechanical, in which the slowest intellect is always sure to succeed best; for the Painter of genius cannot stoop to drudgery … the Grand style of Painting requires this minute attention to be carefully avoided." The kind of attention to detail which characterizes Canaletto's art was in Reynolds's mind consistent with the values of the Dutch school which he considered "certainly of a lower order, that ought to give place to a beauty of a superior kind, since one cannot be obtained without departing from the other". Significantly, in the same essay Reynolds referred to the Venetian school of painting as a whole as "the Dutch part of Italian genius".

For all Canaletto's subtle abilities to render light and shade and the texture of buildings, when devoid of the romantic subject matter of Venice his work paradoxically seemed increasingly at odds with the prevailing tide of Italianate classicism that obsessed so many English patrons of his generation. There was the added irritation of English imitators like Samuel Scott, Francis Harding, Joseph Baudin and many others able to produce considerably cheaper imitations of his work. These factors may begin to explain why Canaletto produced such a surprisingly small number of pictures during his nine years in England.

BIBLIOGRAPHICAL NOTE

The most important source of information on the Venetian history painters in England is Edward Croft-Murray's *Decorative Painting in England, 1537–1837*, 2 vols, London 1962 and 1970, together with George Vertue's Note Books (*Walpole Society* XVIII, XX, XXII, XXIV, XXVI, XXIX, XXX, 1930–50). Much is also to be found in Francis Haskell's *Patrons and Painters: A Study in the Relations Between Italian Art and Society in the Age of the Baroque*, revised edition, London 1980. One of the earliest attempts to tackle the subject can be found in F.J.B. Watson, 'English Villas and Venetian Decorators', *Journal of the Royal Institute of British Architects* LXI, 1954, pp.171–77. On Amigoni see John B. Shipley, 'Ralph, Ellys, Hogarth, and Fielding', *Eighteenth Century Studies* I, no.4, 1968, pp.313–31; Ronald Paulson, *Hogarth: High Art & Low; Volume Two, 1732–1750*, New Brunswick (NJ) 1992, pp.77–81, and Leslie Hennessey, *Jacopo Amigoni (c. 1685–1752). An Artistic Biography with a Catalogue of his Venetian Paintings*, unpublished PhD. dissertation, University of Kansas, 1983, pp.33–58. The literature on Canaletto in London is extensive and referred to elsewhere in this catalogue but the present author has explored some of the reasons for Canaletto's relative lack of success in London in 'Topography or Art: Canaletto and London in the mid-eighteenth century' in M. Warner (ed.), *The Image of London: Views by Travellers and Emigrés, 1550–1920*, London, Barbican Art Gallery, 1987, pp.29–45. For Pellegrini at Kimbolton see Edward Croft-Murray in *Apollo* LXX, 1959, pp.119–24, and for him at Burlington House and Narford Hall, Norfolk, see George Knox in *Burlington Magazine* CXXX, 1988, pp.846–53. On Marco Ricci see Annalisa Sonino, *Marco Ricci*, Milan 1981, and Christopher Gilbert, 'A Nobleman and the Grand Tour: Lord Irwin and Marco Ricci', *Apollo* CXXXIII, 1966, pp.358–63. Sebastiano Ricci is the subject of an important monograph by Jeffrey Daniels (Hove 1976), and of a useful article by George Knox, 'Sebastiano Ricci at Burlington House: a Venetian decoration "alla Romana" ', *Burlington Magazine* CXXVII, 1985, pp.601–09. Finally, for Bellucci, see Eric Young, 'Antonio Bellucci in England and Elsewhere', *Apollo* XCVII, 1983, pp.492–99.

Canaletto and the English print market

DAVID ALEXANDER

Canaletto was in England for the best part of a decade and painted many different views of well known urban scenes and country houses during his stay. Yet there are relatively few English prints of his paintings; what is more, only a couple of those engraved during his stay can be described as fine prints. In attempting to explain this it is necessary to examine his likely attitude to prints after his paintings and to look at the English print market at the time of his visit, in order to establish how topographical prints came to be engraved. First, however, one has to examine the print market in Venice and the part Canaletto had played in it prior to his departure for England.

The best known views of Venice available during Canaletto's youth were the 103 views in Luca Carlevaris's *Le Fabriche et Vedute di Venetia* (The Buildings and Views of Venice), published in 1703; many views by other artists appeared in subsequent years.[1] By 1725 Canaletto was established as a view-painter of exceptional power; he soon made his name among British visitors, in large part because of the interest in him shown by that insatiable collector, Joseph Smith, who also acted as agent and dealer. During the 1720s Canaletto painted a series of twelve views of the Grand Canal for Smith which were engraved by Antonio Visentini.[2] That this project was, in some form at least, under way as early as 1730 is suggested by a letter from Smith to a Staffordshire gentleman, Samuel Hill, in which he presumably refers to this set: "The prints of the views and pictures of Venice will now soon be finish'd. I've told you there is only a limited number to be drawn off, so if you want any for friends, speak in time".[3] In fact the set was not to come out until 1735, issued by Giambattista Pasquali, in whose firm Smith had a major stake, with a Latin title reflecting its international appeal, *Prospectus Magni Canalis Venetiarum* (Views of the Grand Canal, Venice). Its real purpose probably went beyond the simple sale of prints; it seems that Smith may have had the views painted and engraved in order to attract the attention of potential British patrons. If this was the case, as Francis Haskell has commented, "the scheme was remarkably successful": in the late 1730s Canaletto painted twenty-four Venetian views for the Duke of Bedford, another set of twenty-two which were eventually dispersed in 1931 from the collection of Sir Robert Harvey, and several for the Earl of Carlisle.[4]

Prints of Venice sold so well that further sets appeared. In 1741 twenty-one prints by Michele Marieschi were published under the title *Magnificentiores Selectioresque Urbis Venetiarum Prospectus* (The More Magnificent and Select Views of the City of Venice). The following year Visentini's series appeared in an enlarged edition of thirty-eight plates, and was reissued in 1751. Among the English buyers at this time was the Oxford don, Joseph Spence, a scholar of modest means who was working on a treatise on the relationship between "the works of the Roman Poets and the remains of the ancient Artists". He went to Venice for the second time while acting as tutor to the young Lord Lincoln in 1741 and laid out the modest sum of 12 crowns 80 baicos – about 10 shillings – on "Canaletti's Views".[5] Unfortunately we do not know which he bought, but his description at least shows that he was conscious of buying prints designed by Canaletto.

Canaletto himself was a printmaker of genius; he began to etch about 1735 and thirty-one of his Venetian architectural subjects were issued as a set entitled *Vedute Altre prese da i Luoghi altre ideate . . .* (Views, some after nature, some imaginary . . . [fig. 1]) which Canaletto dedicated to Smith soon after he became British Consul in Venice in June 1744.[6] That Spence saw, let alone bought, any of Canaletto's early etchings is highly unlikely. These were aimed at the relatively small number of Venetian collectors, outstanding amongst whom was Anton Maria Zanetti the Elder, who appreciated artists' etchings. However, they seem to have made surprisingly little impact at the time either upon British visitors to Venice or on print collectors in Britain.[7] It was Visentini's prints which were of importance to Canaletto's career rather than his own etchings, which did not appear until shortly before Canaletto decided to go to England.

One reason Spence may have spent relatively little on prints of Venice when he was there is that he might have been able to buy such prints in England. Foreign prints were imported in great numbers, and many Venetian views would have been available in the London print shops. There was actually one engraver with Venetian links, Josef Wagner, working in London in the 1730s in association with Jacopo Amigoni; possibly he sold prints from Venice.[8] The market for prints of Venice was strong enough by the mid–1730s for a fan-painter, Joseph Baudin, to publish in London a set of six views of Venice engraved for him by Louis-Philippe Boitard, the draughtsman and engraver who engraved the plates of ancient sculpture in Spence's book, which finally appeared in 1747 with

the title *Polymetis*.

Baudin's prints, which measure nearly 13 by 19 inches (32.4 × 47.7 cm), are signed "Canaleti Pinx; Jo.s Baudin del" and have the publication line "Publish'd by Joseph Baudin April y.e 22.d 1736, according to act of Parliament". Under the terms of the Engravers' Copyright Act, which had come into force the previous May, prints had to bear the date from which copyright was claimed. It is clear from the wording that the prints were based upon drawings made by Baudin; it does not follow that he had worked directly from paintings and it is possible, especially in view of the fact that no painted originals have been satisfactorily identified for all of these six prints, that he was working from drawings sent from Venice. The Act, known as "Hogarth's Act" after its prime mover, was primarily intended to give artists such as William Hogarth protection against the pirating of prints which they themselves published of their own designs, and there was some uncertainty how much protection it really gave publishers over designs by other artists; this may be the reason why Baudin stressed that he had made the drawings on which the prints were based. Like many English prints of the time this set also bore French titles; there was a flourishing print trade between London and Paris, not least because so many of the line engravers in London, such as Boitard, were of French origin.

These prints would have involved Baudin in considerable investment, but he could expect the prints to produce an income for many years. A mezzotint portrait, describing him as "Publisher of the Views of Venice", was engraved by Andrew Miller in 1738; this was obviously a further attempt to draw attention to the project. It is worth mentioning the way in which a number of artists' portraits had been engraved, mostly by John Faber II, the leading mezzotint engraver who had taught Miller. Several of these, for example that of Samuel Scott, may have served to raise the public profile of the artist and draw the attention of potential patrons.[9] In the days before public exhibitions it was not easy to break into the painting profession: hence the way in which many painters also made use of the print market by engineering, often with a subsidy to the engraver, the publication of portraits which they had painted.[10]

Baudin's prints were successful enough for him to bring out a further complementary set of six prints in 1739, which may be based on paintings rather than drawings, since they are

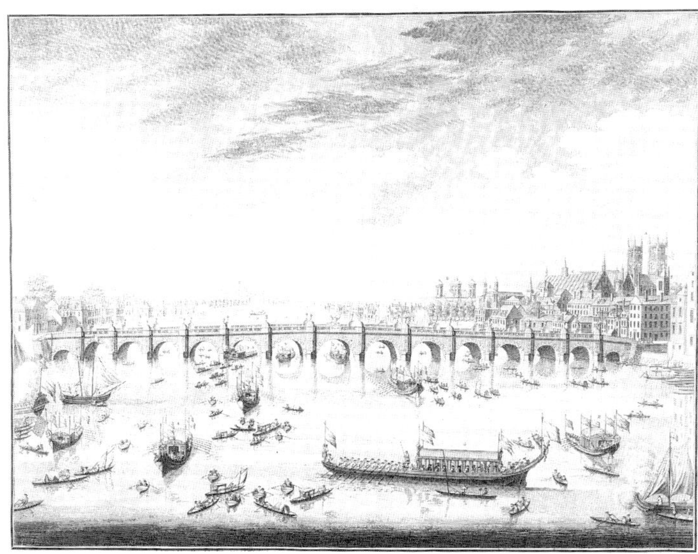

Fig. 13 Remigius Parr after a drawing by Samuel Wale based on a painting by Canaletto, *Westminster Bridge from the north on Lord Mayor's Day*, line engraving, 1747

related to pictures which seem to have been brought to England. The enterprise had clearly prospered for Baudin; in 1744 George Vertue noted of Baudin that "of late years – so much imitated Canaletti. Views of Venice having coppyd several & published prints of them. has also taken to drawing & painting Views here".[11] This second set was engraved by the veteran English engraver Henry Fletcher rather than Boitard, who had by then on his own account engraved and published a plate, dated 1738, of the inside of the Pantheon in Rome, after a painting by Pannini in the collection of Lord James Cavendish.

Boitard's example in producing a print of one of the famous buildings of antiquity was later followed by the English landscape painter Thomas Smith of Derby. He painted four pictures of the Colosseum and other Roman ruins from drawings by Giambattista Busiri, which he had engraved by Francis Vivares, probably the best landscape engraver then at work in London, and which he published in 1745 and 1746. Better known than these were four large composite prints of Roman antiquities based on pictures by Pannini which were published by Arthur Pond and John and Paul Knapton; for 12 shillings purchasers obtained a good idea of all the principal monuments, even though they might in the process have become thoroughly muddled about the topography of the city.[12]

Thomas Smith did not issue other prints of antiquities; his energies were directed into painting and publishing a series of fine prints of northern English scenery, which he launched in the early 1740s. Over the next twenty years he published some thirty large prints based on his own paintings. This was the most important series of English topographical prints to be published singly – rather than in book form – apart from the great enterprise of the brothers Samuel and Nathaniel Buck, whose thirty-year project to make prints of all the principal monuments and towns of England was completed in the early 1750s. These are immensely valuable as a record but except for the large panoramas of towns they had no pretensions to be fine prints.[13] Smith's project also represented the most important case of a landscape painter taking advantage of Hogarth's Act of 1735 to benefit from the sale of prints after his own pictures, in which the often conflicting demands of landscape and topography – on the one hand for beauty and on the other for accuracy – were neatly balanced. The majority of Smith's plates were engraved by Vivares, who had until that time been chiefly employed in engraving landscapes by the Old Masters, first for Pond and then published by himself.[14] Vivares does not appear to have engraved a single contemporary picture prior to his work for Smith. It was important for painters who issued prints of their own work to have them well engraved since this made the prints less vulnerable to competition from similar prints produced by the printsellers. Several printsellers, notably John Boydell (1749–1804), were publishing English views at this time; the shilling views produced by Boydell, who never became a very good engraver, were very matter-of-fact depictions which made no attempt to appeal to serious print collectors. As David Solkin has pointed out, they suggest his early training as a land surveyor and were aimed at people like himself, urban tradespeople of limited means.[15]

It is clear from this discussion that when Canaletto arrived in 1746 the best topographical and landscape prints after contemporary pictures were those initiated and published by painters themselves, launching subscriptions for prints in the way that Hogarth had been doing for his narrative paintings since the early 1730s. For Canaletto such a course of action was both impracticable and unnecessary. As a stranger in a new country he was in no position to arrange subscriptions; these required a great deal of organization and a familiarity with the print-buying fraternity of aristocracy, gentry, clergy, officials and city merchants. He would have needed to be able to invoke the assistance of a number of people of a higher social status to encourage their own peers to subscribe. Such undertakings often took years to carry through; there is no suggestion that Canaletto's residence in England was anything but a temporary one. In addition topographical prints obviously had a special appeal to people of the particular county; although prints of views outside London, such as the country seats of Canaletto's noble patrons, would have to be engraved and printed in London and the subscription organized there, many of the buyers would be those living near the house depicted.

Nor did Canaletto need to concern himself with printselling ventures, whether to increase his reputation or to secure clients. His reputation had gone before him and he already had good contacts with many of the aristocratic families most likely to commission pictures in England. He did not even need to arrange the engraving of a mezzotint portrait of himself as we have seen other painters doing; this was not merely unnecessary, it might have been counterproductive, increasing the professional apprehension which his arrival apparently provoked. No engraved portrait of him appeared in England.

The first prints to be published of paintings done by Canaletto in England were two large ones of Westminster Bridge, the first new bridge in London for centuries. The prints were published by a leading bookseller, John Brindley, who advertised the first [fig. 13] in March 1747:

This Day is published, Price 2s 6d
On a large Sheet of Writing, Imperial Paper, 23 Inches
and a Half by 18,

THE South-east Prospect of Westminster Bridge, Representing the different Arches, the principal Buildings near adjoining each Shore, also on the River, the Magnificent View of the Lord-Mayors Shew, on the 29th October, his Lordship and Bretheren in the City Barge, attended by the different Companies, all finely engrav'd from a Beautiful Painting of Canaleti's.

Published by John Brindley, Bookseller to his Royal Highness the Prince of Wales, in New Bond-street; and sold by all the Booksellers and Printshops of London and Westminster, the Cities of Oxford, Cambridge, York, Bath, Bristol, and all the Principal Towns in England.

For the Curious, a few will be colour'd from the original Painting.[16]

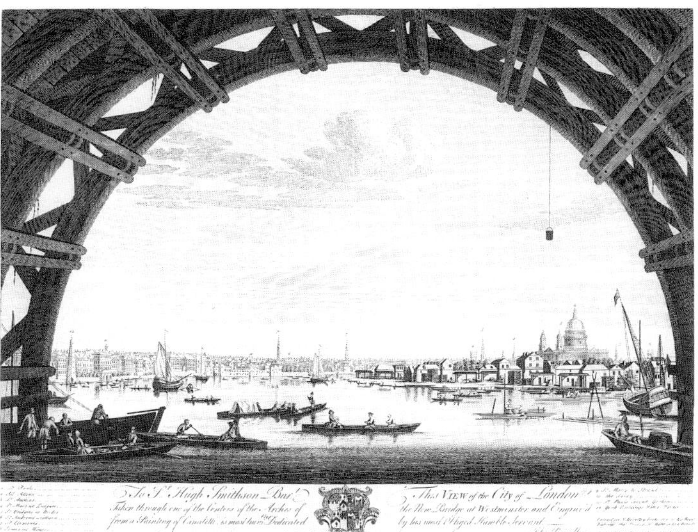

Fig. 14 Remigius Parr after a drawing by Samuel Wale based on a painting by Canaletto, *London seen through an arch of Westminster Bridge,* line engraving, 1747

Interestingly Brindley soon slightly altered his advertisements, emphasizing that this was "the finest bridge in Europe" and adding that the print was "Publish'd according to Act of Parliament": in effect warning against piracies.[17] There was a great deal of interest in the new bridge throughout the country, hence the stress on its general availability. As a bookseller Brindley was able to take advantage of the established network for distributing London books to the provinces.

It is significant that Brindley did not name the engraver, Remigius Parr, in his advertisements. Parr was not an engraver of the first rank; he had been extensively employed by the booktrade, notably on architectural prints, but it is significant that this print seems to be the first which he had ever engraved from any painting, let alone a contemporary painting. Perhaps because of this he was set to work from a drawing of the painting rather than the painting itself. Parr was selected presumably because of his experience as an architectural engraver; the print was being sold as an image of a new bridge which symbolized the progress being made in improving the capital city rather than as a fine engraving. In a sense this was also a 'festival print', since it gave prominence to the spectacle of the Lord Mayor's barge, together with those of nine livery companies identified in the very cluttered inscription area; these gave the print colourers greater scope to introduce brighter colours than was normally possible with prints of London.

Brindley was right to be apprehensive about copies, given the interest in the subject. A longer but very similar print was engraved by Thomas Willson and published by Henry Overton late in 1747, described as "Drawn on the Spot by a Skilful hand, in August 1747". There are sufficient differences in the prints – the boats are different since the Lord Mayor's show is not depicted – that it would have been impossible for Brindley to have gone to law successfully on the grounds of plagiarism, even though the engraver may well have worked from Parr's print. Another similar large print, unsigned and dated, was published by John Bowles as *The North Prospect of Westminster Bridge*, and there were other smaller versions. It was not only the engraving which was copied; several English artists painted views which may have been based on the print, notably Samuel Scott.

Whether Canaletto played any part in the publication of Brindley's print is difficult to say. Since Lord Mayor's Day took place each year in October, the appearance of the advertisements in April 1747 show that he had witnessed the event in the autumn of 1746. What Canaletto did was to anticipate the completion of the bridge, showing it not as it was in October 1746 but as it was assumed it would be when finished; he was not to know that in Spring 1747 one of the piers would settle and that the bridge would not formally be opened until November 1750 [see cat. nos. 6, 7, 8, 13]. Canaletto painted several pictures of the bridge, some as speculations. Had he had a commission for this picture (now in the Yale Center for British Art, New Haven), whose first owner is unknown, at this early point in his visit, or was it one of those painted as a venture? There is no dedication to an owner on the print, which raises the possibility that the engraving had been arranged between Brindley and Canaletto, who might have thought that the publicity from such a print would be helpful in finding a buyer and attracting new clients. The claim that a few prints "will be colour'd from the original Painting" may simply be a figure of speech rather than a claim that the colourists would work from the painting; the normal practice was for one or more copies of the print to be coloured from the painting and for the colourists to work from these master copies; had the painting been in

Brindley's shop he would surely have mentioned this. It is worth noting that the drawing from which the engraver worked was by Samuel Wale, who is named on the print, rather than by Canaletto. However, this may not be significant; Wale was an immensely experienced draughtsman who would have known better than Canaletto what kind of drawing would be of most help to an engraver who had never previously engraved on this scale.

Brindley followed up the first print with a second, slightly smaller one [fig. 14], which was published on 3 June 1747, and advertised as:

> Address'd to Sir HUGH SMITHSON, Bart.
> A Most beautiful View of the *City of London*, taken through one of the Centers of the Arches of the New Bridge at Westminster, and engrav'd from a Painting of the Famous CANALETTI; *great Care has been taken to have this Print well Executed*, the size of which is upwards of 21 Inches by 16, very proper for the ornaments of Gentlemen and Ladies Apartments, Noblemen's-Halls, &c. in the Country. . . . [18]

The rest of the advertisement was similar to the earlier ones, and the price remained at 2s 6d, which was good value and should have brought a large sale; by contrast Ravenet's engraving of Pond's portrait of the Duke of Cumberland published later in the month, with an image size of about 14 by 11 inches (35.5×28 cm), cost 3s.[19] It is interesting that this advertisement makes more of Canaletto's name, that emphasis is laid on the standard of engraving, and that the print is dedicated to Smithson, later Earl of Northumberland, who owned the picture [cat. no. 6]. Aesthetically this is a much more effective print, largely because of the striking use which Canaletto made of the wooden centrings, shortly to be removed as the bridge approached completion. The print is also better presented and the lettering bolder. Whereas the earlier print could, frankly, have been designed by anyone, this is recognisably after Canaletto. It does not seem to have been copied – perhaps because it was so distinctive – though there is a small version of it in the corner of John Bowles's undated *North prospect*.

After Brindley's two engravings it was three years before there were any further prints after Canaletto, and these are something of a come-down after the first two impressive, if not very sophisticated, prints. The artist was very busy working for private patrons. Most of these had high social status; if any

Fig. 15 Anthony Walker after a drawing by Canaletto,
A view of the new bridge over the Thames at Walton, line
engraving, after 1755

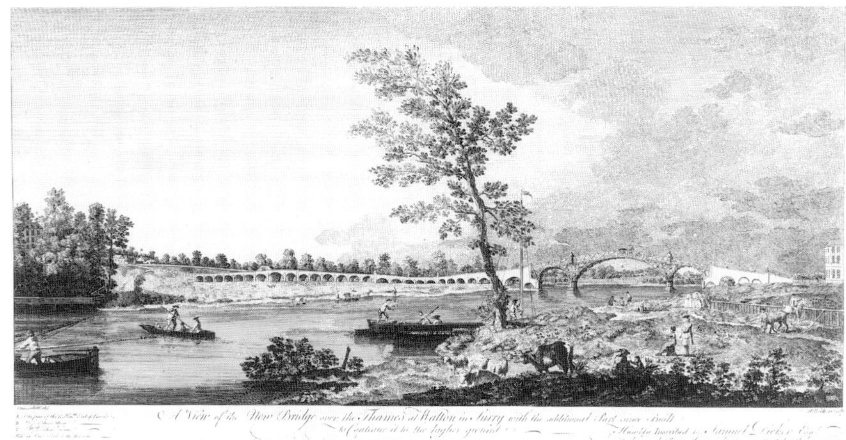

were approached by publishers asking for permission to have pictures engraved they clearly did not consent. They might have agreed had permission been sought to engrave a Poussin or Teniers on their walls, which would have increased their prestige as collectors; there was not the same reflected glory in showing that one had a Canaletto. Thus Vivares, for example, did not engrave a single plate after Canaletto, even though in 1753 he engraved two plates after pictures in English collections by Francesco Zuccarelli, the Venetian landscape painter already becoming popular with the English. Zuccarelli became widely known through high quality English prints after his paintings by Vivares, Bartolozzi, William Byrne and others. It is possible of course that publishers did not consider that prints of the pictures which Canaletto was producing would sell well enough. As a landscape engraver Vivares probably did not regard Canaletto's work as suitable for his burin. Topography was considered inferior to landscape, especially if landscape could be presented as history painting, as it was by Richard Wilson or Zuccarelli. The qualities which made Canaletto's paintings so arresting, notably his skill as a colourist, were ones which did not come across in prints, and his marvellous clarity was lost except in the finest prints; the market was not yet ready for a comprehensive survey of the city, made up of large-scale prints of the highest standard, which would be equal to the sets of Venetian views produced for visitors. Although there were numerous prints of London many of them were illustrations to historical works; even the Bucks produced only ten prints of London, and it was only with the development in the 1770s of aquatint, which enabled artists to

produce large prints themselves, that surveys such as Thomas Malton's became viable. In the middle of the century prints of Old Master pictures were still the ones which sold best at the top end of the market, together with portraits and pictures of the War of the Austrian Succession, which came to an end in 1748.

Between 1750 and 1753, however, a group of a dozen prints, mostly engraved areas measuring just over 9 × 15 inches (23 × 38 cm), and frequently hand-coloured, were issued after Canaletto's London views. These were "Perspectives", designed not only to be framed or kept in albums and portfolios but also to be looked at through optical viewing devices, which gave the prints a three-dimensional effect. The machines were of various types, the most popular being the diagonal mirror; the viewer looked through a large lens at a mirror, hinged from the top of the device at 45 degrees, in which the print was reflected.[20]

Initially most of the London prints aimed at this market were published by members of the two great printselling families, Bowles and Overton, but in the late 1740s Robert Sayer, who took over the business of Paul Overton, became the principal publisher, and it was he who published nearly all the optical views designed by Canaletto. The first two, *A view from Somerset Gardens* engraved by Edward Rooker, and *A north-east view of Westminster*, engraved by J.S. Muller (Miller), were taken from paintings belonging to Thomas West, but most of the others are inscribed "Canaleti delin" and were based on drawings, probably commissioned by the publisher. On 2 December 1751 Sayer, publishing jointly with Henry Overton, issued

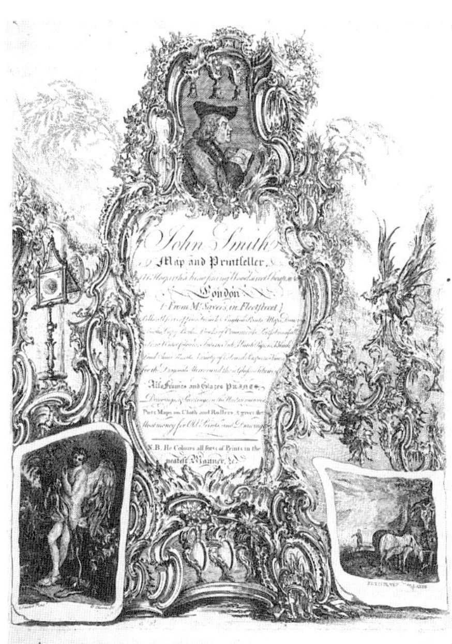

Fig. 16 B. Clowes, trade card of John Smith, printseller, line engraving, engraved area $9\frac{1}{4} \times 7$ ins (23.5 × 18 cm)

a set of four views of Vauxhall Gardens, the most famous resort in London; these were engraved from drawings by Canaletto, made probably after he had returned from his visit to Venice at the end of 1750 and the beginning of 1751. It seems that by then he was finding more difficulty in obtaining commissions for paintings and may have welcomed the relatively small sums obtained by selling or lending his drawings to the print-seller, especially as the prints may have brought him requests for painted versions of them. Most of these prints were new compositions; one exception is a view of *Northumberland House*, engraved by T. Bowles after a picture belonging to Smithson, by then Earl of Northumberland [fig. 8], which is signed "Canaleti Pinxt et Delint"; in other words Canaletto also made the drawing (now in Minneapolis) [fig. 27] for the engraver. Canaletto does not seem to have been asked to make drawings for new prints of Venice; prints of his Venetian views were still available. Among them would have been the six prints engraved by Fabio Berardi published by Wagner, who went with Amigoni to Venice in 1739. At least one English print may have been engraved while Canaletto was in London: *A View of the Great Canal of Venice from the Church of the Holy Cross*,

engraved by John Boydell, presumably from the print in Visentini's 1742 edition, was published by William Herbert whose shop was on London Bridge. Although Canaletto does not seem to have found his later years in London as profitable as the first ones he was still not tempted into publishing prints on his own account. He would have been aware, though, that other painters were doing this, notably George Lambert who launched a subscription in 1754 for a set of four prints, finely engraved by P.C. Canot and James Mason, of pictures of Mount Edgcumbe and Plymouth painted for Lord Mount Edgcumbe.[21]

Before Canaletto finally returned to Venice one fine print after his work did appear, *A View of the New Bridge over the Thames at Walton* [fig. 15], engraved by the very talented draughtsman Anthony Walker, who gave elegance to everything he engraved. This print is very closely related to a drawing which is inscribed, apparently by Canaletto, to the effect that he had drawn it from the picture painted in 1755 for Samuel Dicker, who had paid for the bridge [see also cat. no. 35]. The print does not have a publisher's name, merely the name of a Covent Garden printseller, J. Jarvis, as the seller; it has an unsigned dedication to Dicker. Had Walker been the publisher it would be reasonable to expect that he would have signed the dedication and be named as the publisher in order to secure copyright; the fact that it is unsigned suggests that the print may have been instigated by Dicker himself. If this was indeed a semi-private plate it may explain why it does not seem to have had a very wide distribution, which is a pity, given the print's great superiority to the other English prints by which Canaletto was primarily known to the English public.

Optical prints were widely distributed and sold by most printsellers, including one of Sayer's former employees, John Smith, who set up at Hogarth's Head in Cheapside, producing a splendid trade card which shows a diagonal mirror on the middle left-hand side [fig. 16]. It should be emphasized that the prints after Canaletto were only a few among many which appeared – in 1753 Sayer issued a catalogue of 206. The prints did not do much for Canaletto's reputation, and it is revealing that although Sayer went on selling them until he retired Canaletto's name was not used to promote them and does not appear at all in his 1766 or 1775 catalogues. Nor did John Boydell, who emerged in the 1760s as the most important print publisher in London, ever include prints after Canaletto in any of his catalogues. It is not surprising that Canaletto was unrepresented in the ambitious series of prints which Boydell began to issue in the late 1760s, *Sculptura Britannica: The Most Capital Paintings in England*, since that was, initially at least, made up exclusively of history paintings. Boydell did not commission any new prints of Canaletto's paintings, and he did not acquire the two large plates after Canaletto: how long Parr's plates were printed from and into whose hands they fell is not known. Boydell became adept at acquiring fine plates initially published by others and in due course added to his stock the plates which had first been published, at considerable risk and expense, by Scott, by Lambert and by Richard Wilson; the last two did not put their names on the prints as the publishers and posterity gained the impression that it was Boydell who had first brought them out.[22]

It has been argued here that the absence of fine engravings after Canaletto can in part be explained by the fact that he could or would not operate in the way that his English colleagues had to if fine prints of their work were to appear. The best prints of contemporary topographical or landscape paintings produced at the time were generally the result of initiatives taken by painters themselves. We can only regret that at the time he was in England the English print market was not sufficiently developed to have done justice to such a distinguished visitor.

NOTES

I would like to acknowledge the suggestions of Ruth Bromberg, Ralph Hyde and Giorgio Marini.

1. For engraved views of Venice see *Vues Venitiennes du XVIIIe siècle*, exhibition catalogue, Geneva, Musée d'Art, 1973. Giorgio Marini has drawn my attention also to *Vedute . . . in der venezianischer Graphik des 18. Jahrhunderts*, catalogue by Peter Dreyer, Berlin 1985.

2. See M. Levey, 'Canaletto's Fourteen Paintings and Visentini's Prospectus . . .', *Burlington Magazine* CIV, 1962, pp. 333–41.

3. W.H. Chaloner, 'The Egertons in Italy and the Netherlands 1729–1734', *Bulletin of the John Rylands Library, Manchester* XXXII, no. 2, 1949–50, p.161.

4. F. Haskell, *Patrons and Painters . . .*, revised edition, London 1980, p.305.

5. S. Klima (ed.), *Joseph Spence: Letters from the Grand Tour*, Montreal and London 1975, p.434.

6. For Canaletto's etchings see Ruth Bromberg, *Canaletto's Etchings*, revised edition, San Francisco 1993.

7. For Zanetti see Haskell, *Patrons and Painters*, 1980, and the recent work of Alessandro Bettagno.

8. Giorgio Marini, Bromberg Fellow at Worcester College, Oxford, 1992–94, is working on Wagner.

9. Samuel Scott Bicentenary, exhibition catalogue, London, Guildhall Art Gallery, 1972; it is suggested, p.3, that the print of Scott, engraved and sold by Faber ca. 1731–32 after a painting by Hudson, was "published as an advertisement".

10 The relationship between artists and the print trade is discussed in D. Alexander and R.T. Godfrey, *Painters and Engravings: The Reproductive Print from Hogarth to Wilkie*, exhibition catalogue, New Haven, Yale Center for British Art, 1980.

11 *Walpole Society* XXVI (Vertue Note Books V), 1937–38, p.30, cited by W.G. Constable (revised J.G. Links), *Canaletto*, 2 vols, Oxford 1976; the prints of Baudin's two sets are listed *ibidem*. For Baudin see H.F. Finberg, 'Joseph Baudin, Imitator of Canaletto', *Burlington Magazine* LX, April 1932, pp. 204–07.

12 See L. Lippincott, *Selling Art in Georgian London: The Rise of Arthur Pond*, London 1983, pp. 140–44.

13 Panoramic views of English cities are the subject of a forthcoming book by Ralph Hyde.

14 For Vivares see E. Miller, 'Landscape Prints by Francis Vivares', *Print Quarterly* X, 1992, pp.273–81.

15 D.H. Solkin, *Richard Wilson: The Landscape of Reaction*, exhibition catalogue, London, Tate Gallery, 1982, p.30, where a typical example of one of Boydell's views is illustrated.

16 *General Advertiser*, 26 March and 27 March, 1747. For this and other prints after Canaletto see H.F. Finberg, 'Canaletto in England', *Walpole Society* IX, 1920, pp. 21–76.

17 *General Advertiser*, 31 March and 6 April, 1747.

18 *General Advertiser*, 1 and 3 June, 1747.

19 *General Advertiser* from 28 May 1747; Lippincott, *Selling Art*, 1983, fig. 10.

20 See C.J. Kaldenbach, 'Perspective Views', *Print Quarterly* II, 1985, pp.87–104.

21 A subscription for the prints was being advertised by mid January 1755 (*Public Advertiser* from 12 January; *Whitehall Evening Post* 16–18 January) at a guinea and a half, with a statement that the prints, which were published on 5 May, would be not less than two guineas to non-subscribers; Lambert published a further six, less expensive prints himself. The Mount Edgcumbe prints were reissued by a consortium of printsellers, including Sayer and Boydell.

22 Wilson published six Welsh views engraved by Mason and others by means of a two-guinea subscription in 1767 (*St James's Chronicle*, 9–12 May 1767).

Framing the Modern City: Canaletto's Images of London

MARK HALLETT

Today, Canaletto enjoys a curiously inert and undeveloped identity in the history of art. He has become canonized as both the last representative of the Italian Old Master tradition and as the most sophisticated recorder of eighteenth-century urban life. He is described as a painter who effortlessly yoked the modern city into the realms of ambitious representation, painting it with what Zanetti, shortly after the artist's death, described as a "beautiful clarity and ease of colour and brushwork".[1] This type of abstracted, formalist rhetoric continues to dominate critical discussion of the artist, and is frequently deployed to rescue his work from the supposed constraints of a purely topographical imagery. Meanwhile, the main body of art historical research on Canaletto has concentrated on establishing a secure chronology of artistic production, tying his paintings, drawings and etchings to the narrative of his Italian and English careers.

Now seems an appropriate moment to begin developing new arguments about his work's complex exchanges with different ideological and cultural agendas in mid-eighteenth-century England, and to re-interpret its functions within an urban society constantly subject to re-definition and re-representation. It also provides an opportunity to explore the production, promotion and appeal of the printed images generated by his paintings and designs, ones disseminated along a circuit of consumption geared to a public existing far beyond the confines of the aristocratic gallery. A useful starting-point in terms of both of these preoccupations is the subject that Canaletto first represented on his arrival in England in 1746, one which he repeatedly returned to, and which also formed the focus of a related series of prints and drawings: Westminster Bridge [see cat. nos. 6, 7, 8, 13].

After discussing the imagery of this iconic structure of the modern city, I shall go on to investigate Canaletto's representation of urban space, and his construction of spectatorship. I shall argue that a central painting of his English career, *Whitehall and the Privy Garden from Richmond House* [cat. no. 9], offered a new pictorial definition of aristocratic authority in the metropolitan environment, one that sought to reconcile the signs of élite status with the spaces of popular and bourgeois culture. I shall end by looking at a very different category of Canaletto's English work, the designs he executed for printsellers in the early 1750s, and suggest that they conformed to a new identity for the engraved urban prospect, as a spectacular commodity operating within the bourgeoning sphere of commercialised leisure.

The erection of Westminster Bridge was the major public building project of mid-eighteenth-century London. The need for an alternative conduit for commerce, transport and communication to the dilapidated and overladen London Bridge had been voiced for years; however, it was the impetus provided by a collection of civic-minded and commercially astute members of the Westminster élite specifically organized to coordinate political action on the matter, and meeting regularly at the Horn Tavern in New Palace Yard, that provoked parliamentary legislation. This "Society of Gentlemen" lobbied for and helped ensure the passage of a bridge-building bill in 1736. A body of nearly 200 commissioners was set up to supervise proceedings, and in 1738 work began according to a plan executed by Charles Labelye, a Swiss engineer who subsequently managed the project until its completion in 1750.[2]

The scheme for a new bridge met with sustained and vociferous opposition from the beginning. Petitions to Parliament from the Lord Mayor, Aldermen and Commons of the City of London complained that their traditional status as commercial guardians of the river would be undermined, and that trade and jobs would be sucked out of the east of the capital. The discontent voiced by the Thames watermen was even more acute. For decades, the Thames had been distinguished as an environment in which hierarchies of class, language and decorum that operated in the city itself were temporarily destabilized, if not suspended, and where a boisterous, foul-mouthed and insubordinate river culture constantly overrode the supposedly deferential relationship between the boatmen and the hundreds of passengers they ferried from bank to bank. As well as threatening their livelihood, the bridge promised to arc over this problematic space, and consign the watermen to an emasculated cultural periphery. They responded with a sustained campaign of sabotage and disruption throughout the building of the bridge, climbing on to the scaffolding to threaten the masons, sinking boats, and ramming their barges into the newly raised piers. Criticism also focused on the extensive programme of urban redevelopment around the Westminster approaches to the bridge, supervised by Labelye's assistant Thomas Lediard. Scores of houses were demolished, their occupants bought or forced out, and itinerant and petty trade driven from the streets. The area was rebuilt with broad avenues and palatial houses designed to provide "handsome and convenient lodgings for Members of Parliament and other persons of distinction".[3] Clearly, then, the bridge operated at the centre of a wider, dramatically interventionist project of slum clearance and gentrification, one which reorganized both architectural structure and social space in the interests of a dominant and ruthless urban élite.

By its defenders, the bridge was described as a testament to a modern ideal of civic enlightenment where, as Labelye wrote, "public good, and public spirit, have got the better of private interest".[4] For the entrepreneurial aristocrats who were to form the core of Canaletto's early patronage in England, it was both an iconographically loaded monument to civic responsibility and, throughout its extended metamorphosis from proposal to structure, a flamboyantly modern fixture in the metropolitan environment of commerce and reconstruction that they sought to exploit anew. Part scaffolding, part neo-classical sign, it promised, in Labelye's words, both a "very great ornament to the capital of the British empire . . . and a considerable means towards the increase of Trade, Manufacture and the Useful Arts".[5] The bridge's uncluttered, neo-Palladian design, with its gently curved façade of gleaming white Portland stone and subtle neoclassical detail, linked it to the ideas of an antique culture celebrated in terms of patrician virtue, social order and physical rationality. Furthermore, the bridge's identity as a metaphorical blueprint of urban stability was supplemented by its simultaneous celebration as a marvel of contemporary engineering and as the most explicit site of the modern in the capital. The monumental scale of the technological intervention that was necessitated by the building scheme – the newly invented machines, the webs of wooden supports that propped up the arches – dominated much of the discussion about the bridge as it emerged out of the water. Crowds of people came to stare, and a boating tour around its environs – which temporarily offered a lucrative if ominous new business sideline to the watermen – became an essential part of the polite touristic circuit of the city.

Within the hierarchies of élite taste, and in the theoretical treatises that helped underpin them, the prospect of the English metropolitan waterfront had long been defined as a somewhat debased category of landscape painting and disallowed any pretensions as a site of artistic ambition. The genre's domination by the pictorial conventions of Dutch landscape painting (duplicated by both Dutch and British artists working in London) distanced it from the models of landscape painting — perhaps best exemplified by the works of Claude Lorrain – that enjoyed high cultural status in mid-eighteenth-century England. Why then did Westminster Bridge become a repeated subject of aristocratically sponsored representation? It is clear that this phenomenon arose out of a collective élite demand for the promotion and dissemination of a positive pictorial codification of a project that, as we have seen, was fraught with conflict and opposition. It has recently been established that almost all of Canaletto's early English patrons were Commissioners of the bridge.[6] In particular, the artist executed a series of paintings and drawings for Sir Hugh Smithson, a leading voice in the "Society of Gentlemen", and an active member of the Board of Commissioners throughout the project. For Smithson, the painting of an urban environment that had previously been associated with a theoretically lowly Dutch and native pictorial tradition was newly legitimised through its redefinition as an elevated site of urban regeneration and civic pride. It was a practice further sanctioned by the involvement of Canaletto, whose provenance and celebrity immediately tied his images of the bridge and the city to a particularly privileged pictorial category. His views of Venice had become prized if over-subscribed trophies in the cultural baggage of numerous English Grand Tourists from the 1720s onwards [see cat. nos. 2 and 3], and George Vertue, the contemporary chronicler of the London art scene, noted on his arrival that "the Multitude of his works done abroad for English noblemen & Gentlemen has procurd him great reputation … he is much esteemed and no doubt but what Views and works He doth here, will give the same satisfaction".[7]

In his view of *London seen through an arch of Westminster Bridge* of ca. 1747 [cat. no. 6], Canaletto's first painting for Smithson, the artist clearly redeployed many of the conventions of his Venetian river views. Like them, the city is depicted as a rhythmic assemblage of architectural landmarks and the more muted façades of dockland commerce, a topographic strip juxtaposed with a river-space that supports harmonious narratives of polite passage and marine trade. Canaletto's distinctive shorthand of masts and sails here helps geometricize and order a traditionally dissonant social space, and within it the couples on the boats are pictured as temporary tourists, pulled towards the mathematically precise urban prospect. The bridge itself,

more radically, is defined as a structure that both frames and receives the gaze of the spectator outside the image. Indeed we are pictorially assaulted, shadowed and distanced by the compositional force of this arched internal frame. Why was this dramatic pictorial strategy employed here?

To answer this, we need to turn briefly to categories of early eighteenth-century Venetian art other than the topographic prospect: the *capriccio* and the *veduta ideata*, which were often equivalently geared to the affluent foreign traveller. Marco Ricci's *Capriccio with ruins* [fig. 17] was typical of the genre in its concentration on the motif of the arch, which here frames spaces in which it is relentlessly redeployed. Its gigantic, looming presence both denies and organizes the viewer's access to pictorial space, and constructs the spectator as an educated, if isolated, tourist. We stand outside, and are asked to interpret as well as enter, to assimilate the workers and the shards of antique ruins in terms of a vicarious historical – and art historical – tourism, one that renders the men lifting the ladder, and standing on a plank holding a rope, as picturesque fixtures of a nostalgic, theatricalized landscape. The *veduta ideata*, on the other hand, dramatized the continuing relevance and potential of classic forms. The most ambitious Venetian practitioner of this genre was Piranesi, whose series of *vedute* known as the *Prima Parte* had been published in 1743. Canaletto's internal arch was a direct appropriation from one of Piranesi's engravings from the series, his *Monumental bridge* [fig. 18], which reinscribed Palladio's projected design for the Rialto Bridge in Venice on a grandiloquent and heavily revised basis. Piranesi's image juxtaposes the shadowy figures of contemporary boatmen with the reinflected glories of an older Italian architectural tradition, one that is associated throughout the series with the grandeur of ancient Rome as well as with the most distinguished Venetian precedents. In it, figural narratives are entirely subordinate to the architectural vocabulary generated across the retreating façade, itself framed by a semicircle of stone, the symmetry of which is interrupted only by the desultory signs of an occluded Arcadia – the hanging branches of ivy and amputated stumps of trees breaking through the water's surface.

The pictorial conventions and narrative associations of both genres were frequently redeployed in painted representations of mid-eighteenth-century London. Particularly relevant here are the paintings of Antonio Joli, a close colleague of Canaletto who had made an earlier trip from Venice to London. His *Capriccio with a view of the Thames and St Paul's* of ca. 1746 [cat. no. 41] uses a wholly artificial arched structure – a skeletal version of a Renaissance church's domed crossing – as a screen that is superimposed on and across the river, defining the city in relationship to the most prestigious traditions of public architecture. Like Canaletto's painting, it provides a framing pictorial rhetoric for a 'new' prospect of London. Here it encloses a polite space of viewing, conversation and etiquette, and reconstructs the Thames as a legitimate scenic context for urbane discourse, one monitored and responded to by the Roman statues in the alcoves – two surrogate viewers – who further yoke the image to the neo-classical references and connotations that were used to redefine mythically the city as a 'new Rome'.[8]

Canaletto's painting, in its reinflection of Piranesi's pictorial strategy, operated as a close equivalent to Joli's adaptation of the *capriccio*. Most importantly, it again helps secure the city prospect as a subject worthy of ambitious representation. More shockingly, perhaps, it fuses the central motif of the arch – with its blatant iconographic reference to a series of images dealing with the ideal forms of antique culture – to a minutely detailed record of the bridge's building accessories: the scaffolding, pieces of rope, patches of painting and, of course, the celebrated hanging bucket. A quotidian allegory of modernity is thus mapped across the framing signifier of classical architecture. Importantly, it is one untroubled by the actual, corporeal presence of the bridge workers themselves – they are withdrawn from the image. The representational enmeshing of the arch with the scaffolding thus provided an internal, mutually reinforcing symbolic juxtaposition that correlated precisely with the dual readings of the bridge as both a bearer of tradition and an icon of modernity. Underneath the bridge, the dissident subculture of the watermen is drained as a network of commercial and cultural independence. Joli's image had distanced the boatmen and populated its uncluttered foreground with genteel couples. Canaletto's, rather differently, foregrounds the working culture of the Thames, but defines the watermen – ferrying the polite across the river, and utterly dominated by the structure that looms over them – as representatives of an already marginalised community, clinging to the shadowed edges of the river. As such, they become, like the anonymous figures of the *capriccio*, emptied symbols of a

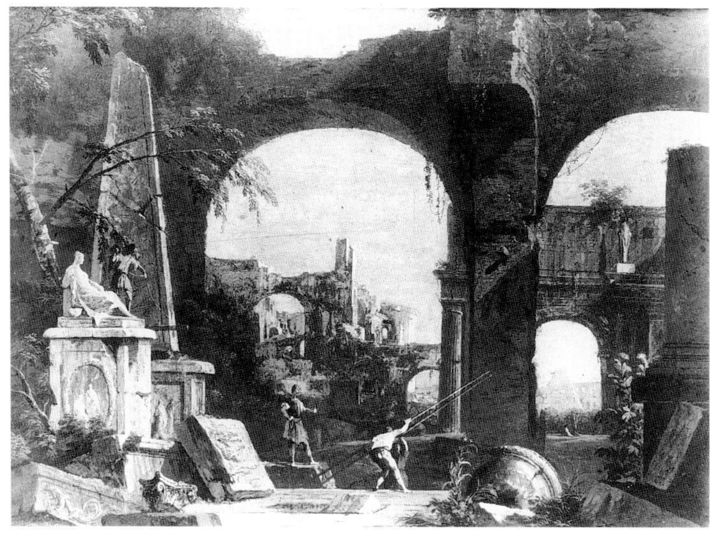

Fig. 17 Marco Ricci, *Capriccio with ruins*, tempera on leather, $13\frac{1}{4} \times 18$ ins (33.7×45.7 cm), Her Majesty the Queen

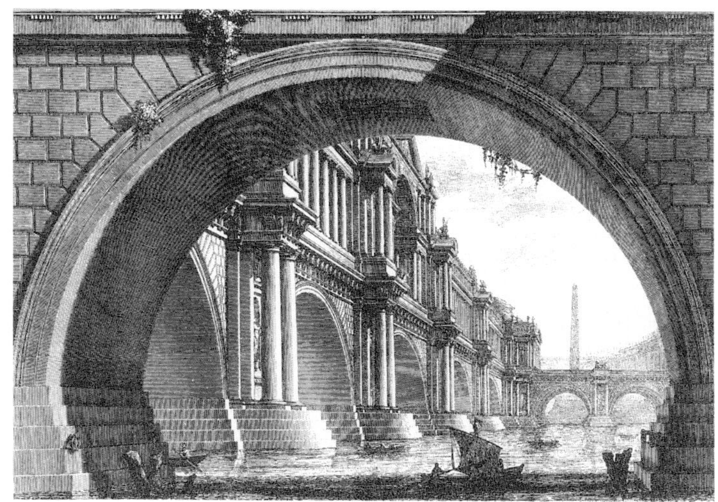

Fig. 18 Giambattista Piranesi, *Ponte magnifico . . .* (Monumental bridge), etching from the series known as the *Prima Parte*, 1743

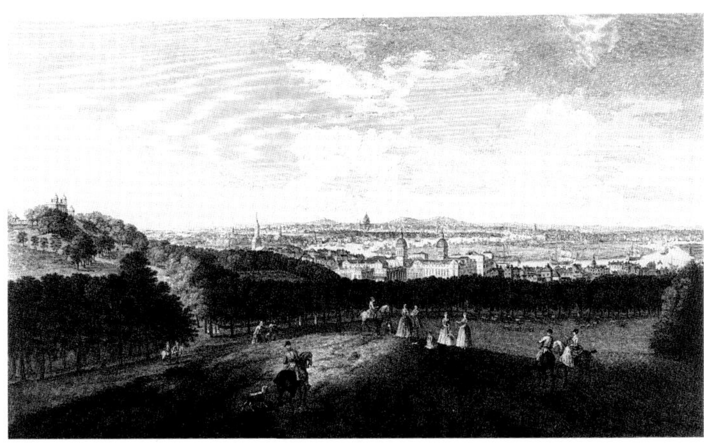

Fig. 19 John Wood after Peter Tillemans, *The view from One Tree Hill in Greenwich Park*, engraving, 1744

redundant culture that is redefined in picturesque terms. Similarly, the viewer is the one figure who operates outside these local details of class and environment, a floating spectator given a withdrawn but wider 'public' perspective, and a set of art historical references, that allows him to begin deciphering the pictorial dialectic of modernity and tradition inscribed across the arch and social space beyond.

In *A Letter on Curiosity* of 1730, an anonymous author had asked, "why, I say, should [owners] not be persuaded to publish Prints of their fine Pictures, or other things? this being both amusing and reputable, as well as instructive (often also profitable) to the Proprieter, and beneficial to the publick."[9] Remigius Parr's engraving of Canaletto's painting, executed after a drawn copy by Samuel Wale, produced for the publisher John Brindley, and released very soon after the completion of the original painting [fig. 14], fulfilled this rhetorical suggestion. The print was dedicated to Smithson, and clearly operated as an important vehicle for his civic agenda. Equally, it was promoted as an affordable marker of urbane taste, geared to both metropolitan and provincial demand, advertised as "a Most beautiful view of the city of London, taken through one of the Centers of the Arches of the New Bridge at Westminster, and engrav'd from a painting by the Famous Canaletti; *great Care has been taken to have this Print well executed* ... very proper for the ornaments of Gentlemen and Ladies Apartments, Noblemen's-Halls, &c., in the country. Care will be taken to convey this ... into all the different great Towns in England."[10]

Parr's engraving fitted into a modern formulation of the urban view in graphic culture. In the decade or so before Canaletto's arrival in England, we can trace the emergence of a category of print that rearticulated the city prospect as a respectable accessory in the private spaces of polite society as much as a decorative badge of civic pride. A useful indication of this new exchange is provided by John Wood's engraving of *The View from One Tree Hill in Greenwich Park* [fig. 19], after the painting by Peter Tillemans, which was published by Arthur Pond in 1744. Here, the traditional topographic strip of the capital is distanced by, and interpreted across, a manicured space of conversation and leisure, one dominated by the signs of landed culture — the hunt, the rolling expanse of landed property, the picnicking women. Given the vocabulary of the advertisement for Parr's engraving — the appeal to a polite audience, the explicit link to a painted original, the marketing of "a most beautiful view of the City of London" — we can see that his image was promoted in similar terms to those assumed by Pond. Equally obviously, Parr's image offers a radically different depiction of the capital. Whereas Wood's engraving rendered the city as a naturalised adjunct to the English landscape, Parr's allows no hint of the Arcadian. Wood's image had integrated the city into a mythically fixed, unchanging hierarchy of aristocratic power — one which the bourgeois consumer could vicariously share through purchase. Parr's, on the other hand, shows a city in flux, and a view newly crowded by an exclamatory iconography of urban change.

As such, it reproduced many of the features of another well established category of graphic culture, one that even more specifically focused on the paraphernalia of incompletion: machinery, abandoned designs, inventions, scaffolding, tools, labour, the fragments of modern structures rather than the completed whole. The Westminster Bridge project generated a spate of engravings that recorded the subsidiary and ephemeral by-products of the bridge's long gestation: projected wooden centres [fig. 20], rejected designs, even the strange contraptions invented to facilitate progress — the pile-driving machine designed by James Vanloue, a watchmaker, for instance [fig. 21], and William Etheridge's underwater sawing machine. Canaletto's painting and Parr's engraving, in their preoccupation with the details and detritus of the bridge's temporary infrastructure, thus shared the iconography of images that dramatized bridge-building as a process, an event, a narra-

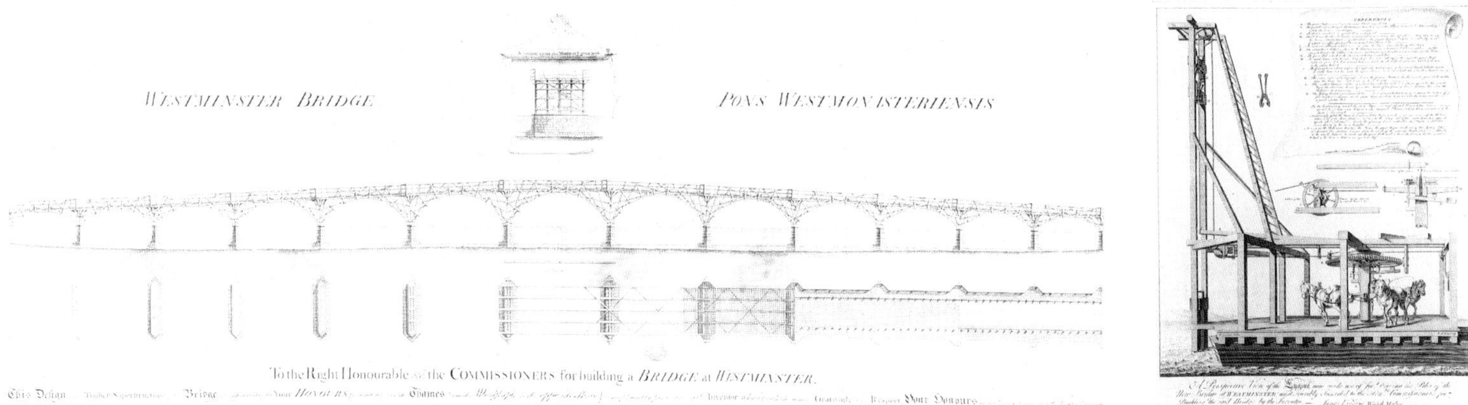

Fig. 20 Pierre Fourdrinier after James King, *A design of the timber superstructure of Westminster Bridge*, engraving, 1738

Fig. 21 John Jure, *A perspective view of the engine now made use of for driving the piles of the new bridge at Westminster*, engraving

tive of technological innovation within which the worker was rendered a dwarfed accessory to the machine; an imagery that, we can suggest, was to reach a kind of apotheosis in Edward Rooker's or Piranesi's engravings of London's next great bridge-building project, that at Blackfriars [fig. 30].

These references to the mechanical, the unfinished, and to the traces of plebeian labour were, as I have already argued, mediated in the painted image by the formal and compositional strategies of certain categories of Venetian painting. In the print, these potentially disruptive details — even in an engraving, the hanging bucket could be (mis)read as an ironic and inappropriate emblem of the popular — are further controlled by two extra-pictorial mechanisms. The introduction of a numbered index of modern buildings within and without the image relates the minutiae of construction to a completed series of public buildings, and thus to a broader, well established programme of civic renewal and patrician benevolence catalogued across the horizon. More explicitly, the anchoring of the accompanying text by Smithson's coat of arms freights the reproduced image with the heraldic vocabulary of an ancient representational code, and thus signals its status as a sanctioned — if newly commodified — adjunct of aristocratic culture.

So far, I have focused on the imagery of an iconic structure of the modern city. Did Canaletto's paintings of less obviously symbolic sites within the capital generate equivalent readings, and similarly provide the urbanised aristocratic community with a modern, pictorial rearticulation of their presence and status within the social spaces of the metropolis? *Whitehall and the Privy Gardens from Richmond House* [cat. no. 9] was painted in 1747 for the Duke of Richmond, one of the wealthiest and most influential peers of his day. Like Smithson, he was both a Commissioner of the new bridge (being built only a few hundred yards away from the site of the painting) and was actively involved in a variety of civic institutions, including the London Hospital, the Society of Antiquaries, the London Infirmary and the Royal Society. He was also a substantial patron of the arts; even before Canaletto's arrival he had bought several painted urban prospects, and was Antonio Joli's main private sponsor in the 1740s.

In Canaletto's painting, the view from one of the Duke's rear windows opens out on to an urban prospect that had, years before, been a central environment of royal power: Whitehall Palace. In the middle distance stand two towering remnants of an older court culture — the Holbein or Treasury Gate on the left, and the Banqueting House on the right. But they were, indeed, remnants — the Palace had burnt down in 1698, and in its emptied place the Privy Gardens had emerged in the eighteenth century as an important site of polite display and conversation. It is one bounded on the left of the image by the expanding avenue of Parliament Street, currently undergoing redevelopment, and on the right by the backs of aristocratic houses: directly opposite, Lady Pelham's recent brick conversion of a cow-shed and laundry building, and behind the tree that spreads over the roof of Richmond's courtyard the town house of the Duke of Montagu.

It is quickly apparent that the painting insistently organizes the view into a fractured hierarchy that operates primarily through the pictorial and physical compartmentalization of three different social spaces, which are defined as separate yet interconnecting. On the lower right, the wall that arrows towards the viewer encloses a space that remains partly inscribed by a traditional code of social deference: the Duke of Richmond himself is portrayed, walking through his own privately possessed property, being bowed to by a liveried servant. An older, hierarchical pattern of a paternal, landed culture is reinflected within the urban zone. Yet even while this exchange remains sealed off from – and thus untainted by – the narratives of the city, it is linked to them: the opened door at the end of the darkened tunnel (yet another arched conduit for interpretation) opens out to a public space operating independently of aristocratic control, and the Duke's display of open-armed grace is a gesture both mimicked and modified in the various episodes of polite personal contact in the bourgeois sphere. This process of internal displacement, or de-emphasis, for the depicted aristocratic body is even more radically indicated by the Duke's immediate environment: he is shown not in front of his magnificent house, but standing next to the servants' quarters, among the everyday details of the house's working subculture: a man putting a key into a door, chickens, a ladder, a washing line, a pole lying against a wall, curtains in the windows; bits and pieces.

Within the painting, however, the courtyard remains a fragmented, marginal space: it is that of the Privy Garden which dominates the image. Perhaps most immediately striking about the Garden are the physical markers of a highly codified system of social and bodily decorum – the paths that cross the tended lawns, the bollards that arc alongside a modern pavement, wooden barriers that men lean on, posts that prevent the gilded carriage from breaking into the pedestrianised grids of a space that remains part park, part square. Along these spatial demarcations, we are presented with the narratives of urbane perambulation, within which the individual is defined both as independent – a number of figures are depicted alone – and yet subtly locked into a network of visual and conversational exchange. The Privy Garden is pictured as a place where the polite (a term blurring the boundaries, as the Garden did, between bourgeois and élite culture) could cluster with acquaintances, enjoy in public a gender-specific conversation (all the groups in the image are single-sexed), or merely stand at a fence gazing across the lawn, casually ignoring or absorbing the components of an already formulated urban picturesque – the workers tending the hedge, the poor families clinging to the edges of the cut grass. Here again the poor become unthreatening fixtures operating at the fringes of the modern touristic thoroughfare.

In the distance, Parliament Street is indicated as a parallel public space, linked to the garden by another doorway, but also cut off from it. And here I think we can suggest how the demands of this kind of image were somewhat different to those that helped condition the depiction of Westminster Bridge: the view from the Duke's house, his own private prospect, invoked a set of priorities other than those of the celebratory imagery of the bridge. *Whitehall and the Privy Garden* was never engraved, and did not operate as a pictorial vehicle promoting urban reconstruction in the same way that Smithson's painting did. It articulated an aristocratic view over the city, one within which the street is incorporated – as yet another space being transformed – but also distanced as a representationally problematic area of the popular, the crowded and the dirty.[11]

The Duke of Richmond's image both signals a new bodily rhetoric of aristocratic restraint within the city and within painting, and offers the compensatory metaphor of the all-seeing eye. Within the picture, he is rendered as merely one figural component of social organization, an equivalent as well as a model for the individuals, couples and groups who circulate around the park and enter the servants' quarters. In depicting him as such, the painting, we can suggest, correlates to a broader shift in the way aristocratic identity was pictorially signified in mid-eighteenth-century England. The ostentatious display of personal status suggested in the grand portrait, or the conventional view of the great landowner in front of his country house, could be deemed both vulgar and problematic within an urban culture where the continuing hierarchies of class were complicated by new forms of capital, communication and social identity. Canaletto's image, I would argue, answered to a need on the part of élite culture for a form of self-representation that corresponded to, and helped mediate, the contemporary dynamics of aristocratic power in the city. The Duke's presence is thus suggested as one that complements rather than contradicts the narratives of the modern urban environment, and the modern city is mythicized as a space punctuated not only by the signs of aristocratic status and decorum but also by codes of bourgeois emulation that have become naturalised, and by the laundered narratives of popular domesticity.

However, the displacement of the aristocratic figure within the hierarchies of the painting, its seeming de-evaluation to the level of miniaturized portrait, is recovered at the level of spectatorship. Canaletto's prospect is clearly intended to map that of the Duke's: this is his view out of his window. There is thus a central process of doubling here. The Duke's occluded perspective within the image is extended and replenished by his perspective from without it, which reasserts aristocratic authority through the channel of the disembodied eye, and through an embryonic mechanics of surveillance. If the space that he looks over, unlike that which surrounded his rural properties, was no longer one that he owned as an economic commodity, it is one that he can continue to appropriate, from on high, at the level of hegemonic observation, which here functions as an appropriate metaphor for the strategies of social and spatial ordering operating on a broader basis in mid-century Westminster. Figural displacement is balanced by the rearticulation of the mythically disinterested vision (and practice) of the aristocratic spectator, one that is able to retain a sense of the public sphere — here, organized along a tripartite spatial schema — even as it is constructed from within the privatised space of the household.

I would like to end by suggesting that the designs Canaletto executed specifically for engraving formed part of a quite different exchange between the viewer and the representation of the urban environment, one in which the voyeuristic dialectic between private viewing and public space that we have begun to trace in the Whitehall image had become explicitly commodified. As we have already seen, Canaletto's engagement with the print market in London began immediately after his arrival in the city, and by the early 1750s he was providing a number of drawn images that were specifically geared to the demands of the print publishers, and in particular Robert Sayer, with whom he was most closely associated.

Sayer's catalogue of 1753 was entitled "Two Hundred and Six PERSPECTIVE VIEWS adapted to the DIAGONAL MIRROUR, or OPTICAL PILLAR MACHINE". Immediately striking is the promotion of these images in terms of their

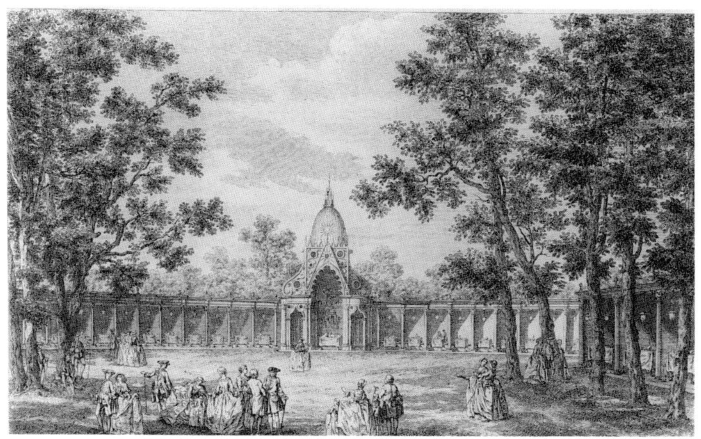

Fig. 22 J.S. Müller after Canaletto, *A view of the Temple of Comus, etc, in Vauxhall Gardens*, engraving

integration into the workings of the "optical pillar machine", which represented a central component of a new mechanics of viewing. By the early 1750s, the diagonal mirror — also known as a zograscope — had become a widely adapted device intervening in the exchange between the viewer and the print. The Oxford English Dictionary describes it as "an optical instrument, consisting of a vertically suspended convex lens in front of a pivotally adjustable mirror mounted on a stand, designed for the viewing of prints in magnified form and with stereoscopic effect". Images appeared to be at some distance from the observer, which enhanced the illusion of space and depth. The zograscope — promoted by entrepreneurs like Sayer as a central conduit of a modern form of aesthetic appreciation — redefined the printed prospect as a spectacular commodity as well as a site of engraved representation. The "diagonal mirror" image pulled the viewer into a space beyond the graphic that offered, however clumsily, an illusion of three-dimensionality approximating to the visual experience of the city in a way that the fixed image could not match. Such a reconfiguration of the image — one that situated it outside the conventional etiquette of high art — correlated to a new bourgeois framework of visual pleasure, thoroughly reconstituting the "prospect" as a product to be consumed alongside the other illusory and theatrical commodities of commercialised leisure.

Unsurprisingly, perhaps, many of the images designed for the "diagonal mirror" depicted the theatricalised and artificial environment of the pleasure garden, and amongst the engravings listed by Sayer are those that Canaletto designed of Vauxhall Gardens [fig. 22]. Indeed, the compositional strategies encouraged by the zograscope – a drastically widened foreground linked by a perspectival device (here the avenues of trees) to a monumental backdrop – are perfectly exemplified in these prints. Another new category of commercialised leisure – the pleasure garden – is shown as deploying a modern simulacrum of the *capriccio* and a panoptic grid of dining-boxes to frame and articulate a circuit of polite pleasures revolving around talk, observation, etiquette and emulation. Looking at the view through the diagonal mirror offered a voyeuristic rhetoric of spectacular participation, one that temporarily denied the viewer's fixity in the private sphere. Yet if the viewer is pulled in a particularly convincing way into the narratives of the garden, he or she is also defined as someone who is doing this by peering into a domestic machine. The image of the outside, of the public sphere, and of the other equivalent bourgeois bodies operating within it, is here not metaphorically screened by a window, but mediated by a luxury household accessory. What is perhaps crucial was that the visual and pictorial practice codified by the pleasure garden – the magnified preoccupation with display and spectatorship, the fusion of high art with the mechanics of ornament and illusion, the self-conscious sense of participating in a commercially organized form of polite leisure – is mirrored precisely in codes of aesthetic consumption operating in the private sphere, which is thus defined as an equivalent, rather than a resistant, site of spectacle and modernity. In these images the conventions of ambitious representation – Canaletto's designs clearly draw, for example, on the model of Watteau – are directed to a quite different agenda to that promoted by Smithson and Richmond. This worked further to break down the cultural independence of the art object, and redefined it as a subsidiary component in an extended relay of visual exchange, one that operated outside the dynamics of traditional appreciation, and that could be subscribed to – given the possession of suitable "optical glasses, on various principles" – through the payment of a shilling across a print-shop counter.

NOTES

1. Quoted by Francis Haskell in 'The Taste for Canaletto', in K. Baetjer and J.G. Links (ed.), *Canaletto*, New York, Metropolitan Museum of Art, 1989, p.31.

2. For a detailed account of the bridge's history see R.J.B. Walker, *Old Westminster Bridge: The Bridge of Fools*, 1979.

3. *Some Observations on the scheme offered by Messrs. Cotton and Lediard*, 1738, p.22.

4. Charles Labelye, *A Description of Westminster Bridge*, 1751, p.25.

5. Charles Labelye, *A Short Account of the methods made use of in laying the foundations of the piers of Westminster Bridge*, 1739, p.82.

6. See Walker, *op. cit.*, p.237.

7. Quoted in W.G. Constable (revised J.G. Links), *Canaletto*, Oxford 1982, p.145.

8. For a survey of equivalent imagery of the city see M. Warner (ed.), *The Image of London*, London, Barbican Art Gallery, 1987.

9. Quoted in Iain Pears, *The Discovery of Painting: The Growth of Interest in the Arts in England, 1680–1768*, London 1988, p.176.

10 Quoted in Walker, *op. cit.*, p.239.

11 Significantly, a later version of the same scene by Canaletto [fig. 6] more explicitly dramatizes the street as an arena of renewal, one again dominated by the familiar iconography of scaffolding.

CATALOGUE

ABBREVIATIONS

C/L W.G. Constable (revised J.G. Links), *Canaletto* 2 vols, Oxford 1976;
3rd edition with supplement by J.G. Links, Oxford 1989. All
references are to the third edition unless otherwise stated.

CONTRIBUTORS

JF   Jane Farrington
ML   Michael Liversidge
SW   Stephen Wildman

Chronology of Canaletto's Career

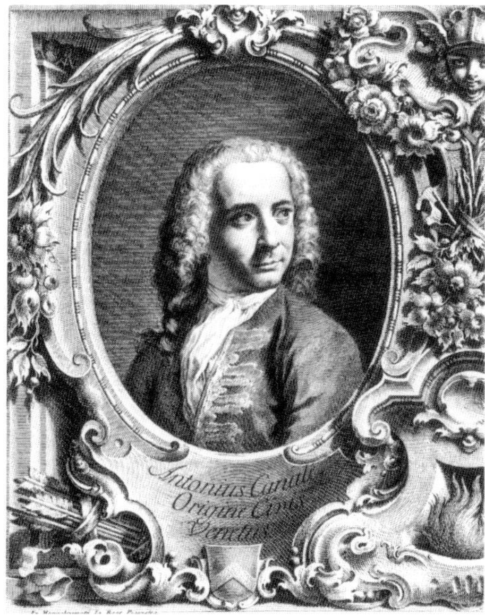

Fig. 23 Antonio Visentini, portrait of Canaletto, from the *Prospectus Magni Canalis Venetiarum*, engraving

1697 Born Giovanni Antonio Canal on 17 or 18 October and baptized 30 October at San Lio, Venice. Son of Bernardo Canal, painter of theatrical scenery and member of the Collegio dei Pittori. Canaletto's first employment was scene-painting for the Venetian theatre.

1719 Went to Rome as his father's assistant and worked on stage designs for two Scarlatti operas.

1720 Returned to Venice where listed in the annual register of painters.

1722 Earliest view-paintings date from this period.

1725 Stefano Conti, a textile merchant in Lucca, commissioned four paintings from Canaletto of Venetian views.

1726 In a letter of 8 March 1726, Owen McSwiney wrote to the Duke of Richmond about his series of allegorical paintings of tombs stating that Canaletto had painted the "perspective and landscape" for two in the series [see cat. no. 1].

1727 In November McSwiney wrote again to the Duke of Richmond stating that Canaletto had been painting views for him – two of which he subsequently sold to the Duke.

1730 The Venetian view-painter Luca Carlevaris died. Joseph Smith first recorded acting as an agent for English buyers including Samuel Hill of Staffordshire who acquired two Venetian views painted in that year [cat. nos. 4 and 5].

1735 Antonio Visentini's engravings after twelve views of the Grand Canal by Canaletto were published together with the only authentic portrait of the artist [fig. 23]. The paintings had been commissioned by Smith. Two other engravings after paintings entitled *Nautical contest* and *Venetian market* were also added. The title page was inscribed: *Prospectus / Magni Canalis Venetiarium / addito Certamine Nautico et Nundinis Venetis.*
At about this time, Canaletto's nephew Bernardo Bellotto joined his studio. In the early 1740s, they made a tour of the Brenta Canal together and visited Padua.

1741 About this time Smith encouraged Canaletto to take up etching and devote more time to drawing. Outbreak of the War of the Austrian Succession.

1742 Smith published a second edition of *Prospectus* containing 24 more engravings. Canaletto signed and dated five large views of Roman subjects for Smith's collection.

1743–44 Smith commissioned a series of thirteen "pieces over doors" probably for his villa at Mogliano.

1744 Canaletto's father dies. On 6 June, Smith appointed British Consul in Venice. Some time after that date, an album of 28 etchings of Venice by Canaletto published and dedicated in the frontispiece to Consul Smith.

1745 Canaletto signed and dated a drawing of the Campanile in St Mark's Square, Venice, after it had been damaged by lightning on 23 April 1745.

1746 At the end of May, Canaletto arrived in London, persuaded to come to England, according to Vertue, by Jacopo Amigoni who had worked in the city 1729–39. Vertue also states that Canaletto was interested in financial investment and that "he had brought most part to putt into the Stocks here for better Security. or better interest than abroad". Canaletto arrived with a letter from Consul Smith to Owen McSwiney asking him to arrange an introduction for Canaletto to the Duke of Richmond. However, Canaletto's first commission was probably from Prince Lobkowicz of Bohemia who was visiting London. Canaletto painted for him Westminster Bridge in its final stages of building and a view of the Thames.

1747 Sir Hugh Smithson probably commissioned two oils [fig. 2 and cat. no. 6], one of which was published as an engraving in 1747 dedicated to Smithson. A third commission to paint Windsor Castle was completed on 11 June 1747 [fig. 3]. Besides his commission from Smithson, another painting of Westminster Bridge was engraved and published early in 1747 [fig. 13]. In May 1747, two arches of Westminster Bridge began to settle necessitating repairs which Canaletto recorded. Probably in the late summer, Canaletto was permitted to make a drawing from the Duke of Richmond's house close to Westminster Bridge and shortly afterwards he began two paintings for the Duke [cat. nos. 9 and 12].

1748–49 Payments to Canaletto from Lord Brooke's account for paintings and a drawing of his seat at Warwick Castle are dated July 1748 and March 1749 [cat. nos. 21 and 22]. Two views of Badminton [figs. 4 and 5] were probably also painted in the summer of 1748.

1749 In July, Canaletto advertised an invitation to see a *View of St James's Park* at his lodgings in Silver Street [cat. no. 19]. He was commissioned to paint the procession of the Knights of the Bath from Westminster Abbey which occurred on 26 June 1749 [cat. no. 27] and was probably also commissioned by the Earl of Chesterfield to paint three *capricci* for the music room of his new Chesterfield House.

1750 Antonio Joli left London for Madrid and at the end of the year Canaletto returned to Venice.

1751 In August Vertue records that Canaletto had been in Venice for eight months and was back in London where he had advertised a public viewing at his lodgings of a painting of the Thames with Chelsea Hospital and Ranelagh Gardens. While in Venice, he had invested in property. Two paintings and five drawings of London in the Royal Collection [see cat. nos. 7, 14, 15, 16, 17] suggest that Canaletto took them back to Venice or executed them there from sketches and sold them to Smith. (Smith sold the bulk of his collection to George III in 1762–63.)

1752 Two payments in March and July from Lord Brooke are probably for the two views of the East Front of Warwick Castle [cat. nos. 23 and 25].

1754–55. Canaletto signed and dated five out of six pictures commissioned by Thomas Hollis including *Old Walton Bridge* [cat. no. 35]. One of a group of *capricci* is dated 1754. They were probably commissioned for Ockham Place, Surrey [see cat. nos. 37 and 38]. Canaletto returned to Venice.

1760 The artist was observed sketching in the Piazza San Marco by two Englishmen, John Crewe of Crewe Hall and John Hincliffe, his tutor.

1762–63 Consul Smith sold the major part of his collection, including his many works by Canaletto, to George III.

1763 Canaletto elected Prior of the Collegio dei Pittori (the Venetian Academy).

1764 Elected to the Committee of Twelve of the Collegio.

1765 Signed and dated a *capriccio* which he presented as a reception piece for the Academy of Fine Arts.

1766 Inscribed a drawing of the interior of San Marco: "Aged 68 Without Spectacles, The year 1766".

1767 Last recorded attendance at a meeting of the Collegio dei Pittori on 23 August.

1768 Died intestate on 19 April and buried at San Lio "con Capitolo" (with twelve priests and candles). Left 28 "medium and small" pictures, a few clothes and household possessions. Also left the equivalent of about £80 in cash and the property he had bought during his 1751 visit to Venice from London.

1770 Joseph Smith died aged about 96 years.

1 Canaletto with Giovanni Battista Cimaroli (active 1718–33) and Giovanni Battista Piazzetta (1683–1754)

An allegorical tomb in honour of John, Lord Somers

Oil on canvas, ca. 1726
110 × 56 ins (279.4 × 142.2 cm)
C/L 516
Private collection on loan to
Birmingham Museums and Art Gallery

This picture is the earliest example of a commission from Canaletto for a British client. Owen McSwiney (ca. 1684–1754) was an Irish entrepreneur and theatrical impresario in London until driven by bankruptcy to the Continent. Once in Venice, he formed a business association with the English merchant Joseph Smith, later to become Canaletto's most important client. McSwiney appears already to have been acting as agent for the Duke of Richmond's art collecting and it was probably at the Duke's instigation that McSwiney commissioned from a number of Venetian and Bolognese painters a series of allegorical paintings of tombs. These "Monuments to the Remembrance of a Set of British Worthies" were intended to commemorate the leading political figures of the Protestant cause and the Whig Settlement. A total of twenty-four paintings were completed, ten of which were sold to the Duke for his dining room at Goodwood where they were described by George Vertue in 1747.

Canaletto contributed to both this work and the *Tomb of Archbishop Tillotson* (Newhouse Galleries, New York, in January 1993) and is likely to have executed most of the architecture and landscape background. They are, therefore, significant works in the context of his early career and style of the 1720s. Although already establishing a successful position as a painter of views and *capricci*, Canaletto was perhaps eager to contribute, however insignificantly, to the whole series because he saw the opportunity of an association with a British client.

Lord Somers, who became Lord Chancellor (1697–1700), was famous for his eloquent defence of the Whig cause during the Trial of the Seven Bishops (1688).

In a letter to the Duke of 8 March 1726, McSwiney wrote:

That of Ld Sommers in a sacrifice on Religious

Ceremony (at this monument) in acknowledg^{mt} of the service done the Church, for his pleading the Cause of the Bishops etc, The perspective and lands^{cps} are painted by *Canaletto* & Cimeroli. The figures by Geo. *Battista Piacotta*.

The picture is not recorded at Goodwood and is likely to have been among the tomb paintings bought by the collector and connoisseur Sir William Morice by 29 November 1729. JF

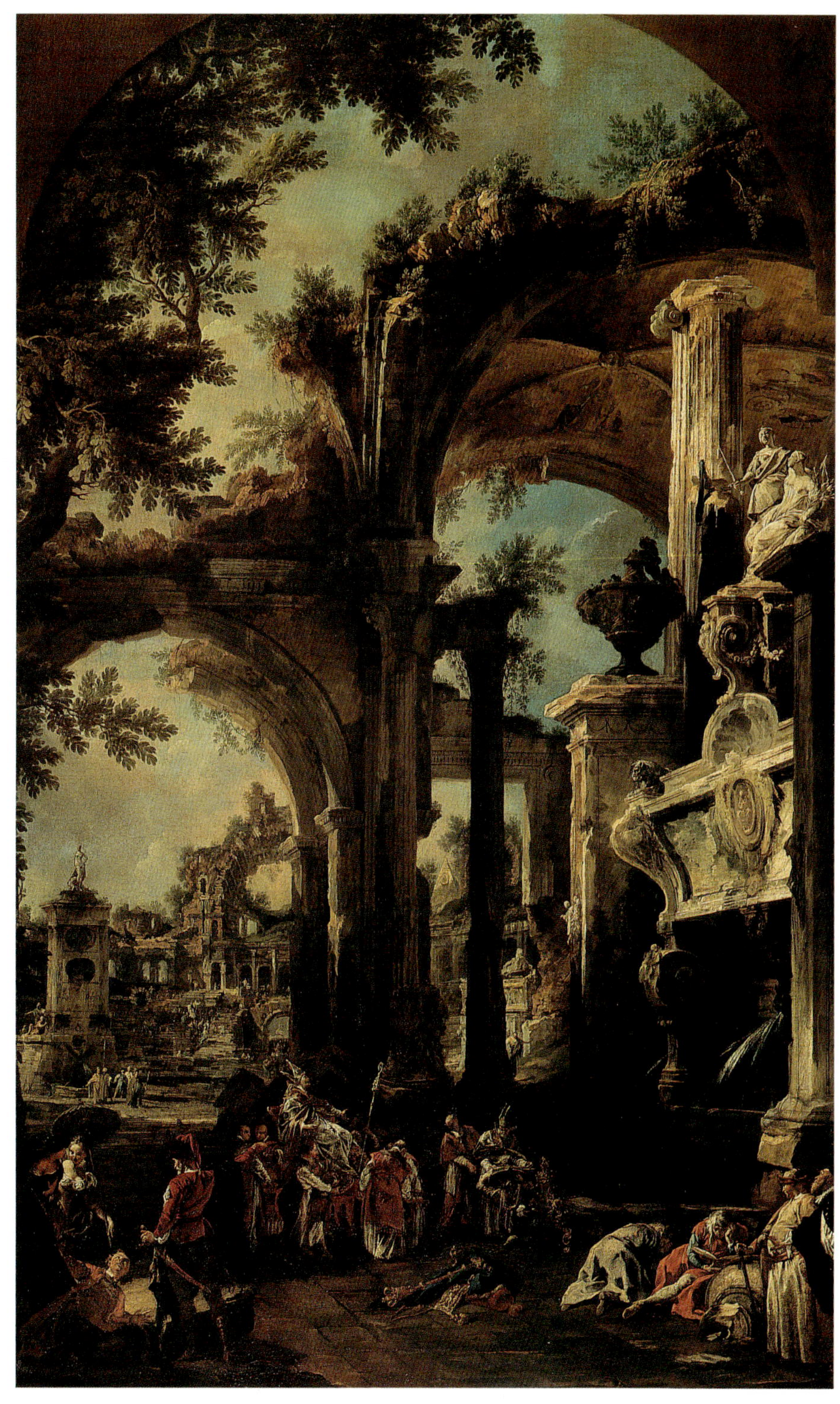

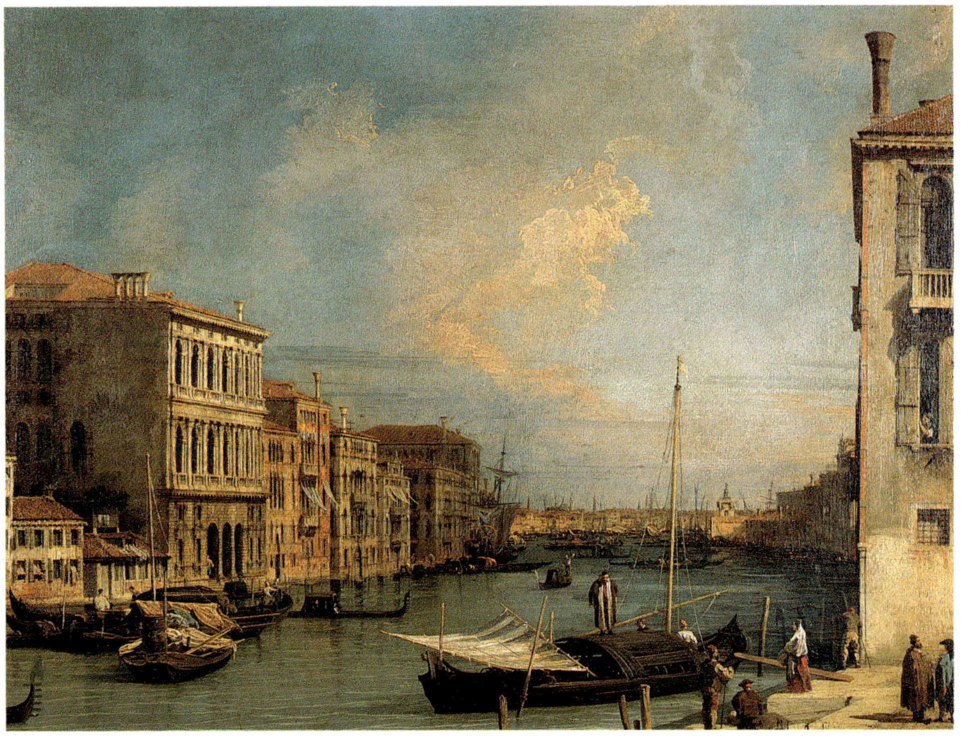

2 Canaletto

The Grand Canal, Venice, looking east, from Campo San Vio

Oil on copper, 1720s
$18\frac{1}{8} \times 24\frac{5}{8}$ ins (46×62.5 cm)
C/L 192

Viscount Coke and the Trustees of the
Holkham Estate, Holkham

3 Canaletto

The Grand Canal, Venice: the Rialto Bridge from the south

Oil on copper, 1720s
$17\frac{7}{8} \times 24\frac{5}{8}$ ins (45.5×62.5 cm)
C/L 226

Viscount Coke and the Trustees of the
Holkham Estate, Holkham

To the cultivated Englishman of the eighteenth century, Venice's beauty and exoticism derived partly from its being a city of the past. The Venetian Republic had once been a great trading power with the East but now, in its fading glory, it became associated with the sensual pleasures – music, theatre, courtesans and carnivals. Whether or not Englishmen had visited it on the Grand Tour, astute agents like Joseph Smith and Owen McSwiney recognised a market in England for picturesque views of its most famous landmarks.

Nine copperplates by Canaletto have survived. They represent a change of style in Canaletto's early career which may show the influence of McSwiney. A lighter palette, sparkling light and accurate topographical detail of Venetian sites would appeal to English clients already familiar with an established tradition of topographical art in Britain. Copperplates also had the advantage of being robust and portable. These two examples were almost certainly bought by the Earl of Leicester (died 1759) and a household inventory records their transfer from London to Holkham in 1760. They were both copied and published as engravings by Joseph Baudin along with ten other paintings by Canaletto.

The detail in both views accentuates the exotic, foreign appearances of the city – the gondolas, striped awnings, colourful native costume, eccentric chimney-pots and medieval shopfronts of the Rialto Bridge. The ragged cloth draped over the bridge and balconies together with stained and peeling plaster suggests picturesque decay. The apparent accuracy of what is depicted is accentuated by the liveliness and convincing grouping of the figures (and dogs) – something at which Canaletto excelled. English clients would also have liked the earthy detail of a man urinating at the foot of the bridge. JF

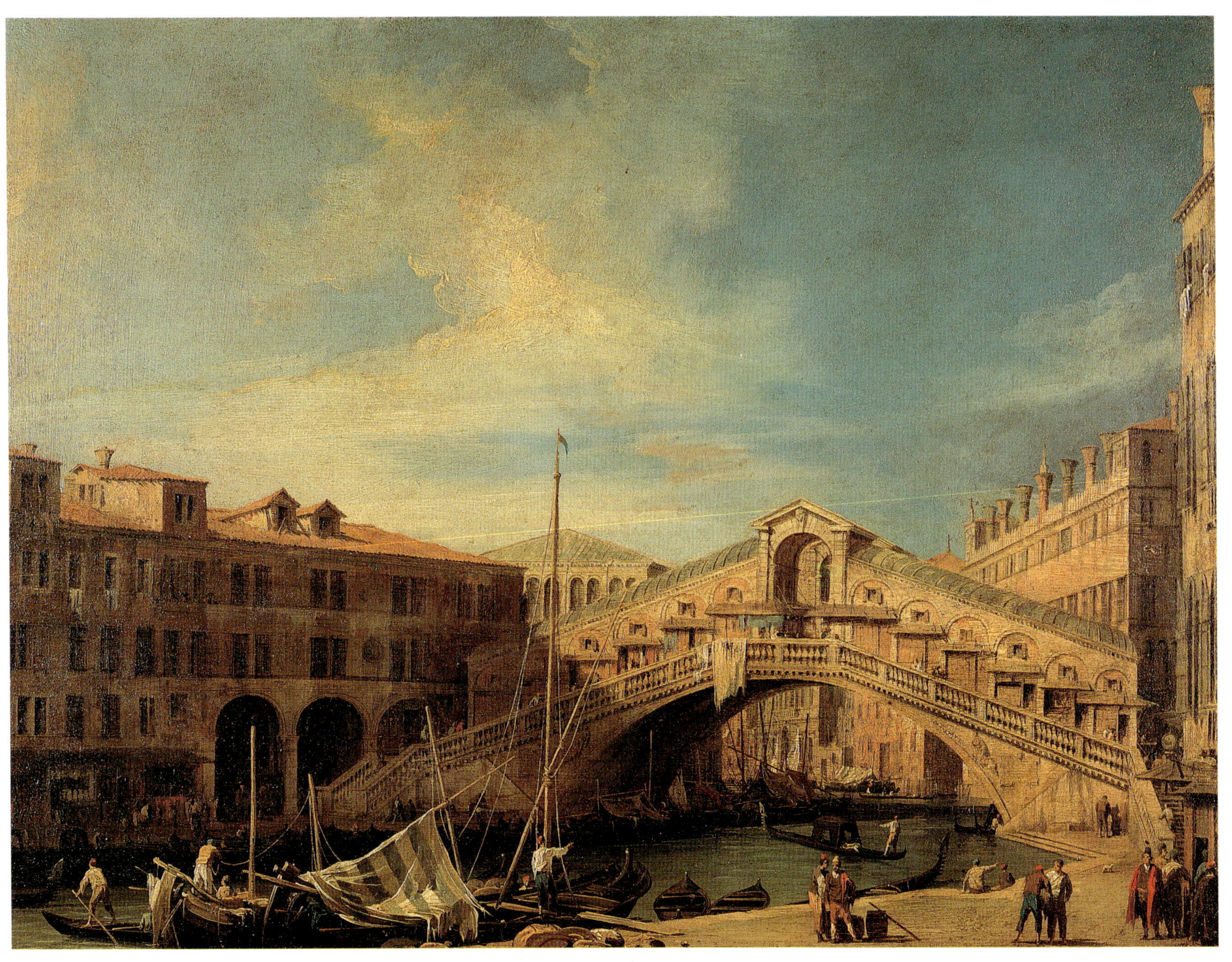

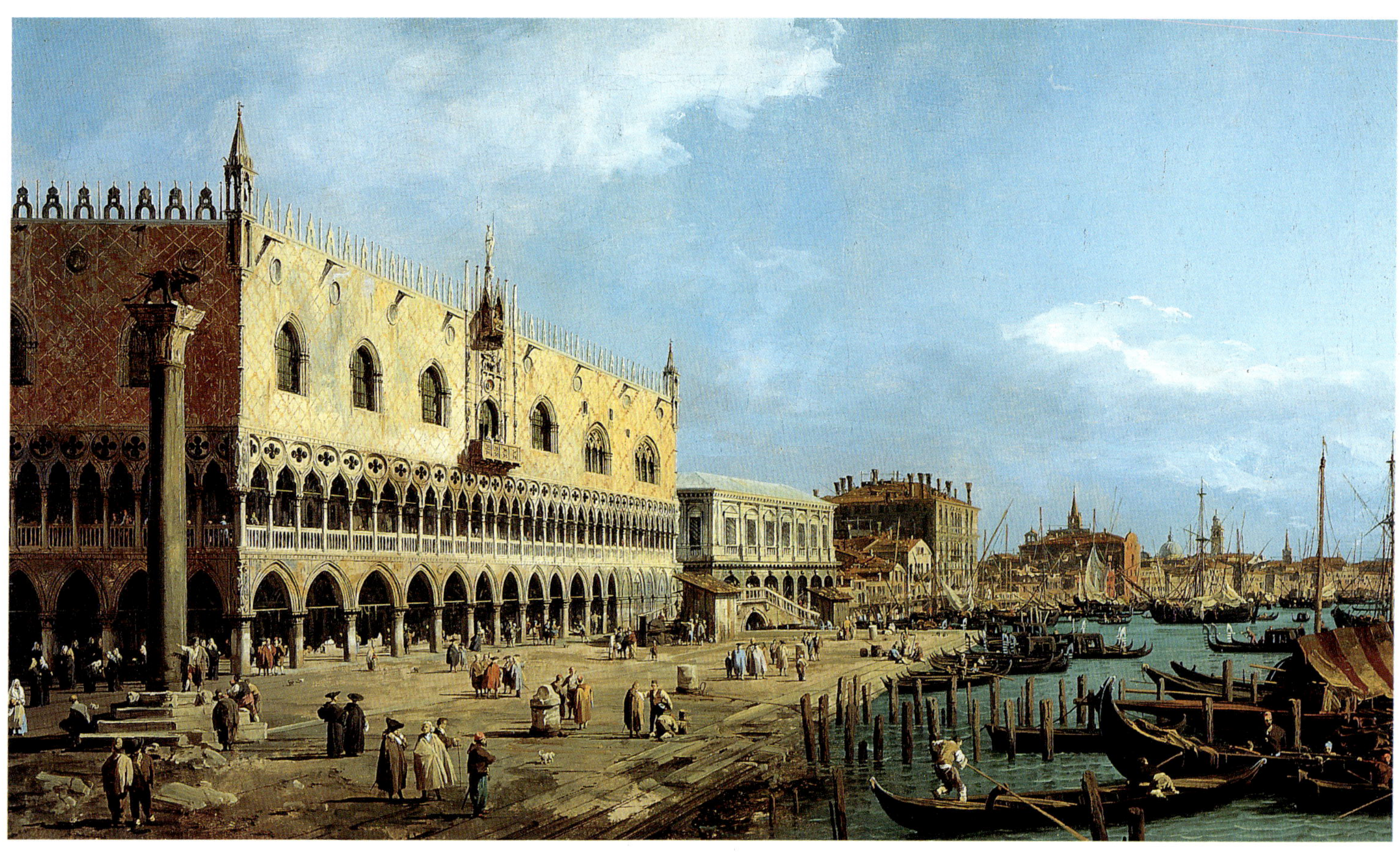

4 Canaletto

The Riva degli Schiavoni, Venice, looking east

Oil on canvas, ca. 1730–31
23 × 40 ins (58.4 × 101.6 cm)
C/L 111

The National Trust (Egerton Collection), Tatton Park

5 Canaletto

The Molo, Venice, looking west

Oil on canvas, ca. 1730–31
23 × 40 ins (58.4 × 101.6 cm)
C/L 97

The National Trust (Egerton Collection), Tatton Park

This pair of views showing perhaps the two most famous buildings in the city, the Doge's Palace and Santa Maria della Salute, were commissioned by Samuel Hill of Staffordshire through Joseph Smith. In a letter of 17 July 1730, Smith wrote:

At last I've got Canal under articles to finish your 2 peices within a twelvemonth; he's so much follow'd and all are so ready to pay him his own price for his work (and which he vallues himself as much as anybody) that he would be thought in this to have much obliged me, nor is it the first time I have been glad to submit to a painter's impertinence to serve myself and friends, for besides that resentment is lost upon them, a rupture with such as one excellent in this profession resolves 'em either not to work for you at all, or which is worse, one gets from them only slight and labour'd productions, and so our taste and generosity is censured – tho' both unjustly.

Smith's assessment of Canaletto's charac-

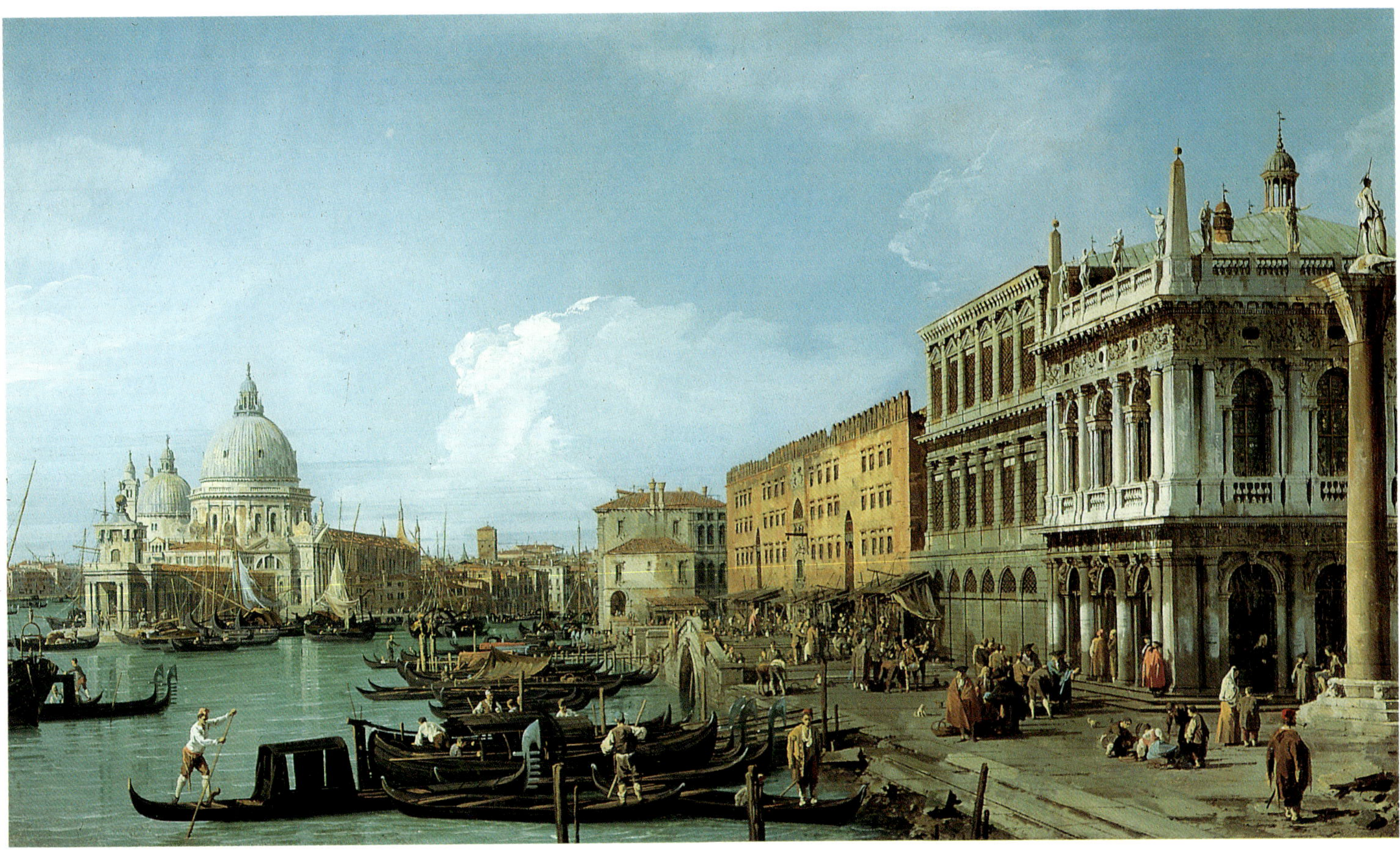

ter and behaviour should not be taken too literally. It was in an agent's interest to make a client think that an artist was difficult and that the agent performed an essential role in negotiating a commission. Nevertheless, there seems to have been some delay. Hill's nephew, Samuel Egerton, was apprenticed to Smith and on 15 December 1730 he wrote that Smith "had at last prevailed with Canal to lay aside all other business till he had finished the 2 pictures you order'd when you was last here …". Samuel outlived his elder brother and inherited his uncle's estates. He transferred the Canalettos to the family seat, Tatton Park, where they remain today.

Canaletto had already painted the famous view of the Riva degli Schiavoni several times for English clients. The column of St Mark has been arbitrarily moved to suit the composition so that it stands against the west rather than the south façade. The quay in the foreground is in disrepair and the crowded shipping creates a picturesque but chaotic effect. The prow of the Doge's galleon anchors the composition at lower right – a device that Canaletto re-used many times in his Thames views. A cross-section of classes is identifiable in both pictures, from beggars, boatmen, priests, gentlemen in coloured cloaks and tricorne hats to civic officials in

long black gowns. This colourful mix of class was also characteristic of Canaletto's depiction of London street-life. The accuracy of detail in, for example, the ramshackle booths with slatted roofs that line the façade of the granaries on the Molo, in contrast with the luminosity of light that reflects from the water, make these views as captivating now as they were in the mid eighteenth century. JF

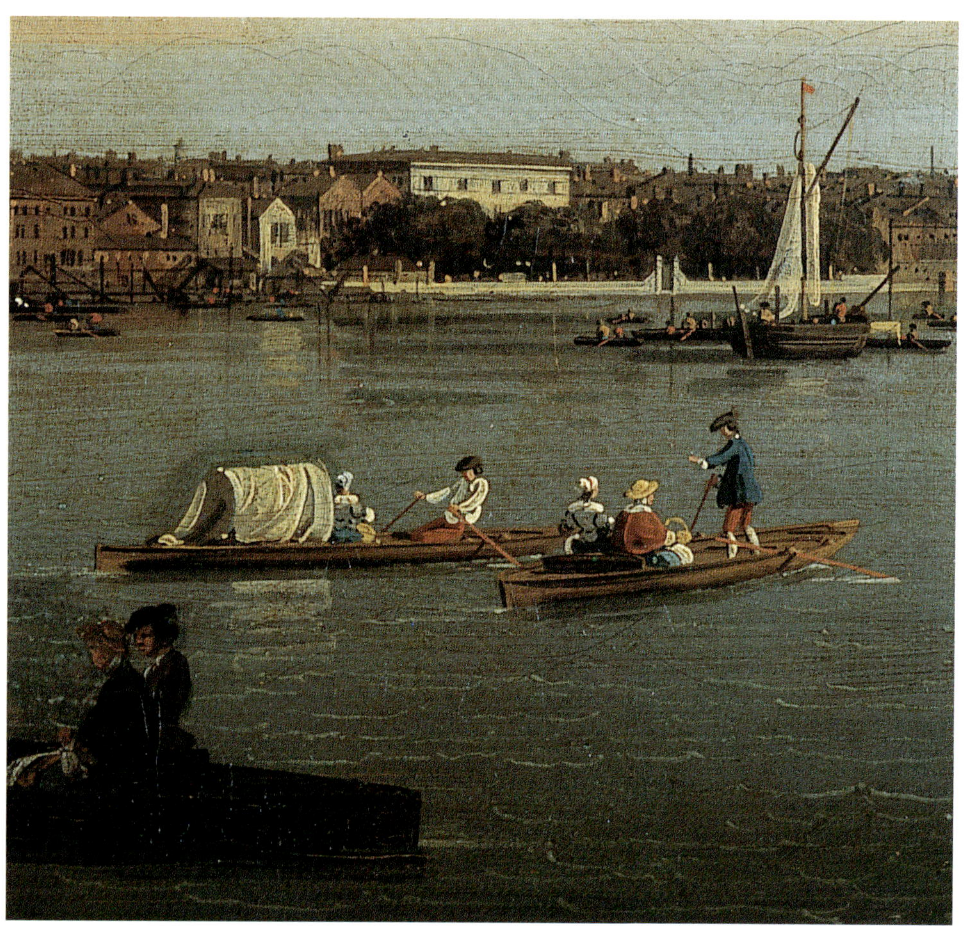

6 Canaletto

London seen through an arch of Westminster Bridge

Oil on canvas, ca. 1747
$22\frac{1}{2} \times 37\frac{1}{2}$ ins (57 × 95 cm)
C/L 412

Collection of the Duke of Northumberland

This inventive and original composition was almost certainly commissioned by Sir Hugh Smithson, himself one of the Commissioners of the new Westminster Bridge. When Sir Hugh's wife's brother died in 1750, Lady Smithson became heir to all Percy titles and seats. Sir Hugh became Earl, then Duke of Northumberland and the most important of Canaletto's first patrons in England. The painting was copied as an engraving and published in 1747 by John Brindley with a dedication to Sir Hugh Smithson. Two related drawings survive [cat. no. 7].

Canaletto shows the arch still supported by its wooden centring and the suspended workman's bucket suggests that building work is still in progress. Perhaps Canaletto linked the composition visually with his views of Venice depicted through an archway and often with a lantern suspended above. Nevertheless, the dramatic boldness of this composition must have come as a revelation to English contemporaries such as Samuel Scott. The arch is placed slightly to the right to avoid a heavy flattening effect and the eye is led in from the left by a clever grouping of small and large boats belonging to the watermen. The accurate panoramic depiction of the London skyline includes the Water Tower and York Water Gate on the left, the spire of St Clement Danes in the centre and St Paul's Cathedral on the right. It has been suggested that Canaletto has depicted the fourth arch from the Lambeth side.
JF

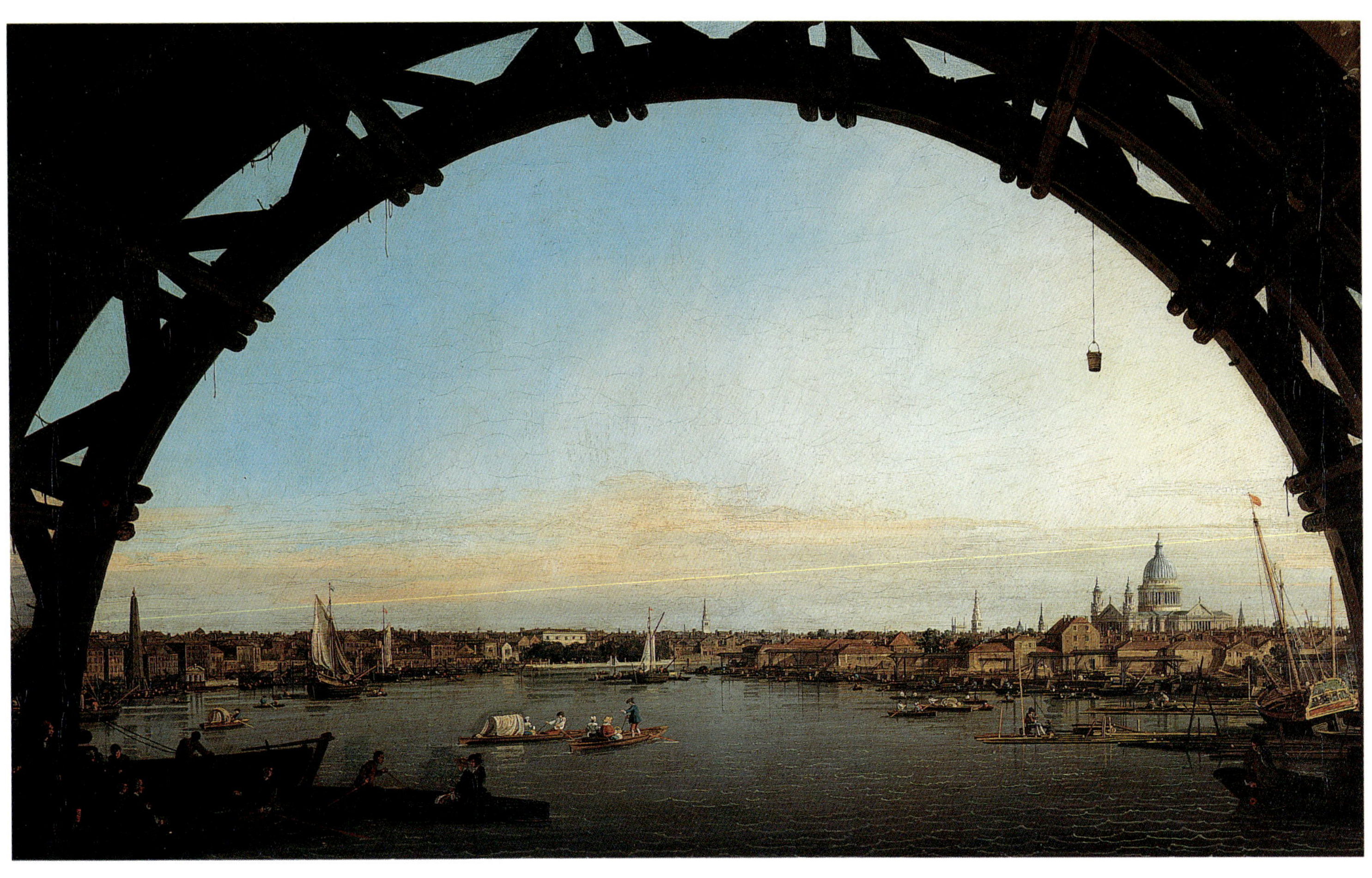

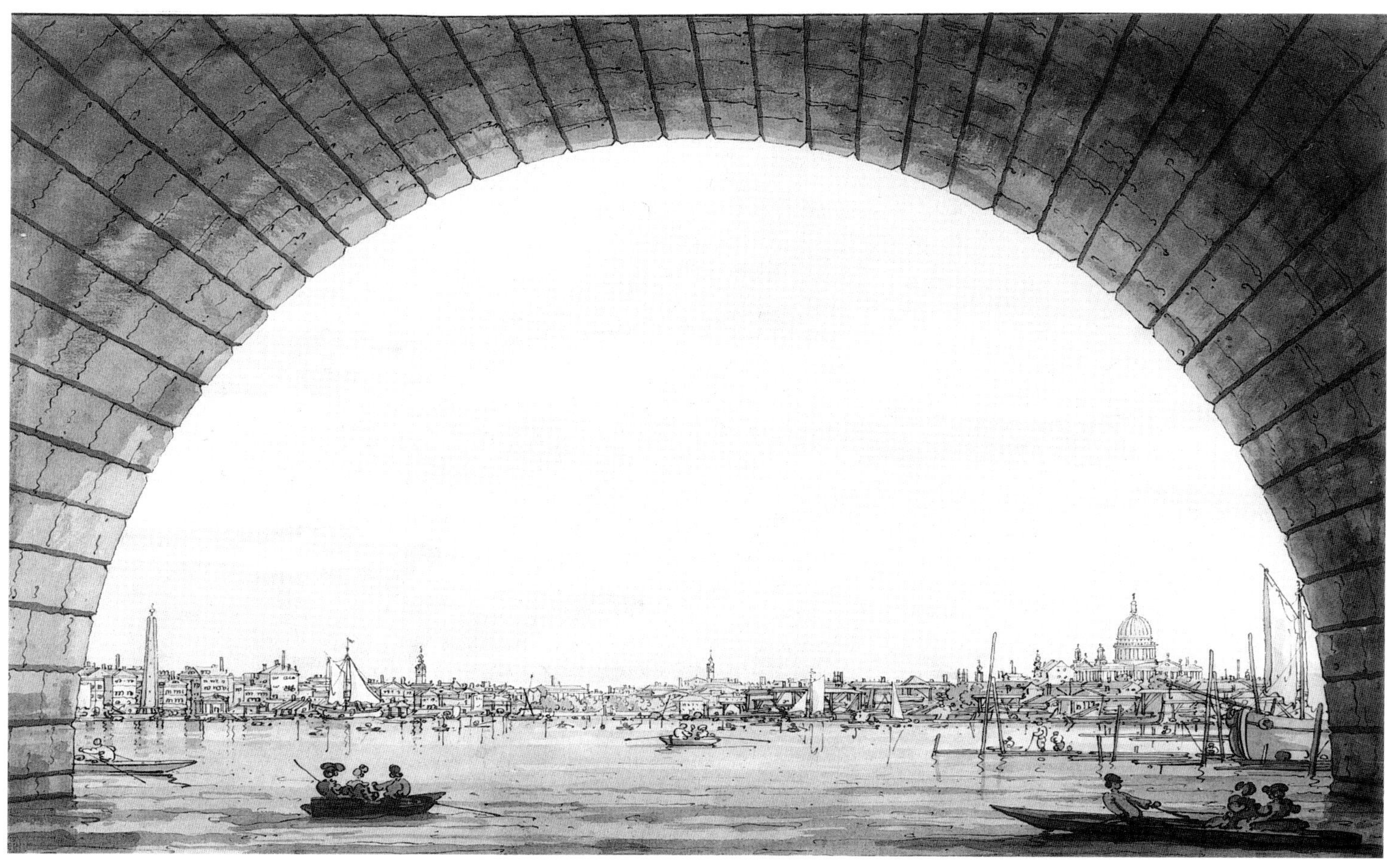

7 Canaletto

London seen through an arch of Westminster Bridge

Pen and brown ink with grey wash over
pencil, ca. 1747–50
$11\frac{3}{8} \times 19\frac{1}{16}$ ins (29 × 48.4 cm)
C/L 732

Her Majesty The Queen

The drawing is closely related to the oil
[cat. no. 6] but the centring in the arch has
been removed. It is likely to have been
done later and taken back to Venice where
Canaletto subsequently sold it to Consul
Smith. An almost identical but probably
earlier version is in the Albright-Knox Art
Gallery, Buffalo. There are far fewer boats
and figures in the drawing but they are
delineated with a lively pen line and there
are delicate touches of wash over the water
and stonework. Unlike the painting, the
arch is placed in the dead centre of the
composition. JF

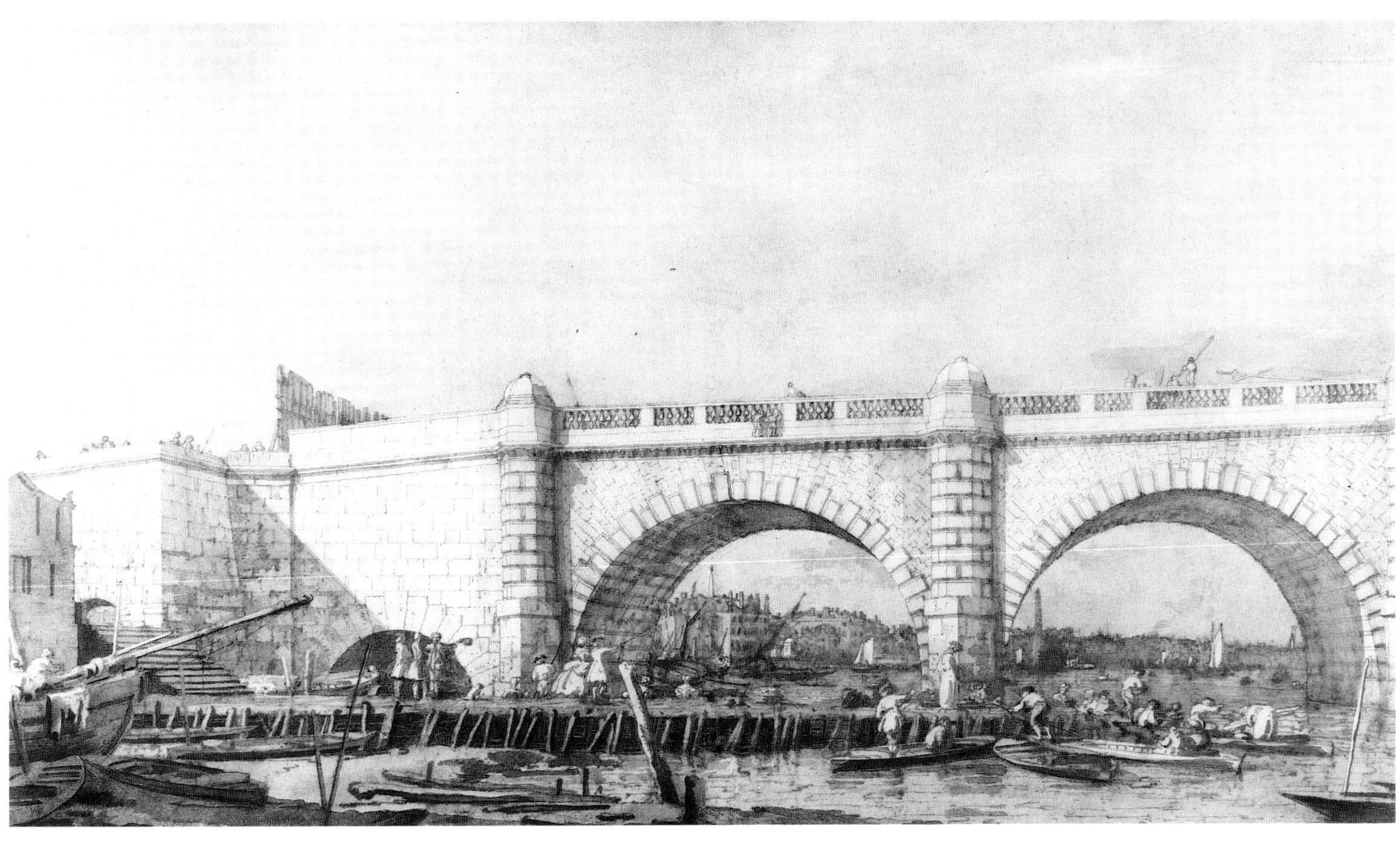

8 Canaletto

The western arches of Westminster Bridge, London

Pen and brown ink with grey wash, ca. 1747
$16\frac{3}{16} \times 28\frac{13}{16}$ ins (41.2 × 73.2 cm)
C/L 752

The Trustees of the British Museum, London

There is no reason to doubt the topographical accuracy of this drawing which shows the western abutment arch and the adjoining two arches as building work on the bridge had reached its final stages in the summer of 1747. However, the drawing could be earlier than that as the bridge was initially opened to traffic on 25 October 1746 and, before that time, the public were prevented from crossing by large wooden barricades, one of which is depicted here. The huddle of figures by the barrier as well as those sightseeing on the bank suggest mounting interest and excitement at the impending opening. The balustrade, which was built to a height of six foot nine inches apparently for fear of suicide attempts, caused many complaints: views of the river were invisible except from the top of a coach. JF

9 Canaletto

Whitehall and the Privy Garden, London, from Richmond House

Oil on canvas, 1747
42 × 46 ins (106.7 × 116.8 cm)
C/L 438
The Trustees of Goodwood House

Canaletto arrived in England in May 1746 with a letter from Joseph Smith to Owen McSwiney asking for an introduction to the Duke of Richmond. Smith had shrewdly decided that the Duke would be a likely patron. He already owned one of McSwiney's tomb paintings to which Canaletto contributed [cat. no. 1] and in the same year of 1727 he ordered a pair of Venetian views on copper. He was also a Commissioner for the new Westminster Bridge which was to provide Canaletto with his first important commissions.

This request for an introduction was passed on to the Duke's friend and former tutor, Thomas Hill, who wrote on 20 May 1746:

The only news I know to send you, is what I had this day from Swiney at the Duke of Montagu's, where we dined, & he, I think, got almost drunk. Canales, alias Canaletti, is come over with a letter of recommendation from our old acquaintance the Consul of Venice to Mac in order to [effect] his introduction to your Grace, as a patron of the politer parts, or what the Italians understand by the name of *virtu*. I told him the best service I thought you could do him w^d be to let him draw a view of the river from y^r dining-room, which in my opinion would give him as much reputation as any of his Venetian prospects.

The Duke followed Hill's advice but there appears to have been a delay of a year before Canaletto was permitted to sketch from a window of the Duke's London residence. The result was what are considered to be the masterpieces of Canaletto's English period, the pair of views at Goodwood [see also cat. no. 12] and *Whitehall and the Privy Garden, London, looking north* (Duke of Buccleuch) [fig. 6].

The view of Whitehall is fascinatingly untidy and is a reminder that there were few great modern public buildings at that time in London. The significant years of urban improvement were to follow

Canaletto's final departure from London in 1755. In the modest courtyard of Richmond House, a liveried servant bows to the Duke himself who wears the blue Garter riband. Chickens and a washing line are visible and, a few yards from the Duke, a soldier urinates against the exterior of the wall. In the background, Inigo Jones's Banqueting House stands left of centre beyond the lawn. The spire of St Martin-in-the-Fields is visible as well as one of the turrets of Northumberland House. On the left is the Holbein or Treasury Gate, one of the last buildings to survive of Tudor Whitehall, which was demolished to ease the increasing flow of traffic in 1759. Perhaps Canaletto knew that he was recording the appearance of a city that was undergoing rapid change. JF

10 Canaletto

Whitehall and the Privy Garden, London, with Montagu House and the Thames beyond

Pen and brown ink with grey wash, 1747
14½ × 29⅜ ins (36.8 × 74.7 cm)
C/L 754
Private collection

This panoramic drawing was made from one of the first-storey windows of Richmond House in the summer of 1747. John Hayes has pointed out that the Plantation Office on the left is in the process of being demolished[1]. It was still occupied in May but demolition had been completed by December. The drawing relates to both the Goodwood oils [cat. nos. 9 and 12] and also *Whitehall and the Privy Garden looking north* (Duke of Buccleuch) [fig. 6], and Canaletto may have contemplated a large

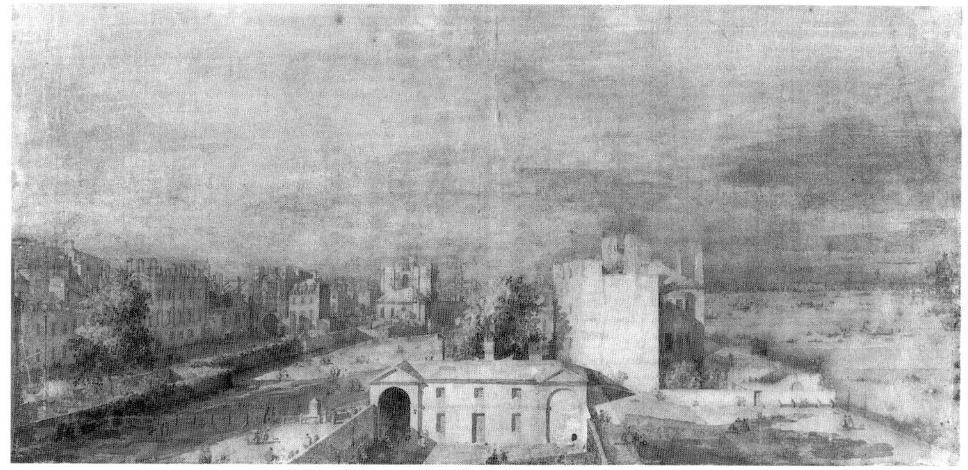

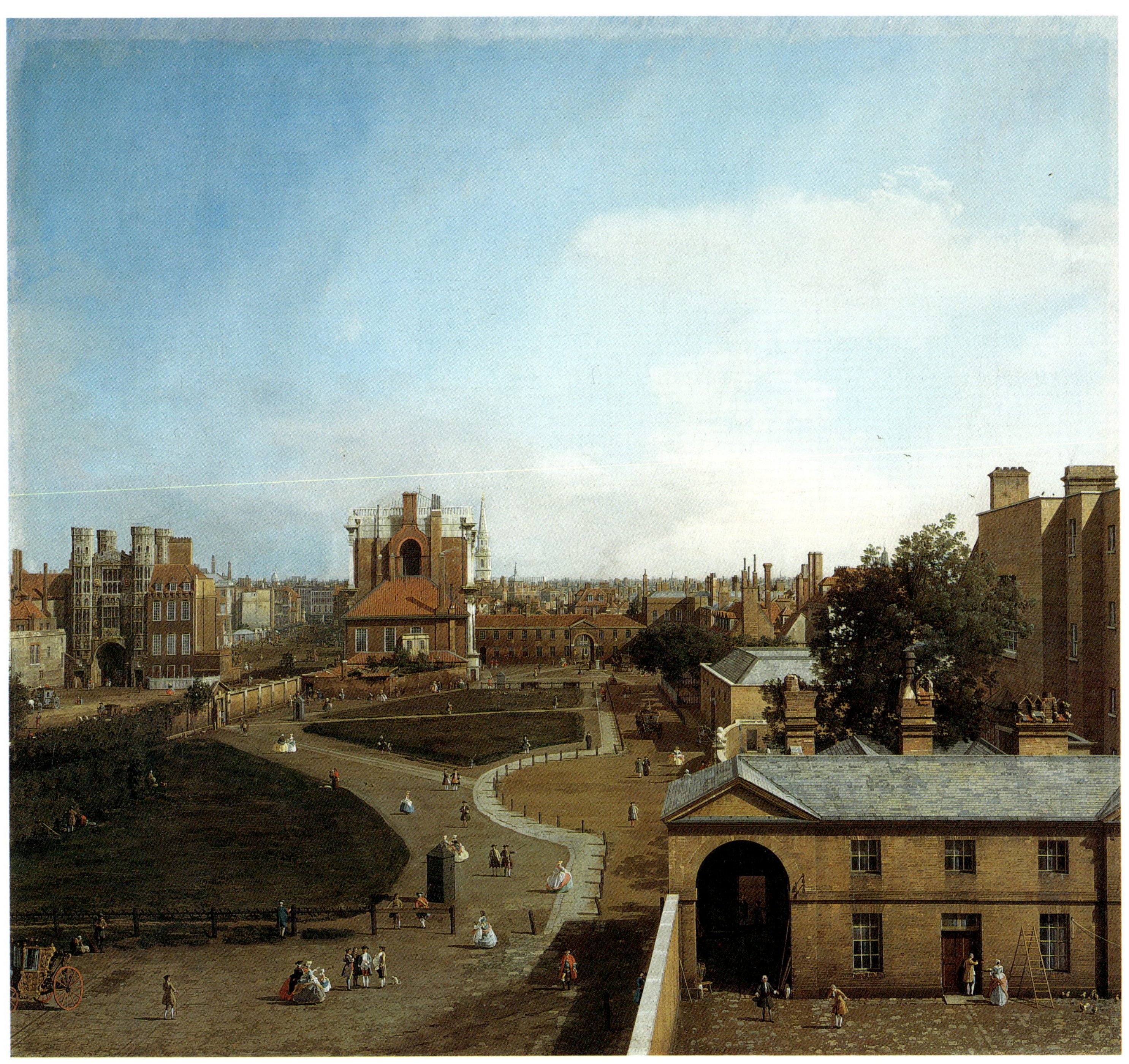

panoramic canvas of the same view. The drawing differs from all three oils in being lit from the left. Although damaged and faded, the delicate washes create a sense of space and distance over the London skyline. Together with the three oils and one more related drawing [cat. no. 11], it is evidence of the care and topographical accuracy Canaletto achieved for this important commission from the Duke of Richmond. JF

1. John Hayes, 'Parliament Street and Canaletto's Views of Whitehall', *Burlington Magazine*, October 1958, pp.341–49.

11 Canaletto

The Thames and the City of London from Richmond House

Pen and brown ink with grey wash, ca. 1747
$13\frac{1}{4} \times 21\frac{1}{4}$ ins (33.7 × 54 cm)
C/L 744

Private collection

The drawing is inscribed, verso, probably by Canaletto: "Vista del Tamigi / dal Duca de Richmond, a Londra". It is related to one of the pair of oils painted for the Duke of Richmond showing views from his London house [cat. no. 12]. The drawing includes more of the Duke's private garden and terrace and a more extensive, panoramic view of the Thames alive with a variety of shipping. Like the oil to which it relates, it is one of the best works produced by the artist in his English period. The delicacy of wash, the lively pen line and sense of luminosity recall Canaletto's wash drawings of the Venetian lagoon. JF

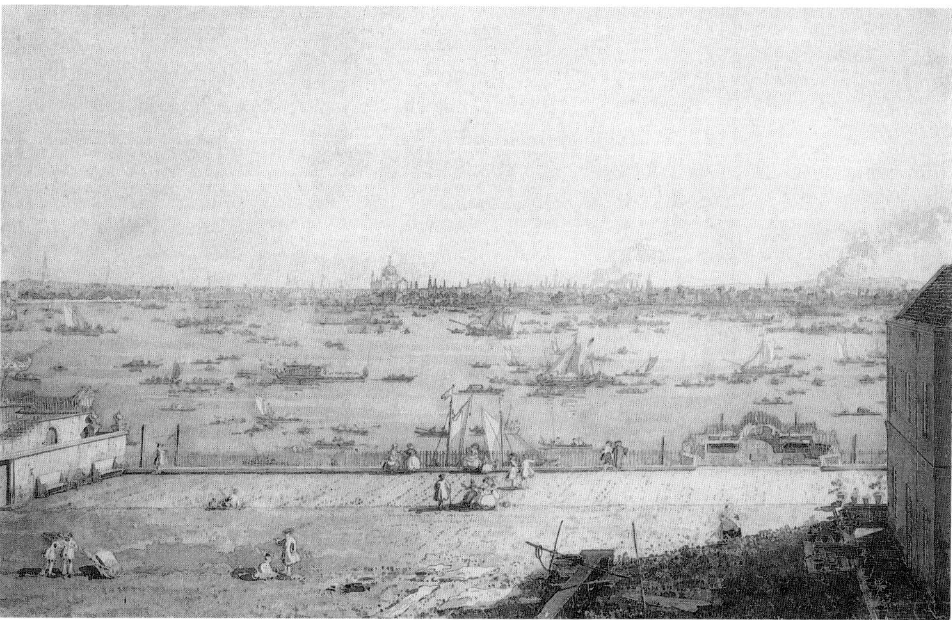

12 Canaletto

The Thames and the City of London from Richmond House

Oil on canvas, 1747
$41\frac{3}{4} \times 46\frac{1}{4}$ ins (106 × 117.4 cm)
C/L 424

The Trustees of Goodwood House

The viewpoint for both this painting and its pair [cat. no. 9] was probably an upper back window of Richmond House but Canaletto may have exaggerated the perspective. Both pictures were presumably destined for a specific location. This view looks north-east and encompasses a breathtaking panorama of the Thames. The great dome of St Paul's, the civic barges and the curved sweep of the river make it impossible not to draw comparisons with Canaletto's vision of Venice and perhaps the Duke saw himself playing a significant role in transforming London into a great modern republic and trading power on Venetian lines. It is a view that indicates power and privilege. The foreground shows the private garden terraces of Richmond and the neighbouring Montagu House with its own water gate. It has already been observed that in the reign of George II the Whigs were more interested in building private fortunes rather than public buildings.[1]

Unlike his first London commissions of Westminster Bridge, Canaletto succeeds in creating a tangible sense of light and atmosphere which is northern rather than Mediterranean. The pair of Goodwood paintings provide an unforgettable image of mid-eighteenth-century London. JF

1. Brian Allen, 'Topography or Art: Canaletto and London in the mid-eighteenth century' in *The Image of London*, exhibition catalogue, London, Barbican Art Gallery, 1987, pp.32–33.

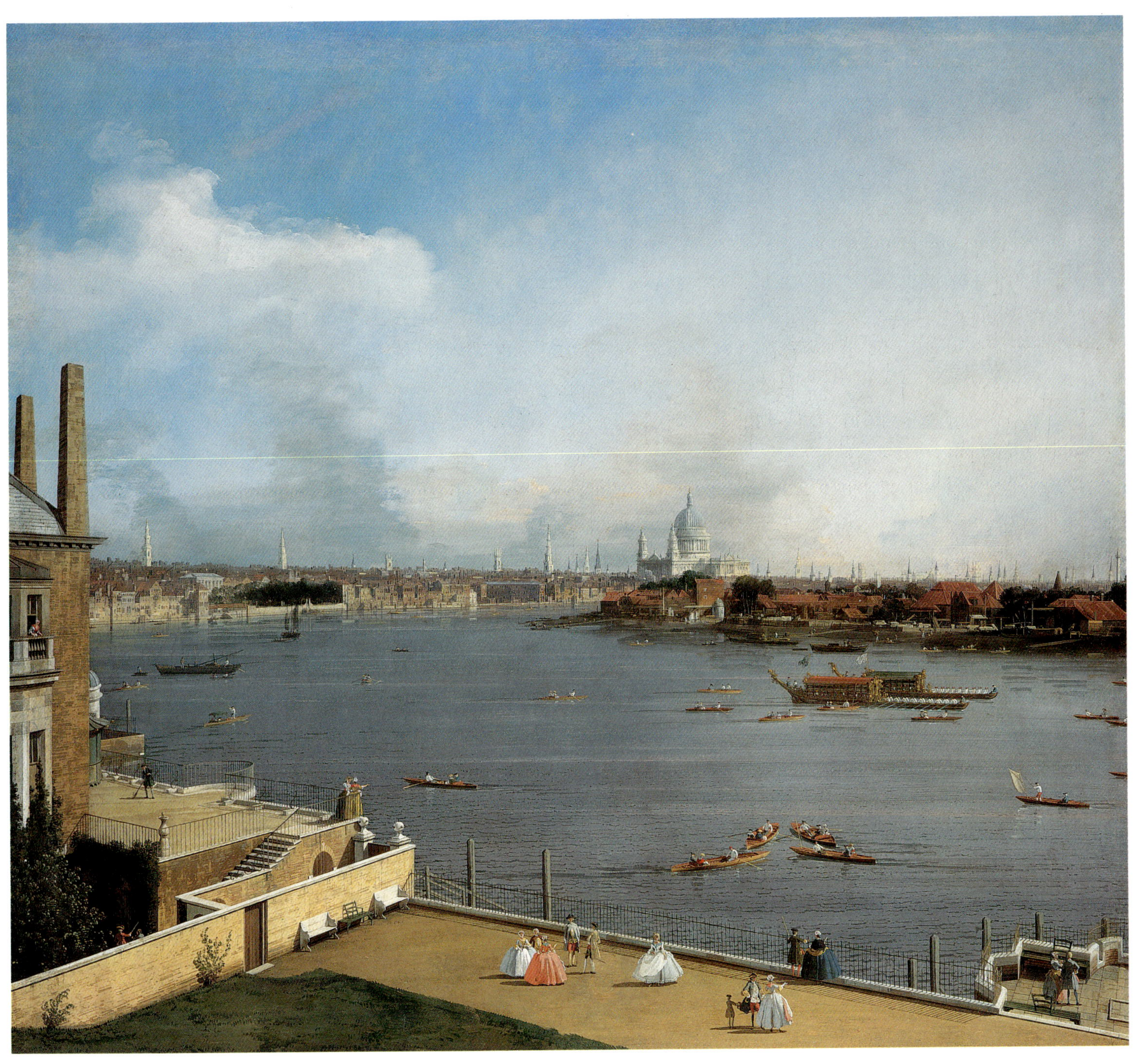

13 Canaletto

Westminster Bridge, London, from the north: the Master of the Goldsmiths' Company's Procession

Oil on canvas, ca. 1750
18 × 30 ins (45.5 × 76 cm)
C/L 436a

Private collection

Apart from Sir Hugh Smithson's commission [cat. no. 6], virtually nothing is known about the original buyers of the many paintings and drawings by Canaletto depicting Westminster Bridge in various stages of construction. However, an inscription in Canaletto's hand was recently discovered on the verso of a similar version of this painting (Artemis Group) which reads: "Antonio Canaleto fecit. con Ogni Stima e Rispeto / All'Eccellentissimo Sigr Gulielmo Vescovo / di Deri". This must refer to William Barnard who became Bishop of Londonderry in 1747. It is not clear what connection Barnard had with the Master of the Goldsmiths' Company, John Blackford, who was sworn in at Westminster in May 1750. It is quite possible that there is an inscription hidden by a relining on the version exhibited here which would reveal more.

The Lord Mayor's blue-topped City Barge appears to the right of centre with its eighteen oarsmen. According to the *Gentleman's Magazine*, the Master of the Goldsmiths' Company travelled in the City Barge attended only by the Goldsmiths' Barge. However, Canaletto has added more civic barges in the composition either for aesthetic effect or at the request of his patron. It is not difficult to make comparison with Canaletto's similar civic processions along the Venetian Grand Canal dominated by the magnificent Bucintoro.

However, the artist often chose a much higher imaginary viewpoint for his Thames views, perhaps showing the influence of earlier topographical painters of the City.

In Canaletto's many depictions of Westminster Bridge, it is often shown as it was destined to appear and not as it actually appeared. The bridge had been opened initially on 25 October 1746, although repairs soon became necessary because of subsidence caused by faulty underpinning. Two arches were dismantled in 1748–49 and the repair work continued until the bridge was finally re-opened on 18 November 1750. Canaletto shows the bridge complete with statues of two river gods, Thames and Isis, in the centre; these had been designed but were never executed. He also depicts domed, octagonal alcoves surmounting each pier although these were constructed on only four piers at each end and four in the middle.

In addition to the civic barges, the river is crowded with small pleasure craft. In the background can be identified, from the right, Westminster Abbey with part of St Margaret's to the right of the tower, Westminster Hall, the House of Commons with two turrets and St John's Smith Square with four. Against the horizon towards the left is Lambeth Palace. JF

See J.G. Links, 'Canaletto and old Westminster: A city in the making', *Apollo*, May 1992, pp.280–87.

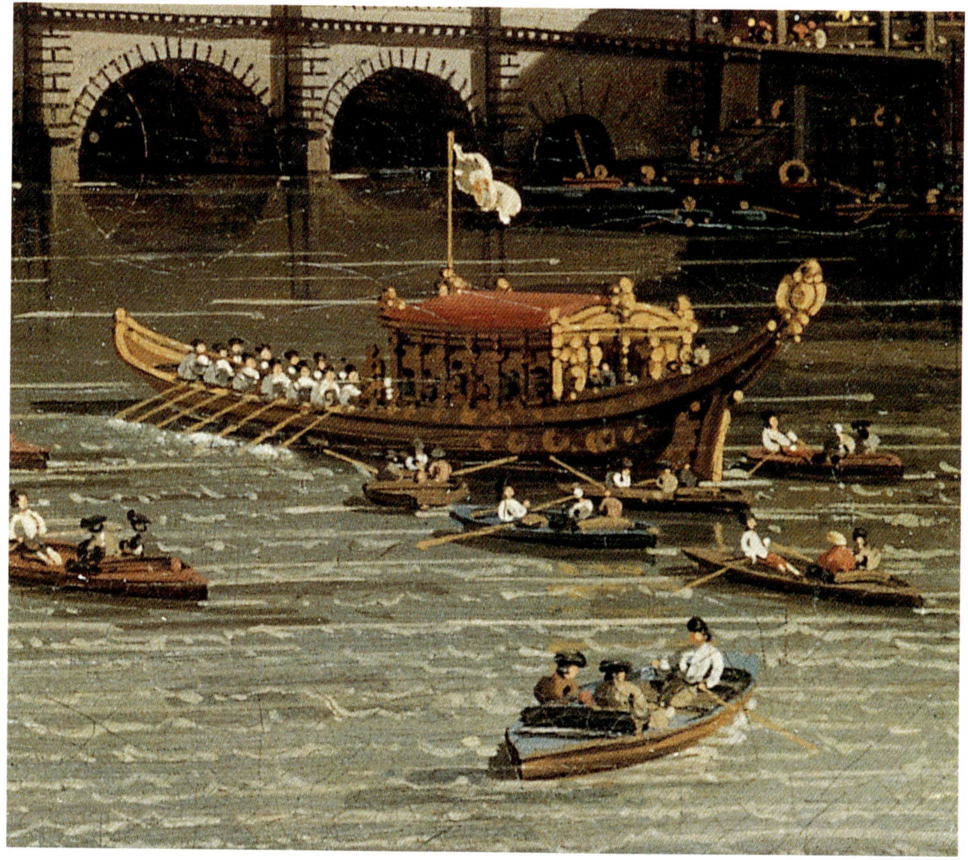

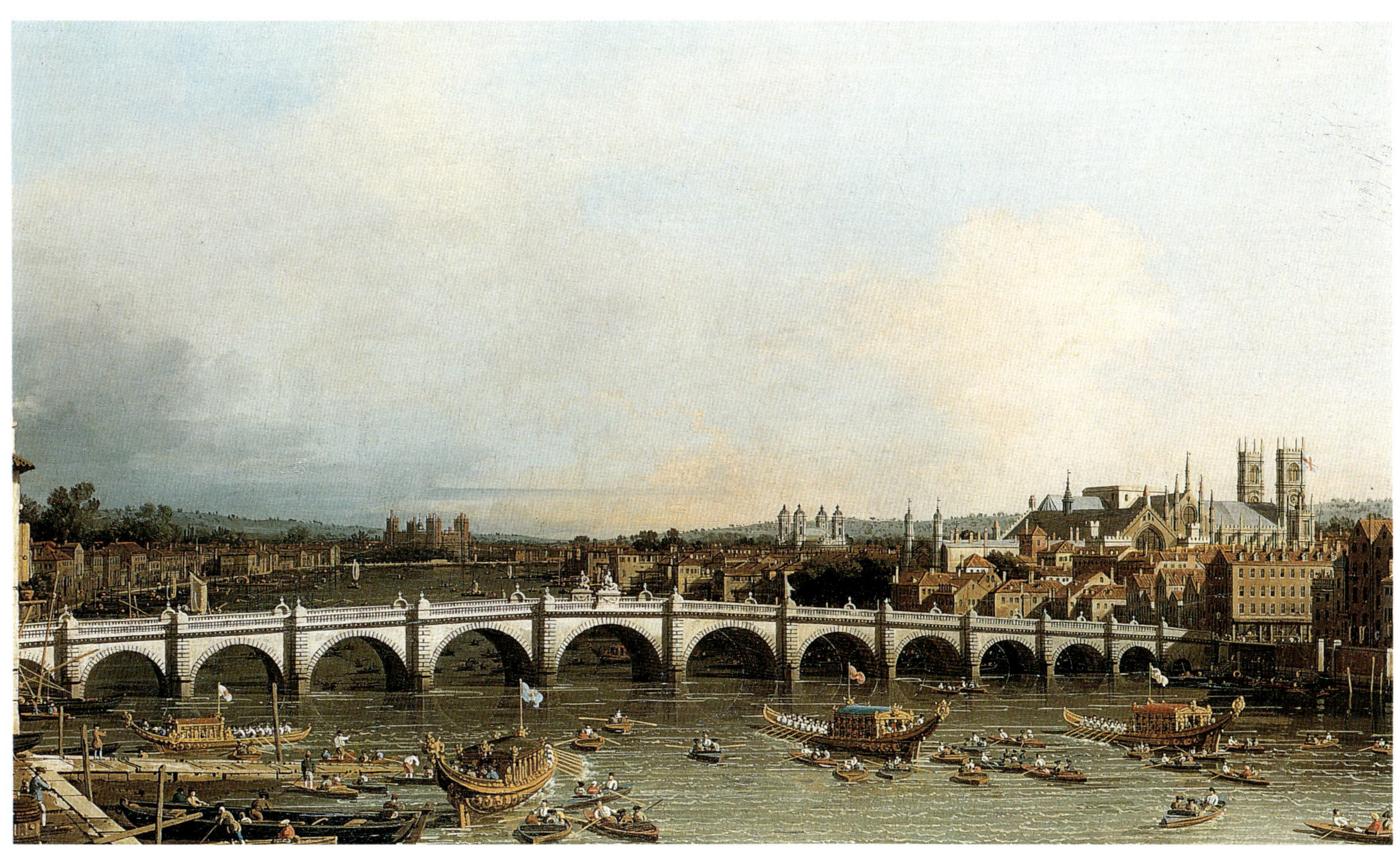

14 Canaletto

The Thames, London, from the terrace of Somerset House, the City of London in the distance

Oil on canvas, ca. 1750
18 × 30 ins (46 × 76 cm)
C/L 428a
Private collection

This picture is the same size as *Westminster Bridge, London, from the north: the Master of the Goldsmiths' Company's Procession* [cat. no. 13] and was probably commissioned from Canaletto as a pendant to it. It is a famous panoramic view of London painted several times by Canaletto and imitated by English followers. The largest version, in the Royal Collection, must have been taken back to Venice 1750–51 or perhaps executed in that city from sketches before being acquired by Consul Smith.

The rapidly developing city of London was described by contemporaries as a modern Rome. Canaletto would have been aware of the English and specifically Whig admiration for the ancient republic of Rome and also for the Venetian Republic of the sixteenth century. English optimism and pride in London's growing power and beauty is cleverly matched by Canaletto's clarity of light and colour on this broad curve of the river which displays an elegant forest of spires dominated by the confident, classical bulk of St Paul's. On the extreme right can be glimpsed the Monument and Old London Bridge.

The broad sweep of the river, the civic barge as well as the dome of St Paul's, beg comparison with Canaletto's Grand Canal views as does the division of public and private space. The houses, gardens, terraces and water gates were privately owned, peopled by the ruling classes and their ser-vants, whereas Canaletto was used to depicting water as a public thoroughfare. The angle of boats and masts balance the composition to the right but also strengthen the line of vision to the focal point of St Paul's. In his English views, Canaletto frequently used the broad crinoline dresses of aristocratic ladies as a pretext for introducing bright eye-catching patches of colour. JF

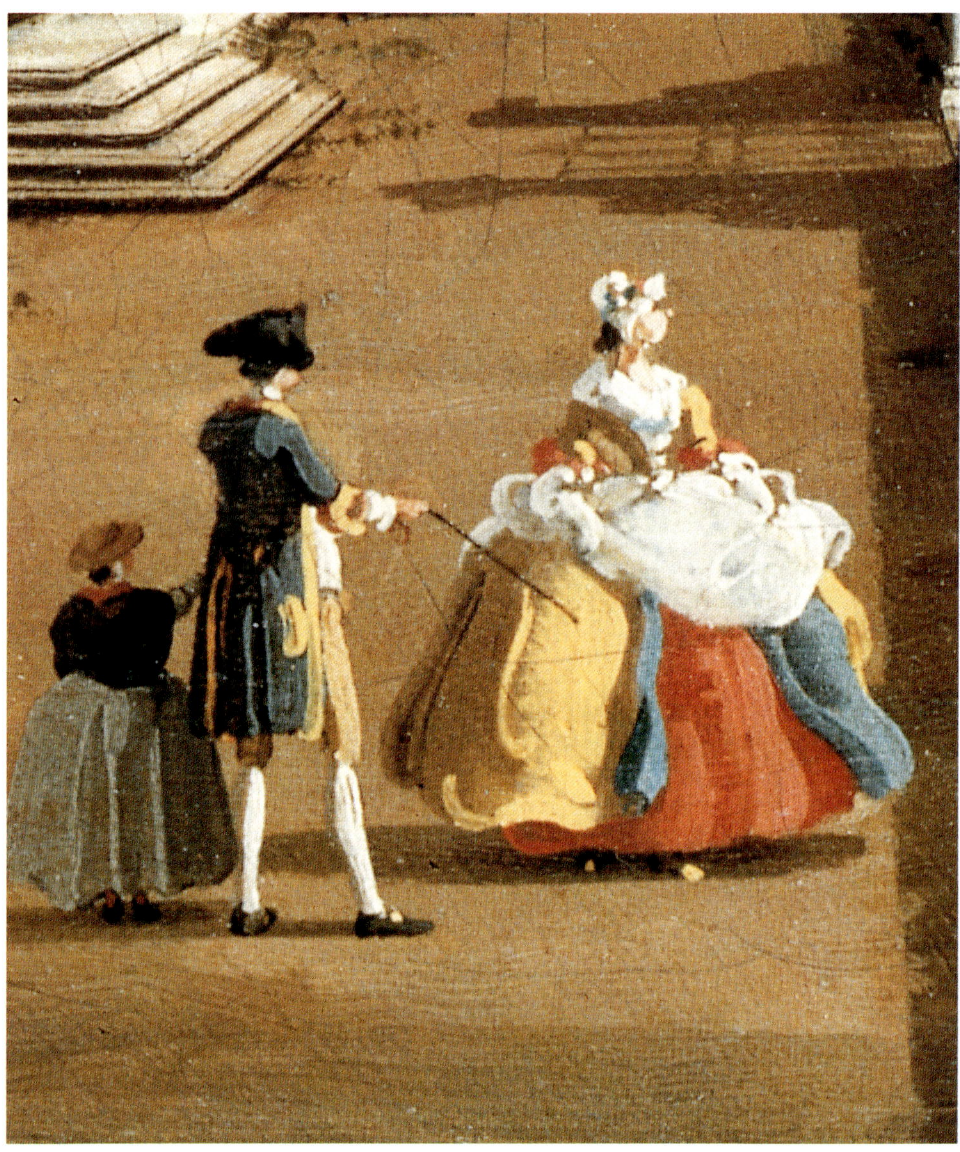

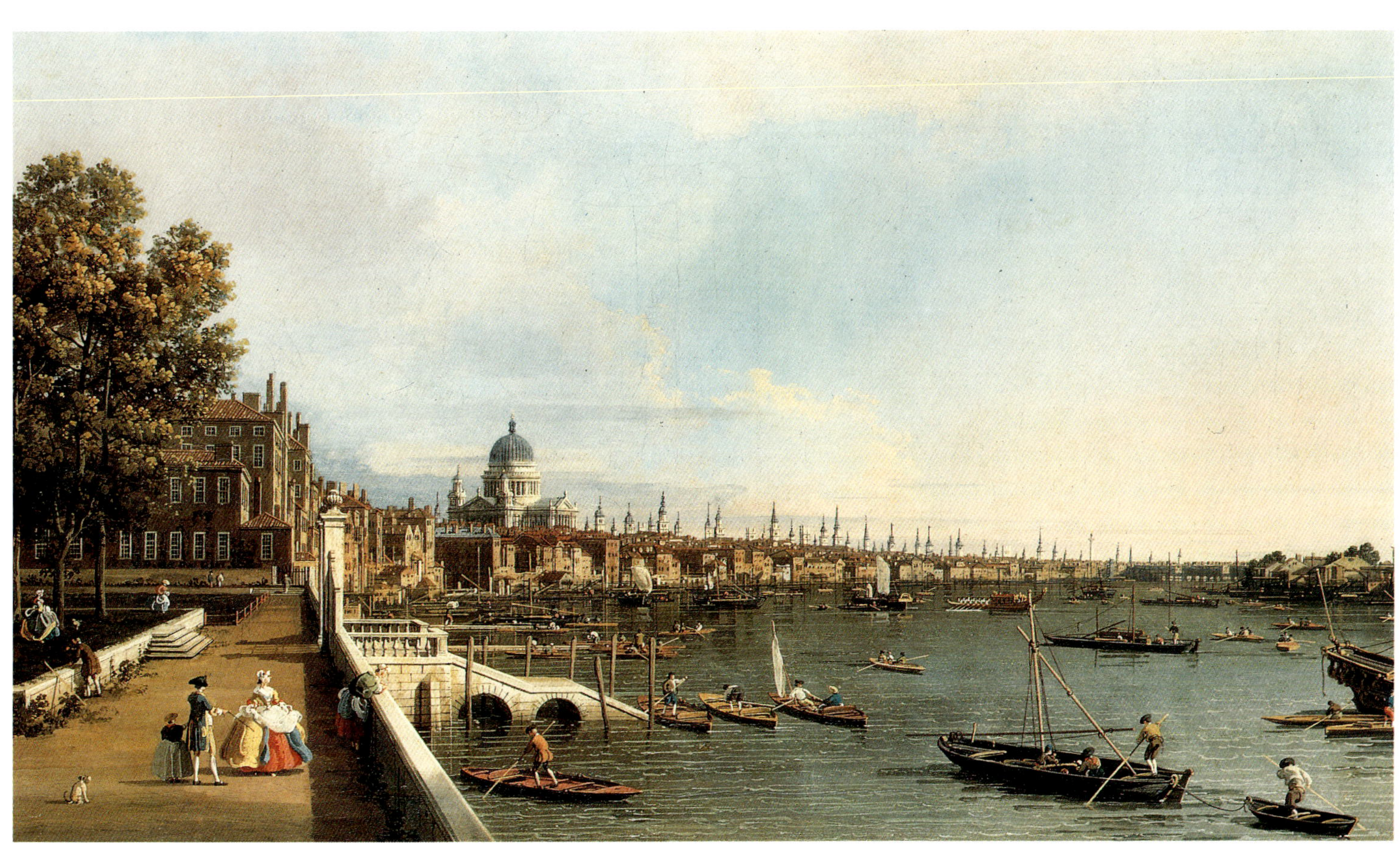

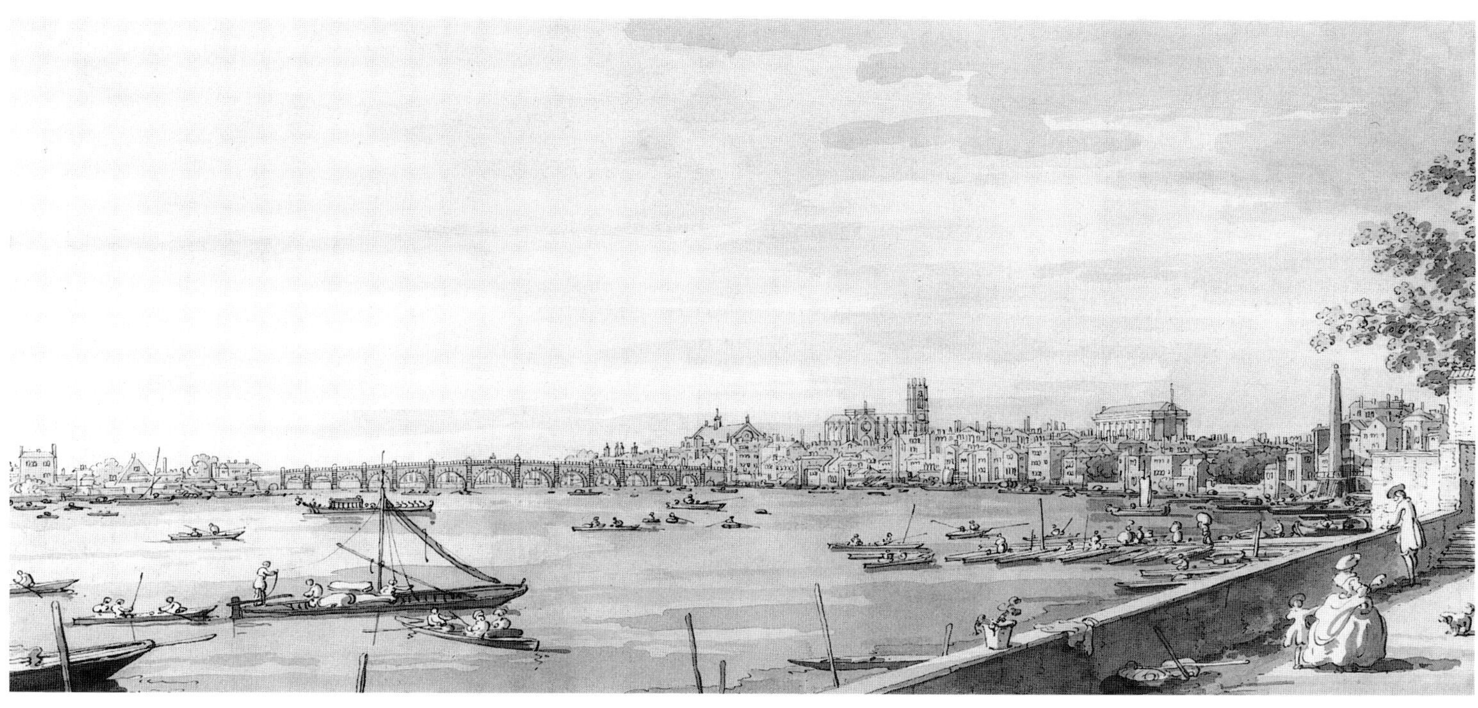

15 Canaletto

The Thames, London, from the terrace of Somerset House, Westminster Bridge in the distance

Pen and brown-black ink with grey wash over pencil, ca. 1750
$8\frac{1}{2} \times 18\frac{3}{4}$ ins (21.5 × 47.5 cm)
C/L 746

Her Majesty The Queen

Westminster Bridge is shown complete and on the west bank can be identified the York Water Tower, the Banqueting Hall, Westminster Abbey and Westminster Hall. This is a pendant to a drawing also in the Royal Collection, *The Thames from the terrace of Somerset House, the City of London in the distance*. Both drawings closely relate to the pair of large oils in the Royal Collection [see cat. no. 14]. It is probable that Canaletto took the pair of drawings back to Venice with him together with the large pair of oils, all of which were acquired by Joseph Smith. This panoramic view, together with its pair looking in the other direction to St Paul's, must have particularly appealed to Smith who had not visited England for many years. There are a number of differences between this drawing and the Royal Collection oil and it relates more closely to a smaller oil (sold Christie's 17 November 1989, lot 3). It is possible that Canaletto made an earlier drawing of this view as there survives a better quality and probably earlier version of its pair in the Courtauld Institute Galleries (Count Seilern collection). The rather Venetian detail of the terracotta plant-pot on the terrace is common to all versions of this view. JF

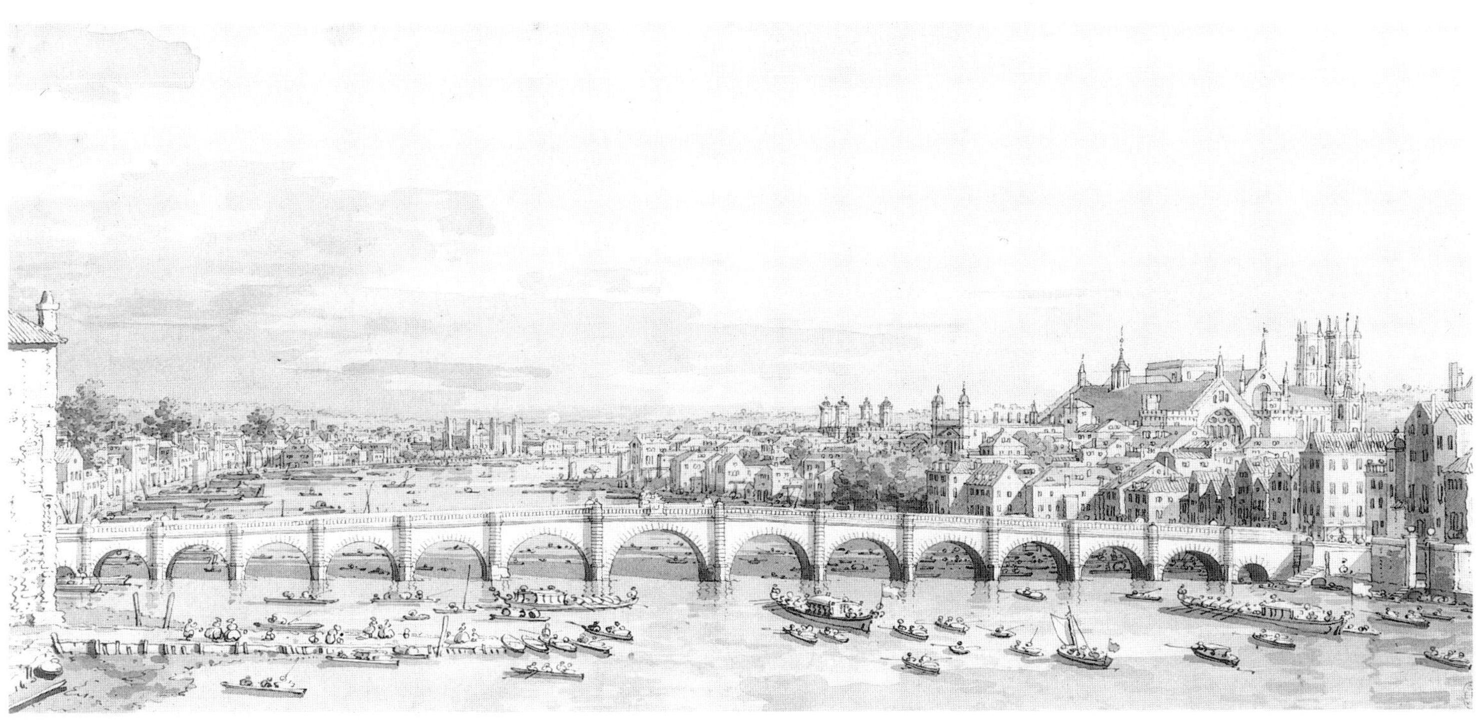

16 Canaletto

Westminster Bridge, London, from the north, Lambeth Palace in the distance

Pen and brown ink with grey wash over pencil, ca. 1750
9 × 12 ins (22.8 × 48.2 cm)
C/L 749
Her Majesty The Queen

This relates to the oil which depicts the Master of the Goldsmiths' Company's procession [cat. no. 13]. If the same event is depicted here, then the presence of fewer civic barges would be historically more accurate. Two other drawings survive, one in the British Museum which omits the barges and one at Stourhead where the boats are similar to the Royal Collection drawing. The Stourhead drawing was acquired by Sir Richard Hoare who was twice Lord Mayor of London and Master of the Goldsmiths' Company. The bridge is shown complete and Canaletto has depicted the octagonal alcoves accurately, as they finally appear with four at each end and four in the middle. The artist presumably took this drawing to Venice in 1750 where it was later acquired by Consul Smith. JF

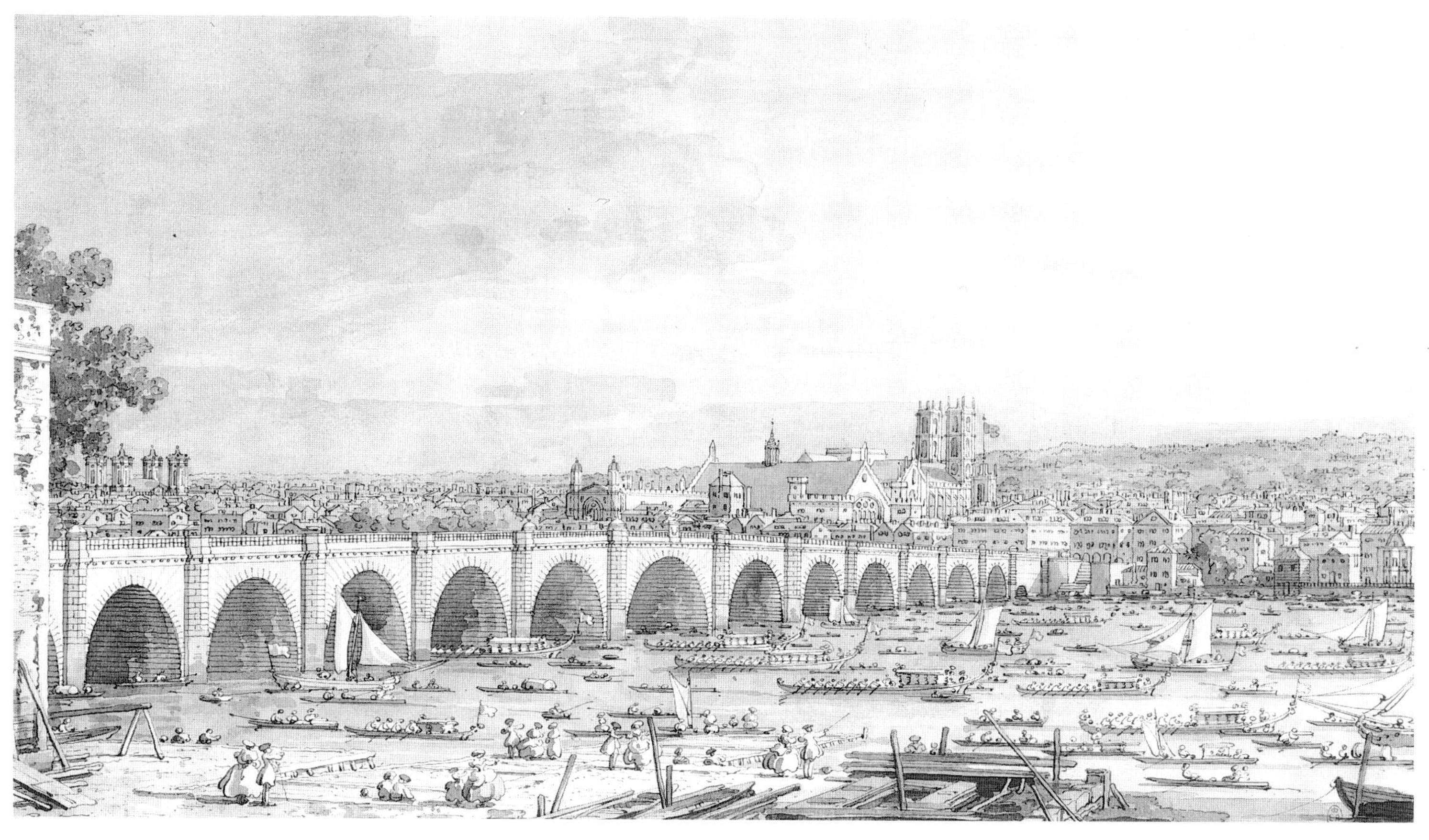

17 Canaletto

Westminster Bridge, London, from the north-east with a procession of civic barges

Pen and brown ink with grey wash over
pencil, ca. 1750
$10\frac{3}{4} \times 19\frac{1}{8}$ ins (27.2 × 48.6 cm)
C/L 750
Her Majesty The Queen

This is a rather schematized drawing in
Canaletto's late calligraphic style which is
enlivened by the numerous oared barges
that process by, watched by groups of
onlookers on the bank. The view is from
Lambeth and, from left to right, can be
seen St John's Smith Square, St Stephen's
Chapel, Westminster Hall, the Abbey and
St Margaret's Church with a flag flying.
The darker washes in the sky and in the
foreground add to the drama of the spectacle represented. The bridge is shown
complete with the alcoves accurately
depicted. A very similar but larger version
is in the British Museum which shows the
bridge with alcoves inaccurately surmounting all the piers, suggesting that it
was executed before the bridge was
finally opened in 1750. JF

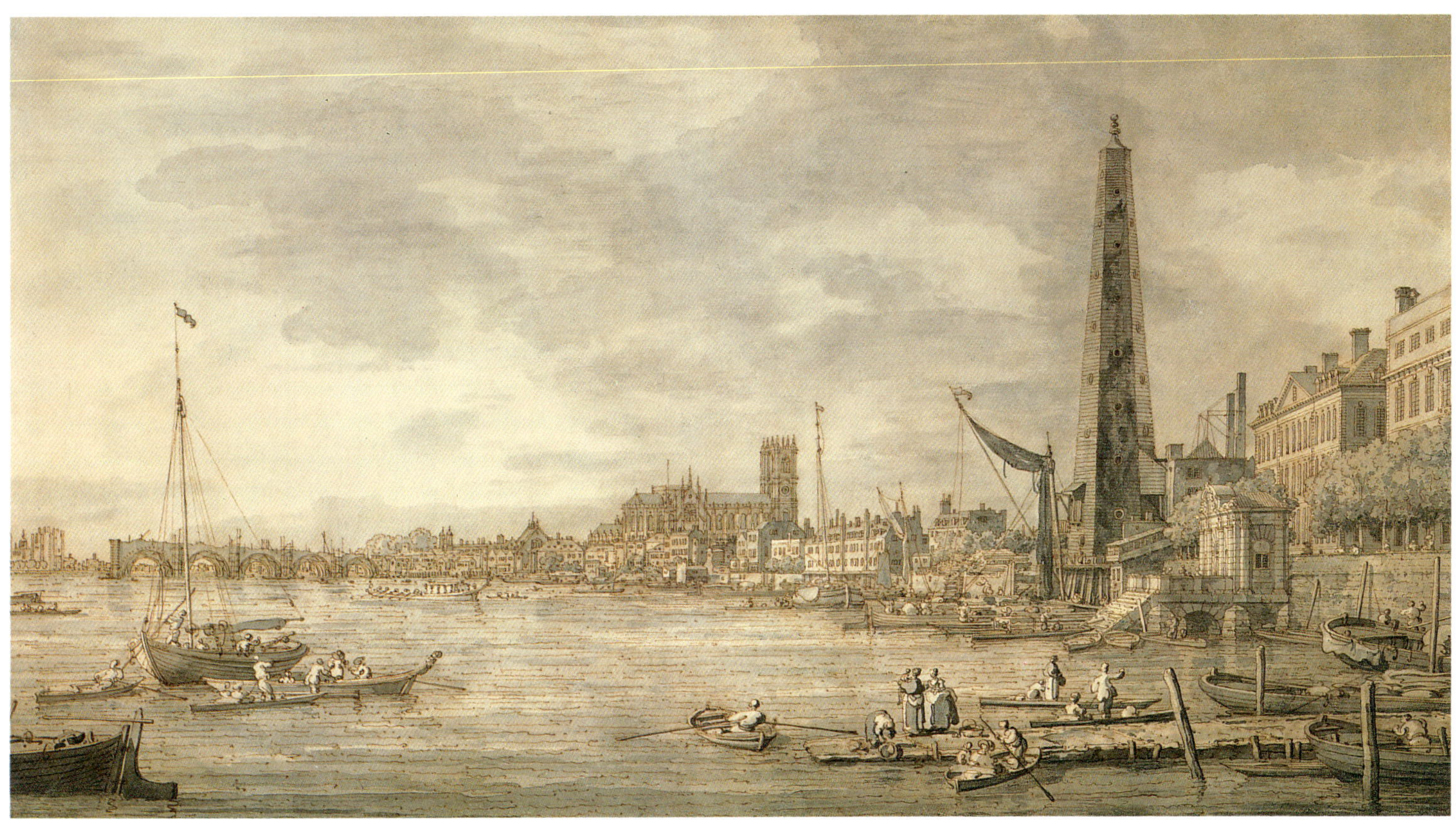

18 Canaletto

The Thames looking towards Westminster, London, from near York Watergate

Pen and brown ink with grey wash
$15\frac{1}{4} \times 28\frac{1}{4}$ ins (38.8 × 71.8 cm)
C/L 747
Yale Center for British Art (Paul Mellon Collection), New Haven

The skyline is dominated not by the Abbey but by the unmistakeable shape of the wooden water tower of the York Buildings Waterworks Company which was one of London's main suppliers of water. Raised from the Thames with horse-driven pumps, water was distributed as far as Marylebone Fields. The tower's distinctive shape can be recognised in many of Canaletto's views of the Thames. The drawing closely relates to two paintings (at Colnaghi's in 1983 and private collection) which all show only five arches of Westminster Bridge completed. This is invention, because when Canaletto arrived in London in May 1746 the bridge was almost finished. Perhaps, as in his other views of the Thames skyline, Canaletto wanted to convey the impression of a historic city expanding into a great modern metropolis. JF

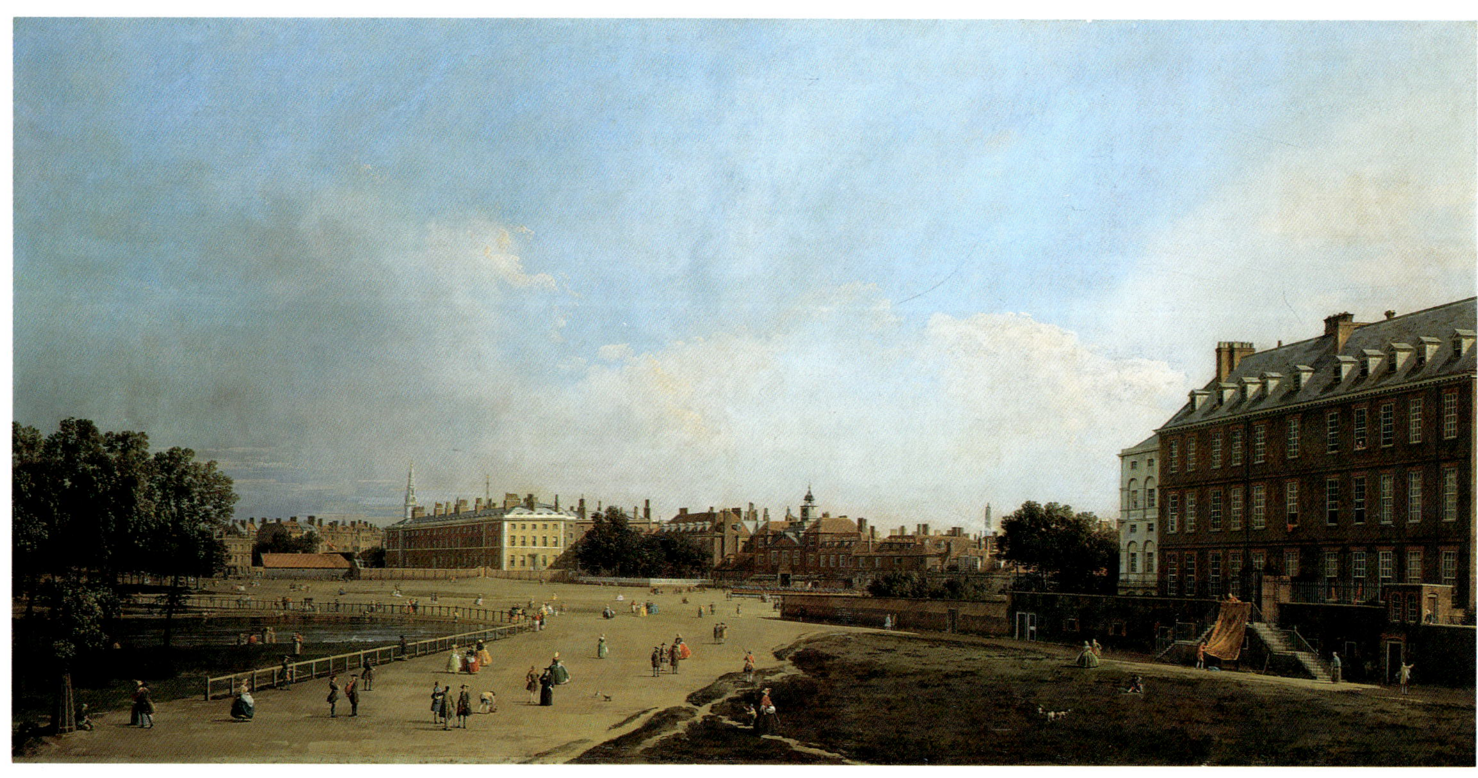

19 Canaletto

The Old Horse Guards, London, from St James's Park

Oil on canvas, ca. 1749
117 × 236 cm (46 × 93 ins)
C/L 415
Sir Andrew Lloyd Webber Art Foundation

On 25 July 1749, Canaletto placed an advertisement in the *Daily Advertiser* which read:

SIGNOR CANALETO hereby invites any Gentleman that will be pleased to come to his House, to see a Picture done by him, being *A View of St James's Park*, which he hopes may in some Measure deserve their Approbation. The said View may be seen from Nine in the Morn-ing till Three in the Afternoon, and from Four till Seven in the Evening, for the Space of fif-teen Days from the Publication of this Advertizement. He lodges at Mʳ Richard Wig-gan's, Cabinet-Maker, in Silver-Street, Golden Square.

This is almost certainly the same painting exhibited here and which is then men-tioned as being in the collection of John Robartes, fourth Earl of Radnor, in June 1756. As with his view of *Whitehall and the Privy Garden* [cat. no. 9], Canaletto must have been aware that an historic site in central London was about to change dram-atically, and although he advertised his new picture, he may have had a specific patron in mind. Elizabeth Einberg suggests that this was Sir Watkin Williams-Wynn (1692–1749), a Tory M.P. and powerful landowner known as a patron of the arts whose house appears on the right of the composition.[1] Unfortunately for Canaletto, in that case, Sir Watkin was killed in a riding accident on 26 September 1749.

The Old Horse Guards building in the centre of the composition was in danger of collapse and plans to rebuild it had been proposed since the beginning of the decade. By the summer of 1749, temporary stables were being erected and demolition must have begun soon after Canaletto completed his painting. The New Horse Guards building, also painted by Canaletto, was completed in 1753.

As with the best of Canaletto's London views, the glimpse he provides of the range of social strata that people a public place is fascinating. Vagrants, beggars, fashionably dressed bourgeoisie, soldiers and nursemaids with children all throng

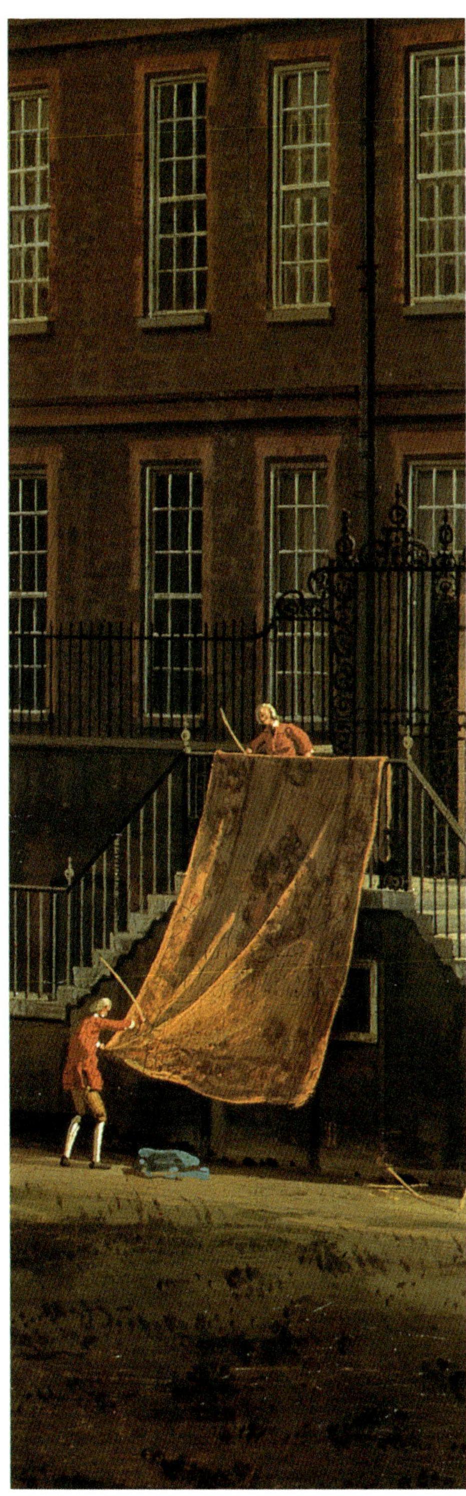

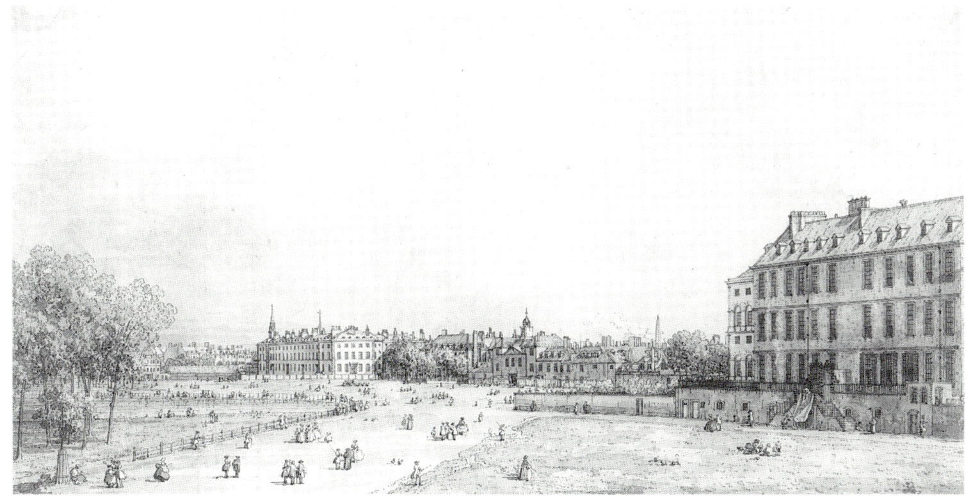

together – the woman with hitched-up petticoats and red heels on the left is probably one of the 'ladies of the town'. A regiment of George II's Life Guards are seen at drill in the background and Canaletto depicts no less than three figures urinating against a wall in different parts of the picture – a commonplace at a time when there were no public conveniences.

Sir Watkin's house on the right was No. 1 Downing Street, next to the London residence of the Duke of Bolton which, in turn, adjoined the Treasury with its private walled garden. On the skyline can be identified the distinctive tower of the York Buildings Waterworks Company and over to the left the white spire of St Martin-in-the-Fields. The high viewpoint and panoramic composition chosen by Canaletto show to advantage his ability to suffuse the picture with a sense of space and light. A detailed drawing of similar high quality also survives [cat. no. 20]. JF

1. Elizabeth Einberg, *Canaletto: The Old Horse Guards from St James's Park ca. 1749*, Tate Gallery Publications 1992.

20 Canaletto

The Old Horse Guards, London, from St James's Park

Pen and brown ink with grey wash, ca. 1749
$13\frac{3}{16} \times 27\frac{1}{8}$ ins (34.6 × 68.8 cm)
C/L 734
The Trustees of the British Museum, London

Closely related to the large oil of the same subject [cat. no. 19], the drawing has a number of differences in figures, in the proportionate size of the trees and in its omission of the regimental drill taking place in front of the Horse Guards building. The figure groupings are closer to Canaletto's later paintings of the New Horse Guards from the same viewpoint and he undoubtedly based these later oils on this drawing. JF

Canaletto and Warwick

Francis Greville, Lord Brooke (later Earl of Warwick), was orphaned at the age of eight years and brought up by his aunt, wife of the Earl of Hertford, whose daughter married Sir Hugh Smithson, later Duke of Northumberland. It was almost certainly Lady Smithson who introduced Canaletto to Brooke. The young Lord Brooke's pride in the castle is shown by the fact that on three occasions he had his portrait painted with plans of the building. In 1744, he extended the castle grounds by acquiring land belonging to the town of Warwick and, in 1748, he employed 'Capability' Brown who worked at the castle for thirteen years.

A series of four payments to Canaletto in Lord Brooke's account at Hoare's Bank (one in 1748, one in 1749 and two in 1752) indicates that Canaletto made at least two visits to Warwick. These resulted in five paintings and three drawings of the castle and two drawings of the town of Warwick. Canaletto painted more views of Warwick Castle than of any other English building.

All eight views of the castle were likely to have been executed in Canaletto's London studio and delivered to Lord Brooke's London house at 29 Grosvenor Square. Canaletto would have undoubtedly made working drawings on the spot in small sketchbooks. However, none of Warwick has survived. JF

See D. Buttery, 'Canaletto at Warwick', *Burlington Magazine*, July 1987, pp.437–45; *idem, Canaletto and Warwick Castle*, Chichester 1992.

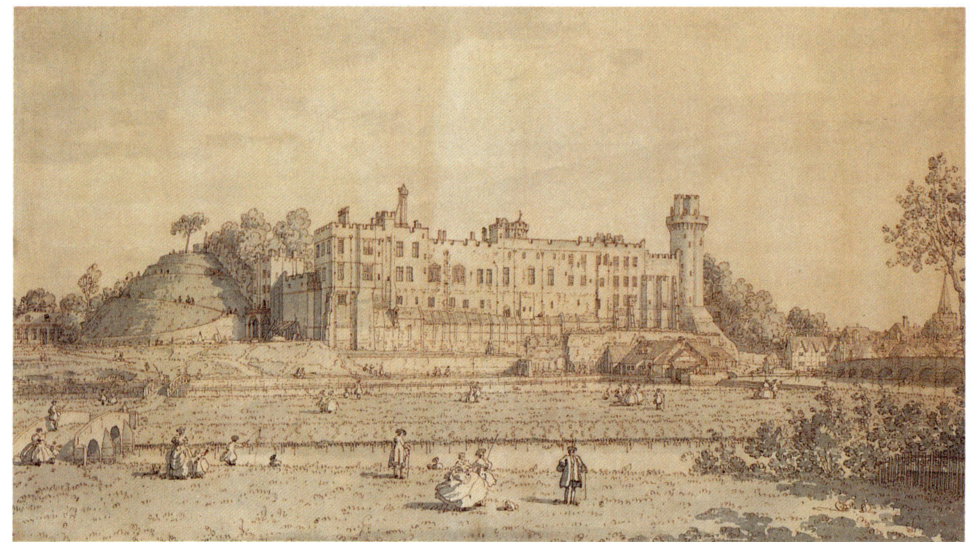

21 Canaletto

Warwick Castle: the south front

Pen and brown ink with grey wash, 1748
$12\frac{1}{2} \times 22\frac{3}{4}$ ins (31.7×57.8 cm)
C/L 758

Private collection

Of the three drawings that survive of Warwick Castle, all are elaborate and highly finished and cannot be regarded as preparatory studies for the oils [see cat. no. 22]. In addition to the four payments recorded to Canaletto in Brooke's account at Hoare's Bank, there is an entry in the 1748 estate account which reads: "To Seignr. Canal for his Drawings of Warwick Castle £10.10". This probably refers to one drawing as Canaletto appears to have charged thirty to forty guineas for an oil and ten for a drawing. This example is closely related to the oil in the Mellon Collection. It shows some of Lord Brooke's improvements to the fenestration and the beginnings of re-landscaping the gardens and Castle mound. The view is more pan-oramic, taken from Castle Park on the other side of the Avon, and includes much lively incidental detail, with figures promenading round the mound to take the view and a lean-to shed at the base of the mound for the workmen and their tools. JF

22 Canaletto

Warwick Castle: the south front

Oil on canvas, 1748
$29\frac{1}{2} \times 47\frac{1}{2}$ ins (75×120.5 cm)
C/L 445

The Thyssen-Bornemisza Collection, Madrid

Canaletto painted three views and made one drawing [cat. no. 21] of the south front, all of which are likely to date from his first visit to Warwick in late 1747 or early 1748. Buttery convincingly argues that this example postdates the smallest oil (private collection, New York) and was commissioned by Lord Brooke to show a new vision of Warwick Castle transformed

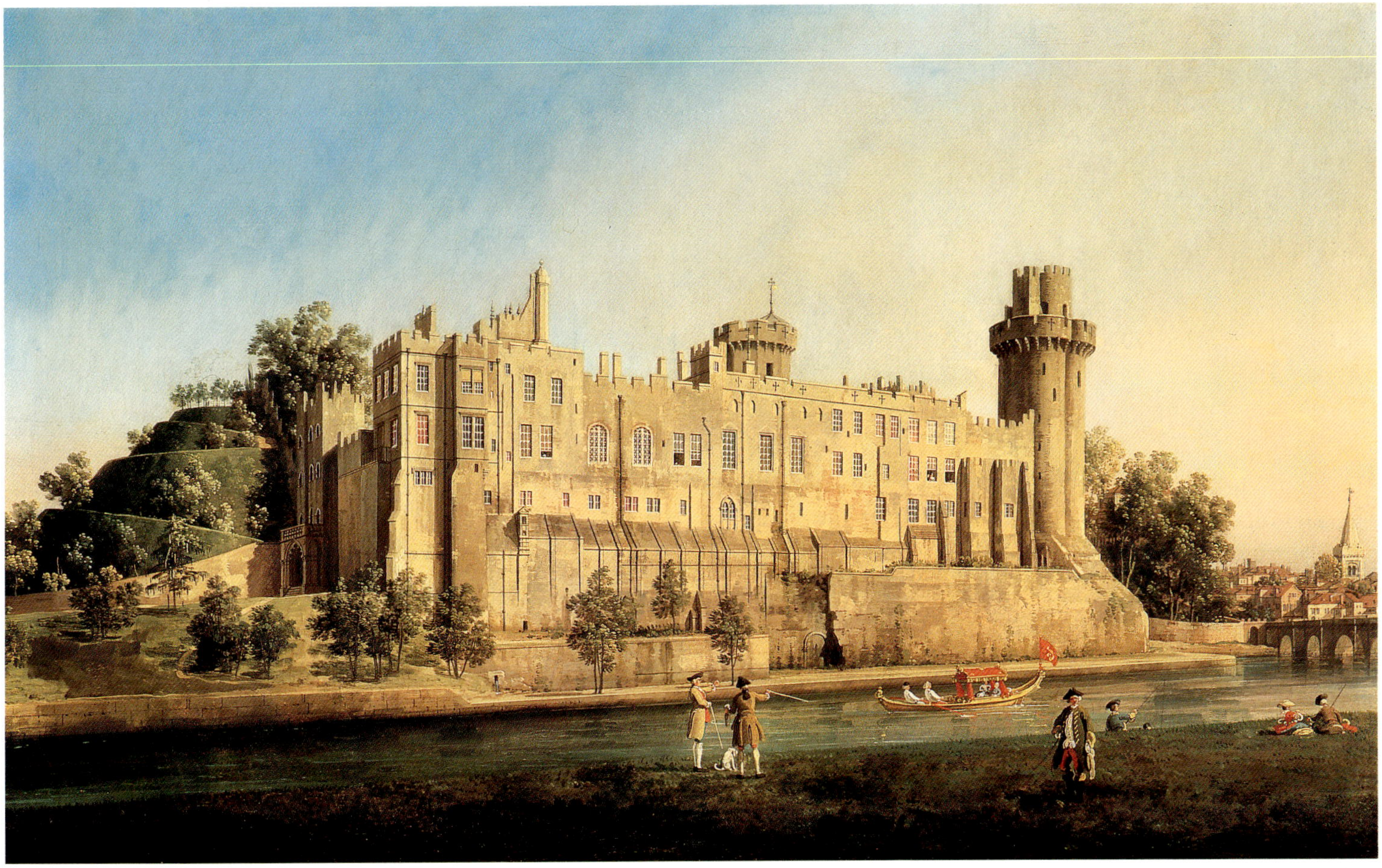

and modernised by his planned improvements. The view is taken from Castle
Meadow and shows the summit of Guy's
Tower projecting over the centre of the
building although it is not actually visible
from this point. To the left there is a
mature and tidy landscape around the
Castle mound. The mill and weir have
been omitted and a number of old-
fashioned Jacobean windows have been
replaced with modern sashes and glazing
bars. The largest windows visible in the
state apartments to the left of centre have
glazing bars in the new gothic taste and
the porch at the base of the mound is also
gothicized. Lord Brooke must have
retained fond memories of Venice, seen on
his Grand Tour, because payments also
exist in the Castle archives for a "pleasure-
boat". Therefore, Canaletto's inclusion of a
gondola is not as far fetched as it might
appear. The third and probably last view of
the south front is now in the Paul Mellon
Collection. JF

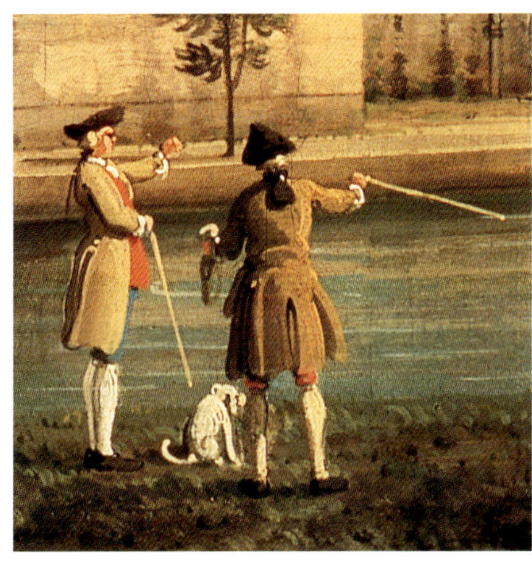

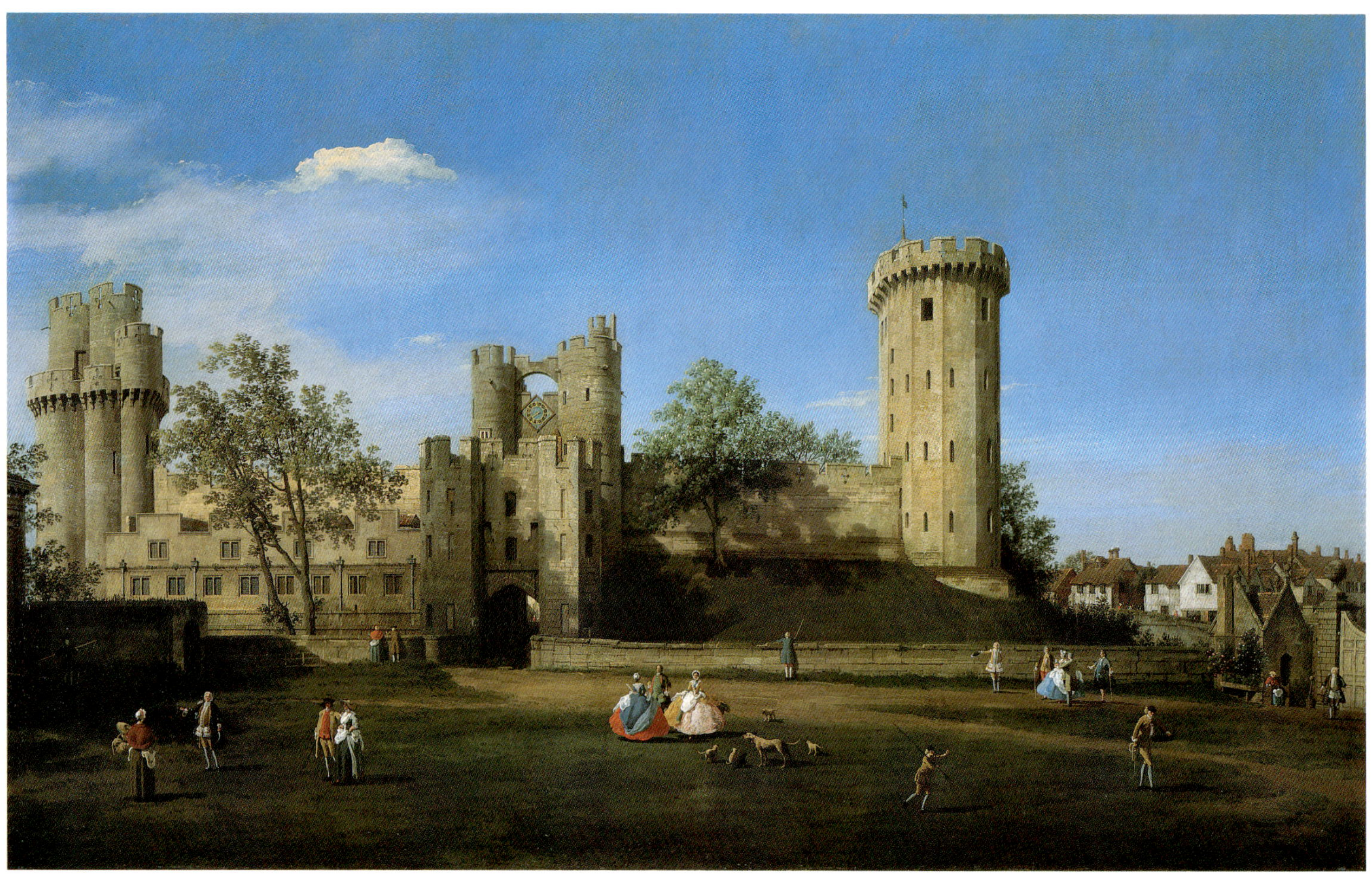

23 Canaletto

Warwick Castle: the east front from the outer court

Oil on canvas, 1752
$28\frac{3}{4} \times 48$ ins (73 × 122 cm)
C/L 446

Birmingham Museums and Art Gallery

Canaletto left England to return to Venice in the autumn of 1750 but had returned to England by July 1751. Pleased with his earlier commissions from the artist, Lord Brooke summoned Canaletto to Warwick again as is shown by the next payment to the artist, dated 24 March 1752, in Hoare's Bank for 32 guineas. The pair of views of the east front with their related drawings [cat. no. 25] can be assumed to be the result of this last commission.

Canaletto has shifted the great battlemented medieval east front to the left of the composition to allow a glimpse of the medieval town of Warwick next to the porter's lodge and main gateway to what was the original approach to the Castle. The imaginary viewpoint looks down on an external walled courtyard with part of the seventeenth-century stable-block glimpsed to the left. The elegantly dressed figures, the low-roofed cottages and the filigree foliage of the trees all serve to accentuate the massive scale of the castle. A porter in livery is visible to the right who appears to have recently admitted an aristocratic group of visitors with their guide. The equally aristocratic bitch in expensive collar with her pups is a particularly delightful addition. The intense blue of the sky perhaps suggests that Canaletto had only recently returned from Venice and had still to adjust to the English light.
JF

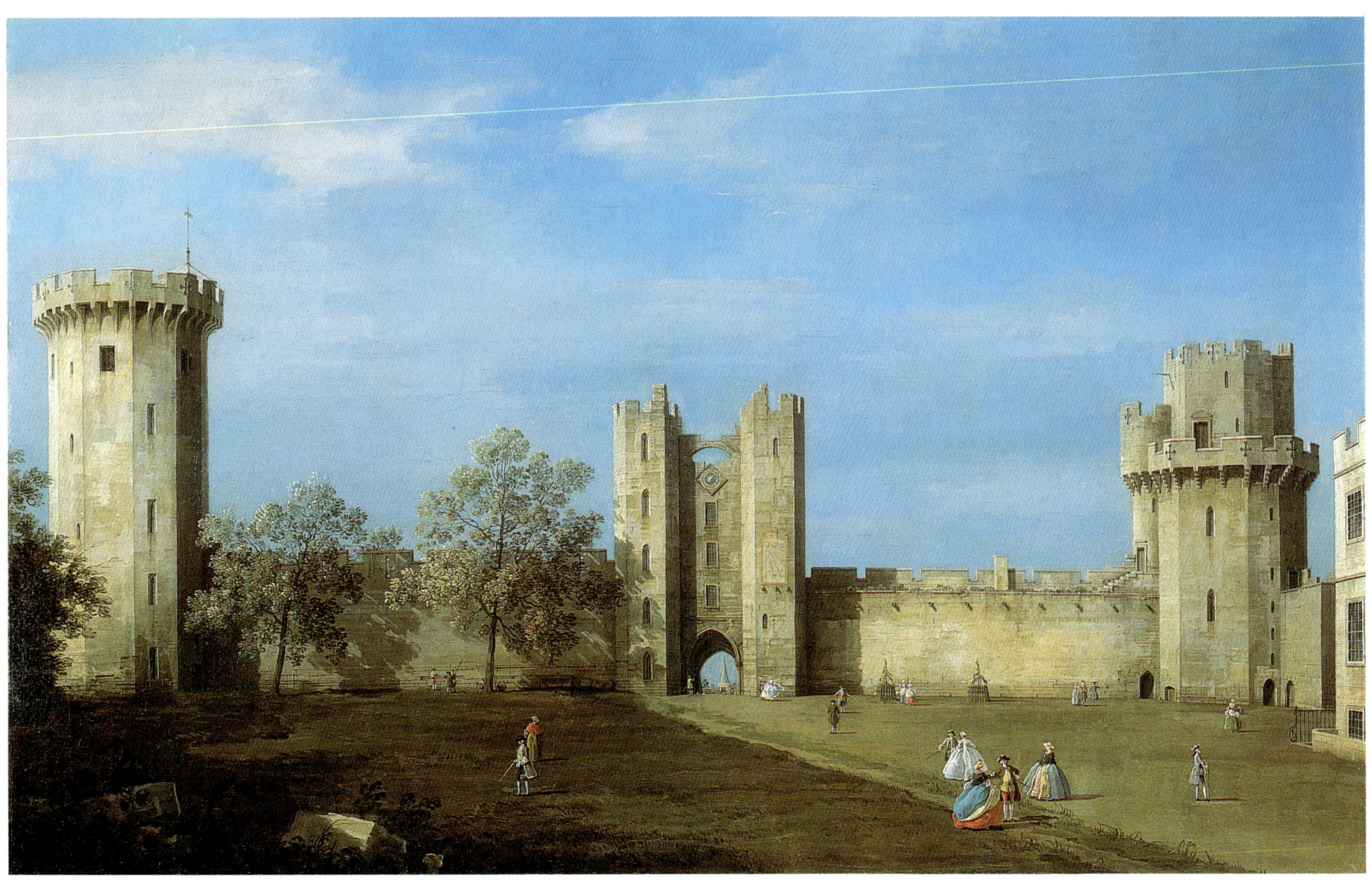

24 Canaletto

Warwick Castle: the east front from the inner court

Oil on canvas, 1752
$29\frac{1}{2} \times 48$ ins (75 × 122 cm)
C/L 447
Birmingham Museums and Art Gallery

This is one of the most starkly simple compositions produced by Canaletto. Guy's Tower, the gatehouse and barbican and Caesar's Tower are spread along the full width of the composition with only a glimpse of more comfortable domestic apartments to the right. The figures, some admiring their surroundings, are dwarfed by the majestic scale and simplicity of the architecture. The eye-catching vignette of St Nicholas's Church spire viewed through the entrance arch is not actually visible from this point. However, doubtless Lord Brooke would consider this to be of trifling importance when showing the picture to his London guests. In 1753, Brooke approved 'Capability' Brown's plans to remove the iron railings visible on the extreme right and to create an oval lawn and coachway. The two newly planted fir trees to the right of the composition are probably early evidence of Brown's landscaping for the courtyard. JF

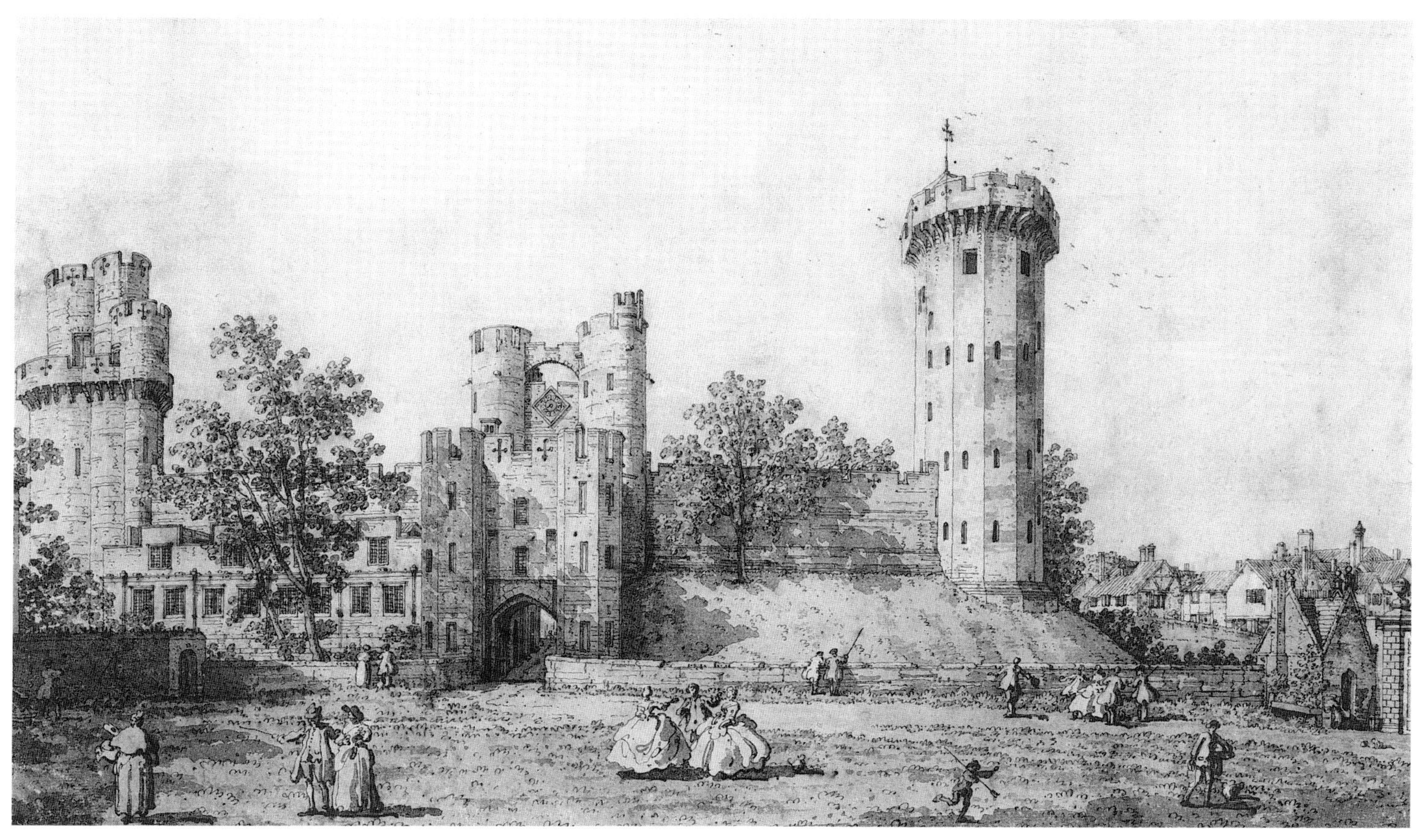

25 Canaletto

Warwick Castle: the east front from the outer court

Pen and brown ink with grey wash, 1752
$12\frac{7}{16} \times 22\frac{1}{8}$ ins (31.6×56.1 cm)
C/L 759

The Metropolitan Museum of Art (Robert Lehman Collection), New York

The composition includes less foreground than the related oil [cat. no. 23] and the towers are higher in proportion to the buildings. There are a number of differences in the figures and the group of dogs is not included but Canaletto has added a flock of birds above Guy's Tower.

A similarly finished drawing which closely relates to the oil of the east front from the inner court [cat. no. 24] is now in the J. Paul Getty Museum, Malibu, California. JF

26 Canaletto

St Mary's Church and Church Street, Warwick

Pen and brown ink with grey wash, 1748 or
1752
14 × 11⅛ ins (35.4 × 28.2 cm)
C/L 757
The Trustees of the British Museum, London

It seems unlikely that Canaletto was commissioned to make two drawings of the
town of Warwick. They were probably
his own initiative and he perhaps hoped
to sell them to an engraver. The mount of
this drawing is quaintly inscribed in the
artist's hand: 'Ingresso nella Piazza de
Varik'. The second drawing, entitled *The
town and Castle of Warwick seen from the gardens of the Priory*, is in the Yale Center for
British Art, New Haven. JF

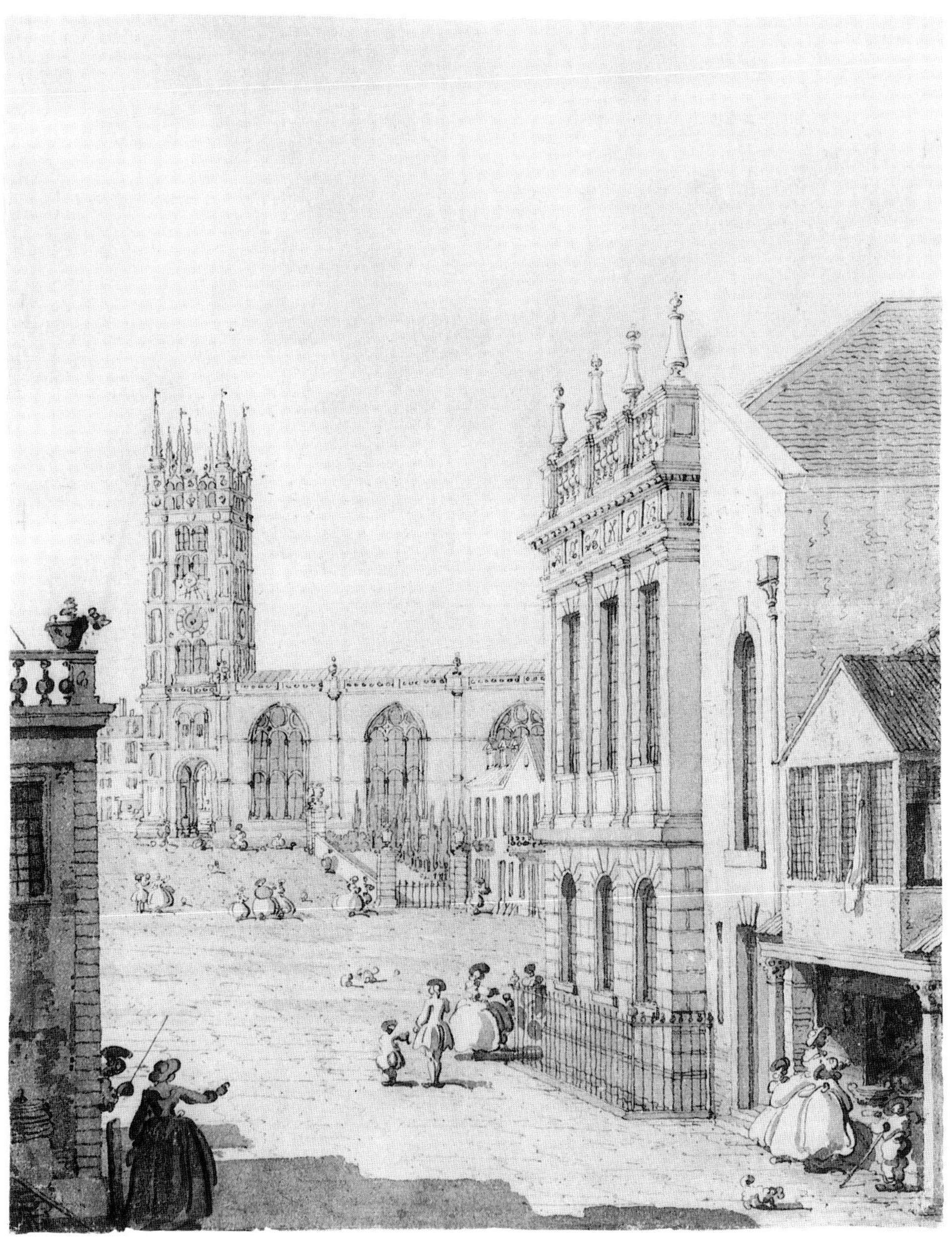

27 Canaletto

Westminster Abbey, London, with a procession of the Knights of the Order of the Bath

Oil on canvas, after June 1749
40 × 40 ins (101.6 × 101.6 cm)
C/L 432
The Dean and Chapter of Westminster

Joseph Wilcocks, Dean of Westminster until 1756, commissioned Canaletto to record the procession of the newly installed Knights of the Order of the Bath from Westminster Abbey to the House of Lords on 20 June 1749. The picture was hung at the Westminster Deanery where it remains today. As well as focusing on the Knights in their ostentatious red and white cloaks and plumed hats, the picture commemorates the completion of restoration work on the Abbey exterior and the construction of the two west towers. Carried out by Wren and Hawksmoor, the project is likely to have continued until 1744–45 although the prominent inscription gives a date of 1735.

It cannot be assumed that Canaletto witnessed the event and he may have relied on visual and written accounts. The fall of light is contrived to spotlight the west front of the Abbey and the procession immediately in front while most of the surroundings and onlookers remain in shadow. A static composition is avoided by moving the Abbey façade to the right so that the eye is drawn along the line of the procession. The red curve of cloaks is countered by a rather obvious patch of sky-blue in the form of a crinolined gown.

On the day itself, the Duke of Montagu, Great Master of the Order, was too ill to attend and was replaced by Lord de la Warr who can be identified standing in line

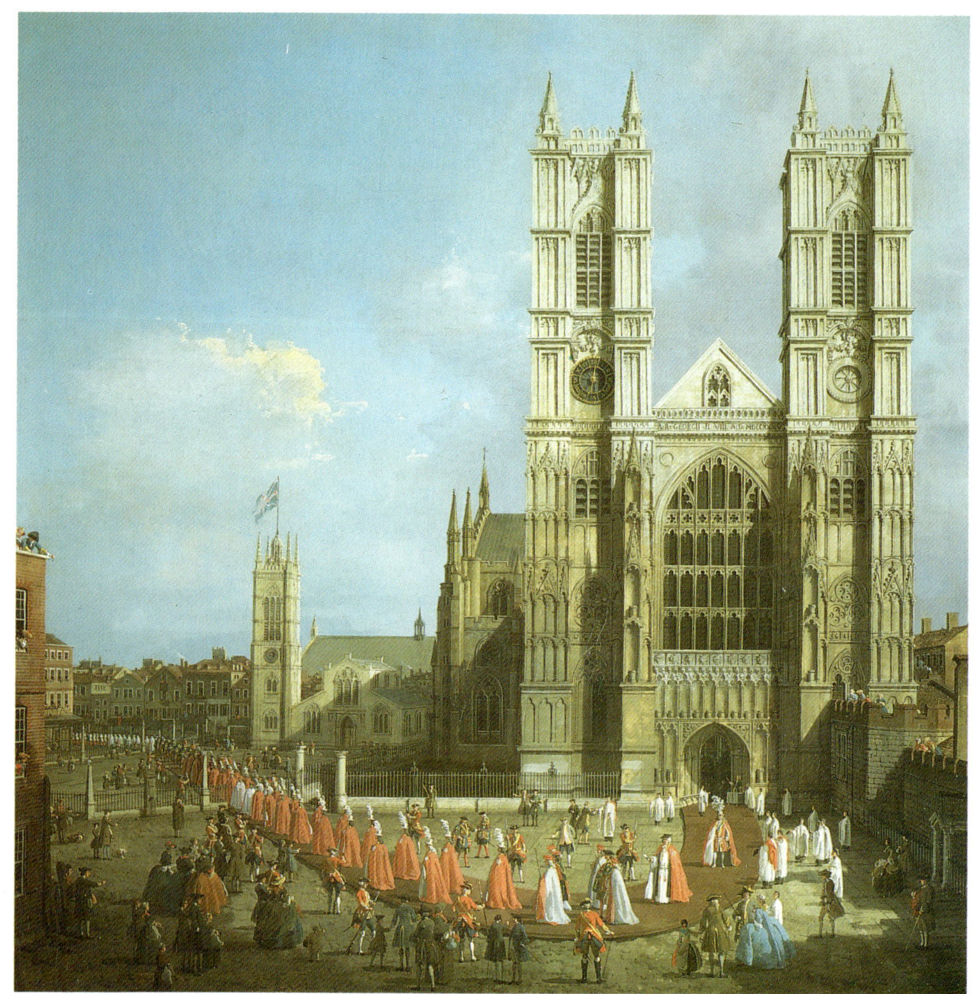

with the west door, preceded in procession by the Dean. Figures in white surplices watch the procession retreating and farther along, at random intervals, the route is lined with Redcoats. The clock indicates a time shortly after midday. JF

28 Canaletto

*The Grand Walk in Vauxhall
Gardens, London*

Oil on canvas, ca. 1751
$19\frac{3}{4} \times 29\frac{5}{8}$ ins (50 × 75.3 cm)
C/L 431
Private collection

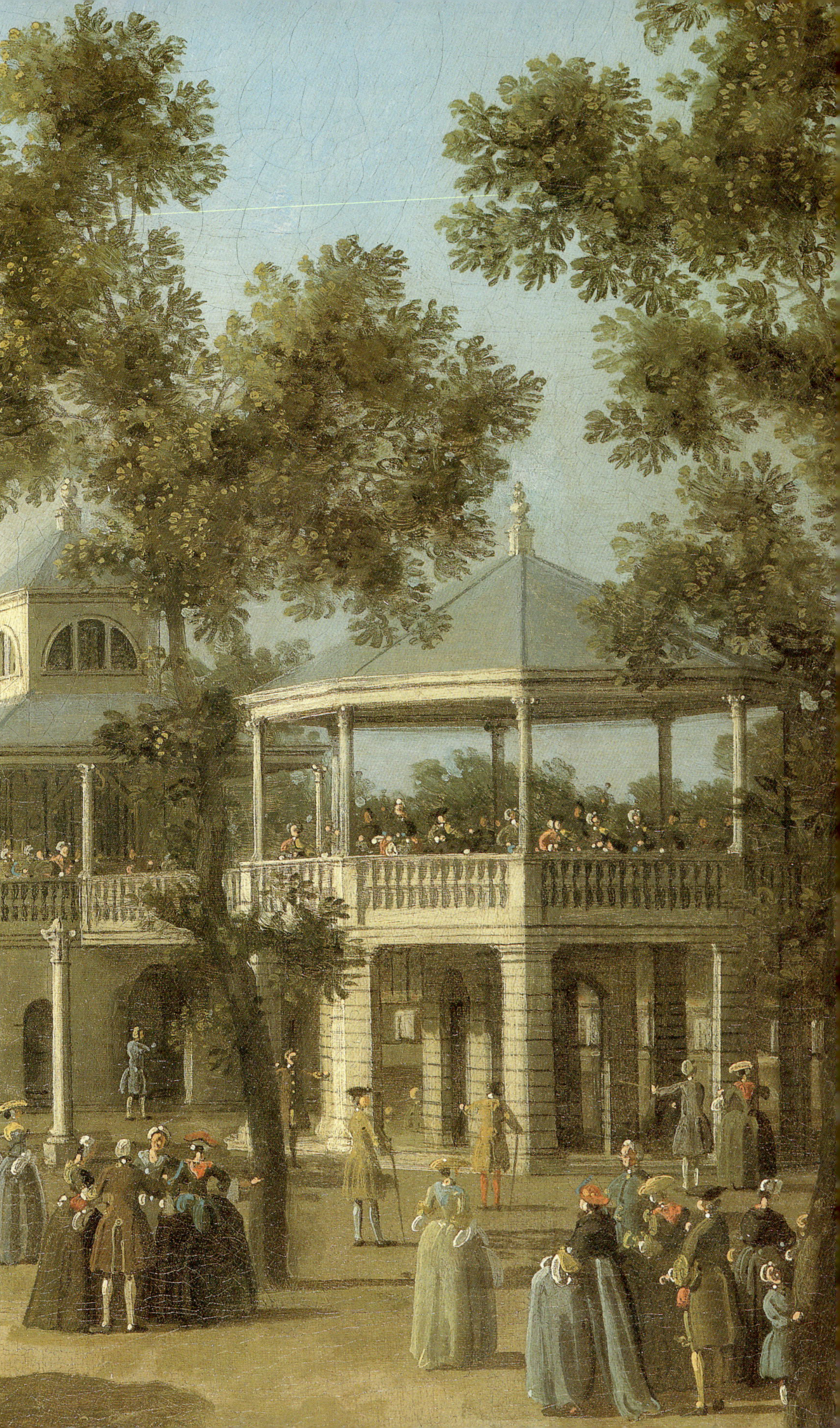

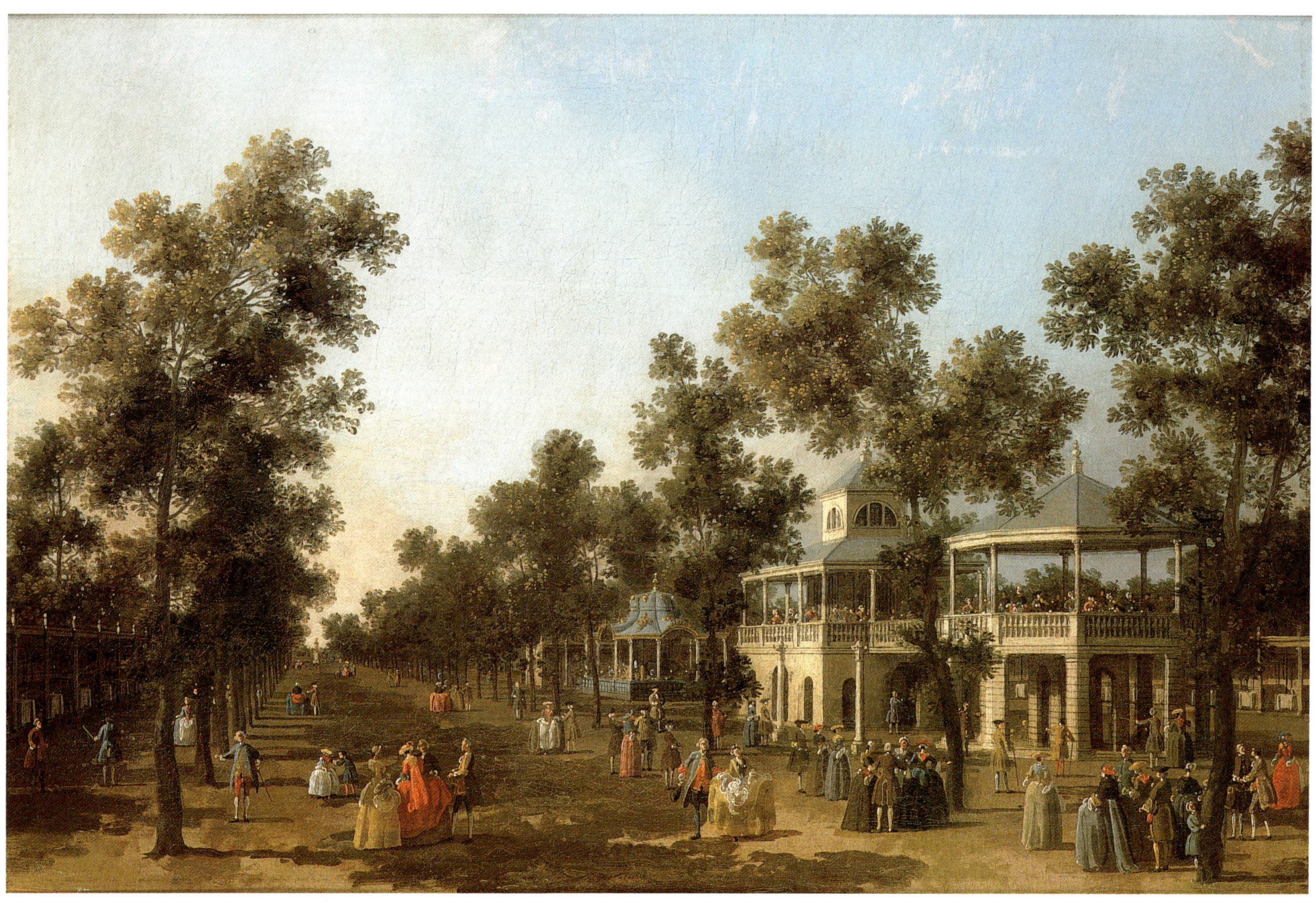

This oil is the only painting by a major artist of this fashionable place of entertainment which was patronised by the Prince of Wales. Vauxhall experienced a revival of popularity after 1750 when the re-opening of Westminster Bridge considerably eased access. Visitors arrived from the later afternoon through the evening and promenaded, listened to music and dined in individual supper boxes by the light of 1500 oil-lamps. Although the scale of the Grand Walk and the proportions of the pavilions have been exaggerated,

Canaletto depicts the view seen on entering the Gardens. To the right stands the octagonal orchestra pavilion, the organ house and the Turkish Dining Tent and, at the end of the walk, a golden statue depicting Aurora, goddess of the dawn, can be seen. To the left, a row of supper boxes is visible.

The foreground is peopled with an elegant if rather stilted crowd but, judging by contemporary accounts, the atmosphere was not always so tranquil and sedate. There was certainly a much greater mix of

class and types from rich to poor – a fact that always took foreign visitors by surprise. No drawings by Canaletto survive and it is possible that both this view and that of Ranelagh [cat. no. 29] may have been painted after engravings which had themselves been copied from drawings by another artist. The fact that the shadows should fall the other way and that the structure of the pavilions shows topographical inaccuracies gives strength to the argument that Canaletto did not sketch the Gardens himself. JF

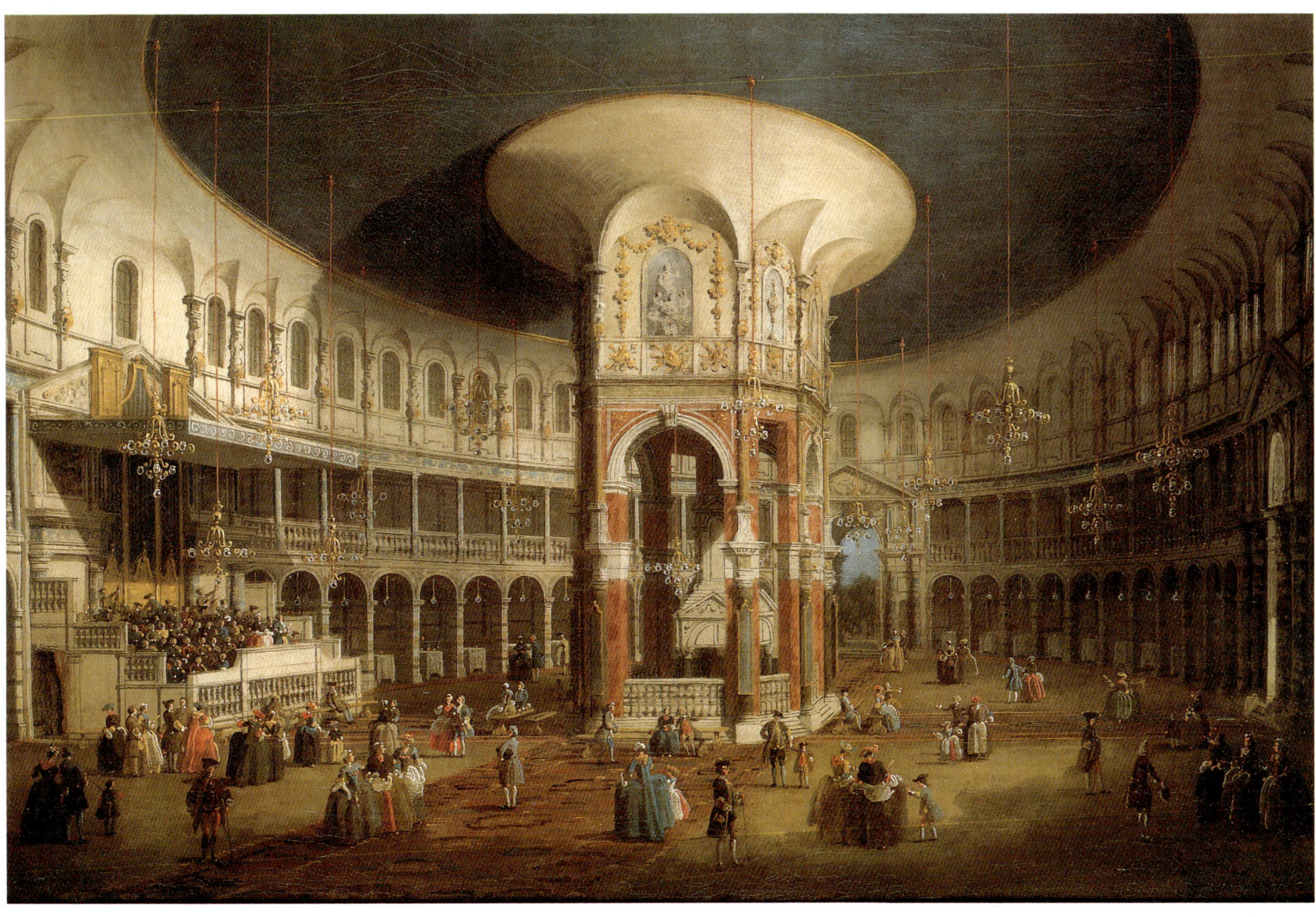

29 Canaletto

The interior of the Rotunda at Ranelagh, London

Oil on canvas, ca. 1751
$20\frac{1}{8} \times 29\frac{7}{8}$ ins (51×76 cm)
C/L 421
Private collection

This view was presumably commissioned as a pendant to the view of Vauxhall.

However, the early provenance of the pair is not recorded. Thomas Hollis commissioned a second version from Canaletto dated 1754 which is now in the National Gallery, London, and which was one of six commissions by Hollis from the artist [see cat. no. 35].

Ranelagh, sited at Chelsea, was opened in 1742 as a rival to Vauxhall Gardens. It was considered to be a more restrained and sedate alternative to Vauxhall and one of its main attractions was the Rotunda. Built entirely of wood, the Rotunda had an

internal diameter measuring one hundred and fifty feet. The raised stand for choir, orchestra and organ was placed on one side and the central architectural structure housed a fireplace and chimney. The surrounding arcade contained supper boxes and, after dark, the interior was illuminated by lamps and chandeliers. "Around these four high pillars [in the centre]", a traveller recorded in 1782, "all of fashionable London revolved like a gaily coloured distaff, sauntering in a compact throng." JF

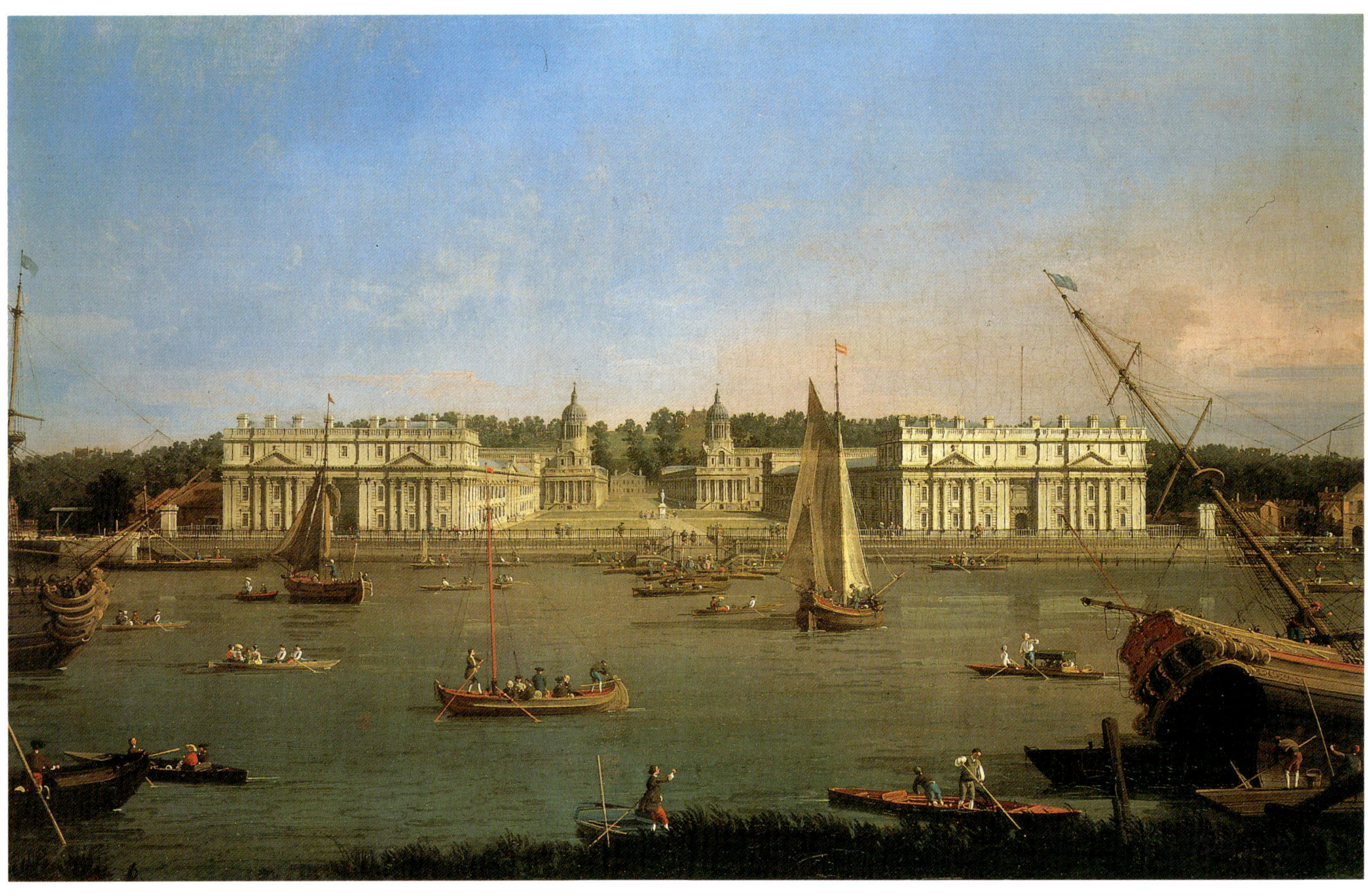

30 Canaletto

Greenwich Hospital, London, from the north bank of the Thames

Oil on canvas, ca. 1752–55
27 × 41⅞ ins (68.5 × 106.5 cm)
C/L 414
The National Maritime Museum, Greenwich

The Royal Hospital was built to the designs of Wren and Hawksmoor and completed in 1752, which presumably inspired Canaletto with the idea to record it, not necessarily with a specific patron in mind. The early history of this picture is not known. A smaller version also survives (private collection). The view, one of the few examples of a London subject which remains largely unchanged today, is taken slightly to the left of centre from the opposite bank. In the centre of the quadrangle is the statue of George II by Rysbrack with Greenwich Park in the background and the Observatory visible on the hill.

Canaletto enlivens the whole composition by the asymmetric shapes of the shipping juxtaposed against the static classical façade. The predominantly cool blue/green palette is punctuated by red on boats and figures, and the angle of hulls, masts and poles leads the eye to the centre. Unlike his Thames views bathed by an even, clear light, the foreground is deliberately darkened in contrast to the silvery light on the building façades. Both the light and the presence of several small craft suggest a summer evening. JF

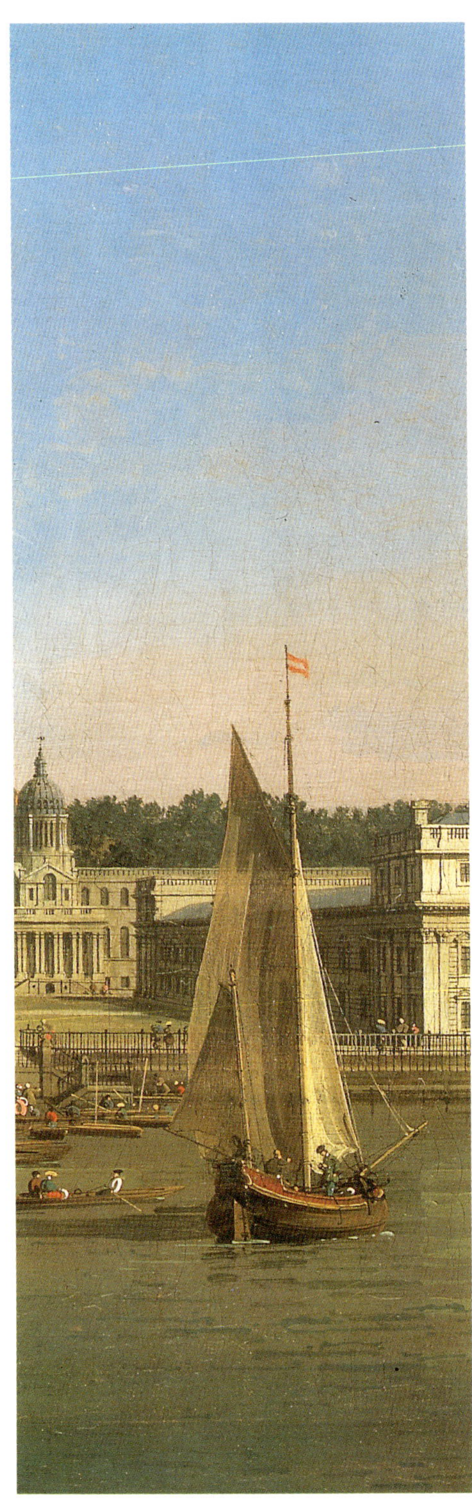

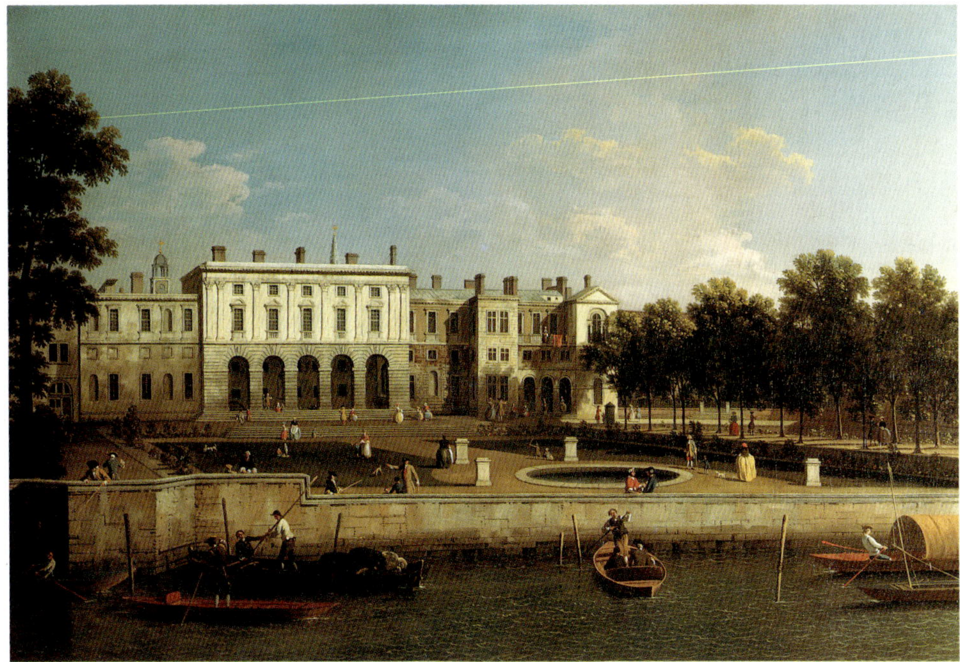

31 Canaletto

Old Somerset House, London, from the River Thames

Oil on canvas, ca. 1752–55
$31\frac{3}{8} \times 46\frac{3}{8}$ ins (79.5 × 118 cm)
C/L 423
Private collection

The original Somerset House built by
Edward Seymour, Duke of Somerset and
Lord Protector of England, dated from
1549. It subsequently became a Royal residence and later in the eighteenth century
was used to house foreign ambassadors. It
was demolished in 1766. The Venetian
envoy occupied the building by 1763 and
this may be one reason for Canaletto's
depiction of it. The formal south façade,
garden and river walk are depicted viewed
from the south bank.

As with other London views, the difference between the public waterway and the
private house and terrace is clearly delineated. The whole composition, although full
of incidental detail, is schematized and
lacking in atmosphere, perhaps adding sub-
stance to Vertue's remarks of June 1749
that the artist was rumoured to be an
impostor and "not the veritable Canelletti
of Venice whose works there have been
bought at great prices or that privately he
has some unknown assistant in makeing or
filling up his peices of works with figures".
There is no evidence that Canaletto
worked with an assistant in London but it
remains a possibility. A surviving drawing
of the same view (Paul Mellon Collection)
includes far fewer figures but both they
and the groups of trees and foliage are
treated in a more lively and subtle manner.
JF

32 Canaletto

Old London Bridge

Pen and brown ink with grey wash
$12\frac{1}{16} \times 24\frac{1}{4}$ ins (30.7 × 54 cm)
C/L 738

The Trustees of the British Museum, London

By the mid eighteenth century, London Bridge was in an alarming state of decay. In 1746, the Lord Mayor, Sir Richard Hoare, set up a court of enquiry to look into the cost of upkeep. Although the bridge was not finally demolished until the next century, Canaletto must have realised that the present appearance of the bridge was likely to change and that there might be a market for images recording its medieval structure of nineteen piers and jumbled, precarious structures of shops and housing. All the houses were removed in 1758 but suggestions by Charles Labelye, architect of Westminster Bridge, to reduce the number of piers raised other problems. The piers occupied five-sixths of the river bed causing the pent-up current to roar through the narrow spaces. This weakened the whole structure and there was a high incidence of drownings. However, the water pressure also turned the waterwheel machinery of the Peter Morris works, visible in the left of the drawing, which provided the City's water supply.

Canaletto's drawing from the west side shows the water, pent up by the bridge piers, almost as still as a lake on which boats float at angles to the sluggish current. A civic barge makes a surprise appearance at the far left purely as a compositional device and the sharp perspective of buildings and shoreline on the right is full of lively detail. On the left-hand skyline can be identified the Old Fishmongers' Hall, the Monument, the Water Tower and the tower of St Magnus. As far as is

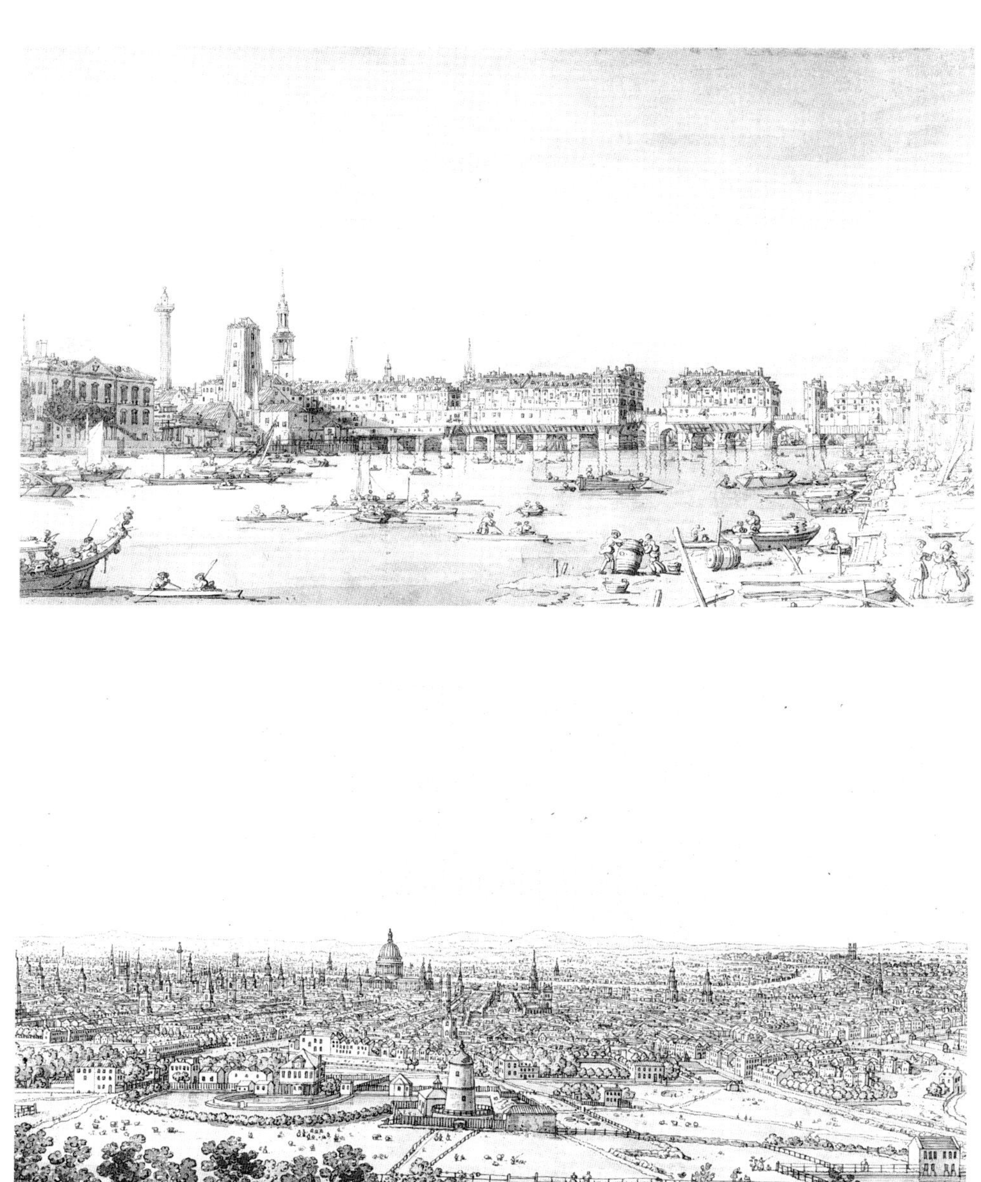

known, no painting or engraving of this image survives by Canaletto. JF

33 Canaletto

A view of London from Pentonville

Pen and brown ink with grey wash,
ca. 1750–51
$9\frac{1}{16} \times 15\frac{5}{8}$ ins (23 × 39.7 cm)
C/L 731
The Trustees of the British Museum, London

In this drawing, Canaletto appears consciously to imitate an old-fashioned panoramic style of topography. The use of line is untypically heavy and static with the exception of the foreground figures and vegetation. Robert Sayer probably commissioned it from Canaletto as it was engraved by John Stevens and published by Sayer in 1751 as *A North View of London*. The topography can be identified by an earlier engraving published in 1730 with a key to the buildings depicted. It is possible that Canaletto based his drawing on the earlier engraving without ever sketching the view himself. It could have been executed just before his departure for Venice at the end of 1750 and suggests he was badly in need of commissions.

The new river head with its water-mill and water house can be seen in the foreground. Reference to the earlier engraving identifies a number of houses that were used in the eighteenth century as health and pleasure resorts in the neighbourhood of Islington and Clerkenwell. In the distance Canaletto depicts the Thames spanned by Old London Bridge and the new Westminster Bridge, the only two bridges across this part of the river at that time. JF

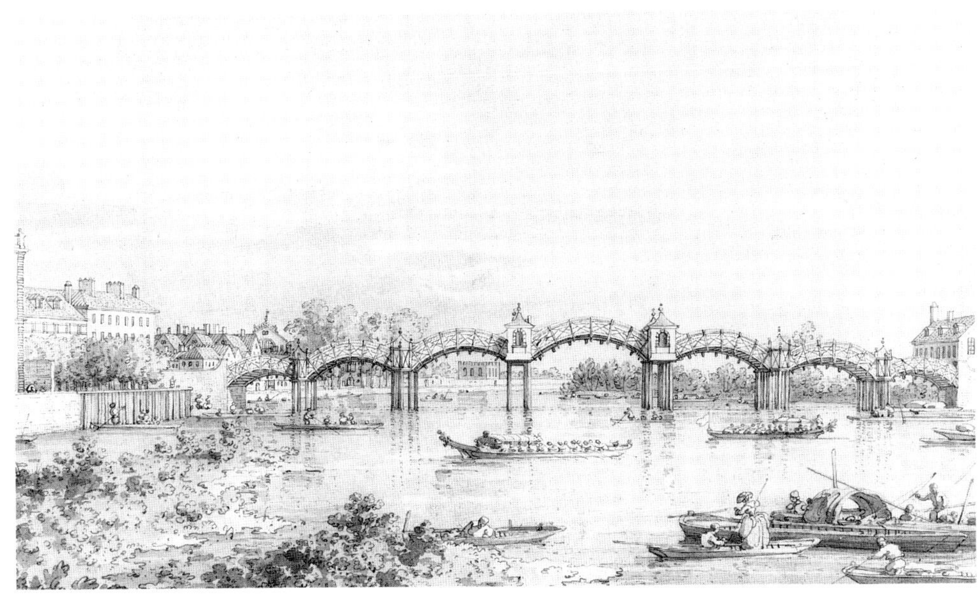

34 Canaletto

Hampton Court Bridge

Pen and brown ink with grey wash, ca. 1754
$9\frac{1}{8} \times 15\frac{5}{16}$ ins (23.2 × 38.9 cm)
C/L 730

The Trustees of the British Museum, London

The wooden Chinese bridge by Hampton Court Palace which opened on 13 December 1753 was designed and constructed by Samuel Stevens and Benjamin Ludgator. Its picturesque structure begs comparison with Old Walton Bridge [cat. no. 35] and Canaletto must have seized a commercial opportunity in recording it. He may have been commissioned by the publisher Robert Sayer who in 1754 produced an engraving by James Hulett closely following this drawing. The two oared barges heading haphazardly in opposite directions seem an unlikely addition and are added for aesthetic effect.

The drawing was bequeathed to the British Museum by Richard Payne Knight, the Regency collector and connoisseur. JF

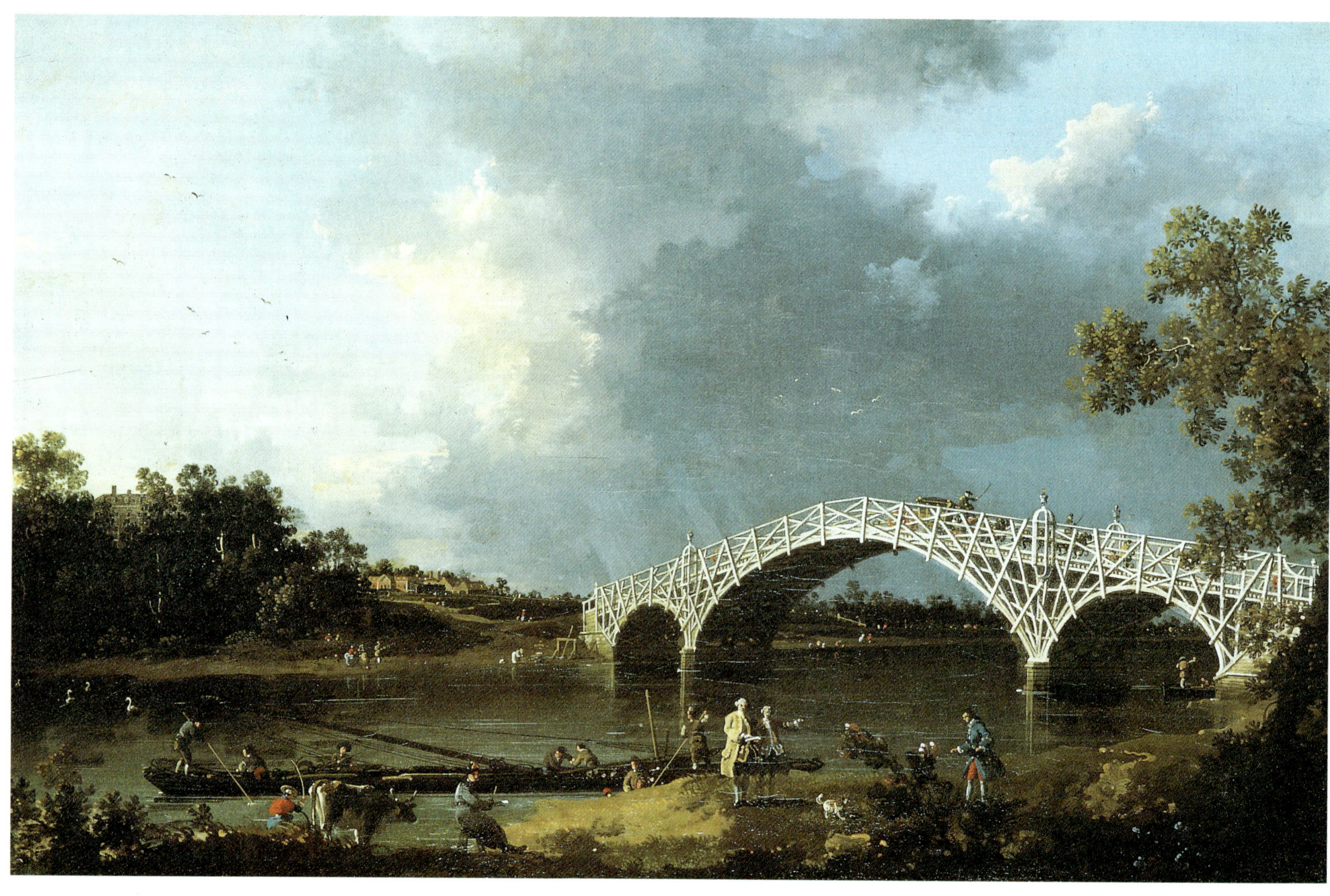

35 Canaletto

Old Walton Bridge

Oil on canvas, ca. 1754
$19\frac{1}{4} \times 30\frac{1}{4}$ ins (48.9 × 76.8 cm)
C/L 441
The Governors of Dulwich Picture Gallery

Perhaps the most charming painting of Canaletto's English period, this is the only one which attempts to convey a fleeting effect of weather characteristic of the English climate. Intriguingly, Canaletto appears to have depicted himself seated sketching on a low stool and wearing a hat and long gown. An old inscription identifies the original owner as Thomas Hollis, the Whig radical, antiquary and collector and friend of Consul Smith. Hollis owned a total of nine Canalettos of which he commissioned six. Canaletto painted a second version of the bridge in 1755 for Samuel Dicker M.P. who also commissioned a drawing (both at the Yale Center for British Art, New Haven). These three works provide the only firm evidence of Canaletto's presence in England from 1754–55.

According to a catalogue of the Hollis collection, Hollis is depicted in the foreground with his friend Thomas Brand, his servant Francesco Giovannini and his dog Malta. A coach travels over the bridge and a boat has lowered its mast in order to pass underneath. The bridge was constructed in 1750 and paid for by Samuel Dicker whose home is visible in the background. It was replaced by a stone one in

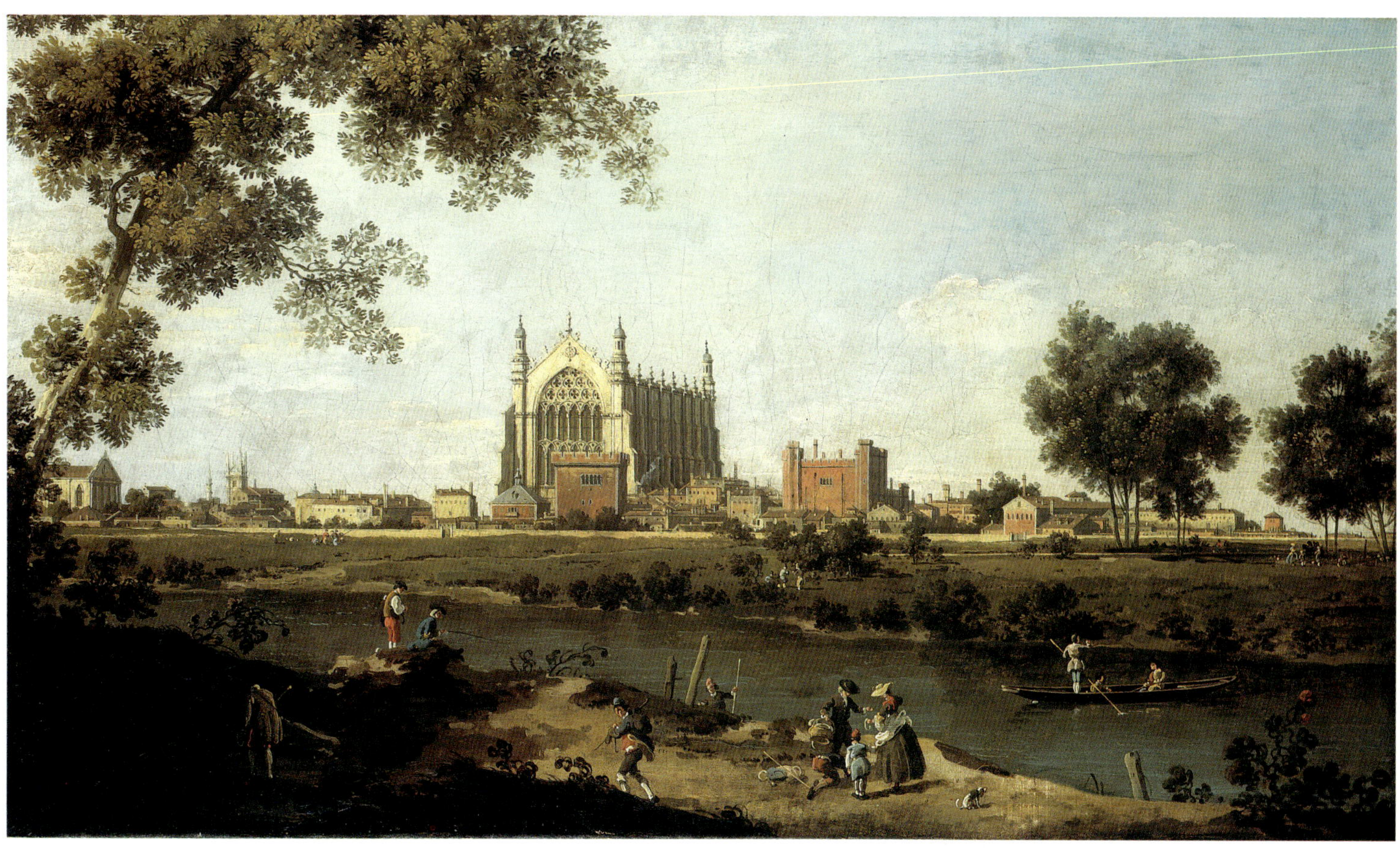

1780. According to earlier records, the wooden bridge was straight, not curved, and had bays of equal width, and so Canaletto's depiction should be viewed more as a *capriccio* in the Venetian tradition.
JF

36 Canaletto

Eton College Chapel, Windsor

Oil on canvas, ca. 1754
$24\frac{1}{4} \times 42\frac{3}{8}$ ins (61.5 × 107.5 cm)
C/L 450

The Trustees of the National Gallery, London

The many topographical inaccuracies in this view of the Chapel from across the Thames, together with the rather unconvincing river landscape in the foreground, suggest that Canaletto may have based it on a drawing or engraving by another hand. Indeed, the odd juxtapositions in scale of the buildings make it more comparable to his *capriccio* landscapes with reminiscences of England [cat. nos. 37 and 38] and the Chapel does appear again in a similar *capriccio, A sluice on a river, with a reminiscence of Eton College Chapel* (private collection). The early history of the painting is not recorded and it is possible that it was painted in Venice after Canaletto's return in 1755. He adopts the familiar compositional device of a dark foreground and trees and foliage to frame and lead the eye to the middle distance. This was a device familiar to English view-painters but which Canaletto was also employing much earlier, for example in the tomb paintings [see cat. no. 1]. JF

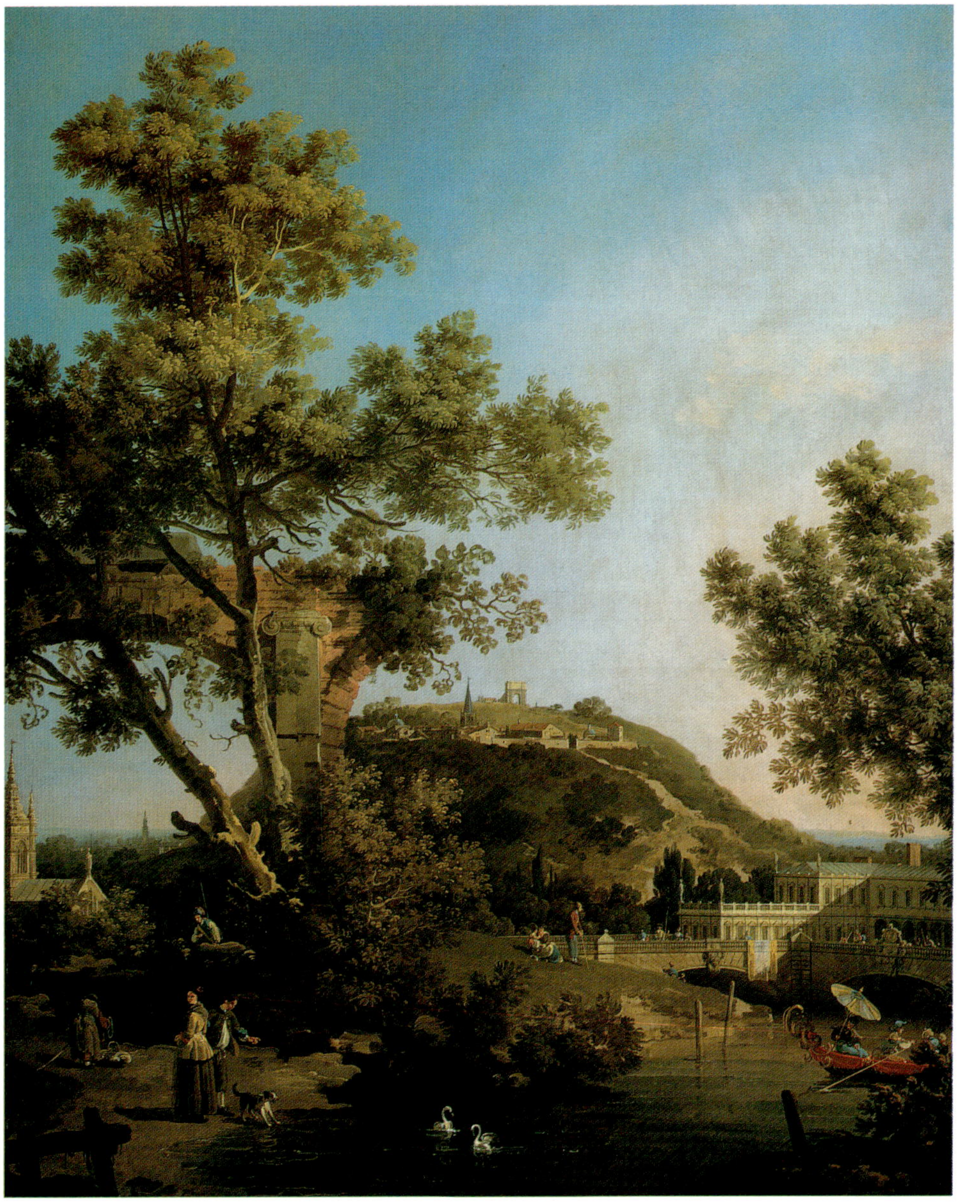

37 Canaletto

*Capriccio: river landscape with a
ruin and reminiscences of England*

Oil on canvas, ca. 1754
52 × 42 ins (132 × 106.7 cm)
C/L 473
The National Gallery of Art, Washington

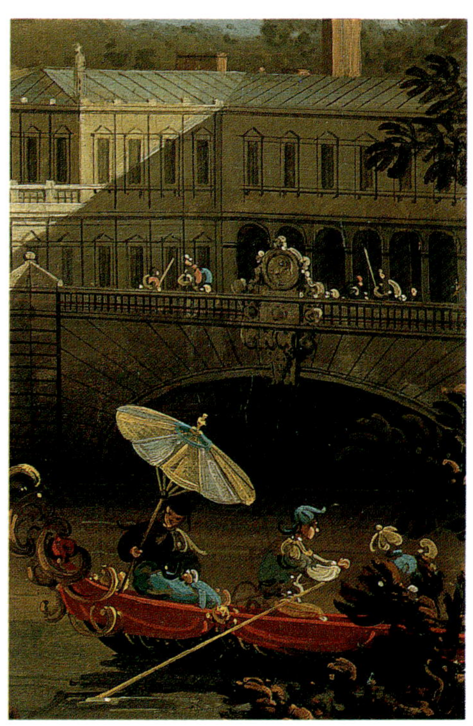

38 Canaletto

Capriccio: river landscape with a column, a ruined Roman arch, and reminiscences of England

Oil on canvas, ca. 1754
52 × 41 ins (132 × 104.2 cm)
C/L 474
The National Gallery of Art, Washington

These two *capriccio* views are part of a group known as the 'Lovelace Canalettos' referring to the fourth Earl of Lovelace who sold six Canalettos in 1937. He was descended from the third Baron King who is said to have commissioned them. He died in 1754. They were probably intended for a specific room at the King family home of Ockham Place, Surrey. Another *capriccio* in the series (private collection) is signed and dated 1754.

Canaletto painted *capriccio* views throughout his career, using architectural motifs seen on the Venetian lagoon and during his travels to Rome, Padua and along the Brenta Canal. The adaptation of this theme to include English trees and buildings produces a delightful rococo effect. Indeed the lady with a parasol in her pleasure boat suggests an equally fashionable *chinoiserie* style which may hint at the decorative scheme of the room for which these works were intended. JF

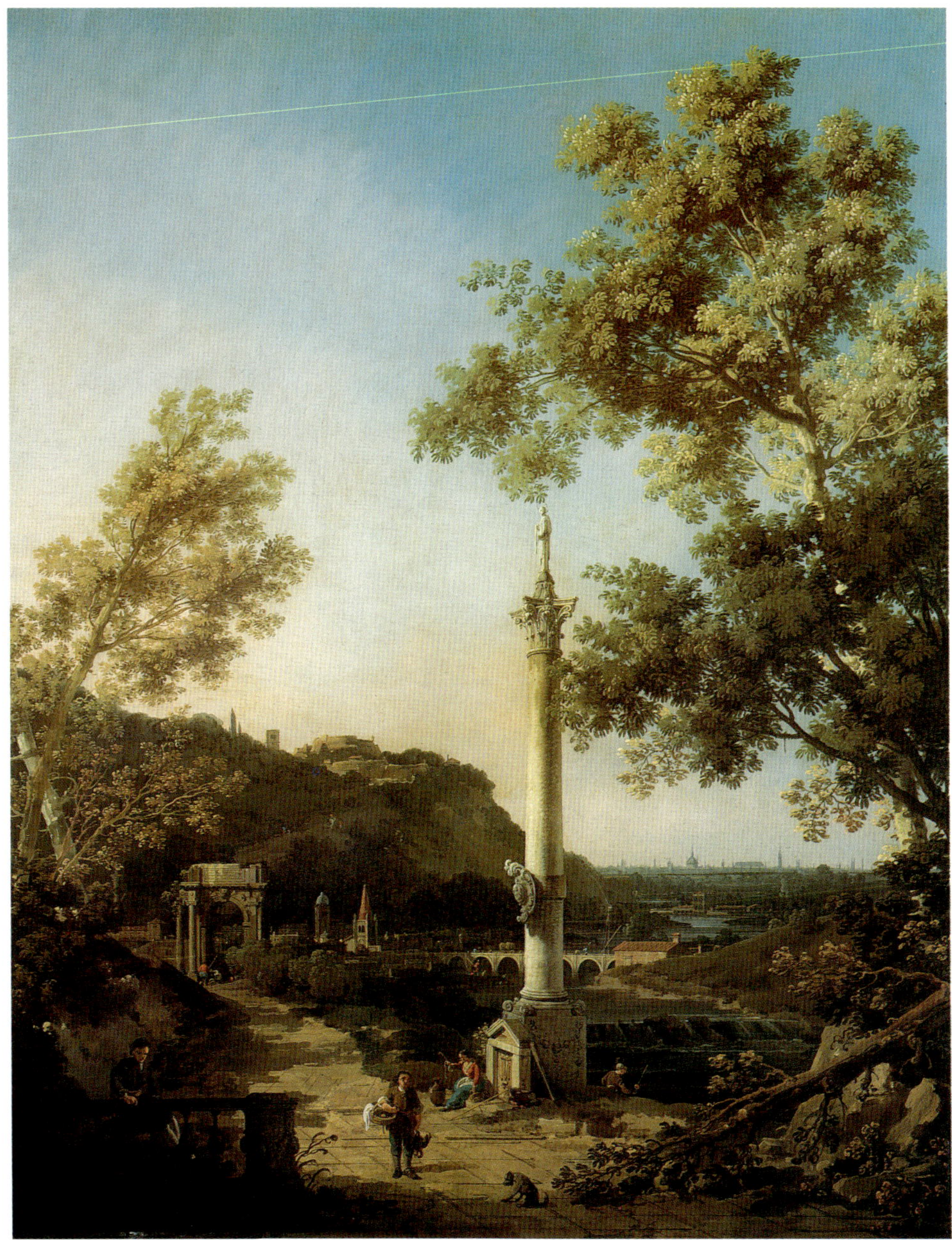

39 Canaletto

The island of San Michele with Venice in the distance

Pen and brown ink with grey wash over pencil
$7\frac{7}{8} \times 10\frac{15}{16}$ ins (20 × 27.8 cm)
C/L 654
The Visitors of the Ashmolean Museum, Oxford

This is the only Canaletto drawing in the exhibition of a Venetian view. It is one of two pen and wash versions by the artist and was much copied and imitated [see cat. no. 117]. Canaletto also repeated the same composition in pen and ink for Consul Smith, in a drawing which entered the Royal Collection in 1763. After the artist returned to Venice in 1755, the composition was engraved in reverse and published by Josef Wagner in his series of six etchings entitled *Sei Villaggi Campestri*. It is a *capriccio* view but the tower of San Michele and the Venetian skyline showing the dome of San Pietro a Castello and the campanile of San Francesco della Vigna are accurate. It has a connection with Canaletto's English period in that the composition was repeated for one of the so called 'Lovelace Capriccios' of 1754–55 commissioned by Baron King for Ockham Place, Surrey [cat. nos. 37 and 38].

The luminosity of the sky is reflected in the surface of the water through the artist's limpid handling of wash. In contrast, the agitated, broken pen line contributes to the freshness and vigour of the image. JF

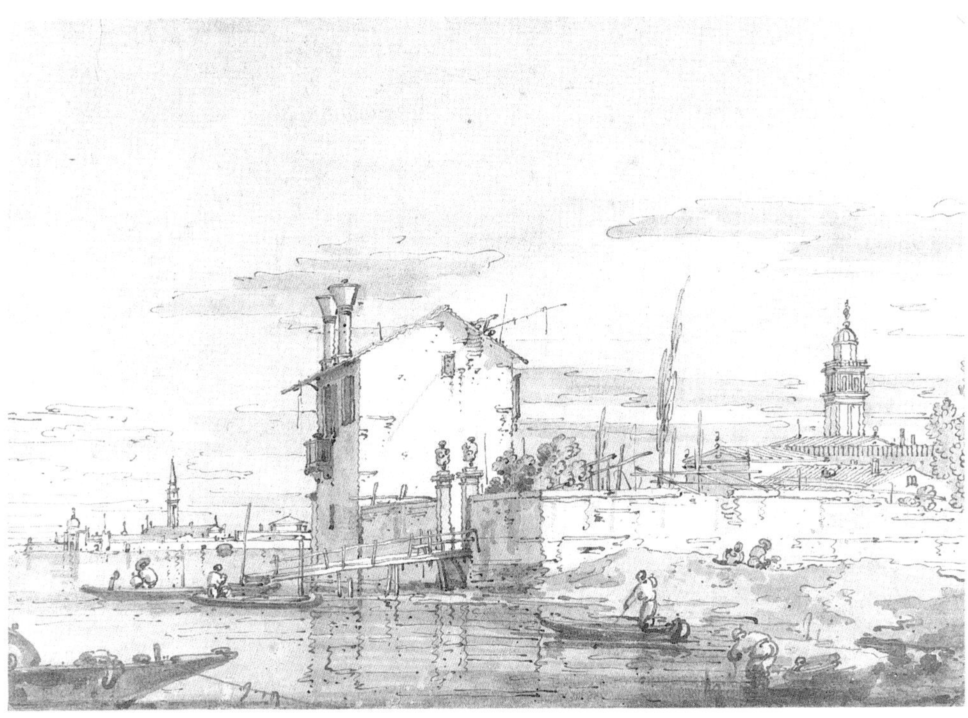

40 Canaletto

Portico with a lantern

Etching
$11\frac{3}{4} \times 17$ ins (30 × 43.3 cm) sheet size
Signed left of centre: A. Canal. f.V.
The arms of the Canal family appear above the basement window of the house to left
C/L p.655
Bristol Museums and Art Gallery

Some time after 6 June 1744, when Joseph Smith was appointed British Consul in Venice, twenty-eight etchings of Venice by Canaletto were published, dedicated to Consul Smith. It must have been Smith who persuaded Canaletto to take up etching for the first time, perhaps at a period when the artist was short of work. Canaletto proved himself to be adept at handling the etching needle. His technique is fluent and direct. Tone is created by the varying thickness of needles drawing through the etching ground and by the spaces between the lines. Even after publication, many of the plates were reworked showing the artist's close involvement and desire to perfect his work.

Prints by or after Canaletto were far more widely accessible to English artists than his paintings or drawings and the impact of this group of etchings should not be underestimated. A number of the etchings, including this one, are imaginary, *capriccio* views of Venice. The formula of a vista framed by an archway with a suspended lantern, which had already been used successfully by Canaletto in paintings and drawings of Venice, influenced, in turn, a generation of British artists [see cat. nos. 101 and 118]. JF

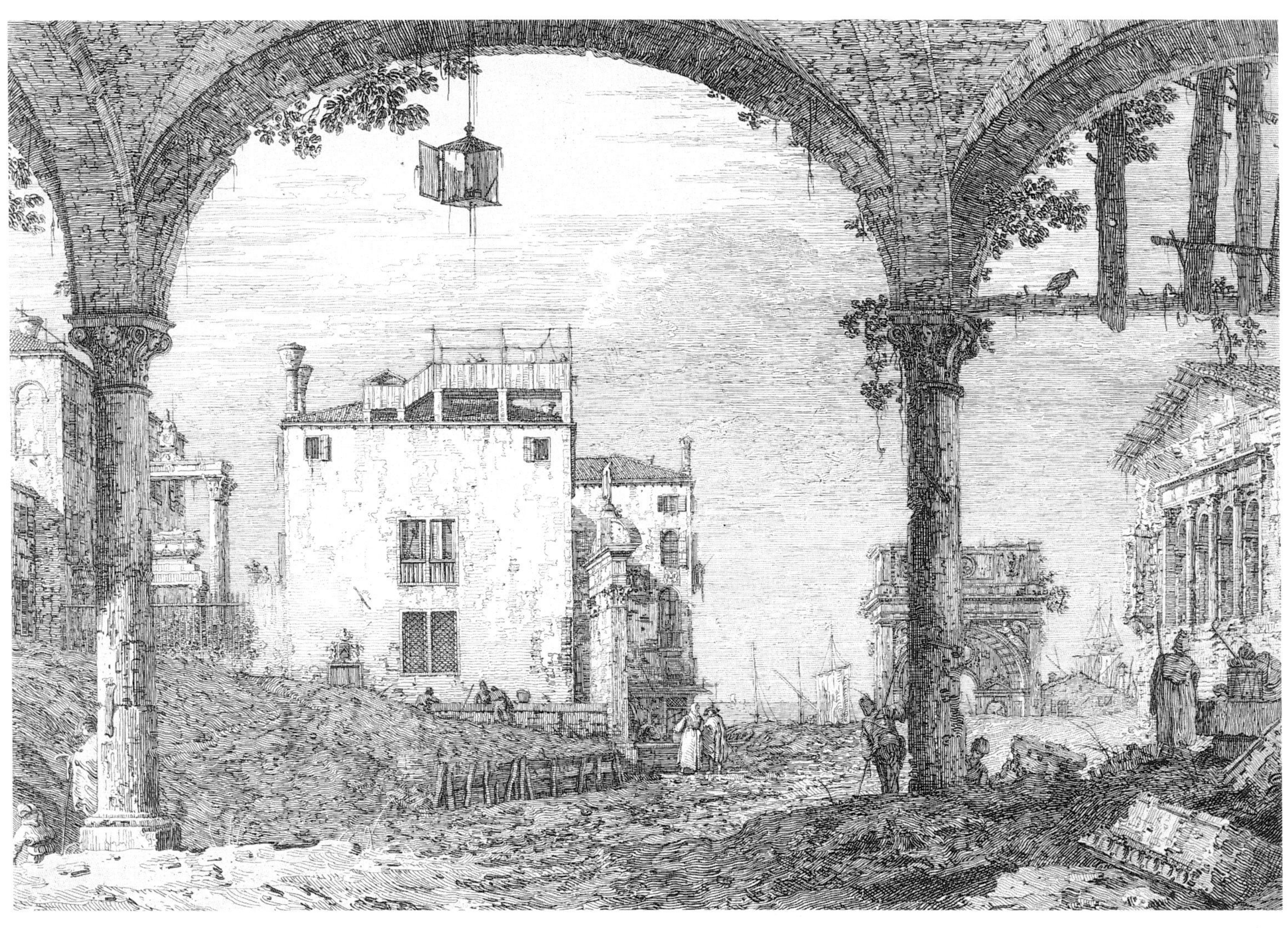

Antonio Joli ca.1700–1777

Canaletto was not the first Italian artist to seek new patronage in England in the first half of the eighteenth century. Several Italians such as Giovanni Antonio Pellegrini and Marco and Sebastiano Ricci came in response to an increasing demand for decorative history painting for the new English country houses being built. According to George Vertue, it was the decorative history painter Jacopo Amigoni, who worked in England 1729–39, who persuaded Canaletto to come to London. However, the only Italian view-painter of any note to work in England both before and during Canaletto's visit was Antonio Joli.

Joli trained as a decorative and theatrical painter and was working in Venice as a view-painter by 1735 where he was already influenced by Canaletto. In 1742, he travelled to Dresden and then London where he was employed as scene-painter and possibly assistant manager at the King's Theatre, Haymarket. He almost certainly knew Canaletto and both artists were patronised by the Duke of Richmond. He left London in 1750 to work for the Spanish court at Madrid before returning to Venice in 1754. The last part of his career was spent in Naples, again working for the court theatre, and there he attracted the patronage of Sir William Hamilton, the British Envoy to Naples. JF

41 Antonio Joli

Capriccio with a view of the Thames and St Paul's

Oil on canvas, ca. 1746
45 × 43 ins (115 × 105 cm)
Signed on the plinth of the statue on the right: A.I

Harari & Johns Ltd., London

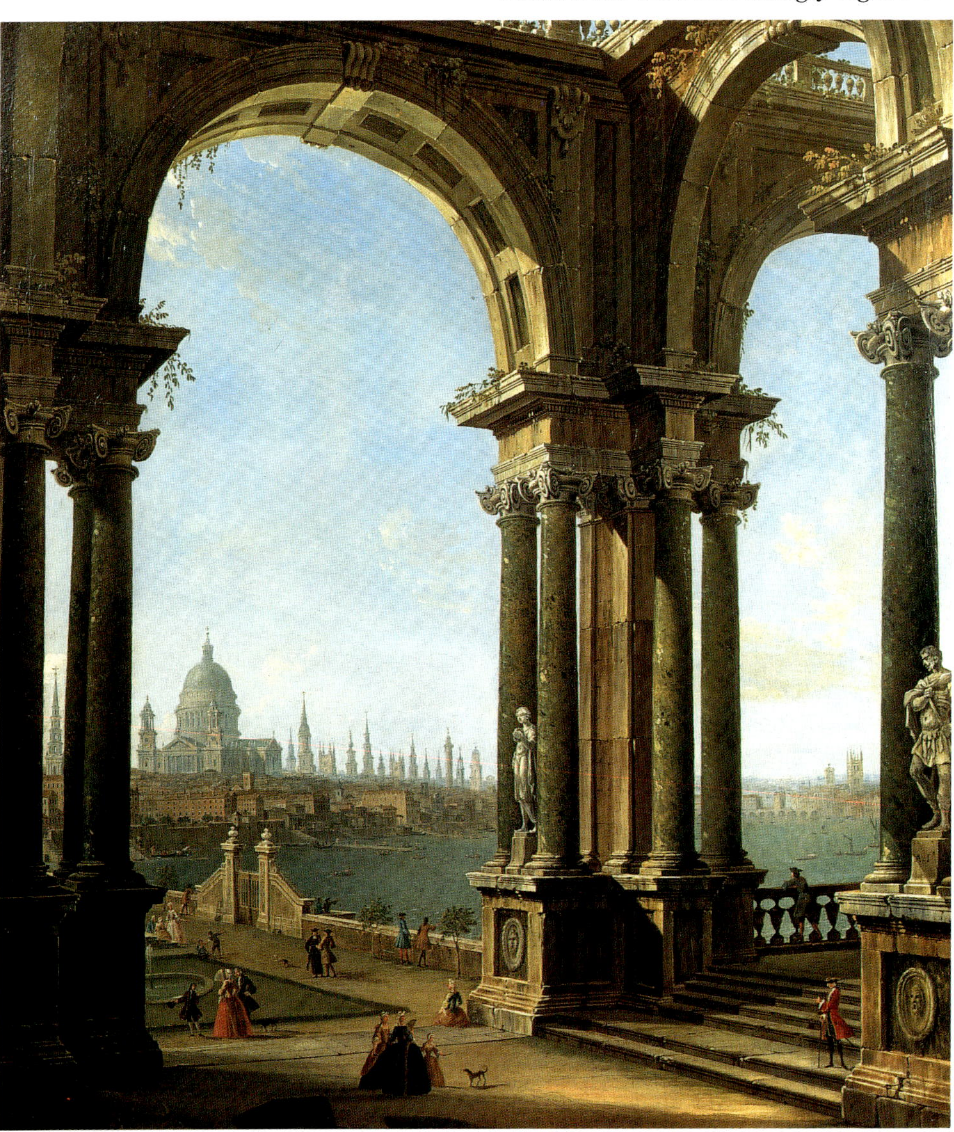

This is one of a group of three similar paintings of which it is the only signed version. A second was sold at Sotheby's, 12 July 1989 (lot 90) and a third is now owned by the Metropolitan Museum, New York. The fantastically proportioned foreground architecture shows Joli's training and skill as a theatrical painter. His lack of interest in topographical accuracy extends to the London skyline dominated by St Paul's. It has been convincingly argued that

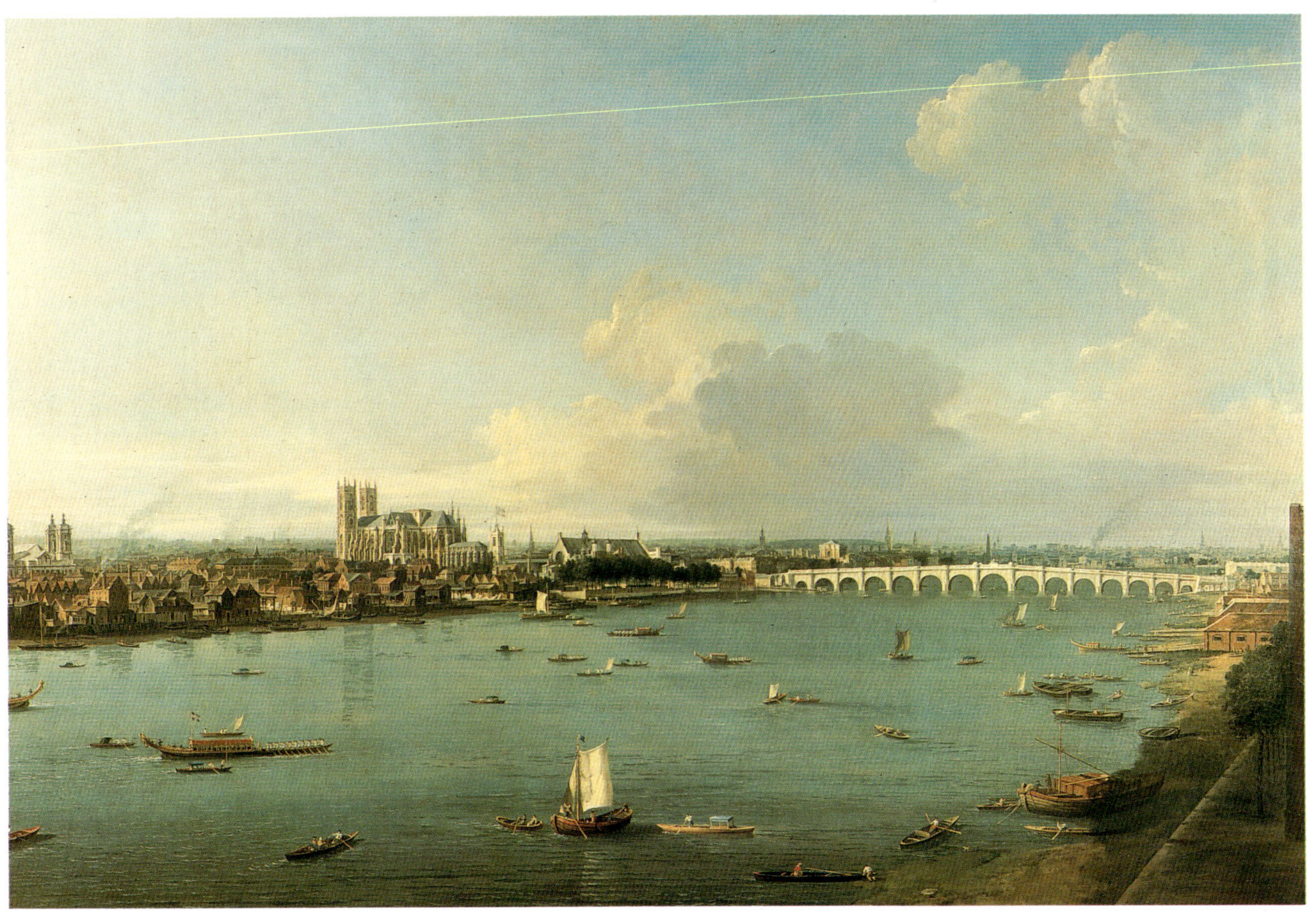

the ruinous state of the classical arcading peopled with antique Roman sculptures and sprouting vegetation is deliberately contrasted with modern London seen as the new Rome.[1] Canaletto produced a rather more subtle portrayal of the same idea in his Thames views which was doubtless equally understood and which had considerably more impact on English view-painters. JF

1. Malcolm Warner (ed.), *The Image of London, Views by Travellers and Emigrés, 1550–1920,* London, Barbican Art Gallery, 1987, p.126.

42 Antonio Joli

The Thames with Westminster Bridge in the distance

Oil on canvas, ca. 1746–47
$46\frac{1}{2} \times 70\frac{1}{2}$ ins (118×179 cm)
Formerly attributed to Canaletto C/L 426

The Governor and Company of the Bank of England, London

This is almost an exact copy of Canaletto's painting commissioned by Prince Lobkowicz in 1746 and now in the National Gallery, Prague. Joli has omitted all but a glimpse of the edge of Lambeth Palace on the right and the Bridge is shown in a completed state. Canaletto had taken considerable trouble, in probably his first commission in England, to show the partially completed bridge in the precise state that it was. In contrast, Joli has included nothing like the same level of detail in buildings and wharfs along the river edge as Canaletto. Joli must have made his copy very soon after Canaletto had completed the original and before Prince Lobkowicz left London. It is an indication of the admiration he felt for Canaletto's skills as a view-painter. JF

Canaletto and English Painters

M.J.H. LIVERSIDGE

There are contrasting opinions about the extent and nature of Canaletto's contribution to English view-painting and topographical drawing in the eighteenth century, and on the degree to which his work still exerted any significant influence in the nineteenth century, when so many English painters found Venice a place of romantic inspiration. It has been argued, for example, that there was already a flourishing tradition of prospect painting in England, extending back into the seventeenth century, from which the urban scenes, views of picturesque antiquities and country house 'portraits' that constitute such a large part of the English landscape artists' output from the 1750s are descended. It is indeed the case that such works are plentifully present in English painting before Canaletto's arrival in London in 1746, but with a few exceptions they are relatively pedestrian affairs which concentrate on factually recording the scene and providing an inventory of its contents. To deny that Canaletto contributed a transforming and reinvigorating stimulus to this aspect of English painting perversely flies in the face of the visual evidence. In 1746 English topographical art was for the most part dull and conventional; ten years later it was revitalised and new painters and draughtsmen were appearing who carried on the tradition in a much more sophisticated and visually responsive form over the next fifty and more years. In the process new influences were felt and absorbed from the developing and changing formulations of English landscape aesthetics as eighteenth-century sensibility gave way to new romantic sensations, but along the way painters continued to draw inspiration from different aspects of Canaletto's art. In the 1740s and 1750s he breathed new life into topographical painting: above all he let the light in on the English view.

To understand how Canaletto's influence was transmitted it is necessary to consider where and in what form English painters could have encountered his work. Some, of course, would have seen his pictures in their patrons' collections. Certainly that was the case with Samuel Scott and William Marlow, the two artists who can be regarded as his most immediate and consistent followers. Both were employed by the Earl (later Duke) of Northumberland who, both as Sir Hugh Smithson before he succeeded to the peerage and afterwards, was Canaletto's most important patron in England and owned six of his pictures, representative of every type of view he painted there [cat. no. 6; figs. 2, 3, 7, 8]. He seems to have been

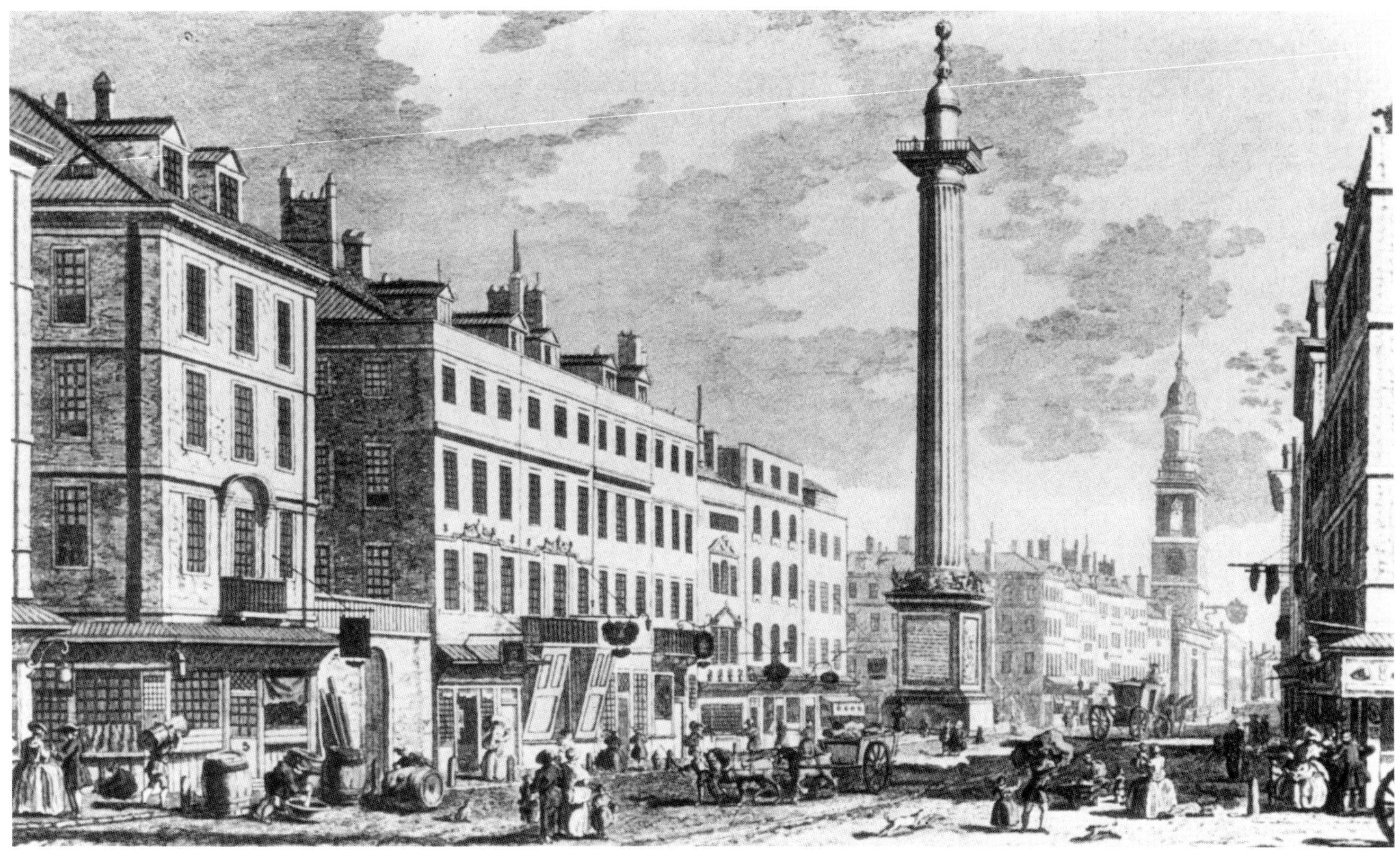

Fig. 24 George Bickham after Canaletto, *A view of the Monument, London*, engraving, 1752

particularly partial to topographical paintings, and both Scott and Marlow painted copies of at least one of his Canalettos, the view of *Alnwick Castle* [fig. 7]. Marlow was sponsored by the Duchess of Northumberland when he travelled in France and Italy in 1765–66, and there is a fine group of his Continental landscapes and views still at Alnwick today; he may also have painted some of the landscapes which decorate Robert Adam's remodelled library in Syon House near London, another Northumberland residence. Samuel Scott seems to have been called on at least once to paint a picture as a pendant to one of Canaletto's. One of the versions of his *Tower of London* [cat. no. 45] corresponds in size to Canaletto's 1749 view of *The Old Horse Guards* [cat. no. 19]: both paintings have the same eighteenth-century provenance (from the fourth Earl of Radnor

of the earlier creation to his friend James Harris M.P. by bequest in 1757 and thence by descent to the Earls of Malmesbury), and from this it is reasonable to conclude that the Scott view was commissioned as a companion to the Canaletto.[1] Another artist who would have seen Canaletto paintings and drawings in his patrons' collections was Paul Sandby, who certainly knew the pictures belonging to the Earl of Warwick (previously Lord Brooke) [cat. nos. 22, 23, 24] and probably the Royal Collection works as well after they were bought from Consul Smith.

The London sale rooms and dealers' shops were another forum in which Canaletto's pictures could occasionally have been seen – and also, no doubt, copies masquerading as the real thing. A thorough review of sale catalogues in the second half of the eighteenth century would certainly reveal a substantial number of items. As it is, in the very incomplete anthology published by Algernon Graves in 1901, eight of Canaletto's English pictures are listed as having passed through London sale rooms between 1774 and 1790, as well as some Venetian scenes. Drawings, too, appeared on the market, like the *View of Old London Bridge* sold in 1766 and "One capital (drawing) by Canaletti, view in St. James's Park, near Whitehall" in the Charles Rogers sale conducted by Thomas Phillips in 1799.[2] The catalogues of the 1765 and 1773 sales of the painter Samuel Scott's possessions are also informative, showing that he owned Canaletto's etchings, "A sketch by Canaletti, and 3 others", and two more views of Venice (whether paintings or drawings is not clear), all sold in 1765; in 1773 among the prints are "Sixteen views in Venice" which probably included engravings after Canaletto, while lot 46 comprised four drawings, "2 of Covent Garden and 2 from Canaletti, by Mr Scott", indicating that he kept copies of the artist's work made by himself for reference. Since William Marlow was his pupil from 1755 to 1759, and in the 1750s Samuel Scott was a leading member of the artistic fraternity in London closely associated with William Hogarth, the part he played in extending Canaletto's influence can be appreciated. The fact that he owned a collection of Canaletto's etchings, possibly the set issued with a dedication to Joseph Smith, is also significant. The brilliant calligraphy and vividly suggestive manner of Canaletto's etchings were influential for the development of English topographical draughtsmanship later in the eighteenth century, and in the drawing style which artists such as Girtin and Turner developed in the 1790s there are clear references to his cursive handling of the etching needle.

Prints were another important means through which Canaletto's influence spread into the mainstream of English topographical art, not least because they were the most readily available form in which his work could be seen and consulted. One example in particular illustrates their impact. In 1752 the printsellers Robert Sayer and Henry Overton issued a fine engraving of *A View of the Monument erected in memory of the dreadfull Fire in the Year 1666* done by George Bickham from a drawing of Canaletto's [fig. 24]. It shows a scene looking down Fish Street towards Wren's church of St Magnus Martyr, presenting the subject with all the appearance of a dignified classical parade. This composition provided a model for numerous

later "perspectives" of city streets in London as well as the provinces. The street itself is crowded with incidental details of figures engaged in their business — carriages, carts, coopers, porters, ladies and gentlemen strolling past shop windows — which animate the scene and give it a feeling of specific locality: it was one of the City's busiest quarters, Fish Street leading directly up from Old London Bridge into the centre of affairs. On this view by Canaletto a succession of street scenes by later artists were modelled to a greater or lesser extent, ranging from Samuel Scott's *Ludlow town* (ca. 1766) [cat. no. 51] and William Marlow's Whitehall views of the 1770s (for example *Whitehall looking north-east* [fig. 25], or his pair of *Ludgate Street with the west front of St Paul's Cathedral* and *Fish Street towards the Monument* which were engraved in 1795), to Thomas Girtin's *St Martin's le Grand* (ca. 1795; engraved 1815) or Turner's view of *The High Street, Oxford* (1810) [fig. 26].[3] Copies of Canaletto's print exist, the earliest known being an oil painting signed W. James and dated 1759. Another prospect by Canaletto which proved especially influential was that of Northumberland House, Charing Cross [figs. 8 and 27], which was engraved in 1753 by Thomas Bowles, published by Sayer and Overton, in which Canaletto invested the junction of Charing Cross and Whitehall overlooked by the newly classicised palatial façade of Northumberland House with something of the architectural grandeur of a Venetian *piazza* or *campo*.[4] This, too, was a view frequently repeated with variations in detail by, among others, Joseph Nickolls, Samuel Scott and William Marlow. Evidence of the enduring popularity of Canaletto's engravings is provided by the fact that six of the Sayer and Overton plates were reprinted and reissued in 1794 by another London firm, Laurie & Whittle.[5]

Probably there were still in the later eighteenth century some of Canaletto's drawings in the hands of London print publishers who had commissioned or bought them. Certainly there were some in circulation which English artists would have seen. It is known that Samuel Scott owned examples, and Paul Sandby was given two of Warwick Castle by, it is assumed, the Hon. Charles Greville (younger son of the Earl of Warwick, for whom they were originally executed) [cat. nos. 21 and 25]. Since both Scott and Sandby were central figures in the professional circles of their time other artists must have seen them. There is not much other evidence from the provenances of surviving drawings with which to reconstruct a

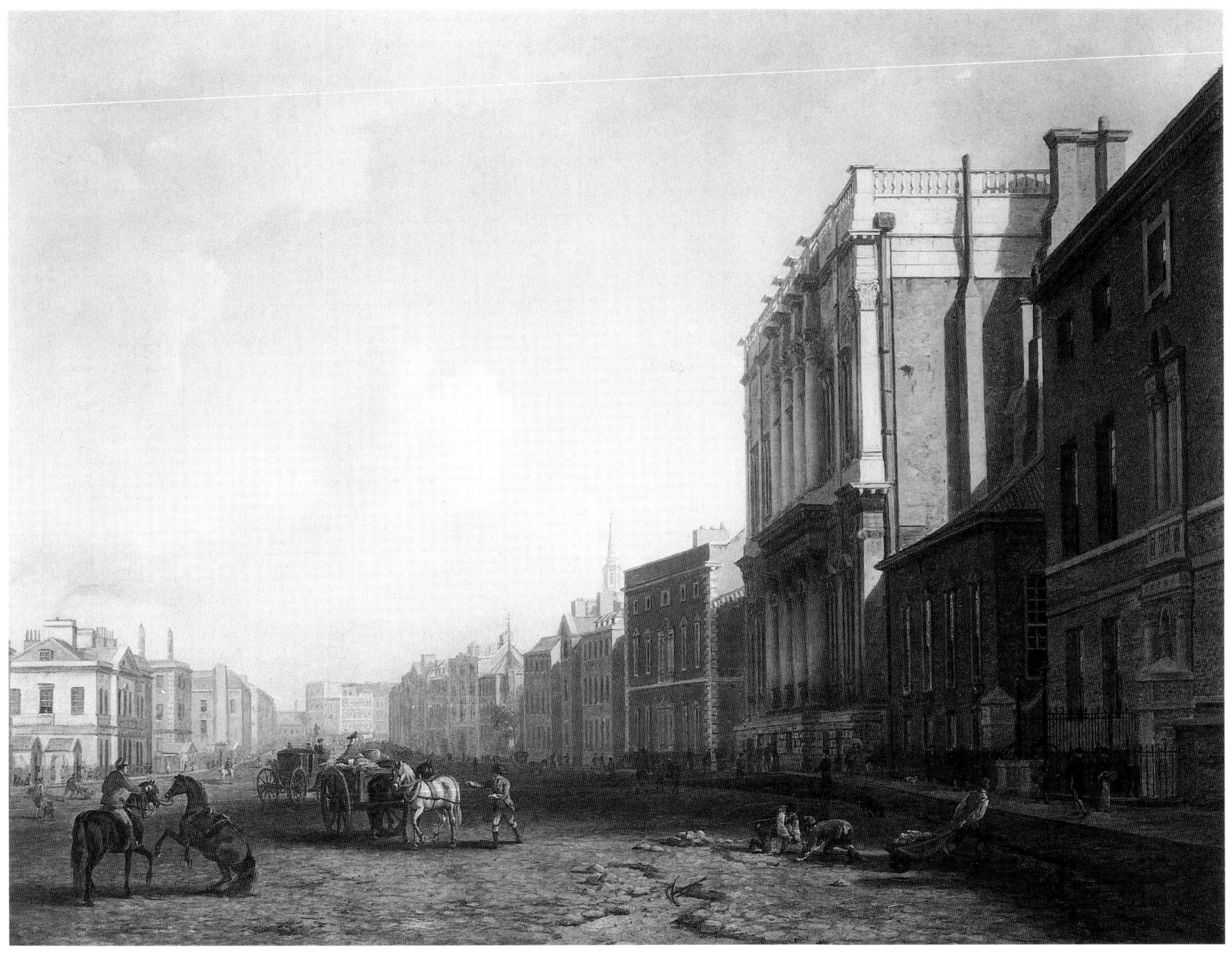

Fig. 25 William Marlow, *Whitehall, London, looking north-east*, oil on canvas, $27\frac{5}{8} \times 35\frac{3}{8}$ ins (70×90 cm), Yale Center for British Art, New Haven

clear idea of precisely who may have seen what, but there certainly were two groups of Canaletto drawings that were available to many of the younger watercolour artists who were beginning their careers in London in the 1790s and early part of the nineteenth century. These belonged respectively to Dr Thomas Monro and John Henderson who were neighbours in The Adelphi in London.

In Dr Monro's sale at Christie's in 1833 there were thirteen Canaletto drawings, including a now lost "View of London from Westminster Bridge".[6] John Henderson had a group of mainly *capricci* drawings, and he also owned some Canaletto paintings of Venetian scenes.[7] Both were prominent patrons and collectors of English landscape painting, and Monro especially had a significant influence on the development of water-

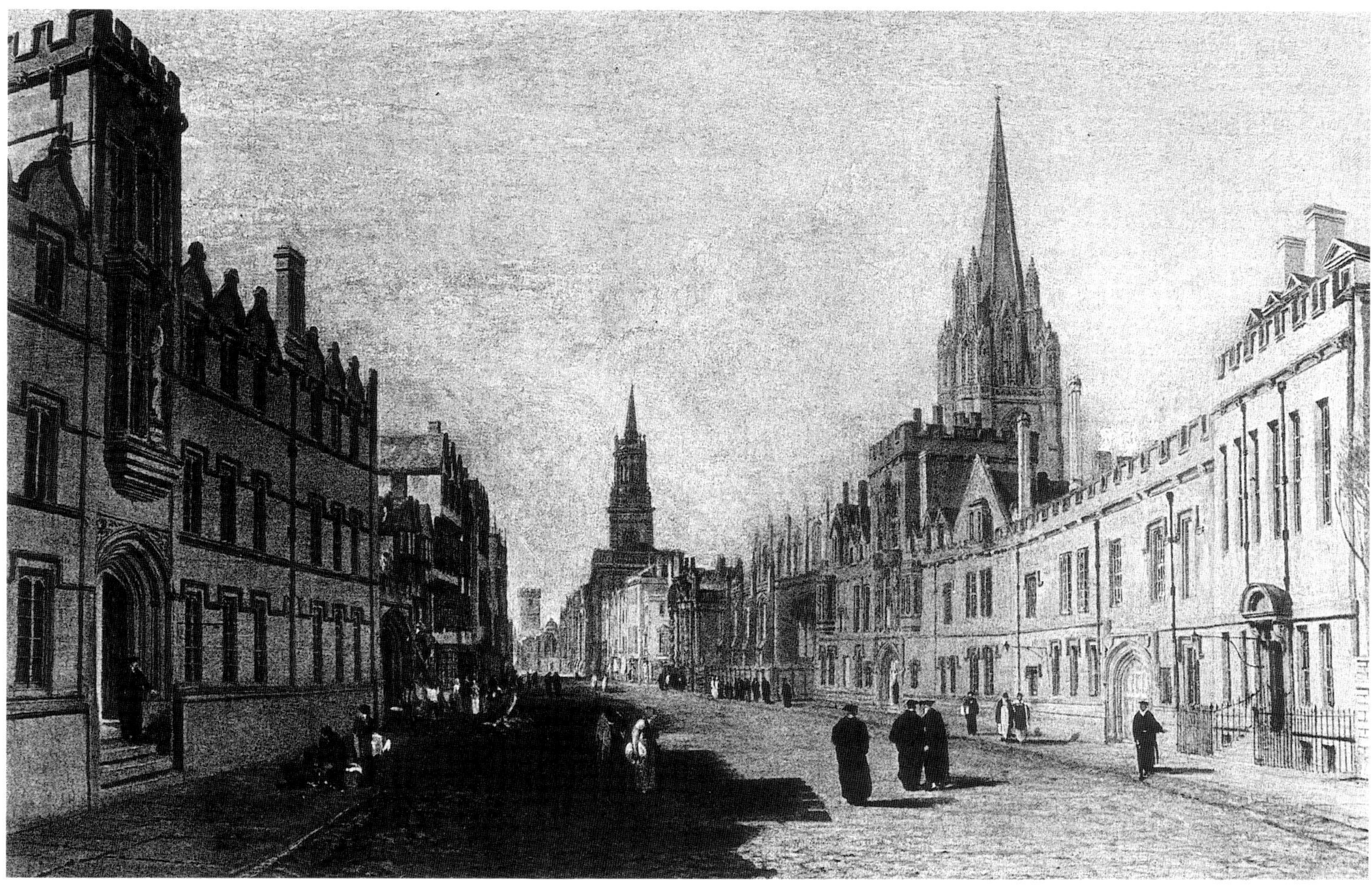

Fig. 26 J.M.W. Turner, *The High Street, Oxford*, oil on canvas, 27 × 39½ ins (68.5 × 100.3 cm), 1810, private collection

colour between the 1790s and 1820s. Joseph Farington, Secretary to the Royal Academy and a notable topographer, records in his diary (for the later eighteenth century and first twenty years of the nineteenth an invaluable source of reliable information and gossip about the art world) that Monro kept a sort of evening "academy" at his house when he would provide hospitality to young painters and have them copy works in his own and his friends' collections. It was here in the mid–1790s that Thomas Girtin and the young J.M.W. Turner met, and many of the leading figures in the English watercolour school also passed through Monro's "academy". His *conversazioni* were also attended by, among others, Paul Sandby, William Marlow, Thomas Hearne and Michael 'Angelo' Rooker.

Canaletto's works were certainly sometimes copied in this circle, and his drawings were evidently admired. It was one of the sources from which a characteristic manner of drawing in a cursively calligraphic technique that ultimately derives from Canaletto's mannerisms must have developed. This idiom is found in Girtin and Turner in the 1790s, and spreads to artists like John Sell Cotman, the Varley brothers, Paul Sandby Munn, William Alexander and others; and what becomes a characteristic of picturesque topographical watercolours about this time, a lively play of dots, dashes and blobs, is a manner loosely descended from Canaletto's draughtsmanship. The connection with the Henderson-Monro circle is firmly established by the existence of four Venetian watercolours by Thomas Girtin

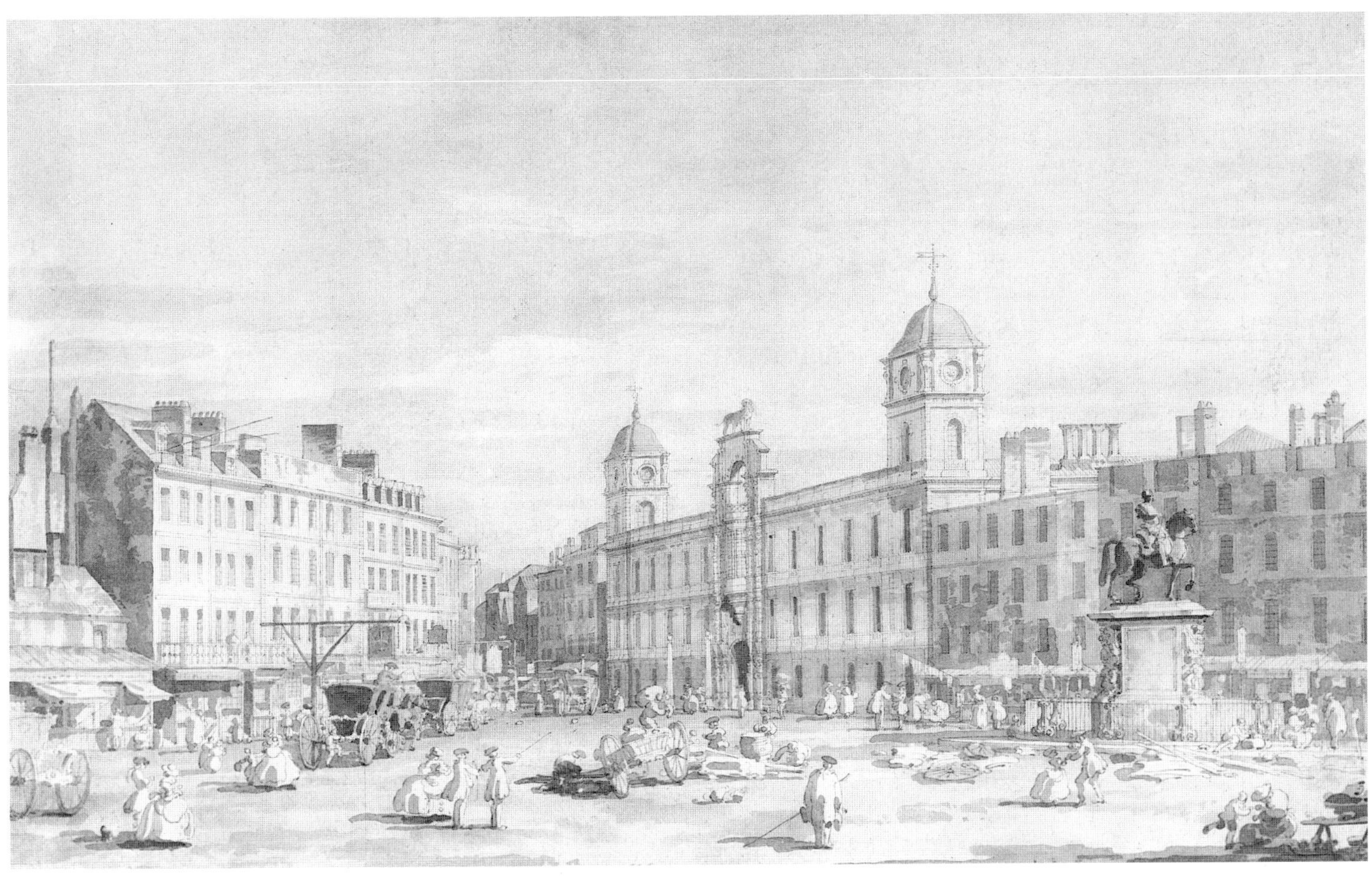

Fig. 27 Canaletto, *Northumberland House, Charing Cross, London*, pen and wash, $11\frac{5}{16} \times 16\frac{3}{4}$ ins (29 × 42.5 cm), ca. 1752, Minneapolis Institute of Arts

now in the British Museum which have a Henderson provenance and which are based on Canaletto prototypes [cat. nos. 108 and 109]. Three of them are copied from Visentini engravings in the enlarged 1742 edition of the *Prospectus Magnis Canalis Venetiarum*, but the fourth is related loosely to a drawing.[8] In the same collection there are drawings by another of Monro's artists, William Henry Hunt, which copy Canaletto originals (in one case an etching) and imitate his technique of drawing in pen and brown ink with grey ink washes; some of these, too, have Henderson or Monro provenances. The same combination of ink outline with a contrasting wash can be found in other artists who knew Canaletto's drawings — Joseph

Farington, for example, and Thomas Girtin.

In rather a different vein, Thomas Rowlandson was another draughtsman who clearly admired Canaletto's drawings, especially his way of doing figures, and who reflects the influence in his own work. Rowlandson is of course known chiefly for his humorous caricatures and satirically robust portrayal of eighteenth-century English life. He was also an accomplished landscape and topographical draughtsman, working in pen and watercolour in a free and lively idiom [cat. no. 98]. There are qualities in his drawing style which clearly show that he had learned from Canaletto's originals. Canaletto is something of a magician with his pen, brilliantly unfurling little figures in curl-

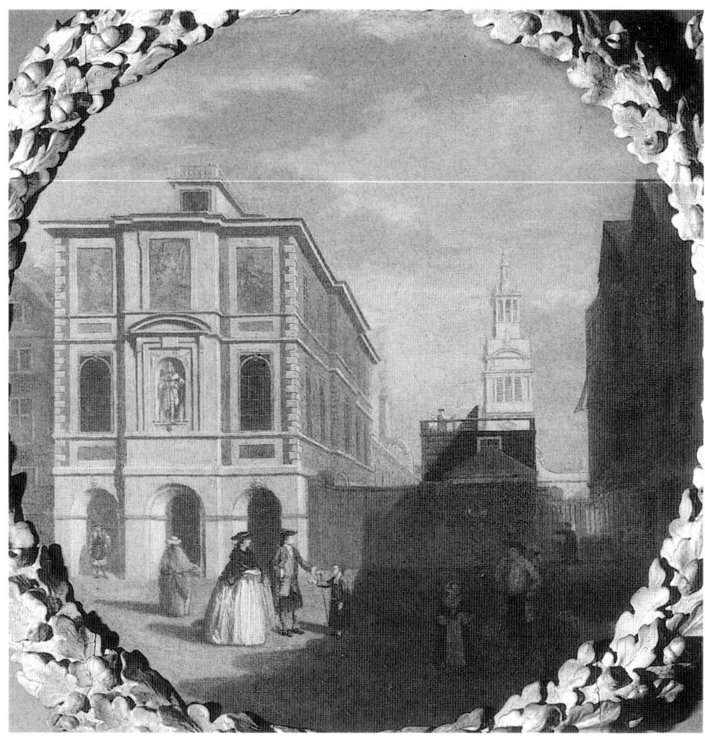

Fig. 28 Samuel Wale, *Christ's Hospital*, oil on canvas, diameter 21 ins (53.3 cm), Thomas Coram Foundation for Children, London

ing rococo lines which define and describe their character in a summarily vivacious fashion. Rowlandson's bounding calligraphy and animated washes have the same technical facility, turned to a somewhat earthier expressive purpose. But there can be no doubt that he had looked closely at Canaletto's drawings.

There is a further direct link between specific Canaletto paintings and drawings and English painters that can be established through the engravers who reproduced his work in the 1740s and 1750s. The two earliest prints of his English subjects to be issued were the engravings of Sir Hugh Smithson's *London seen through an arch of Westminster Bridge* [cat. no 6] and of *Westminster Bridge from the north on Lord Mayor's Day* (1746–47, Yale Center for British Art, New Haven, Paul Mellon Collection) [figs. 13, 14]. Both prints were published (as a pair) in 1747 for the printseller John Brindley. They are inscribed "Canaletti Pinx. S. Wale delin. R. Parr Sculp.", from which it is clear that the engraver actually worked not from the original canvases

but from copies drawn ("delineavit") by Samuel Wale (1721–86). Although he is chiefly known as a book illustrator, Wale worked extensively for print publishers and it is not surprising to find him copying paintings in drawings for an engraver to work from. What is particularly important in the present context, though, is the fact that he painted three of the eight topographical roundels presented to the Foundling Hospital as decorations for the Court Room. Wale's contribution were views of Christ's Hospital [fig. 28], St Thomas's Hospital and Greenwich Hospital, each very precisely drawn and painted in a way that shows he was trying to match Canaletto. Five more roundels completed the set: two by Richard Wilson and one by Thomas Gainsborough [fig. 12] are more painterly and evocative than the rest, but the remaining two by Edward Haytley (Chelsea Hospital [fig. 29] and Bethlem Hospital) are meticulously accurate and suggest the work of a modestly accomplished English artist attempting to do something Canalettesque. It was William Hogarth who conceived the idea of artists presenting specimens of their work to decorate the fine rooms of the Foundling Hospital, which were opened to polite visitors as a permanent 'gallery' of contemporary British art to demonstrate what native talent could achieve. With Canaletto recently arrived in London it is tempting to view the series of roundels as a deliberately planned strategy on the part of Hogarth's circle to divert patrons away from him.[9] Samuel Wale went on to become a foundation member and first Professor of Perspective of the Royal Academy. Thus, through him the knowledge of Canaletto's art and the optical discipline underlying it could have been disseminated further.

The engraver Edward Rooker (1724–1774) is also important in this connection. He engraved three plates from views by Canaletto, two Vauxhall Gardens subjects (1751) and another (1750) from one of the versions of *The Thames from the terrace of Somerset House, the City of London in the distance* [see cat. no. 14].[10] It may well have been this last print, with its companion view (by a different engraver) from Somerset House terrace towards Westminster [see cat. no. 15], which established the site as one of the most popular from which London scenes were drawn and painted in the eighteenth century. Edward Rooker specialised in topographical and architectural prints. As the father of one of the most notable eighteenth-century watercolour topographers, Michael 'Angelo' Rooker (1746–1801), whom he initially trained, and as a close friend of Paul Sandby who taught his son in the 1760s, he is a central figure in the development of English topography in the third quarter of the eighteenth century. Apart from engraving works by other artists (including Paul and Thomas Sandby, and the younger Rooker) he also occasionally produced plates from his own drawings. His most notable set of six London views published 1766–68 show how he transmitted the lesson of Canaletto in his engravings of town and river scenes. Five of the six are based on Sandby's drawings, the other being from one of his son's views. The most dramatic of them, showing *Blackfriars Bridge under construction* [fig. 30], brings together Canaletto, Scott, Marlow and Sandby in its various components.

It would certainly be misleading to give the impression that eighteenth-century English view-painting and topography developed in the way it did solely, or even primarily, because of Canaletto's influence. Samuel Scott was already making accurate drawings in pen with ink and watercolour washes of the London Thames around Westminster Bridge as early as 1742 [see cat. nos. 44 and 52].[11] These establish beyond doubt that he was beginning to develop as a topographical artist before Canaletto's arrival, and their style indicates that he was capable of producing meticulously observed records of architectural detail independently, in the tradition of earlier English draughtsmen. If these contain any indirect influence of a Canalettesque nature it would have to have come from Antonio Joli. Nonetheless, after 1746 (and none of Scott's surviving view-paintings can be dated before the late 1740s) it is surely possible to see in the work of Scott and others the fresh impetus that Canaletto's presence gave to topographical pictures in their treatment, more varied choice of subject, more adventurous compositional devices, and in their livelier disposition of figural content and narrative.

Some lessons at least, though, could have been learned from Canaletto before he actually set up in London. There were, after all, a lot of Canaletto's Venetian views in English collections, and there were also copyists at work in England. One of them is mentioned by George Vertue in 1745:

Mr. Harding. painter of Landskhipes &c & coach painter [...] its hard to distinguish in Time his coppys from the originals. he is continually immitating paintings of Canaletti of Venice Views &c. & also paintings of Paulo Panini with good success.[12]

It is therefore perfectly possible that English painters before

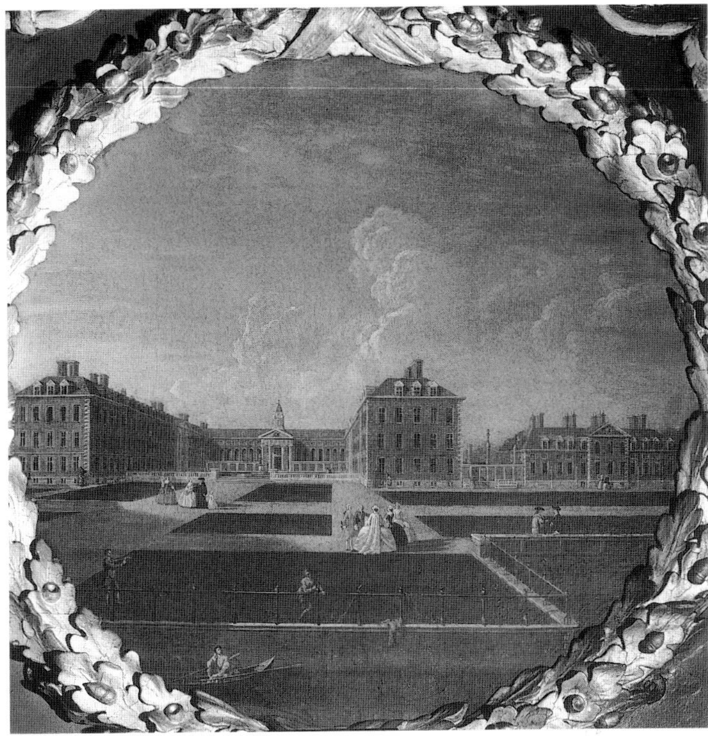

Fig. 29 Edward Haytley, *Chelsea Hospital*, oil on canvas, diameter 21 ins (53.3 cm), Thomas Coram Foundation for Children, London

1746 could have assimilated some features of Canaletto's treatment of topography and reflected it in their own work. Another early copyist who remains an elusive and mysterious figure is William James. He exhibited views at the Society of Artists and Royal Academy exhibitions from 1761 to 1771, but only one painting dated 1759 with a signature "W. James" is recorded. This was a copy of Canaletto's *View of the Monument* [fig. 24]. According to one early source, the artist Edward Edwards who published his *Anecdotes of Painters* in 1808, James had been a pupil or assistant of Canaletto when he was in England. On the basis of this rather tenuous evidence a great many pictures of London and Venice have been attributed to him, but although the paintings themselves make it clear that there was an artist or studio producing variants of Canaletto and Scott themes whether they can convincingly be attached to James is still disputed [see cat. nos. 57 and 58].

By the time Canaletto left England in 1755 he had created a new fashion for view-paintings after his manner, and through the influence he exerted on contemporary English painters he effectively revolutionised the native topographical tradition. Samuel Scott was the first fully to comprehend his example. His particular genius lay in his ability to capture the subtle nuances of effect and atmosphere peculiar to the English climate and which, to some extent, had eluded Canaletto. In a sense he naturalised the Venetian's style and translated his manner into a recognisably English idiom by adapting what he learned from him to the native tradition of topographical painting, producing from the synthesis of the two a newly revitalised current of view-painting in England. This can be seen especially in works like *An arch of Westminster Bridge* (ca. 1750–55) [cat. no. 48] in which he exploits the framed view motif in a way that relates to Canaletto prototypes without, however, exactly following them.[13] Scott was successful enough as a painter to afford to have a house in Twickenham from 1749 while retaining a studio in London. From the 1750s or early 1760s there are some beautifully illuminated views of the Twickenham riverside which are among his most atmospherically sensitive renderings of topography in a Canalettesque vein [cat. no. 53].

Scott's pupil William Marlow carried on from his teacher the Canaletto tradition of view painting to the end of the eighteenth century. His early works, such as the *View of Worcester from the River Severn* [cat. no. 72], are closely dependent on Scott: in the 1760s he was painting a mixture of London views, topographical prospects, country house portraits and occasionally landscapes in which he shows a tendency towards incorporating elements of the new picturesque taste English painters were adopting. In 1765 and 1766 he toured France and Italy, and must have visited Venice because he is one of the relatively few English painters who painted Venetian views (other than copyists imitating Canaletto and other *vedutisti*). From his return to England and throughout the 1770s and 1780s Marlow produced a large number of oils and watercolours of French and Italian subjects of the kind that appealed as souvenirs to those who had made the Grand Tour, but it is in the London views which he continued to paint at the same time that his debt to Canaletto and Samuel Scott is apparent. He carried on where they had left off as the principal painter of new developments and projects, depicting such notable architectural achievements as the new Blackfriars Bridge (completed 1769), Somerset House and The Adelphi which were changing London's riverfront so dramatically in the later eighteenth cen-

tury. At its best his work can be impressively evocative and a late painting like *The Adelphi* (Government Picture Collection; probably exhibited in 1789 at the Society of Artists) [fig. 31] displays a powerful sense of architectural spectacle combined with a fine understanding of light effect and atmosphere that look forward to the more romantic images of the next century. On one occasion a painting by Marlow was mistaken for a 'Canaletto'. In a letter to Sir Horace Mann, Horace Walpole reported in 1771 that "two views of Verona by Canaletti have been sold by auction for 550 guineas – and what is worse it is come out that they are copies by Marlow, a disciple of Scott. Both master and scholar are indeed better painters than the Venetian, but the purchasers did not mean to be so well cheated."[14] One of the copies may be the huge *View of Verona* [fig. 32] by Marlow now in the Courtauld Institute Galleries, London, which is in fact taken from an original by Canaletto's nephew, Bernardo Bellotto, who was often confused in the eighteenth century with his uncle. Since Marlow had by then moved to Twickenham and was a near neighbour of Walpole's the story probably came from the artist. Walpole himself owned works by both Scott and Marlow, but even so his critical estimation of them as "better painters than the Venetian" is somewhat perverse for a connoisseur of his calibre. One wonders, though, how many more 'Canalettos' Marlow might have painted.

By the end of the eighteenth century English topographers and landscape artists had evolved new and infinitely more varied pictorial formulations and interpretive faculties to express their responses and characterize different kinds of scenery and experience. New ideas about picturesque beauty and landscape as a vehicle for feeling and sensation were fundamentally changing what painters were concerned to communicate. Thomas Girtin and J.M.W. Turner were among the first in the 1790s to express a new, reactive sensibility in their work. In both cases, however, their teachers were specialists working in the eighteenth-century topographical tradition who passed on to them pictorial conventions which had become almost canonical in the vocabulary of the picturesque view. Inevitably these included some that ultimately go back to Canaletto and his immediate successors in England, and it is clear from their early draughtsmanship and watercolour technique that they responded to the stimulus of seeing his drawings.

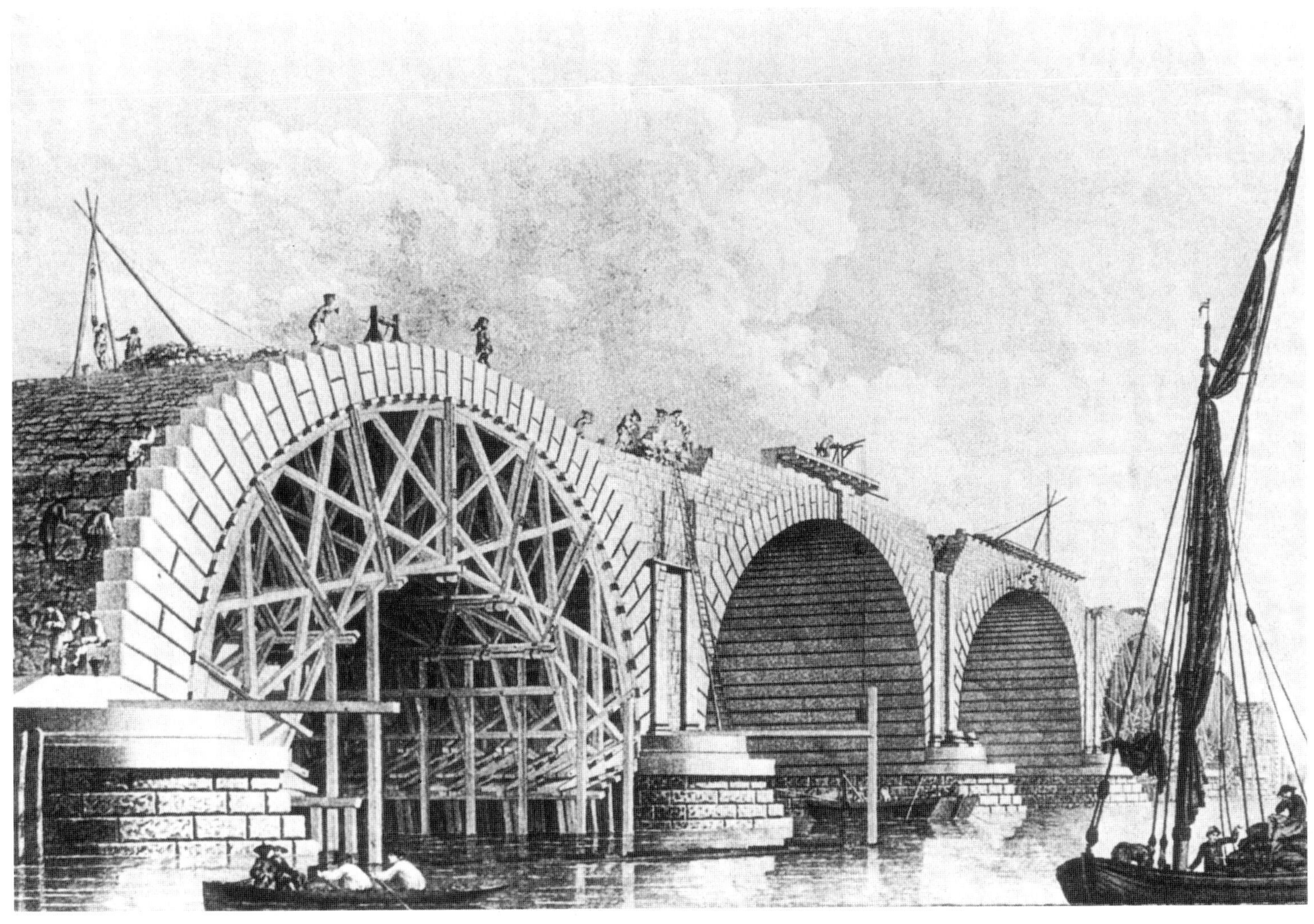

Fig. 30 Edward Rooker, *Blackfriars Bridge, London, under construction*, engraving

Turner carried his interest in Canaletto much further in the nineteenth century. It is well known that his knowledge of the Old Masters was exceptional, and that especially after he became Professor of Perspective at the Royal Academy in 1807 he embarked upon an intensive investigation into their methods and procedures. Topographical scenes of one sort or another still occupied him a great deal, although by now he was transforming them into intensely personal and original statements which express his own imaginatively charged vision. That he may sometimes have reflected on Canaletto seems almost certain. There is one painting, already mentioned above, which has a vicarious connection with the Canalettesque tradition in English painting, his *High Street, Oxford* of 1810 [fig. 26].[15] This was commissioned by the Oxford picture-dealer James Wyatt who also possessed two Samuel Scott London views which Turner may well have seen.[16] That Turner was later to turn his thoughts to Canaletto very directly in Venice is definitively established by his 1833 Royal Academy exhibit, *The Bridge of Sighs, Doge's Palace and Customs House, Venice: Canaletto painting* [cat. no. 116], in which the greatest of Venice's romantic interpreters pays tribute to its most celebrated eighteenth-century *vedute* painter.[17]

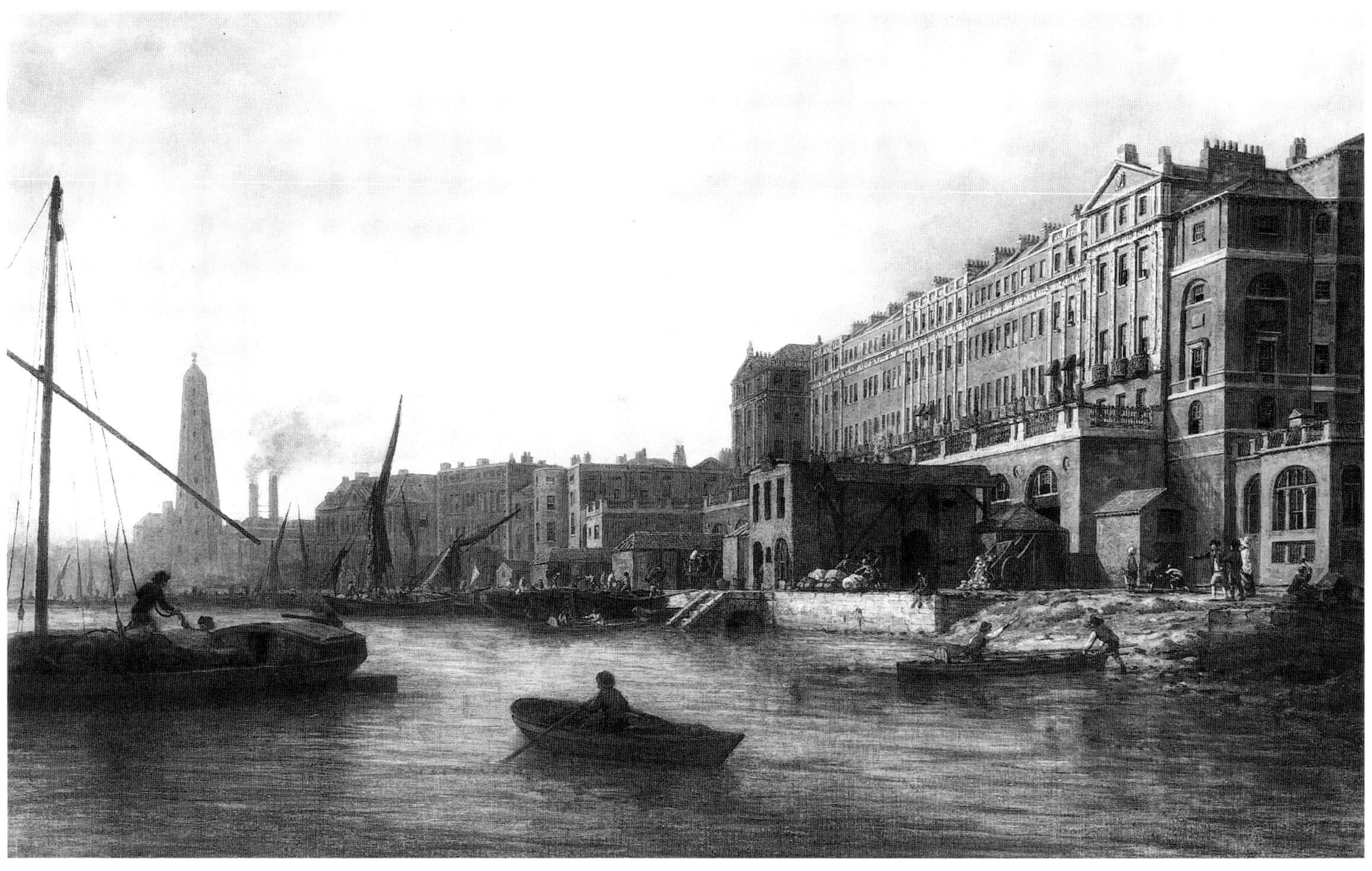

Fig. 31 William Marlow, *The Adelphi, London*, oil on canvas, $41\frac{1}{2} \times 65\frac{1}{2}$ ins (105.4×166.4 cm),
The British Government Art Collection

It was, of course, inevitable that many English visitors to Venice would judge what they saw against Canaletto's portrayal of the city. His pictures became paradigmatic. In 1789 Dr Johnson's friend Mrs Piozzi wrote about how, when she saw Venice for the first time, the experience brough back to her "all the ideas inspired by Canaletti, whose views of this town are most scrupulously exact ... to such a degree, indeed that we knew all the famous towers, steeples, &c before we reached them". By the time of Turner's first visit thirty years later the Venice of Canaletto was still physically the place he had painted but politics and the poetic imagination had changed for ever the associations it aroused. There were no British visitors to speak of from the early 1790s until 1815 during the wars with Revolutionary and Napoleonic France. Venice herself was profoundly affected by the conflict in Europe. In 1797 the Venetian Republic was extinguished after more than a thousand years of independence: first the French, then the Austrians, and finally the French again ruled Venice and her mainland territories. In 1815 the Congress of Vienna assigned the former Republic to the Austrian Empire; not until 1866 did it become part of the newly formed Kingdom of Italy.

The suppression of Venice by the French in 1797 excited widespread attention in England. The fate of La Serenissima at the hands of French tyranny became a symbol of the threat to British liberty, and in the years that followed a new vision of Venice tinged by nostalgia for its past and its romantic

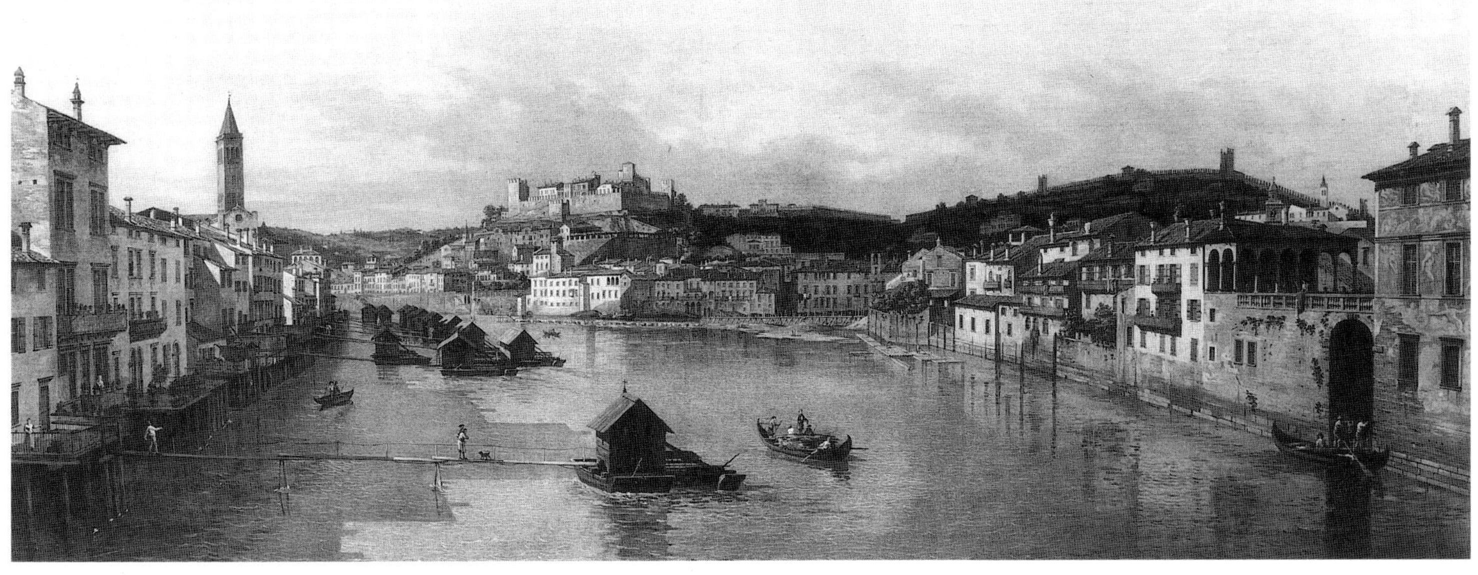

Fig. 32 William Marlow after Bernardo Bellotto, *A view of Verona*, oil on canvas, $54\frac{1}{4} \times 92\frac{9}{10}$ ins
(138×236 cm), Courtauld Institute Galleries (Lee of Fareham Collection), London

enchantment inspired a new generation of poets and painters. This is the spirit that informs the imaginative response encountered in the verses of Shelley, Byron and Wordsworth and which finds expression in the paintings of Bonington, Turner and others. Where Canaletto had painted the city's picturesque beauties and architectural features, the Romantics expressed a different kind of associational feeling aroused by sensation, imagination and attachment. The view gave way to a vision. But if Canaletto had not painted Venice as he did and made it so much part of the English visual repertoire and memory over the preceding century it would probably not have had the particular resonance for the Romantic and later the Victorian imagination that it did.[18]

For the nineteenth century, therefore, it was Canaletto's Venetian scenes rather than his English pictures which chiefly aroused interest in his work. Occasionally, though, when an appropriate subject presented itself, the Canaletto 'tradition' might make its presence felt. One instance where this occurs is in John Constable's sketches and paintings of Waterloo Bridge which the Prince Regent opened ceremonially in 1817. It was some time afterwards that Constable painted the pictures in which he clearly refers back to the work of Canaletto, Scott and Marlow, though not in a directly imitative way. His *Thames and Waterloo Bridge* (ca. 1820; Cincinnati Art Museum) carries on the tradition, reinterpreted in the fresh and naturalistic manner that one should expect of Constable; the preliminary study in the Royal Academy is in its abbreviated suggestion of figures and boats almost uncannily suggestive of Canaletto. From 1820 until 1832 Constable was working on a much grander subject, *The Opening of Waterloo Bridge* (Tate Gallery, London)

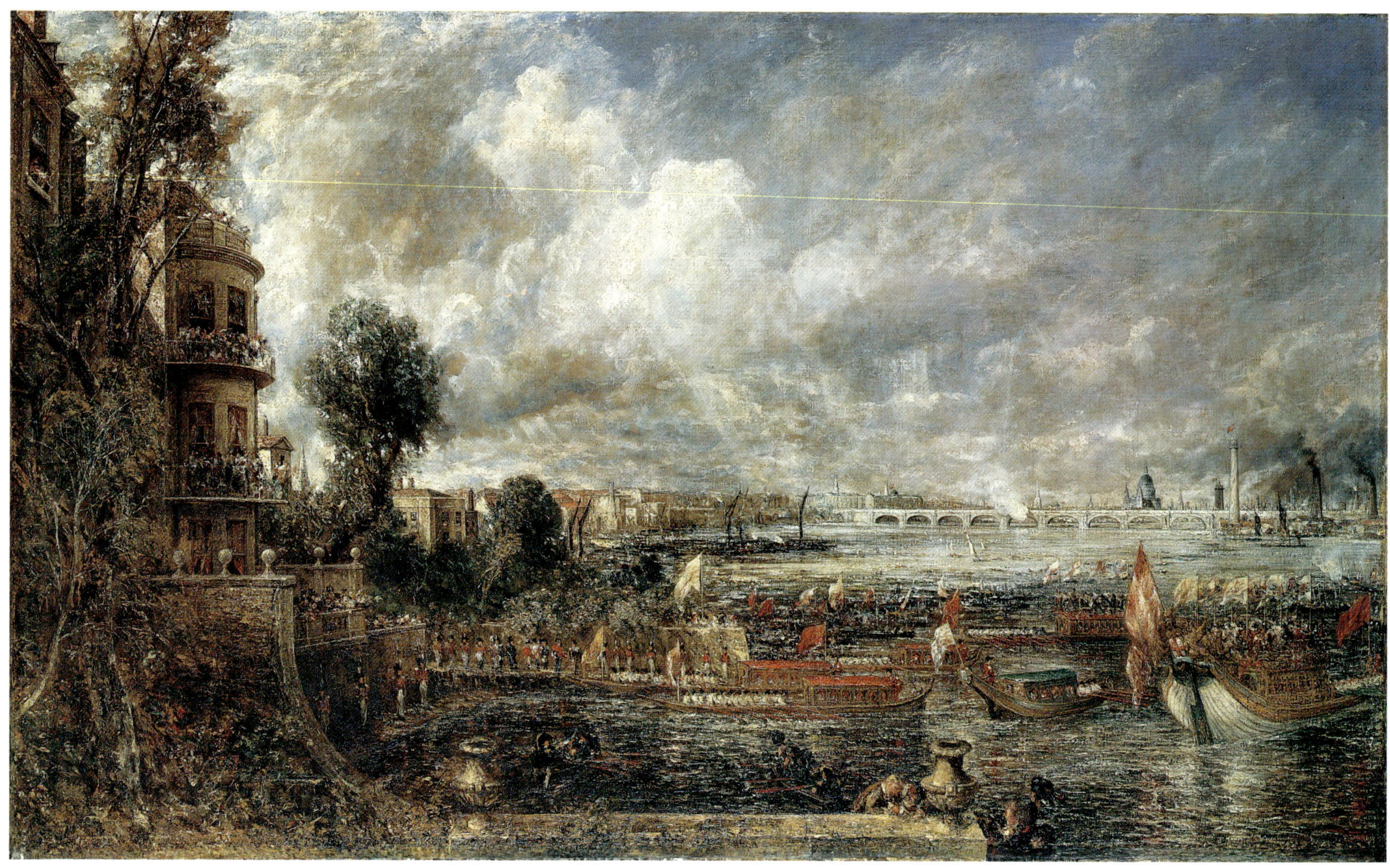

Fig. 33 John Constable, *The Opening of Waterloo Bridge, London*, oil on canvas, $51\frac{1}{2} \times 85\frac{7}{8}$ ins
(130.8 × 218 cm), Tate Gallery, London

[fig. 33]; showing the festive spectacle of state barges setting off from Whitehall Stairs for the ceremonies. A sketch of the subject was seen by Constable's friend Bishop John Fisher in 1822: his reaction to it is described in a letter to Constable from his wife — "He was quite in raptures with your Waterloo, sat down on the floor to it, said it was equal to Cannalletti ...".[19] The commotion of colour and gilded barges on the river are indeed reminiscent of one of Canaletto's water carnivals in Venice, but the weather and breezy effects are distinctively Constable's.

It was not to be long before Canaletto's reputation as an artist received its most savage mauling from an English critic. In 1846 John Ruskin published the second volume of his

Modern Painters in which he places the transfiguring genius of Turner at the pinnacle of landscape painting. For Ruskin Canaletto seemed prosaic in his portrayal of Venice, merely a recorder of facts who signified the decline of the great Venetian artistic heritage — a painter "whose miserable, virtueless, heartless mechanism, accepted as the representation of such various glory, is, both in its existence and acceptance, among the most striking signs of the lost sensation and deadened intellect of the nation at that time ...". Ruskin criticizes Canaletto in several passages: he paints water with repetitive monotony, his reflections are optically false, "the truths of colour are contradicted by ... the thousand", his work displays "want of poetry, of feeling, of artistical thoughtfulness in treatment, or of the various other virtues which he does not so much as profess."[20] In a letter from Venice to his father he describes its beauty as "beyond all I conceived" and adds, "That foul son of a deal board – Canaletti – to have lived in the middle of it all and left us nothing!"[21] Ruskin's influence over artistic and aesthetic perceptions in mid-nineteenth-century Britain was immense. The appeal that Canaletto's pictures had for the public was not by any means extinguished by Ruskin, but what he wrote does represent a change in the intellectual appreciation of his work. Exactly one hundred years had elapsed since Canaletto first arrived in England.

NOTES

1. See Richard Kingzett, 'A Catalogue of the Works of Samuel Scott', *Walpole Society* XLVIII, 1982, pp.49–50 (*Tower of London*, version B).

2. Algernon Graves, *Art Sales*, 3 vols, London 1918–21: the paintings listed include interiors of King's College Chapel, Cambridge, and Henry VII's Chapel, Westminster, views of Horse Guards, Westminster Bridge "with the lord mayor's shew on the water", the Thames from Somerset House, Northumberland House and Warwick Castle – a fairly representative group of Canaletto's English pictures. For the drawings, see W.G. Constable (revised J.G. Links), *Canaletto*, Oxford 1976, II, nos. 738, 742.

3. *Ibid.*, no 739.

4. *Ibid.*, nos. 419, 740.

5. The prints republished in 1794 were: *Northumberland House, Hampton Court Bridge, Ranelagh Rotunda and Gardens, Vauxhall Gardens: the Grand Walk, View of London from Pentonville, St James's Park looking west.* See Constable (revised Links), *Canaletto*, 1976, II, pp.683–85.

6. *Ibid.*, nos. 526, 733 for Monro's drawings.

7. *Ibid.*, nos. 729, 770, 777a, 819, 832 for Henderson's drawings.

8. See T. Girtin and D. Loshak, *The Art of Thomas Girtin*, London 1954, catalogue nos. 221–24.

9. For the Foundling Hospital roundels, see Benedict Nicolson, *Treasures of the Foundling Hospital*, Oxford 1972; and *Manners and Morals. Hogarth and British Painting 1700–1760*, exhibition catalogue by Elizabeth Einberg, London, Tate Gallery, 1987, nos. 163–70.

10. The prints are listed in Constable (revised Links), *Canaletto*, 1976, II, pp.684–85. For Edward Rooker generally, see Patrick Conner, *Michael Angelo Rooker*, London 1984, pp.18–24.

11. Kingzett, 'Works of Samuel Scott', 1982, pp.2–3, catalogue nos. D95, D96, D97.

12. *Walpole Society* XXII (Vertue Note Books III), 1934, pp.126–27.

13. Scott would have known Canaletto's 1746 *London seen through an arch of Westminster Bridge* at least from the 1747 engraving; perhaps he also knew of a composition such as Canaletto's drawing of *The western arches of Westminster Bridge* (ca. 1747; British Museum) in which the view seen through the two arches shown is the same as that in Scott's painting: see Constable (revised Links), *Canaletto*, 1976, II, no. 752.

14. W.S. Lewis (ed.), *The Yale Edition of Horace Walpole's Correspondence*, XXIII, London 1967 (26 April 1771).

15. Martin Butlin and Evelyn Joll, *The Paintings of J.M.W. Turner*, London 1977, no. 102.

16. Kingzett, 'Works of Samuel Scott', 1982, p.53 (*View of the Thames with Montagu House*, version C), p.55 (*York Buildings Water Tower*, version B).

17. Butlin and Joll, *The Paintings of J.M.W. Turner*, 1977, no. 349; for a general account of Turner's Venetian paintings, see Lindsay Stainton, *Turner's Venice*, London 1986.

18. There is a useful anthology of English literary responses to Venice in Dario Calimari (ed.), *English Writers and Venice 1350–1950*, Venice 1981.

19. Constable's Waterloo Bridge paintings and the related studies for them are fully discussed in Leslie Parris and Ian Fleming-Williams, *Constable*, London, Tate Gallery, 1991, pp.206–11 (nos. 102–05), pp.369–72 (nos. 212–13), p.443 (no. 288). Maria Constable's letter is quoted from R.B. Beckett (ed.), 'John Constable's Correspondence (II)', *Suffolk Records Society* VI, 1964, pp.275–76. It is worth noting that Constable owned two books of engravings after Canaletto: a set by G.B. Brustolini and a 1751 edition of Antonio Visentini's plates ('John Constable: Further Documents', *Suffolk Records Society* XVIII, 1975, [Constable's Library]).

20. John Ruskin, *Modern Painters*, II, 1846 (*Complete Works of John Ruskin*, Library Edition, edd. E.T. Cook and A. Wedderburn, London 1903–12, pp.214–16, 513–16).

21. *Ibid.*, p.214 (note 1).

43 Joseph Nickolls
fl. 1726–55

A view of Charing Cross and Northumberland House, London

Oil on canvas, 1746
20 × 30 ins (50.8 × 76.2 cm)
Inscribed lower left: Jo Nickolls Pinx/1746
The National Westminster Bank Collection

In the centre foreground is the bronze equestrian statue of Charles I by Hubert Le Sueur; beyond lies the Strand with the Jacobean brick towers of Northumberland House dominating the scene. Stylistically this painting belongs to the tradition of English town topography that had developed in the seventeenth and eighteenth centuries from Dutch painting. The figures give an idea of the whole spectrum of London society from ladies and gentlemen of fashion to the urban poor, all depicted with a realism and characterization that suggests Nickolls took an interest in Hogarth's work. Of Nickolls himself very little is known. The earliest documented painting by him is a view of the Middle Temple Fountain Courtyard which was engraved in 1738. He has been connected with Twickenham river scenes bearing an inscription and date of 1726, but both the attribution and date have been doubted since they show later features and are more likely to have been done in the mid–1750s.[1] His 1746 Charing Cross view shows that he was an accomplished performer in the same topographical tradition from which Samuel Scott initially emerges in the early 1740s, and comparison with Canaletto's portrayals of Northumberland House [figs. 8 and 27] reveals very clearly how the Venetian's influence was to affect English view-painting. ML

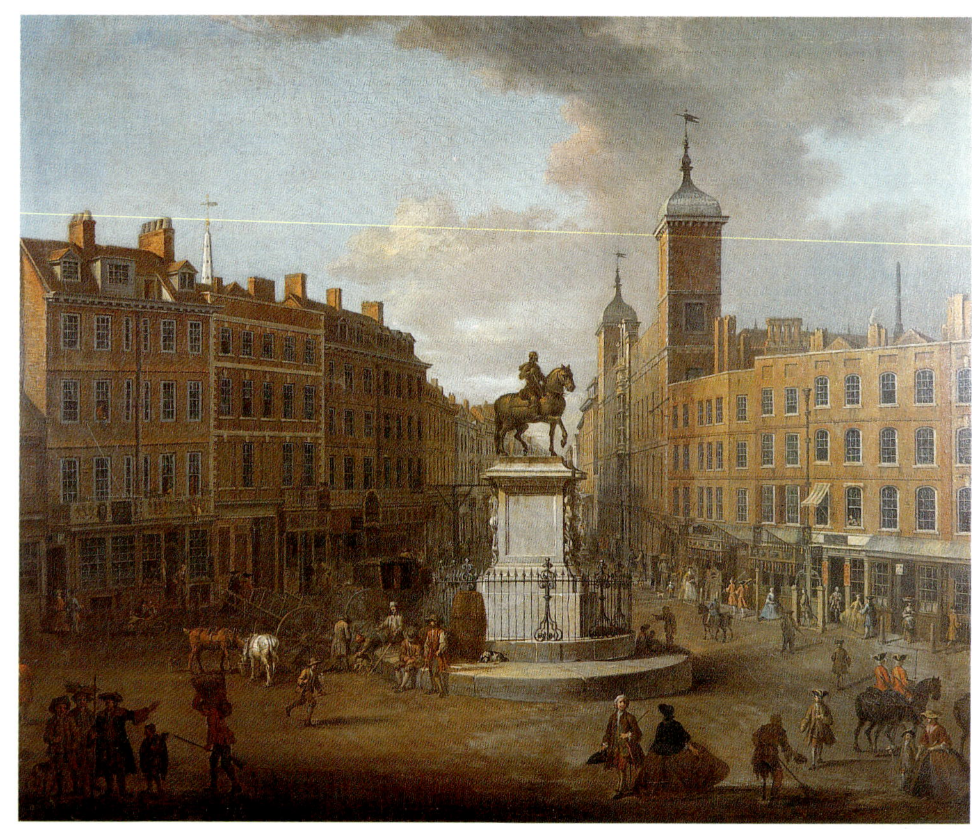

1. See *Manners and Morals. Hogarth and British Painting 1700–1760*, exhibition catalogue by Elizabeth Einberg, London, Tate Gallery, 1987, nos. 113–15; and *Country Houses in Great Britain*, exhibition catalogue, Yale Center for British Art, New Haven, 1979, cat. nos. 17–18.

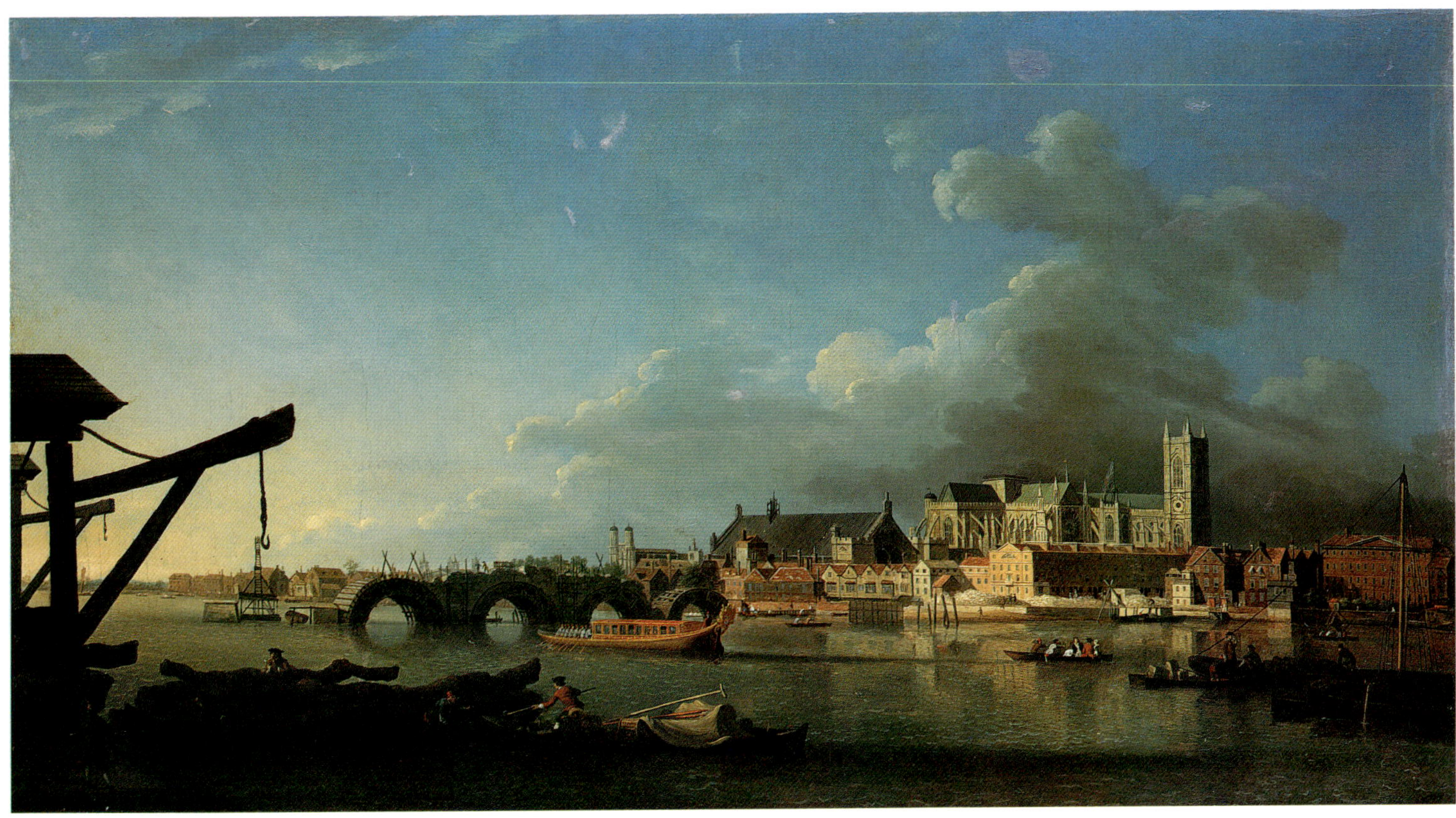

44 Samuel Scott

ca. 1702–1772

The building of Westminster Bridge

Oil on canvas, 1747
$24 \times 44\frac{3}{8}$ ins (61 × 112.7 cm)
Signed lower right: S. Scott

The Metropolitan Museum of Art
(Purchase, Charles B. Curtis fund and Joseph
Pulitzer bequest, 1944), New York

The painting is one of a pair, its companion being one of the versions of a *View of Old London Bridge* which is signed and dated 1747. The view is from a timber yard on the south bank. Westminster Bridge appears as it must have been in 1742. Westminster Abbey has only one of its western towers: the second was not finished until 1744. To the left of the Abbey the long roof of Westminster Hall and beyond it the twin turrets of the old Houses of Parliament (originally the medieval St Stephen's Chapel, burned in 1834) can be seen, and just visible over the third arch from the Westminster side are the four corner towers of Thomas Archer's baroque church, St John's Smith Square. The discrepancy between the date of the painting, 1747, and the topographical evidence indicates that Scott must have referred back to an earlier drawing of 1742. The Livery Company barge apparently practising for the annual Lord Mayor's water procession to Westminster Hall for the swearing-in ceremony is the Ironmongers', of which the Lord Mayor elected in 1741 was a member. The pairing of Westminster Bridge with London Bridge (which had its ancient houses on it until cleared and modernised in 1756) contrasts old and new, ancient gothic with classical Palladian improvements to London's amenities. The river with its boats and reflections of the buildings is one of Scott's most accomplished Thames scenes, and although the houses are rendered with evident awareness of Canaletto the fact that the painting is based on a drawing of around 1742 shows that Scott was developing as a topographical artist independently before Canaletto's arrival. ML

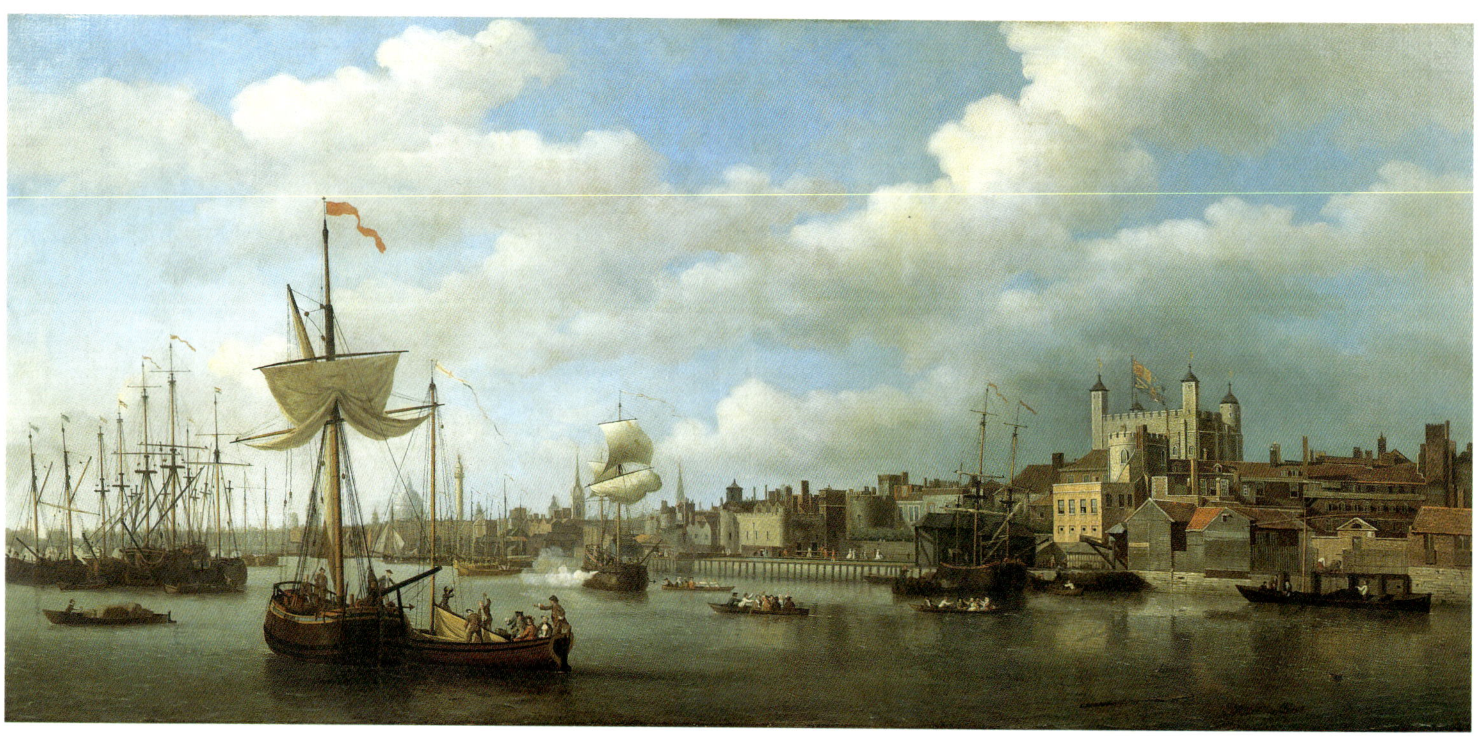

45 Samuel Scott

The Tower of London

Oil on canvas, 1749–50
45 × 98 ins (114.3 × 248.9 cm)
Private collection

The view shows shipping at anchor in the reach of the Thames known as the Pool of London opposite Bermondsey on the south bank, with the buildings on the north extending from the Tower westwards to the Monument, St Paul's and beyond. The careful depiction of the ships is a reminder that Samuel Scott was at the start of his career a specialist in marine subjects following in the tradition of the famous Dutch painters William van de Velde the Elder and the Younger who had worked in England in the seventeenth century. Nearly all Scott's paintings are sea pieces or river views, and he invariably represents ships and boats with meticulous precision. The architectural detail in his paintings, however, is often less accurate. As is often the case Scott's painting is full of information about the activity on the river and the commerce conducted in the yards and on the wharves bordering it. He adds a further 'narrative' episode with the ship saluting the official barge near the centre of the picture. In the handling of light on the buildings and their precise contours the view is comparable to Canaletto. As it shares the same provenance as his *Old Horse Guards from St James's Park* [cat. no. 19] it must have been commissioned as a companion to Canaletto's painting. The composition was one of Scott's most successful works and eight autograph versions are known, the earliest dated 1746. This painting must be later than 1749, the date of the Canaletto to which it is a pair. ML

46 Samuel Scott

A view of the Thames with Montagu House, London

Oil on canvas, after 1749
27 × 46½ ins (68.6 × 118.1 cm)
The Corporation of London, Guildhall Art Gallery

This view shows the north side of the Thames with the houses built in the eighteenth century over the site of part of the former Whitehall Palace which was

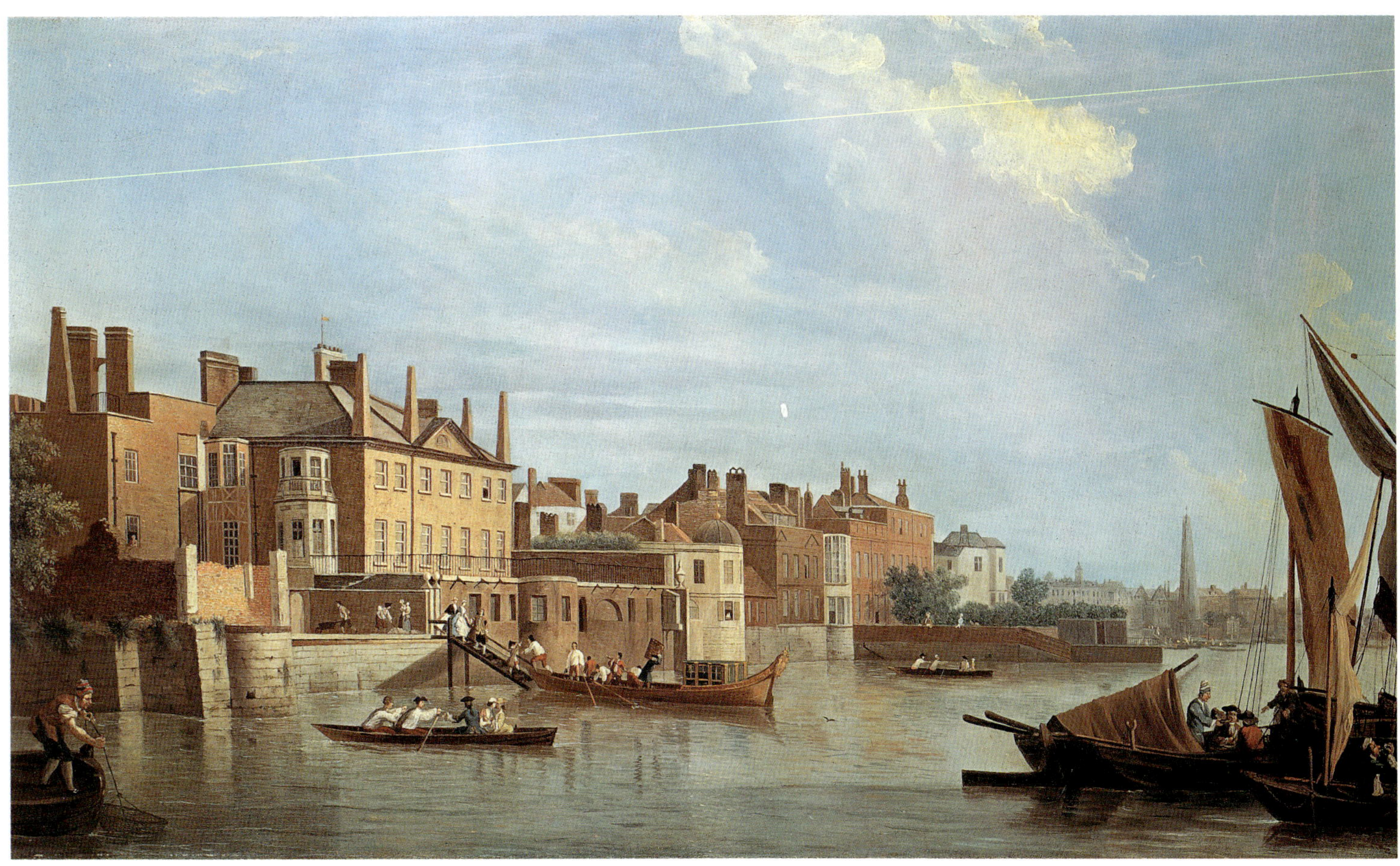

burned down in 1698. On the extreme left is a corner of the terrace of Richmond House from which Canaletto drew the views he painted in 1747 for the Duke of Richmond [cat. nos. 9 and 12]. The pedimented Palladian mansion is the Duke of Montagu's house with, in front of it, the terrace also visible in one of Canaletto's Richmond pair. Beyond the houses can be seen the familiar (to eighteenth-century Londoners) wooden obelisk of the York Water Tower. In this and one other version of the view Scott has omitted the spire of St Martin-in-the-Fields which was visible from his viewpoint; the two other painted versions include it. In the middle fore-ground Scott shows a rowing barge with a coat of arms at the stern taking on an obviously elegant family party from the private Montagu House river stairs – perhaps members of the Duke's family. It is the kind of detail juxtaposing different social classes in the ordered world of mid-Georgian London that Canaletto habitually introduces. In this picture Scott combines elements of Canaletto's style with the English tradition that looks back in some respects to seventeenth-century Dutch townscapes. The picture cannot be before 1749, the date which appears with Scott's signature on what is thought to be the prime version, still in the possession of descendants of the Duke of Montagu. This version together with its companion (*The York Buildings Water Tower*, showing the Thames from York Stairs westwards to Westminster Abbey and Bridge) belonged in the nineteenth century to the Oxford art dealer James Wyatt who commissioned J.M.W. Turner to paint a precisely topographical view of *The High Street, Oxford*, in 1810 [fig. 26], which might also be construed as carrying on the tradition that Canaletto and Scott exemplify. ML

47 Samuel Scott

The High Cross and Cathedral, Bristol

Oil on canvas, ca. 1749–50
23 × 19½ ins (58.4 × 49.5 cm)
Bristol Museums and Art Gallery

The view of Bristol High Cross and Cathedral taken from College Green is based on an engraving by W.H. Toms of a drawing by Richard West which was published in 1743. Scott has changed the composition from a horizontal to a vertical format, cutting off the extensions of the view to left and right in the print. The view shows Bristol Cathedral (originally St Augustine's Abbey) in the truncated state in which it was left at the Dissolution in 1537: the old Norman nave had been taken down in preparation for rebuilding, but not until the mid nineteenth century was a replacement designed by G.E. Street eventually constructed. The High Cross was originally erected in the city centre to commemorate a charter conferring county status on Bristol granted in 1373; later additions were made to it in the seventeenth century. It was removed to College Green in 1736 but dismantled again in 1762 and finally given to Henry Hoare who added it to his pleasure gardens at Stourhead where it may be seen today. This painting belonged to Horace Walpole who hung it in his splendid 'Gothick' gallery at Strawberry Hill, Twickenham. The subject would have appealed to his particular interest in medieval antiquities and gothic architecture. It is difficult to date, but may have been painted for Horace Walpole after he had started work on transforming Strawberry Hill, and after Scott took a property at Twickenham in 1749. The light effects are Canalettesque,

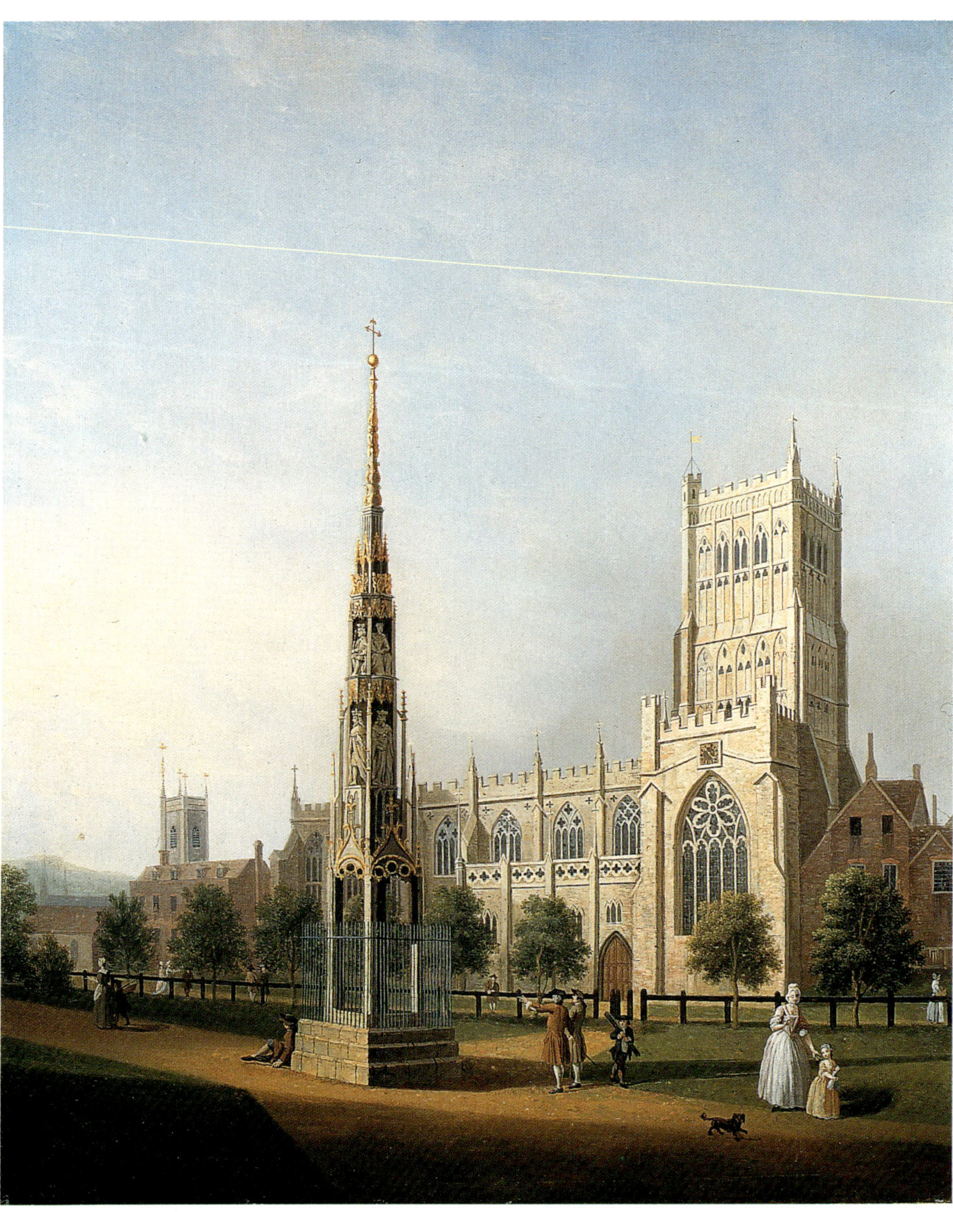

but in this instance Scott is following an engraved model which is stylistically typical of earlier eighteenth-century English topography. ML

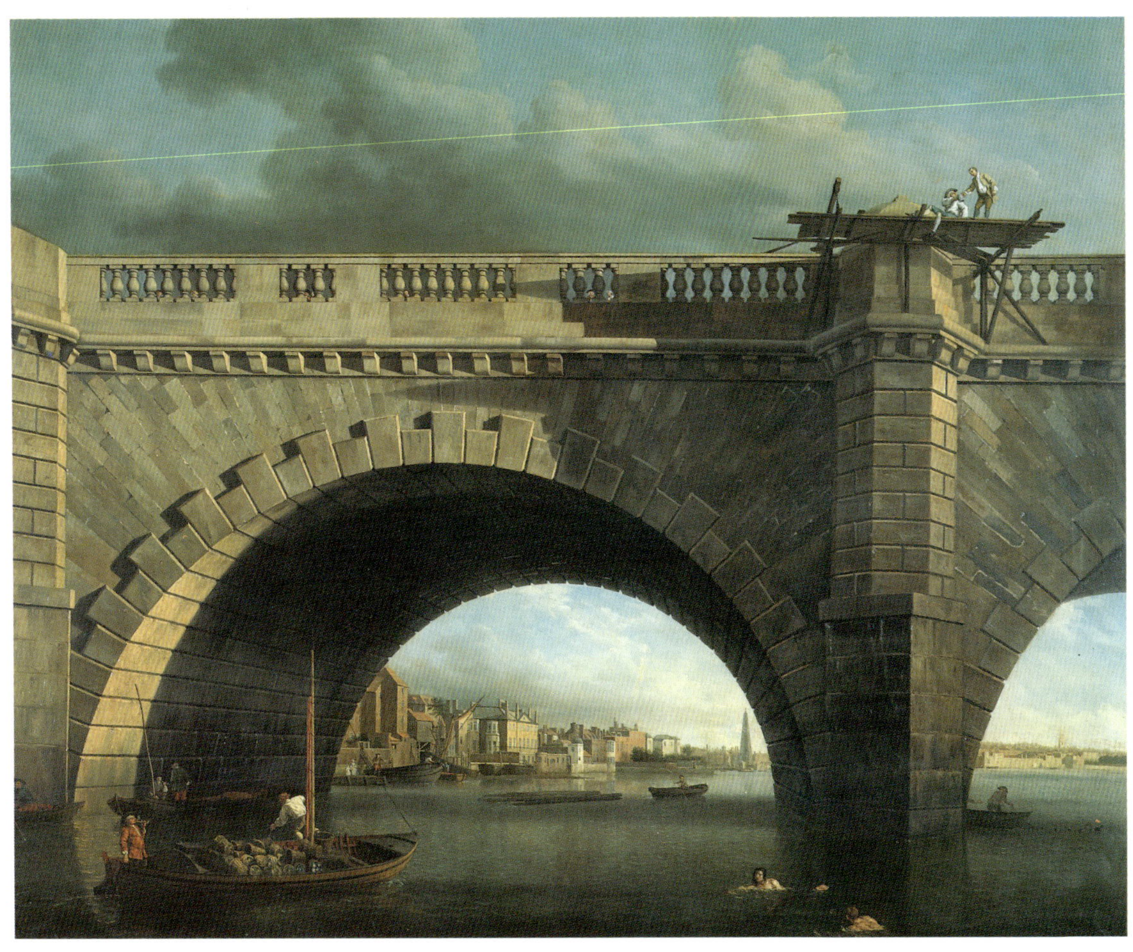

48 Samuel Scott

An arch of Westminster Bridge

Oil on canvas, ca. 1750–55
$53\frac{1}{2} \times 64\frac{1}{2}$ ins (135.9 × 163.8 cm)
The Trustees of the Tate Gallery, London

The picture shows the view through the first and part of the second arches of Westminster Bridge at the Westminster end, looking along the north bank of the Thames past the houses of Whitehall to the York Water Tower. Five versions of the subject are known, each varying slightly in details of the boats, figures and state of completion of the bridge. In this picture the scaffolding on the upper pier was presumably for the topping-off of the domed niches over each pier, work that was carried out in 1747. However, Scott's many paintings in which Westminster Bridge appears cannot be dated by the topographical evidence since he often worked from earlier drawings. The classical balance and other stylistic evidence suggest it was painted around or soon after 1750. Scott's composition is clearly related to Canaletto's *London seen through an arch of Westminster Bridge* [cat. no. 6], and it is also comparable to two drawings by the Venetian, one showing the two western arches of Westminster Bridge [cat. no. 8], the other a later view through an arch of the bridge [cat. no. 7] with the stonework completed and centring removed. The Tate Gallery painting is often considered Scott's masterpiece among his London views: it unites Canaletto's lucid topographical delineation and warm light with a subtle sense of atmosphere that gives it a definitively English accent. ML

49 Samuel Scott

'The Custom House Quay'

Oil on canvas, 1757
54 × 41 ins (137.2 × 104.2 cm)

Inscribed on the frame: Custom House Quay
in the year 1757. Painted by Scott from the
Collection of Sir Edward Walpole.

The Fishmongers' Company, London

Various suggestions have been made
about the location, but none exactly
matches the architecture and Richard
Kingzett has concluded that probably
Scott invented the scene by incorporating
into it elements from different wharf
sites.[1] There is a related drawing (Kingzett D105) in the Victoria and Albert
Museum (FA644) which shows the buildings to the right of the picture. A second,
larger version of the subject is also in the
same collection (1–1866). The painting
focuses on the trade and merchant shipping which made London so prosperous in
the eighteenth century: what commodity it
is that is being loaded is unclear. The figures near the foreground centre might be a
customs official and a shipping agent or
merchantman captain recording a cargo's
details. As usual, Scott documents the
human activity and marine detail with careful attention; the buildings are rendered
with a fine sense of sunlight playing on
different textures and there is a feeling for
atmosphere and effect which translates the
Canalettesque element into a distinguish-
ably English realism. When this picture was
painted William Marlow was an apprentice
in Scott's studio: one of his earliest subjects, *Old Fish Quay beside London Bridge*
(1761: versions in the Royal Collection and
Guildhall Art Gallery), is closely modelled
on *'The Custom House Quay'*. ML

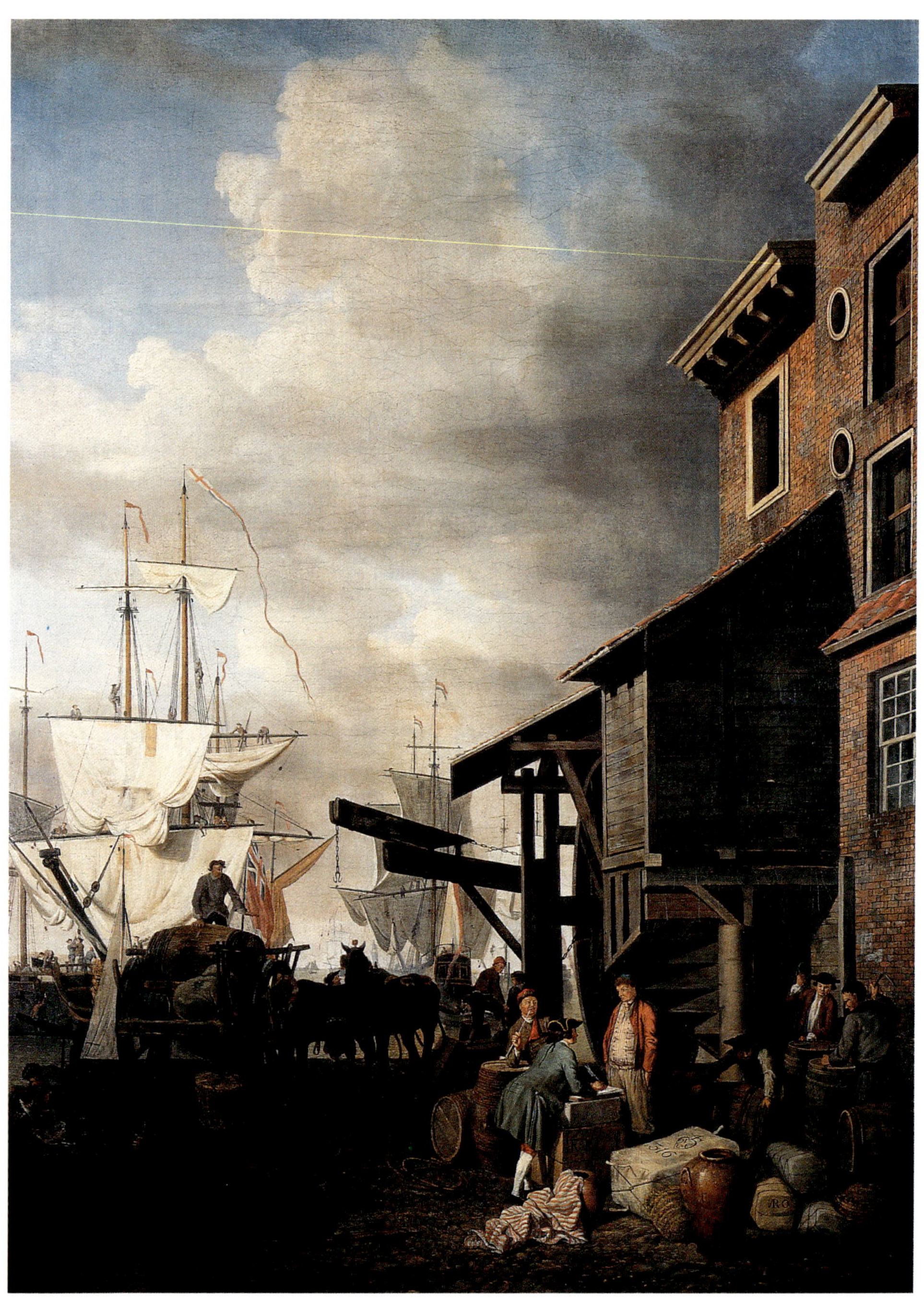

1. R. Kingzett, 'A Catalogue of the Works of
Samuel Scott', *Walpole Society* XLVIII, 1982,
pp.41–44.

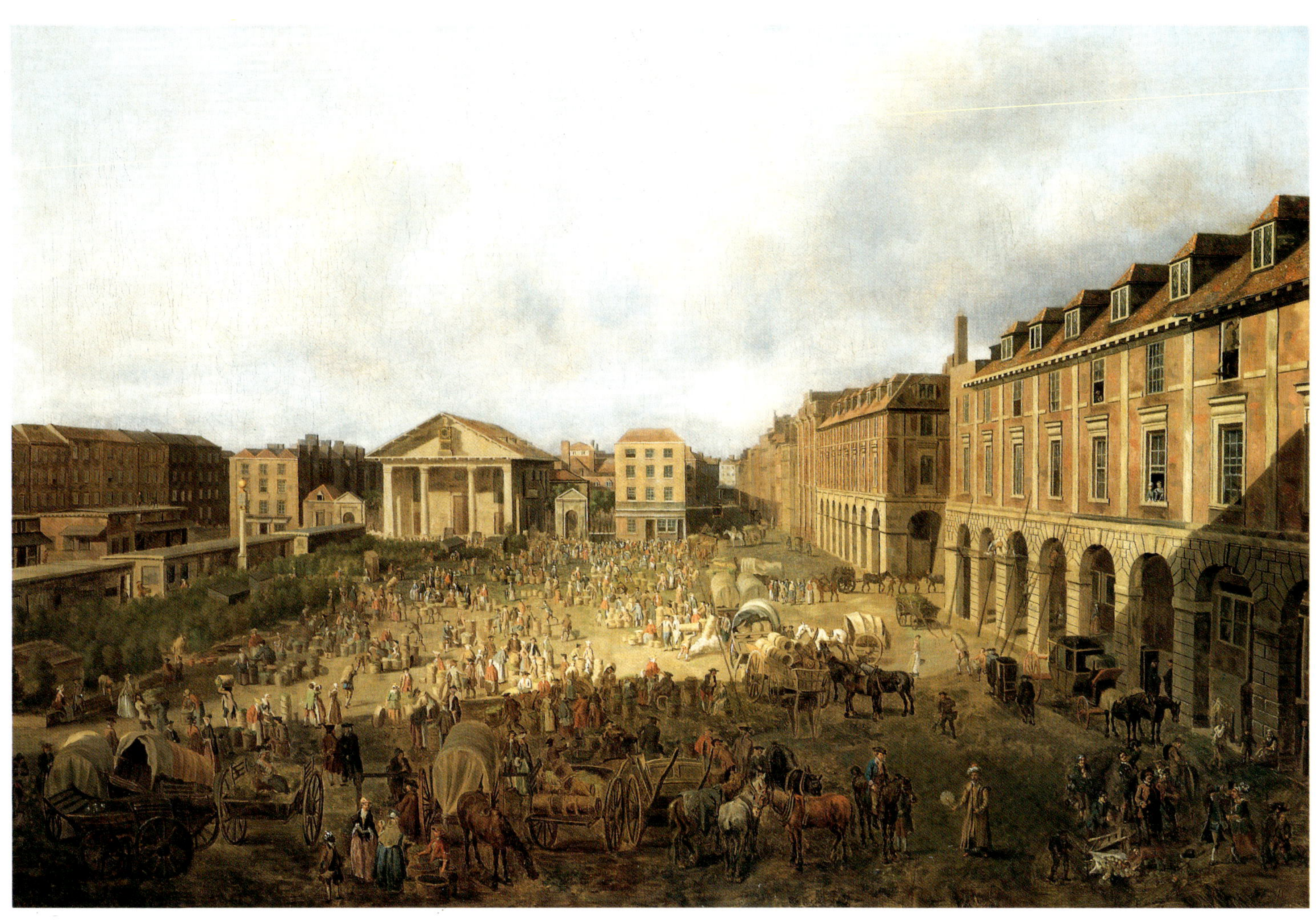

50 Samuel Scott

Covent Garden on market day

Oil on canvas, before 1761
$43\frac{3}{4} \times 66\frac{1}{2}$ ins (111.1×168.9 cm)
The Museum of London

In the 1765 sale of Scott's studio contents before he moved to Ludlow one lot consisted of "Two views of Covent Garden; one on a Market Day; the other on an Election Day". Earlier eighteenth-century artists had found the colourful, crowded spectacle of the Covent Garden market a tempting prospect which afforded the opportunity to depict a richly varied cross-section of London life. Scott's painting is crowded with incident and anecdotal detail. The overall treatment of the Piazza, people and buildings combines the Dutch town scene of the seventeenth century with echoes of Canalettesque views and a dash of seasoning from Hogarth. Across the market place the main architectural feature is the severely plain Tuscan-order temple built by Inigo Jones as the church for the new parish of St Paul's, Covent Garden; on the right are the covered arcades and simple elevations of Jones's houses, the first uniformly classical town house development of its kind in London's history. Samuel Scott lived in the Covent Garden area for much of his life, retaining

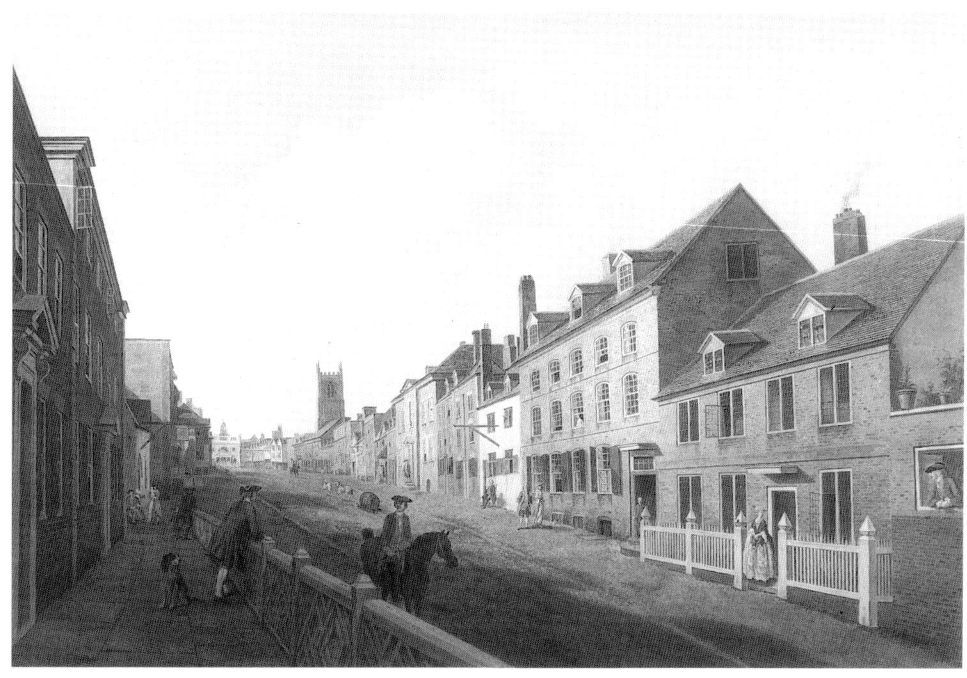

his studio there after he had acquired a property at Twickenham from 1749: the locality was popular with artists. Four Covent Garden paintings by him are recorded, and there are a number of studies of figures in watercolours and ink washes which were used in the paintings. The horses and some figures were done by one of Scott's pupils who stayed with him as an assistant for a time, Sawrey Gilpin. As he was with Scott from 1749 to 1756 as an apprentice and then as an assistant for two or three years the Covent Garden paintings must date from the end of the 1750s. The earliest record of the subject cited by Richard Kingzett is 1761. ML

51 Samuel Scott

Ludlow town

Oil on canvas, ca. 1766
29 × 43¼ ins (73.7 × 109.9 cm)
The Midland Bank Collection

In 1765 Scott retired from his London studio and Twickenham house to Ludlow in Shropshire where his daughter lived. A large sale of his collection was held (Langford & Son, 1–4 April 1765). He stayed in Ludlow until 1769 when he moved again to Bath where he died in 1772. He may have gone to Bath to find a cure for the disabling disease he endured in later life: Horace Walpole describes him as "terribly afflicted with the gout" which "harassed and terminated his life". The view looks up Broad Street to the church of St Lawrence. It gives a fascinating picture of a quiet country market town which

enjoyed some prosperity in the eighteenth century – reflected in the smart brick façades, sash windows and stone pedimented doors of the Georgian town houses fronting the street. At the end of the street an imposing new classical edifice stands as a symbol of the town's civic pride and civility. Indeed, the whole picture seems to convey the orderly values of a well regulated society. Scott kept a large collection of figure studies which he used to populate his scenes and which sometimes recur in more than one painting: here, as Richard Kingzett observed, some of Ludlow's citizens have reappeared from Covent Garden. ML

52 Samuel Scott

Westminster from Lambeth

Indian ink with grey wash and watercolour, 1743
10⅛ × 42⅛ ins (25.7 × 107 cm)
Inscribed lower left: Westminster Abbey Scott; lower right: Westminster Hall
The Trustees of the British Museum, London

This drawing was used for the architectural details of the left-hand part of one of Scott's views of Westminster, of which four painted versions exist, the earliest signed and dated 1746. From the incomplete state of Westminster Abbey's southwest tower the drawing can be dated to 1743. It shows the warehouses and yards beside the river with the finely observed details of the gothic flying buttresses of the Abbey looming over them; the tower from which the Union flag flies is St Margaret's, Westminster. Further along to the east is the long, low roof of Westminster Hall: this part of the river is now, of course, dominated by Charles Barry's Houses of

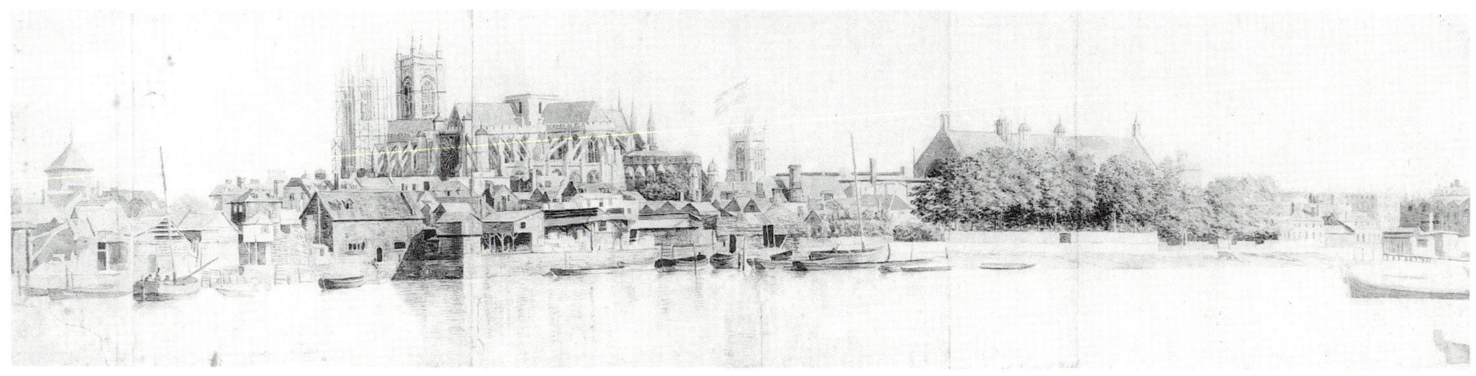

Parliament. The interest of this drawing lies mainly in the fact that it is a good example of the topographical work that Samuel Scott was doing before Canaletto arrived in London, and it illustrates the precise draughtsmanship and delicately sensitive handling of washes that characterize his drawing style generally at all periods of his career. ML

53 Samuel Scott

Twickenham Church and waterfront on the Thames

Pencil with touches of pen and ink and watercolour washes, ca. 1760
$10\frac{1}{4} \times 18\frac{1}{4}$ ins (26.1 × 46.3 cm)
The Whitworth Art Gallery, University of Manchester

At the centre of the drawing is the church of St Mary the Virgin with its medieval stone tower and classical nave built of brick to the design of John James in 1713–15. The Twickenham waterfront is probably drawn from the bank of an island opposite known as the Aight. Scott had taken a property at Twickenham in 1749, but his first dated drawing of a Twicken-

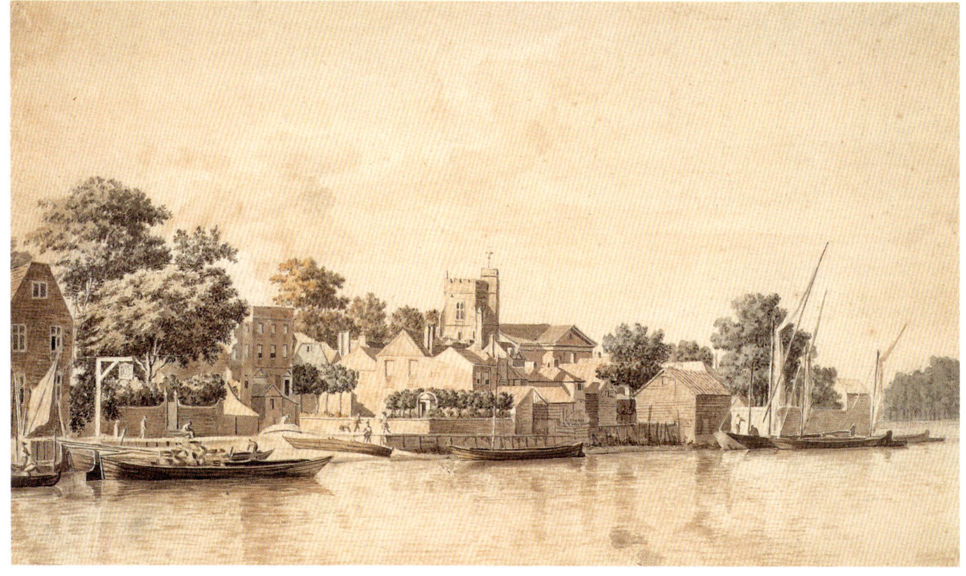

ham subject is inscribed 1758. He painted a number of picturesque river views of Twickenham which can be dated from around 1760.[1] These and his drawings of the same period are among his most delightful and informal works, showing how he adapted the luminous tones and light effects describing the textures of different buildings and foliage that he must have admired in Canaletto's work to the emerging taste for picturesque landscape in the 1750s and 1760s. As a group his

Twickenham paintings and drawings are freshly perceived and convey an atmospheric sensitivity that is peculiar to Scott. ML

1. Richard Kingzett, 'Catalogue of the Works of Samuel Scott', *Walpole Society* XLVIII, 1982, pp.64–67 (paintings), pp.103–05, D106–10 (drawings).

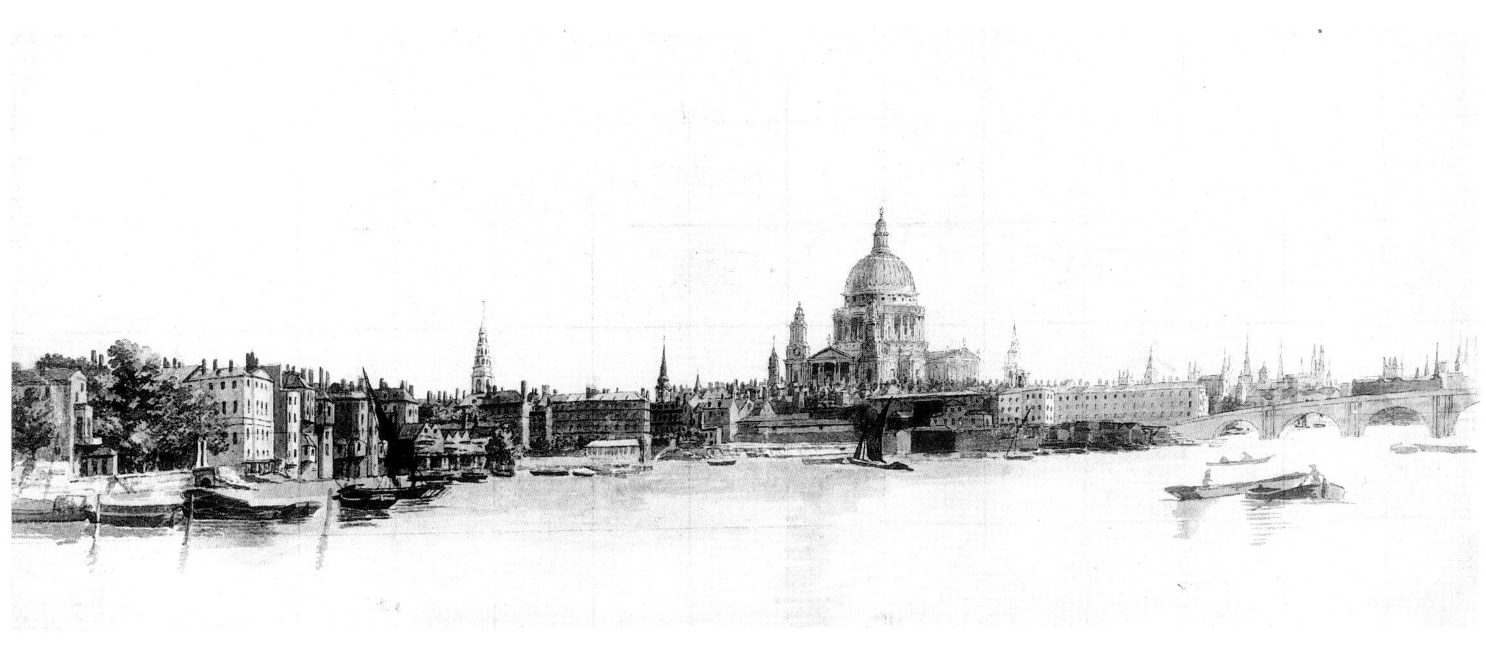

54 Samuel Scott

St Paul's from the River Thames, London

Pen and ink with watercolour, squared for
enlargement, ca.1763–65
$7\frac{1}{8} \times 16$ ins (17.9 × 44.4 cm)
The Trustees of the British Museum, London

This must be one of Scott's latest London
drawings. In 1765 he sold up and moved
to Ludlow where his daughter lived;
Blackfriars Bridge, the first arches of which
can be seen at the right of the view, was
not finished until 1769, having been started in 1760. If, as is likely, the drawing was
made from sketches taken apparently from
a boat more or less opposite Temple Gardens, it cannot have been done very long
before Scott left London. Temple Stairs are
on the extreme left, with the spires of St
Bride's Fleet Street and St Martin Ludgate
leading the eye to St Paul's; further east the
multiple spires and towers of the rest of Sir
Christopher Wren's City churches perform
a delicate ballet across the London skyline.
Comparison with the earlier drawing of
Westminster from Lambeth [cat. no. 52]
reveals how Scott's technique had evolved
over the intervening period, an evolution
in which Canaletto's influence can clearly
be detected. ML

55 Richard Wilson 1713–1782

San Giorgio Maggiore, Venice

Pen and ink with bistre wash, ca. 1751
$6\frac{3}{8} \times 9\frac{5}{16}$ ins (15.7 × 21 cm)
Sir Brinsley Ford, CBE, Hon FRA, FSA

Wilson left England for Italy late in 1750
and spent his first year abroad in Venice
before moving on to Rome at the end of
1751. He had trained as a portrait painter
under Thomas Wright in London and from
about 1736–37 until 1750 worked mainly
as a portraitist. He occasionally painted
landscapes as well, and in 1744 painted a
view of *Westminster Bridge under construction*
(private collection) which owes something
to Antonio Joli and the Venetian *veduta*
tradition. His desire for recognition as a
landscape painter was publicly expressed
by his contribution of two roundels, *St
George's Hospital* and *The Foundling Hospital*,
for display in the Foundling Hospital Court
Room in 1746. In Venice in 1751 he met
Francesco Zuccarelli and was encouraged
by him to paint landscapes in the Venetian
rococo style. He also assimilated ideas
from contemporary view-painting, and in
its technique this drawing suggests that he
experimented with the effects of pen and
wash in the manner of *vedutisti* such as
Canaletto. The sketch is the only known
example in Wilson's œuvre of a drawing
using this technique. It shows Palladio's
church of San Giorgio Maggiore across
from the Piazzetta in front of the Doge's
Palace. ML

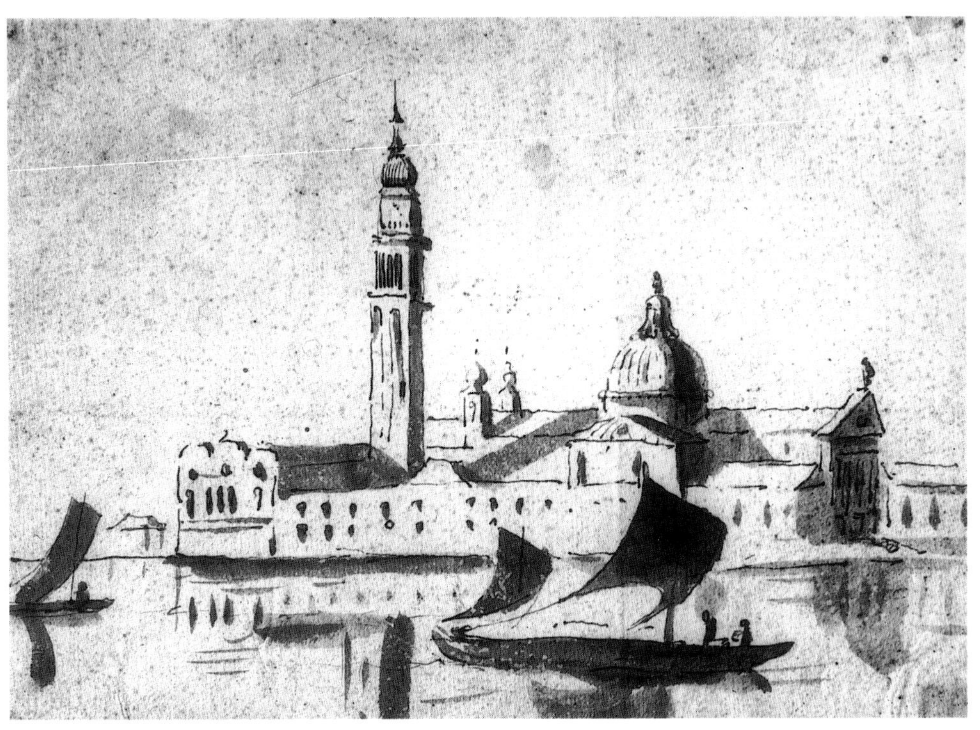

56 Richard Wilson

Cattolica

Black chalk, 1751
$6\frac{1}{2} \times 10$ ins (16.5 × 25.3 cm)
Inscribed upper left: Catolica
Sir Brinsley Ford, CBE, Hon FRA, FSA

Below the arch on the right Wilson has written "Rimini", which lies on the Adriatic coast a few miles north of Cattolica. This drawing must date from 1751 and was presumably made on the journey from Venice to Rome. A letter written from Venice by Wilson to one of his early patrons back in England mentions "Mr Smith ... our Consul here is exceedingly kind to me, he is a very great virtuoso ...".[1] Wilson also states that Smith had secured a portrait commission for him from another English visitor to Venice. Clearly he would have known Joseph Smith's collection of Canaletto paintings and drawings, and may well have met the artist himself who was visiting Venice over eight months from late 1750 to about mid-1751. The abbreviated calligraphic mannerisms Wilson uses in this and other sketches made *en route* between Venice and Rome are reminiscent of certain aspects of Canaletto's draughtsmanship in some of his drawings and etchings, but Wilson's handling is less resolved and he uses a different medium. The drawing style also suggests the influence of Zuccarelli's Venetian rococo forms. ML

1. W.G. Constable, *Richard Wilson*, London 1953, pp.21–22.

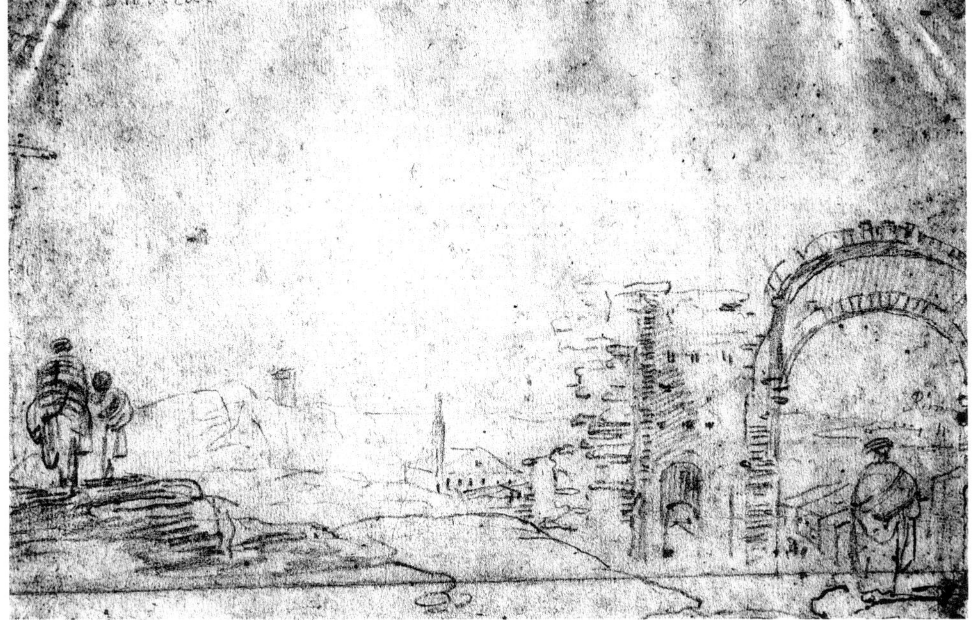

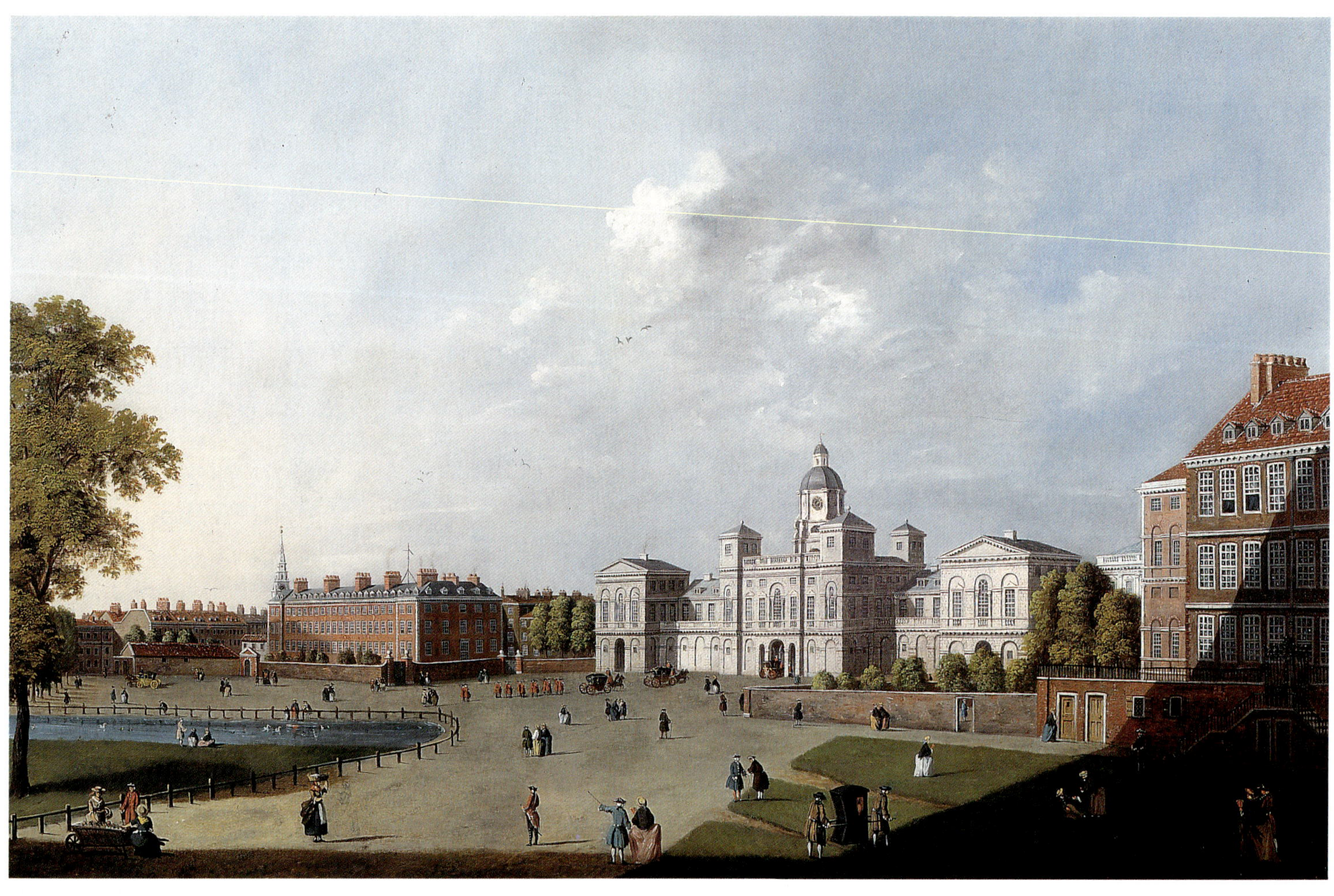

57 William James fl. 1754–71

*Horse Guards' Parade from
St James's Park, London*

Oil on canvas, ca. 1760
$23 \times 37\frac{1}{2}$ ins (58.5 × 95 cm)
Rafael Valls Ltd., London

William James is one of the most elusive
figures in eighteenth-century English
painting. A painter of the name exhibited
at the Society of Artists between 1761
and 1768, showing mostly London views
and English landscapes. Typical examples
were "The west end of Westminster
Bridge" (1767, no. 77) and "Black Fryars
Bridge, as in the year 1767" (1768, no. 74).
Curiously, in 1767 he also showed some
pictures of Egyptian antiquities, and did so
again at the Royal Academy in 1769 and
1770. He last exhibited at the Royal
Academy in 1771, showing a pair of
London views ("Westminster from the
Adelphi" and "Blackfriars Bridge from
Somerset Gardens", nos. 108, 109). The
London subjects indicate an artist who
would fit well with the Canaletto-Scott-
Marlow tradition. None of these pictures
has been positively identified, however,
and only one painting with a signature and
date ("W. James. 1759") has been recorded:
that was a copy of Canaletto's *View of the
Monument, London*, taken from the 1752
engraving [fig. 24], which appeared on the
art market some years ago but cannot now
be traced. From this evidence a large
number of London and Venetian views
imitating Canaletto and Scott have been
attributed to James. He never exhibited
any Venetian subjects, but some justifi-

cation for the assumption that they may be by him is provided by the notoriously malicious artist Edward Edwards (1738–1806), who states in his *Anecdotes of Painters*, published posthumously in 1808, that James was a pupil or assistant of Canaletto when he was in London. This is inherently unlikely, but may repeat a claim by James whom Edwards could have known.

It is clear from the multitude of copies, 'variants' and imitations of London or Venetian subjects attributed to James that more than one hand was at work. Pictures like the present example, clearly based on a known Canaletto source, in this case the 1753 engraving by Thomas Bowles from a drawing by Canaletto of the New Horse Guards, are the most likely to be by James. In its distribution of light and shade, topographical detail and proportions it exactly follows the engraving, differing only in the figures. The new Horse Guards was finished in 1753. ML

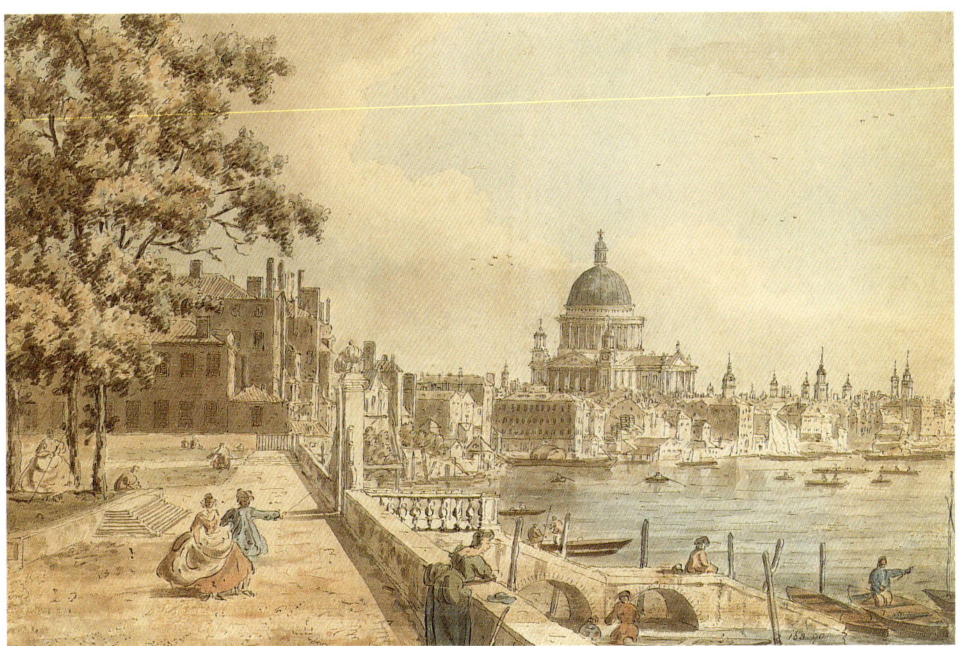

58 William James

St Paul's Cathedral and the River Thames from the terrace of Old Somerset House, London

Pen and ink with watercolour, ca. 1750–60
$9\frac{1}{4} \times 14\frac{1}{8}$ ins (23.5 × 35.9 cm)
The Trustees of the Victoria and Albert Museum, London

The attribution of this drawing rests on its very close similarity to Canaletto's treatment of the same view. Most interestingly, it seems to be closest in some details (the figure seated on the stairs leading down to the water, the woman leaning on the parapet in the foreground, the lady on the path with a gentleman flourishing his cane towards the river view) to Canaletto's drawing in the Royal Collection [cat. no. 15] which was almost certainly purchased by Consul Joseph Smith in Venice in 1750–51. If the attribution to James is secure, therefore, this could indicate that he did have some contact with Canaletto himself. Alternatively, it may have been taken from another painted version of the subject. The pen and ink drawing style clearly emulates Canaletto's calligraphy, while the watercolour washes capture a translucent tonality which follows the colour values of his paintings. ML

59 Thomas Sandby 1723–1798

The garden or river front of Old Somerset House, London

Pen and ink and watercolour, ca. 1770
$20\frac{7}{8} \times 29\frac{1}{2}$ ins (53 × 75 cm)

Inscribed in pencil on the back: T. Sandby
fect

Her Majesty The Queen

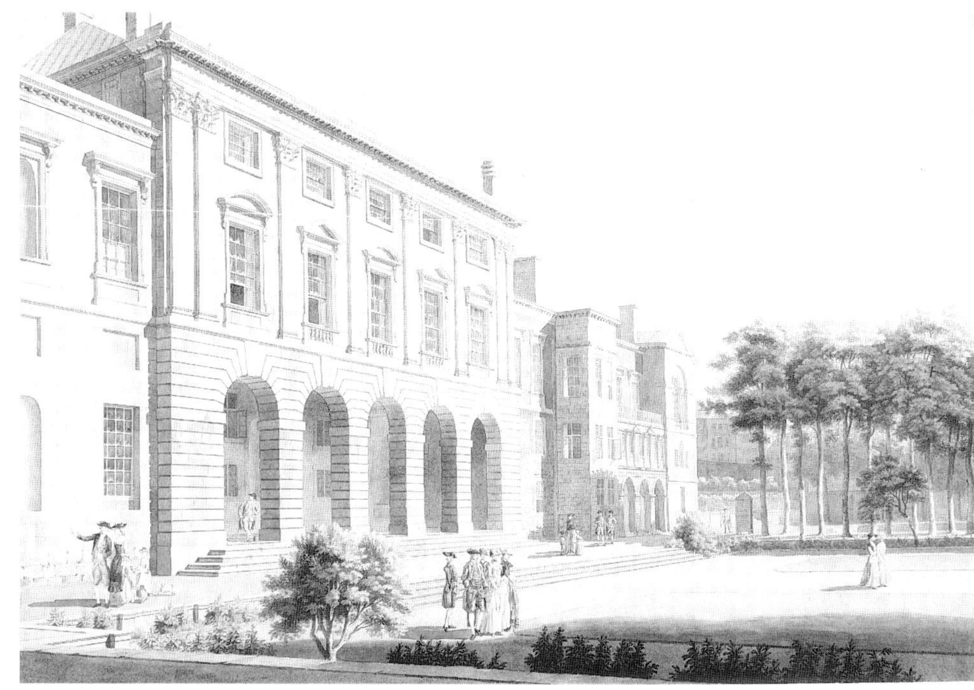

Thomas Sandby and his younger brother
Paul were born in Nottingham where
they were apparently taught to make
survey drawings and architectural perspectives and learned to compose landscapes by copying works from engravings
and draughtsmanship manuals. In 1742
Thomas Sandby joined the Ordnance
Office in London as a military draughtsman. In 1743 he was sent to Scotland
where he studied architectural drawing
with William Adam, the architect to the
Ordnance in Edinburgh. During the
1745–46 campaigns against the Jacobites
Sandby was attached to the Duke of Cumberland's staff and subsequently served
under him in the Low Countries in
1747–48. He became the Duke's personal
Draughtsman in 1750, and worked with
him and his successor on various schemes
for improving Windsor Great Park of
which he was appointed Deputy Ranger in
1765. In 1768 he was appointed the newly
founded Royal Academy's first Professor
of Architecture.

Thomas Sandby's combination of topographical artist with professional architect
and draughtsman is evident in drawings
like this. The meticulous precision with
which the buildings are drawn and their
details defined by the absolute clarity of
the lighting is typical of his architect's
approach. The figures have been added
subsequently and several have been copied
from figure studies by Paul Sandby: the
child in the group on the left is identical to
one of the daughters of Lord Waldegrave
in a drawing by Paul Sandby of about
1770, which provides an approximate date
for this view.[1] Thomas Sandby's treatment
is more purely documentary than Canaletto's *Old Somerset House from the River
Thames* [cat. no. 31], and although he was
clearly aware of the Venetian's London
views his drawings are more representative
of the descriptive English style of topography. ML

1. Luke Herrmann, *Paul and Thomas Sandby*,
London 1986, pp.84–85; Paul Sandby's
drawing is in the Victoria and Albert Museum.

60 Paul Sandby 1731–1809
and/or Thomas Sandby

Chiswick House

Watercolour with pen and pencil, ca. 1770?
19 × 26¾ ins (48.3 × 68.1 cm)

Inscribed verso: Chiswick House by
P. Sandby

Birmingham Museums and Art Gallery

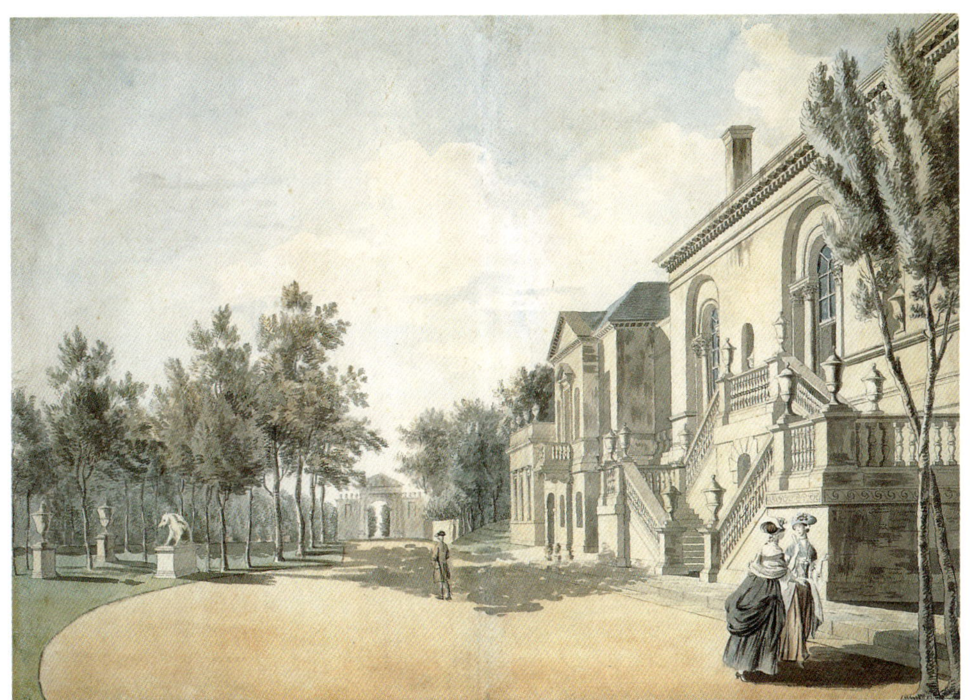

While it would be too simplistic to suggest that Thomas had a hand in all Sandby drawings with a strong architectural element, a watercolour such as this seems a likely candidate as one of the body of works to which the architect brother undoubtedly did contribute (the drawing in the Royal Collection of *The Great Bridge over Virginia Water* inscribed by Paul, "This drawing was made by the two brothers T. and P. Sandby", is one of several pieces of evidence attesting to the partnership).

Thomas Sandby was the Royal Academy's first Professor of Architecture, and in 1770 he delivered six lectures, devoting the last two to "the modern uses of the art, offering suggestions as to the choice of the situation in building both town and country houses, the precautions to be observed in laying the foundations, the distribution of plans, and the applications of decorations, illustrating his suggestions by plans of Lord Burlington's house at Chiswick and of Holkham, and by others of his own design."[1] This watercolour may derive from one of the forty or more drawings which he used as illustrations.

Designed and built by the third Earl of Burlington on his return from Italy in 1719, in association with the architect William Kent, Chiswick House has always been recognised as one of the earliest and most enthusiastic English responses to the architecture of Palladio. This view also includes the classical gateway designed in 1621 by Inigo Jones for Beaufort House, Chelsea, which was brought to the gardens at Chiswick by Lord Burlington in 1738. sw

1. William Sandby, *Thomas and Paul Sandby – Royal Academicians*, London 1892.

61 Paul Sandby

The Round Tower, Windsor Castle

Pencil and watercolour, 1756?
$11\frac{1}{2} \times 20\frac{1}{2}$ ins (29.2 × 57.1 cm)
The Provost and Fellows of Eton College

Like his elder brother Thomas, Paul
Sandby started his professional career as a
military draughtsman. In 1747 he joined
the Board of Ordnance in London and was
sent to work with the Military Survey of
Scotland. His official duties involved
making accurate survey drawings of Scot-
tish topography from which maps and
views suitable for military purposes were
prepared. In the aftermath of the 1745
Jacobite rebellion the Survey was intended
to provide accurate information about the
country as a precaution against another
insurrection. While he was in Scotland
Sandby also made sketches and etchings of
local scenery in which he was able to
develop his skills as a landscape artist and
figure draughtsman. In 1752 he returned to
London and for the next few years he lived
and worked there and at Windsor with his
brother who had been appointed
Draughtsman to the Duke of Cumberland,
George II's son and Ranger of Windsor
Great Park. In London in the 1750s and
1760s Paul Sandby's prolific output
included topographical watercolours, landscape paintings and etchings, and engraved
views; he was also prominently active in
promoting the professional advancement
of the fine arts, participating in the forma-
tion of the Society of Artists in 1761 and
becoming a foundation member of the
Royal Academy in 1768. His earlier topographical drawings are most obviously
influenced by his training in survey work
and by Thomas Sandby's professional
architectural draughtsmanship, but in their
light effects and clear tones they also show

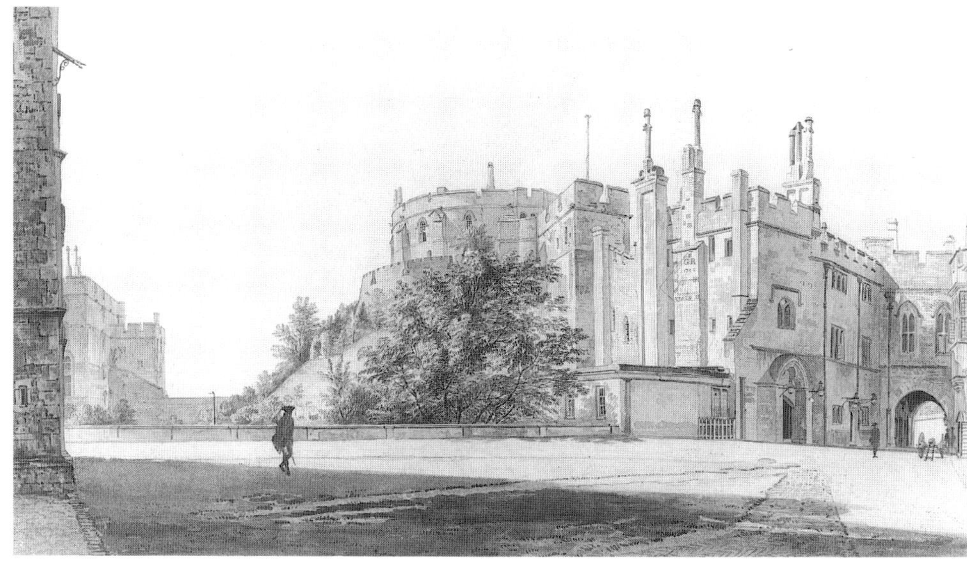

that he admired particular qualities in the
work of Canaletto and his English followers. Above all, perhaps, Paul Sandby
demonstrates how the English topographical tradition was able to accommodate and
absorb aspects of Canaletto's style without
seeming to become derivative or imitative.
This is especially true of the Windsor
watercolours he did from the 1750s to the
1770s, of which this may be a relatively
early example. The date 1756 shown on
the sundial below one of the chimneys
may, it has been suggested, be the date of
the watercolour.[1] ML

1. Luke Herrmann, *Paul and Thomas Sandby*,
London 1986, p.29.

62 Paul Sandby

*The west end of St George's Chapel
and the entrance to the Singing
Men's Cloister, Windsor Castle*

Pencil, pen and ink, and watercolour,
ca. 1765–70
$9\frac{1}{2} \times 12\frac{5}{8}$ ins (24 × 32.2 cm)

63 Paul Sandby

*The entrance to the Singing Men's
Cloister, with Crane's Building,
Windsor Castle*

Pencil, pen and ink, and watercolour,
ca. 1765–70
$9 \times 12\frac{3}{4}$ ins (23 × 32.5 cm)
Her Majesty The Queen

Sandby first exhibited a Windsor subject
at the Society of Artists in 1763 (no. 113:

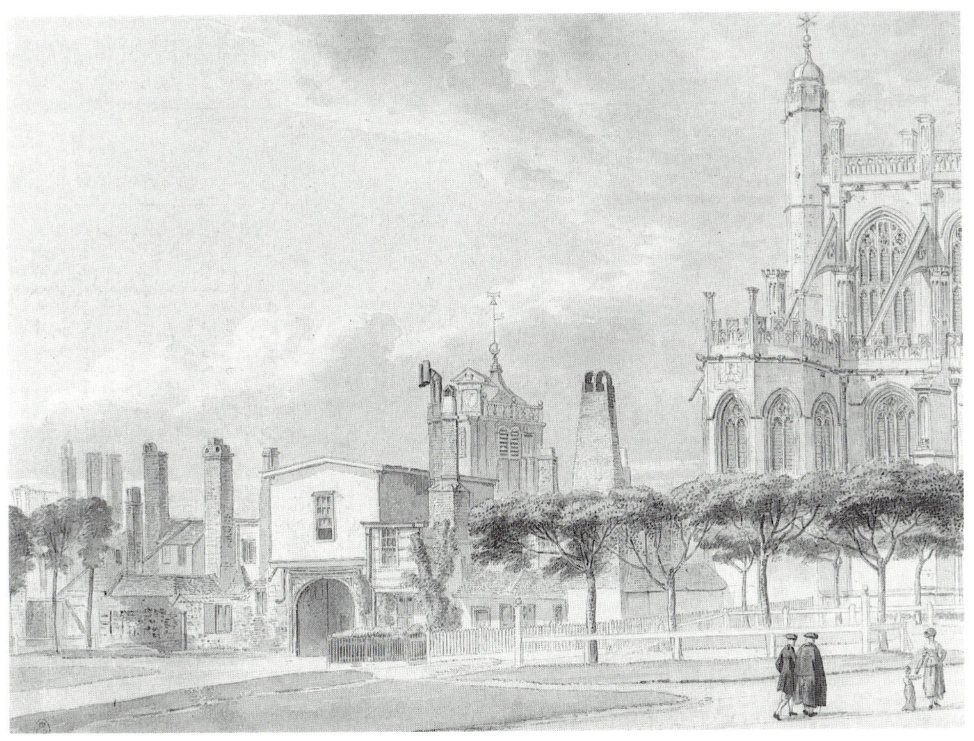

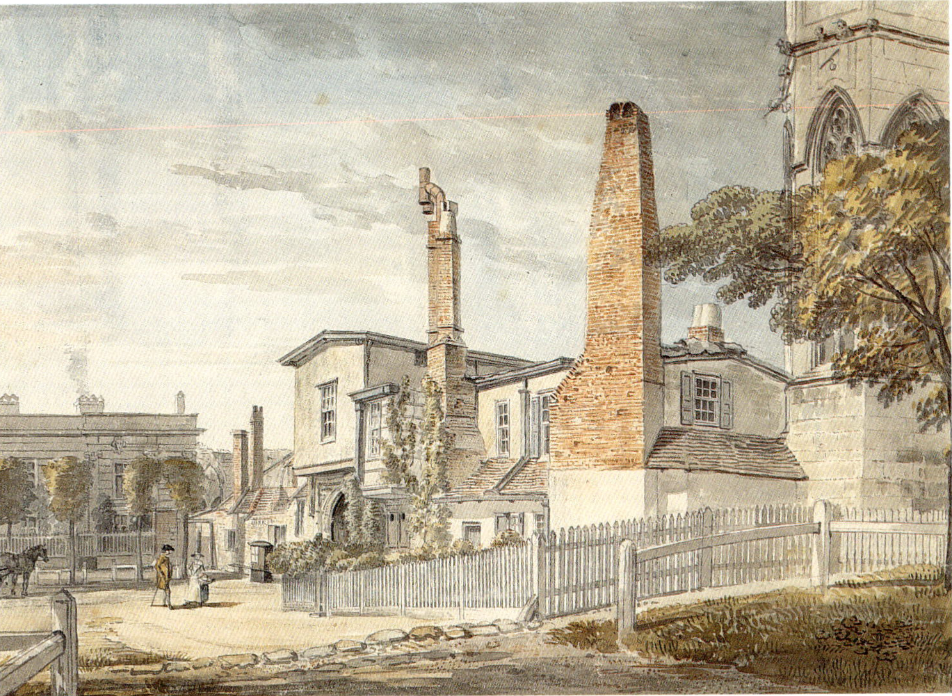

"A gateway in Windsor Castle"). In 1765 he showed three Windsor Castle scenes: a view of "Windsor Castle from the Gateway of a Brewhouse Yard, Datchet Lane", another of "Windsor Castle from Love Lane", and the third described as "Entrance in to the Singing Men's Cloister, and the West End of H.M. Chapel of St George in Windsor Castle" (nos. 232–34). There is a larger, more finished version of the first of these two watercolours at Yale which may be the view exhibited in 1765: its technique of gouache (bodycolour) suggests that it may have been intended for exhibition. Both these drawings were originally in the collection of Sir Joseph Banks, one of Sandby's most important patrons, with whom he made a tour of South Wales in 1773 from which two years later he produced and published a set of twelve aquatint views of architectural antiquities set in picturesque landscapes. A group of Windsor drawings was purchased for the Royal Collection in 1876 when the Banks collection was dispersed. They are particularly fresh and delicate examples of Sandby's topographical drawing, especially notable for the subtlety with which the effects of light and the picturesque details of the architecture are rendered. ML

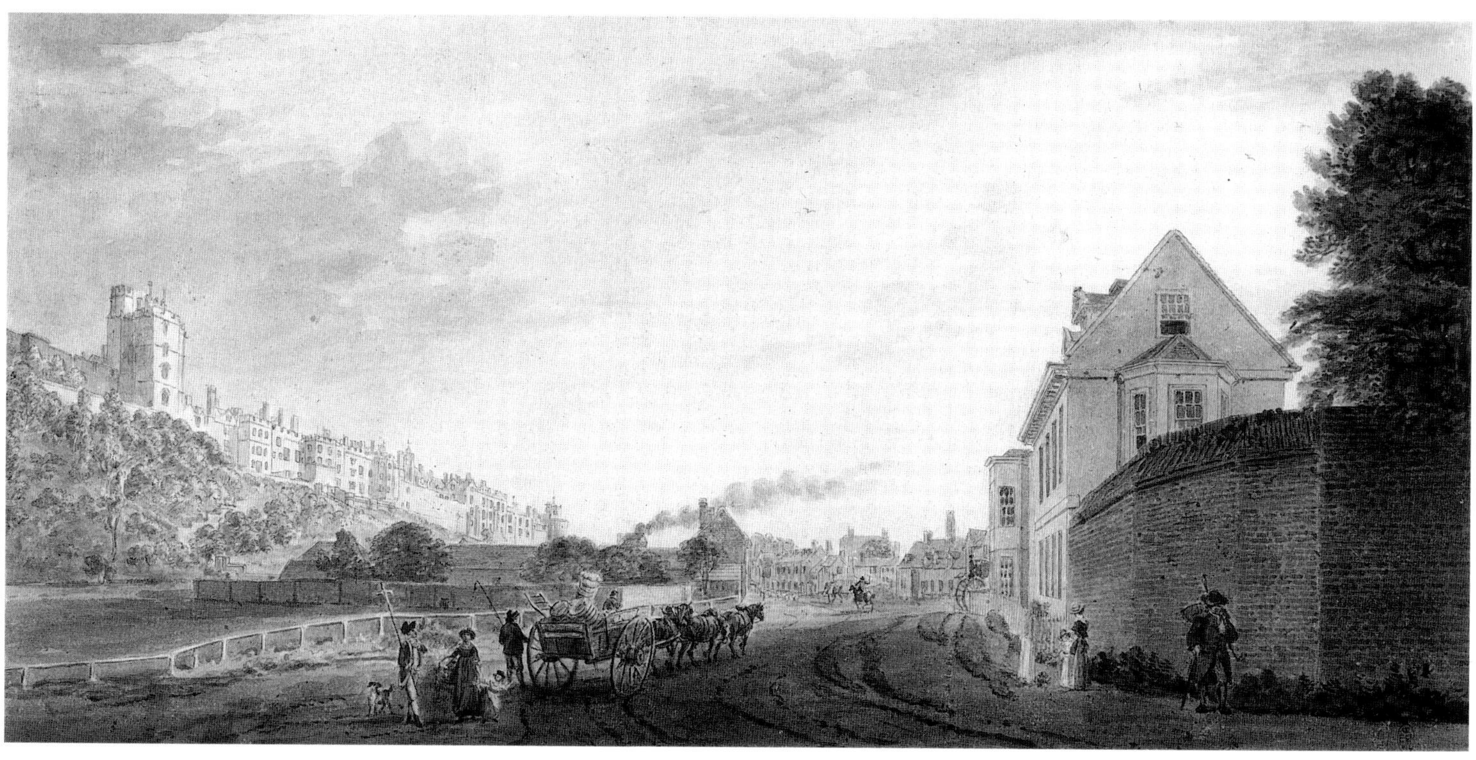

64 Paul Sandby

Windsor Castle from Datchet Lane

Pencil, pen and ink, and watercolour, 1770?
$8\frac{1}{2} \times 17\frac{1}{8}$ ins (21.7 × 43.5 cm)
Her Majesty The Queen

An inscription on the mount, apparently
copied from an earlier hand, gives the
date of this drawing as 1770. The
extended view with its wide foreground is
reminiscent compositionally of some of
Canaletto's prospects, for example those of
the Old and New Horse Guards from St
James's Park [cat. no. 19] and also a picture
such as his *Windsor Castle* painted for Sir
Hugh Smithson [fig. 3]. The introduction of
more picturesque details of the houses
along Datchet Lane and the evening effect
of the setting sun give Sandby's view a
more specifically English character and
shows how he developed the topographical tradition into a more atmospherically
suggestive vehicle. The view of the Castle
shows part of its north front with Win-
chester Tower. ML

65 Paul Sandby

*A view from the gardens of
Somerset House, London, looking
east to the City and St Paul's
Cathedral*

Pencil, pen and ink, and watercolour,
ca. 1755
$8 \times 20\frac{1}{2}$ ins (20.3 × 52.1 cm)

66 Paul Sandby

*A view from the gardens of
Somerset House, London, looking
west to Westminster Abbey and
Bridge*

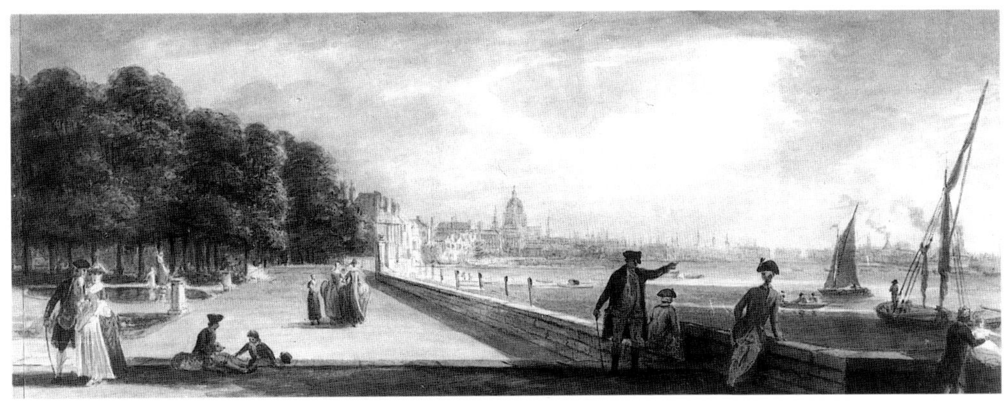

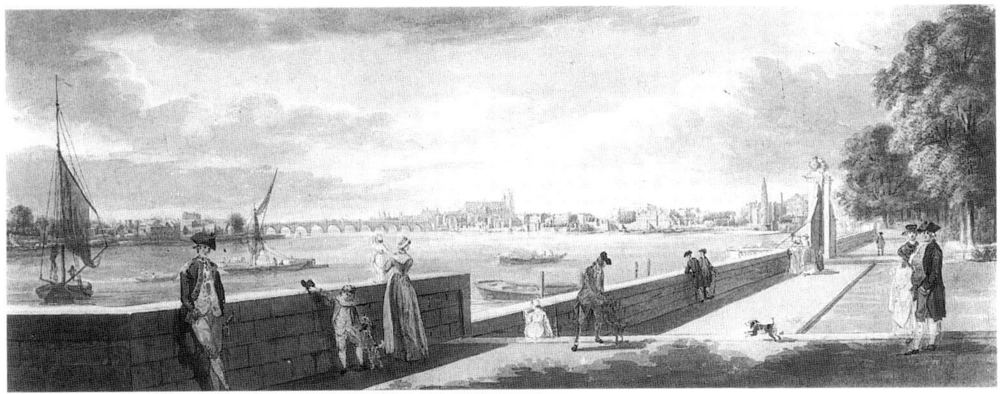

Pencil, pen and ink, and watercolour,
ca. 1755
$7\frac{3}{4} \times 20\frac{1}{2}$ ins (18.7 × 52.1 cm)
Sir Brinsley Ford, CBE, Hon FRA, FSA

The views towards the City and Westminster from the terrace of Old Somerset House were depicted by a number of eighteenth-century English artists in the 1750s, and because Canaletto painted similarly extensive prospects of the River Thames from the same site and engravings were published of one of the pairs of pictures in which he recorded these scenes their repetition by others is generally attributed to his influence. He was not, however, the first to portray the view from Somerset House. A very similar view looking westwards had been engraved by Jean Maurer in 1742, and it has been suggested that Canaletto was very probably influenced in his own choice of some London subjects by images that were already available as prints.[1] Of two other views by Paul Sandby very similar to these in the British Museum, that of Westminster has been associated with the Maurer engraving, and it seems certain that in his early London views he drew upon a varied repertoire of sources.[2] Although he must have been aware of Canaletto's views, his watercolour technique is more responsive to the transient effects of light and atmosphere the English climate produces. Since Old

London Bridge is visible in the distance in the view looking down river past the City these watercolours must date from around the middle of the 1750s. ML

1. Bruce Robertson, *The Art of Paul Sandby*, New Haven, Yale Center for British Art, 1985, no. 9.

2. Lindsay Stainton, *British Landscape Watercolours 1600–1860*, London, British Museum, 1985, nos. 21a, b.

67 Paul Sandby

Warwick Castle from the river

Watercolour over pencil, ca. 1775
$19\frac{3}{4} \times 29\frac{7}{8}$ ins (50.3 × 75.9 cm)
Birmingham Museums and Art Gallery

Sandby exhibited two views of Warwick Castle at the Royal Academy exhibition of 1775 (described, in the tenor of the time, as "stained drawings"). These may probably be identified with the two large watercolours now in the Victoria and Albert Museum and Birmingham collections.

Each was used as the model for one of the *Four Views of Warwick Castle*, a set of sepia aquatints published by John Boydell in 1775–76. One of Sandby's pupils and patrons, the Hon. Charles Greville, younger son of the first Earl of Warwick, purchased the formula for the aquatint process from one Peter Burdett of Liverpool and presented it to Sandby. A 1773 tour of Wales in the company of Joseph Banks and Greville resulted in the artist's highly successful first experiments in the medium, twelve *Views in South Wales*, published in 1775.

Titled on the aquatint *Part of Warwick Castle from the South East*, the view shows the (now ruinous) medieval bridge over the Avon in use: in 1790 this was superseded by a new bridge on the Banbury road. The great west tower of St Mary's, Warwick, rebuilt in 1698–1704 to the designs of Sir William Wilson, which also figures in Canaletto's drawing of the church [cat. no. 26], can be seen through the trees on the right. sw

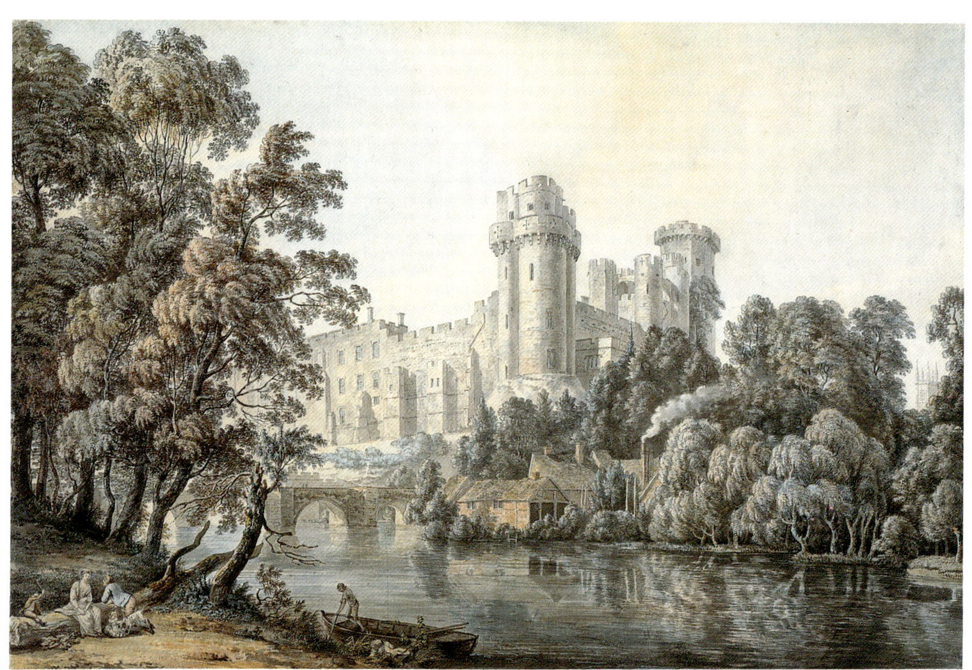

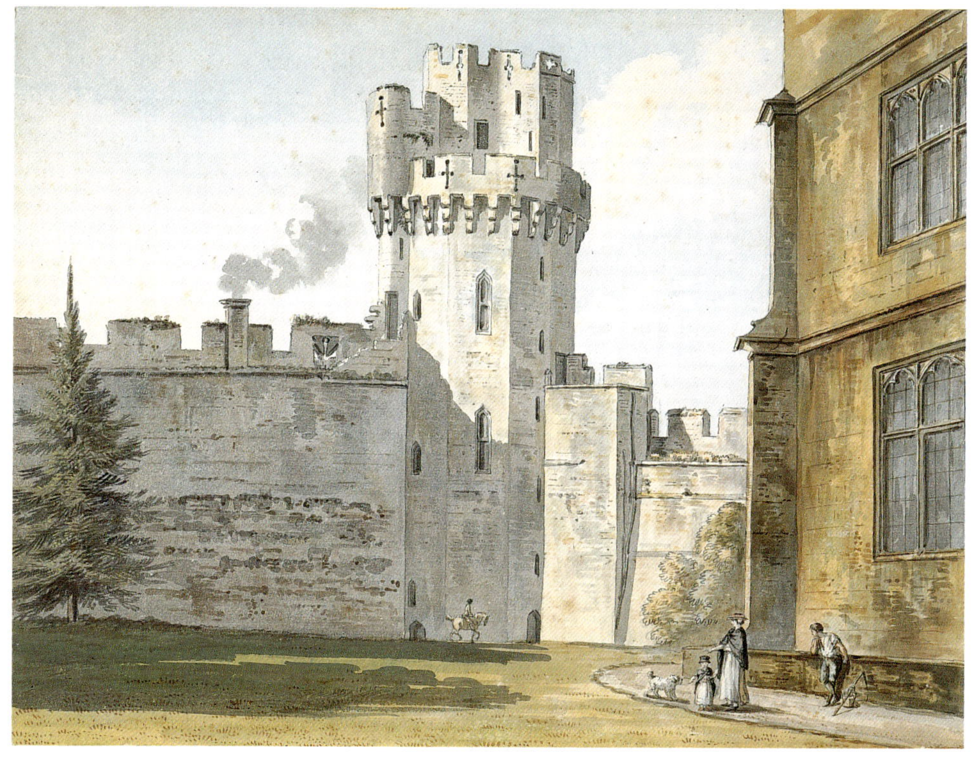

68 Paul Sandby

*Caesar's Tower, Warwick Castle,
from the inner court*

Watercolour over pencil, ca. 1775
$11\frac{3}{4} \times 15\frac{7}{8}$ ins (30 × 40.3 cm)
Inscribed verso: Part of [crossed out] Guy's
Tower in Warwick Castle P. Sandby; and
number: 4
Birmingham Museums and Art Gallery

In its simple but brilliant rendering of
architectural detail and local colour, this
work is quite unlike Sandby's formal style
of finished watercolour, and feels more
akin to the oils of Warwick Castle by
Canaletto, with which he was doubtless
familiar. Presumably dating from the same
time as his work on the exhibition watercolours and aquatints [cat. no. 67] it may
be one of a series of more informal views
either suggested or commissioned by the
artist's patron the Hon. Charles Greville.

   Effectively reproducing the right half of
Canaletto's *East Front from the inner court*
[cat. no. 24], but from closer range, the
composition similarly just includes a corner
of the domestic apartments, showing a
recent insertion of 'Gothick' fenestration.
One of the young saplings shown in the
1752 painting seems happily to have
matured. SW

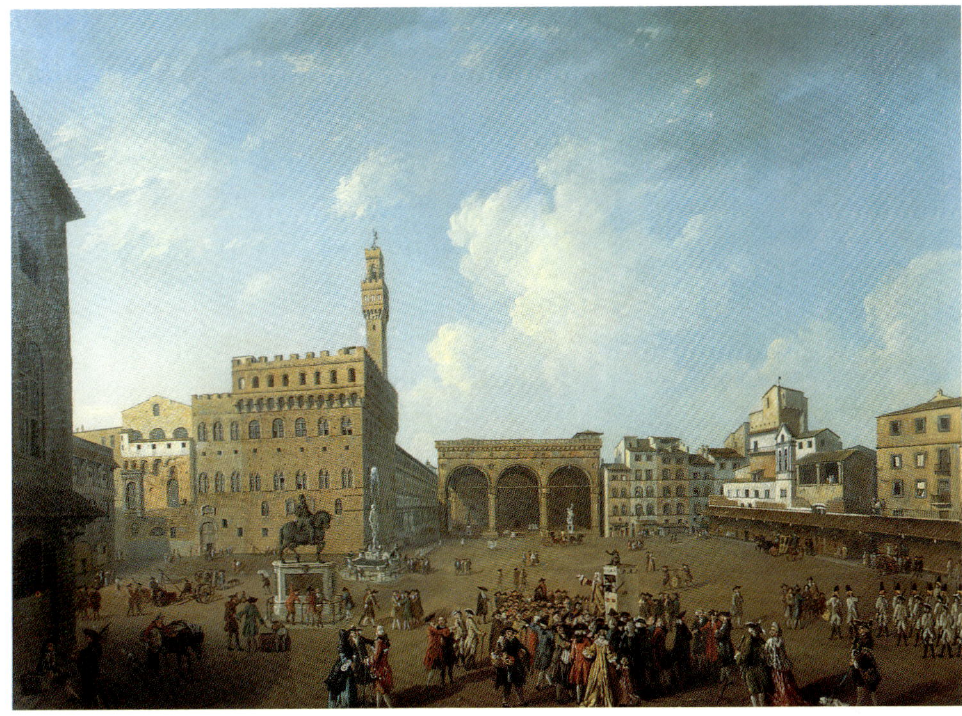

69 Thomas Patch 1725–1782

The Piazza della Signoria, Florence

Oil on canvas, 1763
$34\frac{1}{2} \times 48$ ins (88.2 × 122 cm)
Plymouth Museums and Art Gallery

The view is taken from opposite the
Loggia dei Lanzi in which two of the
most celebrated sixteenth-century Floren-
tine Renaissance sculptures were displayed, Benvenuto Cellini's bronze *Judith
with the head of Holofernes* seen through the
left arch and Giovanni da Bologna's *Rape of
the Sabine* beneath the right arch. On the
left is the medieval Palazzo Vecchio: the
nearer of the two statues just visible in the
shadows flanking the entrance is
Michelangelo's *David*. Beyond, extending
down towards the River Arno, is the long
façade of the Uffizi.

Thomas Patch was born in Exeter and
went to Rome in 1747 where he studied
with the French landscape painter Claude-
Joseph Vernet. At the same time he was
acting as a guide to English visitors and as
an agent in the acquisition and shipment of
works of art. Expelled from Rome by the
Holy Office for heretical activities of some
sort in 1755 he moved to Florence where
he remained, dying there in 1782. As well
as landscapes and views as souvenirs for
Grand Tourists he also painted caricatures
of English visitors including several of con-
vivial company drinking and dining at the
house of Sir Horace Mann, the British
Envoy to the Grand Duchy of Tuscany. In
1760 Patch was in Venice where he very
probably saw the Canaletto paintings in
Consul Joseph Smith's collection. He must
also have seen paintings by Canaletto's
nephew, Bernardo Bellotto, who had
painted in Florence in 1745. ML

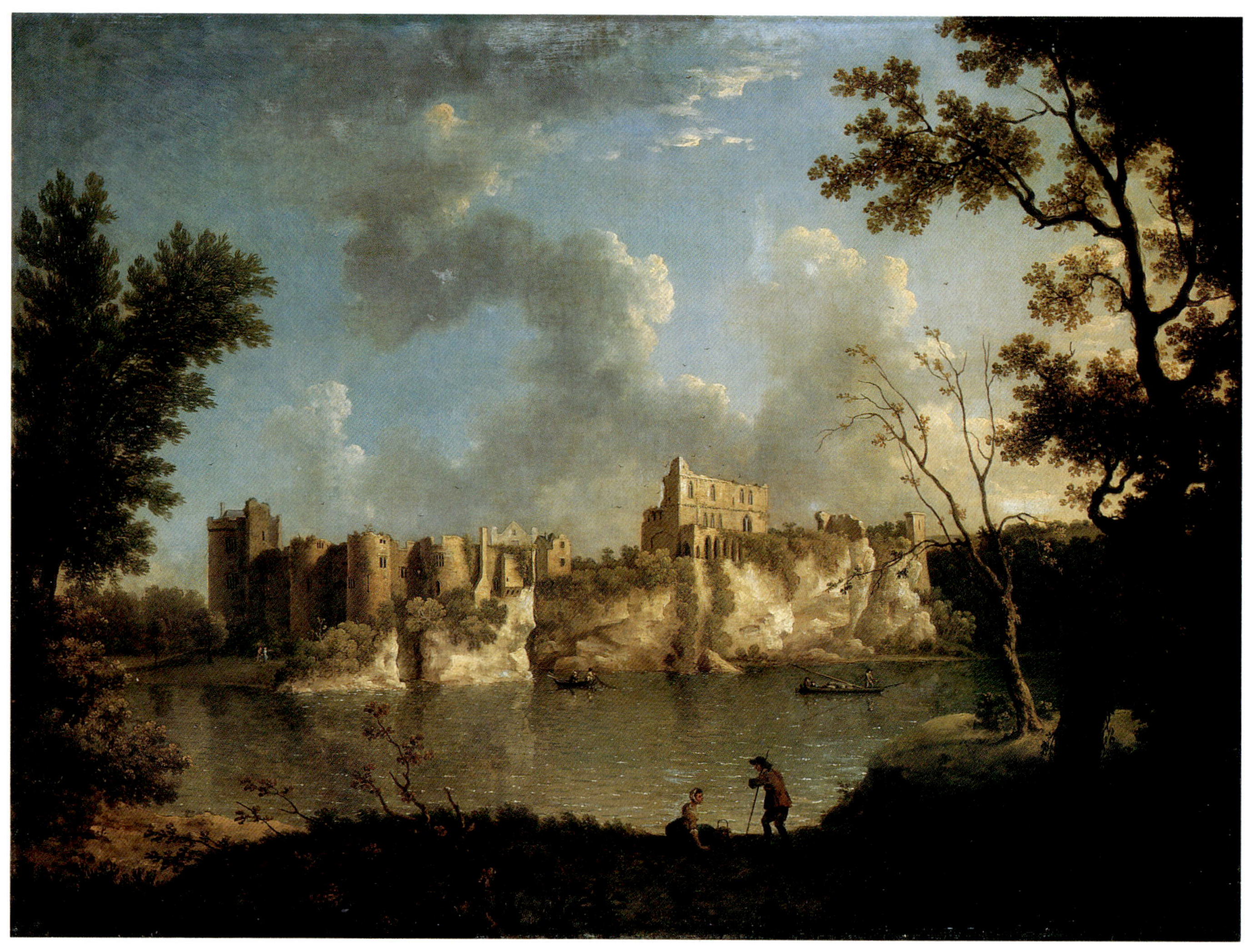

70 John Inigo Richards
1731–1810

Chepstow Castle and the River Wye

Oil on canvas, ca. 1776
$29\frac{11}{16} \times 41\frac{1}{8}$ ins (75.4 × 104.4 cm)
National Museum of Wales, Cardiff

Richards regularly exhibited topographical and rural landscapes at the Society of Artists from 1762 to 1768 and then at the Royal Academy, of which he was appointed a foundation member in 1768, from 1769 until 1809. In 1788 he was elected the Academy's Secretary. He generally applied the principles of picturesque composition to his landscapes and views, and in a painting such as this the architecture and scenery are combined to produce the kind of decorative prospect which becomes a standard convention of so much topographical painting in the second half of the eighteenth century. In his treatment of the picturesquely ruined castle Richards might be compared to artists like Paul Sandby and William Marlow. The latter especially was exhibiting views in the early 1760s which are very similar to this in treatment and handling. This is probably the *Chepstow Castle* Richards exhibited at the Royal Academy in 1776 (no. 248). ML

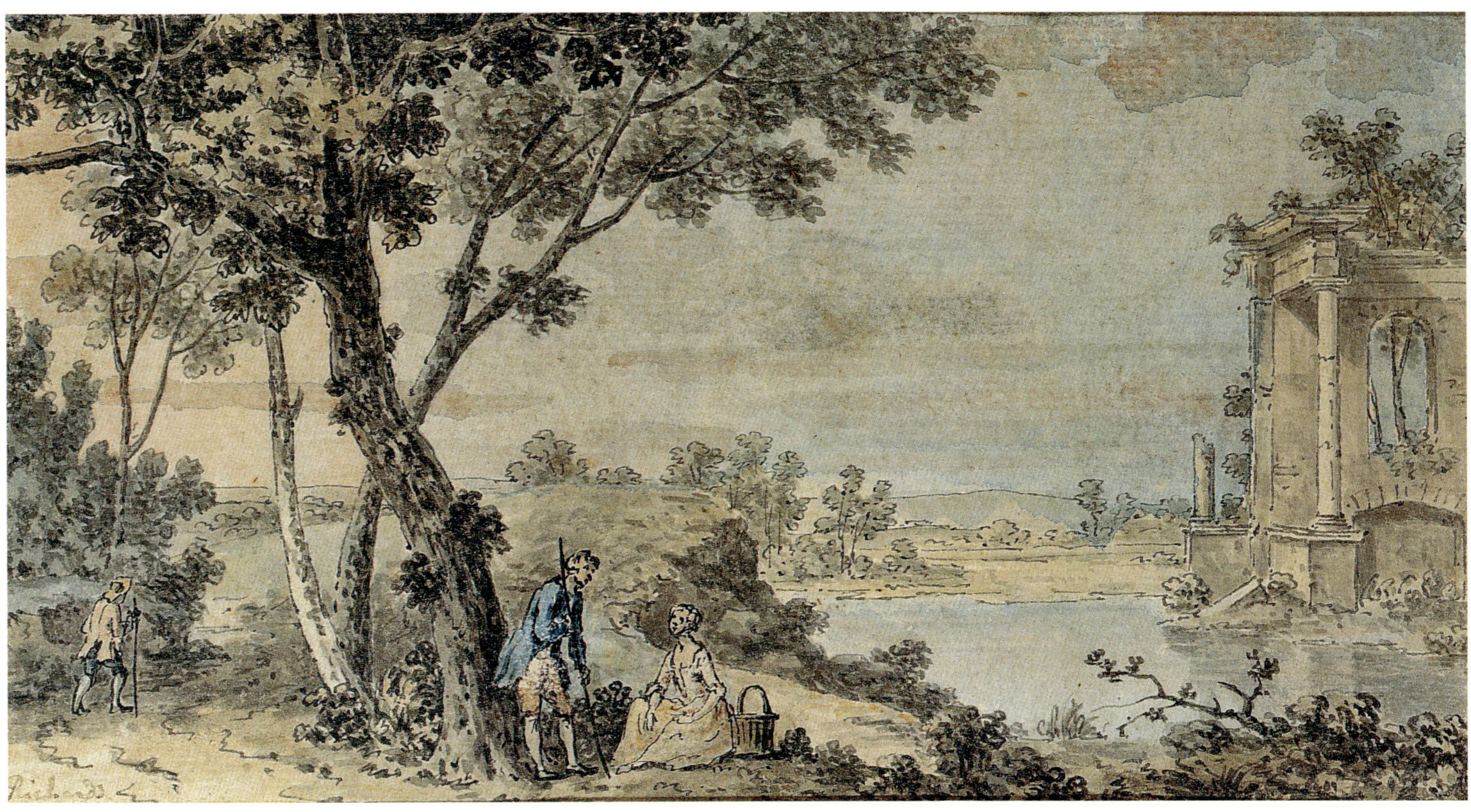

71 John Inigo Richards

*Landscape with figures by a lake
and ruins*

Pen and ink with wash
$5\frac{1}{2} \times 9\frac{1}{2}$ ins (13.9 × 24.1 cm)
Signed lower left: J. Richards

The Corporation of London (National Loans
Collection Trust – the S.C. Turner bequest),
Guildhall Art Gallery

As well as topographical views and landscapes of actual scenery Richards painted
imaginary compositions which included
capricci of Italianate buildings and classical
ruins, pastorals and invented rural subjects.
For some time he worked as a scene-
painter at Covent Garden Theatre, an
experience which no doubt contributed to
his inventive facility. The composition of
this drawing combines pastoral landscape
with ruin *capriccio*. Its rococo charm and
decorative elegance suggest the influence
of the Venetian landscape painter Francesco Zuccarelli who was in England
1752–62 and again 1765–71. The drawing
style may reflect a knowledge of Canaletto's draughtsmanship in details such as the
ruin and the landscape beyond it, but the
foreground figures and the rest of the composition follow English rococo and picturesque conventions. The result is a purely
decorative synthesis of a variety of the
different ingredients which are to be found
in English landscape of the third quarter of
the eighteenth century. ML

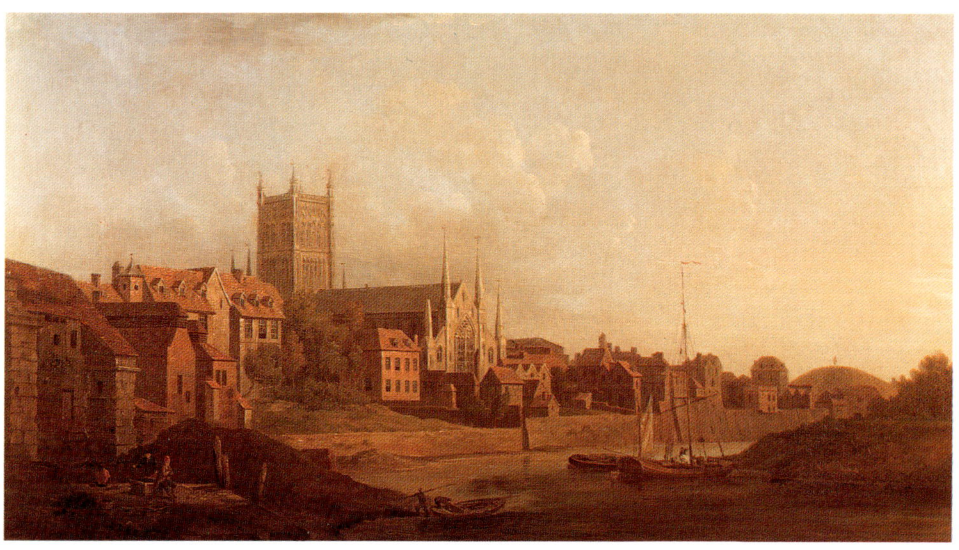

73 William Marlow

*St Paul's and Blackfriars Bridge,
London*

Oil on canvas, ca. 1770–75
$20\frac{1}{4} \times 29\frac{1}{2}$ ins (51.3×74.7 cm)
Signed lower right: W. Marlow
Yale Center for British Art (Paul Mellon
Collection), New Haven

Blackfriars Bridge was completed in 1769
and this view must have been painted soon
afterwards. It is one of the freshest and
compositionally most successful of Marlow's London scenes and one which he
repeated with variations to the boats and
right foreground: there are at least three
oval versions, each paired with a view of
Westminster Abbey and Bridge and differ-
entiated as early morning sunrise (St Paul's)
and evening sunset (Westminster) views.
One of the pairs now belonging to the
Guildhall Art Gallery, City of London, was
originally owned by the actor David Garrick and hung at his house in The Adelphi.
The view is taken from the south bank
opposite Temple Gardens; on the other
side of the river the Carpenters' Company
timber wharf is clearly visible. In the way
he has painted the distant details glimpsed
through the arches of the bridge and the
activity along the waterfront opposite
using a summary notation of abbreviated
dots and dashes of paint for the accents
Marlow's technique evidently derives from
Canaletto. ML

72 William Marlow 1740–1813

Worcester from the River Severn

Oil on canvas, ca. 1765
$21 \times 37\frac{3}{4}$ ins (53.3×95.9 cm)
Worcester Museum and Art Gallery

William Marlow was born in Southwark
in 1740 and studied under Samuel Scott for
five years from 1754 to 1759. He may
have stayed with Scott for a year or two
after completing his formal apprenticeship.
In 1762 he exhibited for the first time,
showing "A View of part of Worcester" at
the Society of Artists. From then until
1765 he painted mainly views and a few
picturesque landscapes with architectural
antiquities, as well as occasional country
house 'portraits'. His style is often very
close to Samuel Scott's, and in early
London pictures from this period he relies
heavily on his teacher's compositional
methods and treatment of architecture. In
the early 1760s he probably also made
some copies from Canaletto: two paintings
reproducing his *View of Alnwick Castle* survive which show that he had some connection with the Earl of Northumberland. In
1765–66 Marlow toured France and Italy;
he was apparently supported financially by
the Countess of Northumberland for
whom he painted a set of Italian landscapes
and coastal scenes. After he returned in
1766 (not in 1768 as is usually stated) he
painted and exhibited a great many French
and Italian subjects in oils and watercolours, but he also continued to produce
London views, English topographical subjects, country house commissions and landscapes in which he follows standard
picturesque conventions. From the 1770s
he was living in a house in Twickenham
which had formerly been Samuel Scott's,
but his success was declining by the 1790s
when his views and landscapes were
becoming rather old fashioned. He seems
to have more or less given up practising
by 1800.

In this early picture the Canaletto-Scott
influence is clearly apparent. There is
another less extended version of the subject which may be the 1762 Society of
Artists picture (sold at Christie's, 16

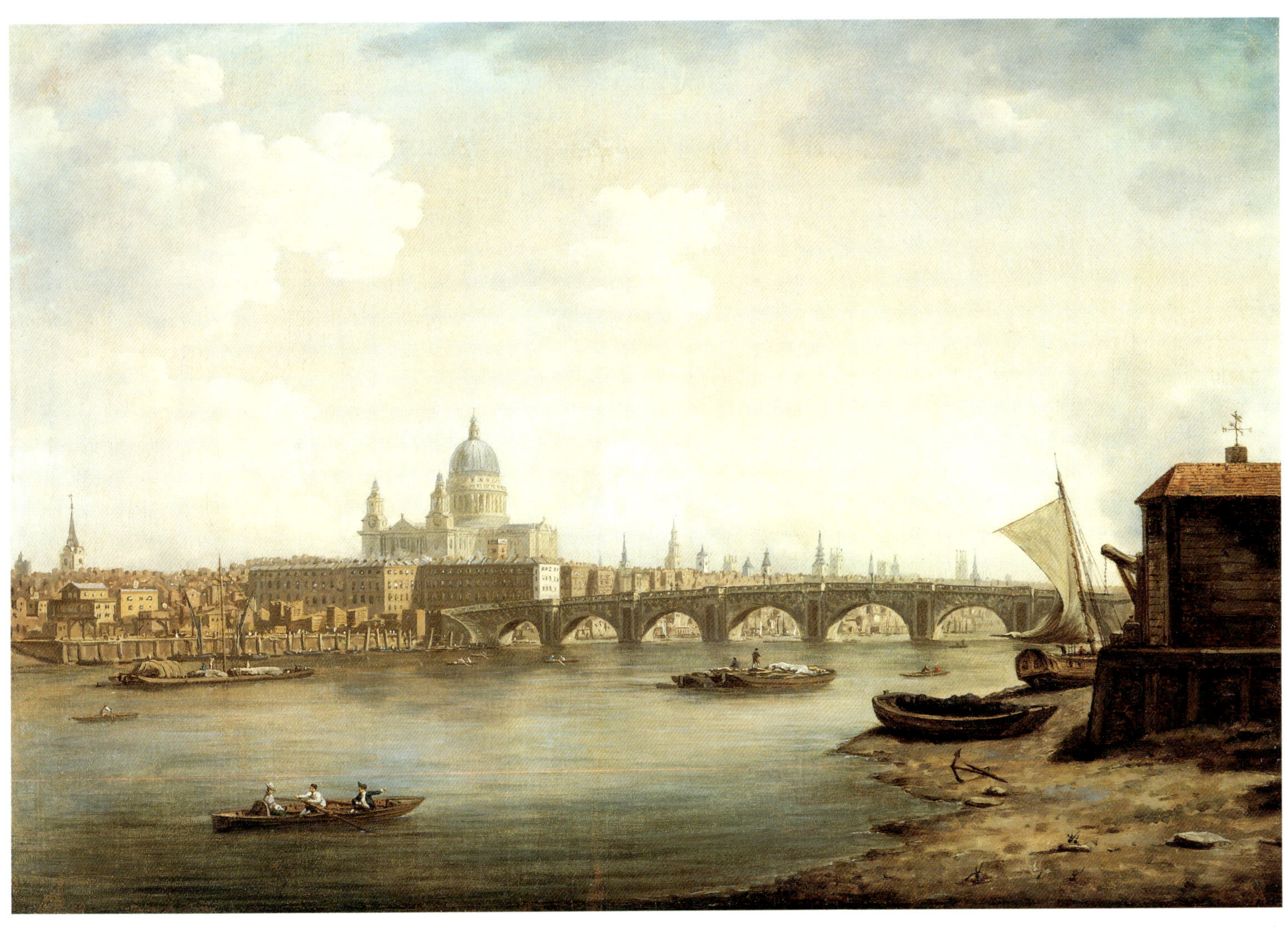

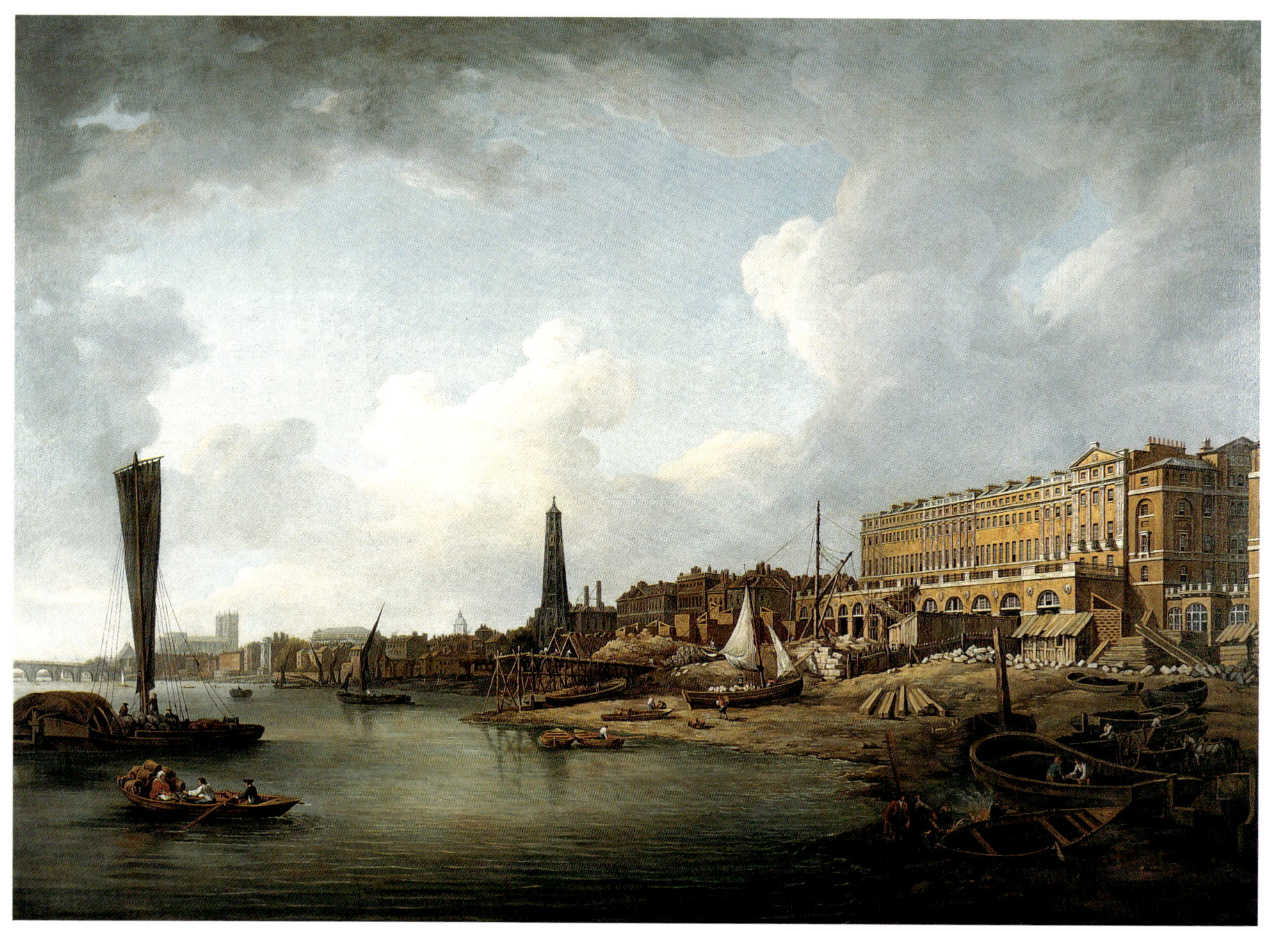

74 William Marlow

The Adelphi, London, under construction, with York Water Tower and the River Thames towards Westminster

Oil on canvas, 1771–72
$54\frac{1}{8} \times 76$ ins (135.3 × 190 cm)
Signed with initials on the stern of the boat to the right: W.M.

The Museum of London

The appearance of London's waterfront between St Paul's and Westminster was radically changed by three major architectural projects carried out over nearly thirty years between 1760 and 1790: Robert Mylne's Blackfriars Bridge, completed in 1769, the Adam brothers' Adelphi project of 1768 to 1773, and the vast new Somerset House built for the Government by Sir William Chambers from 1776. In this view the central Royal Terrace of The Adelphi has been completed, but only one of the streets with houses at right angles to it which terminated with a projecting pedimented facade facing the river. The Adam Street front to the right of Royal Terrace was finished in 1771; the corresponding Robert Street on the other side was added the following year. Of particular interest in this painting are the details of the building materials and organization of the construction site in the foreground. ML

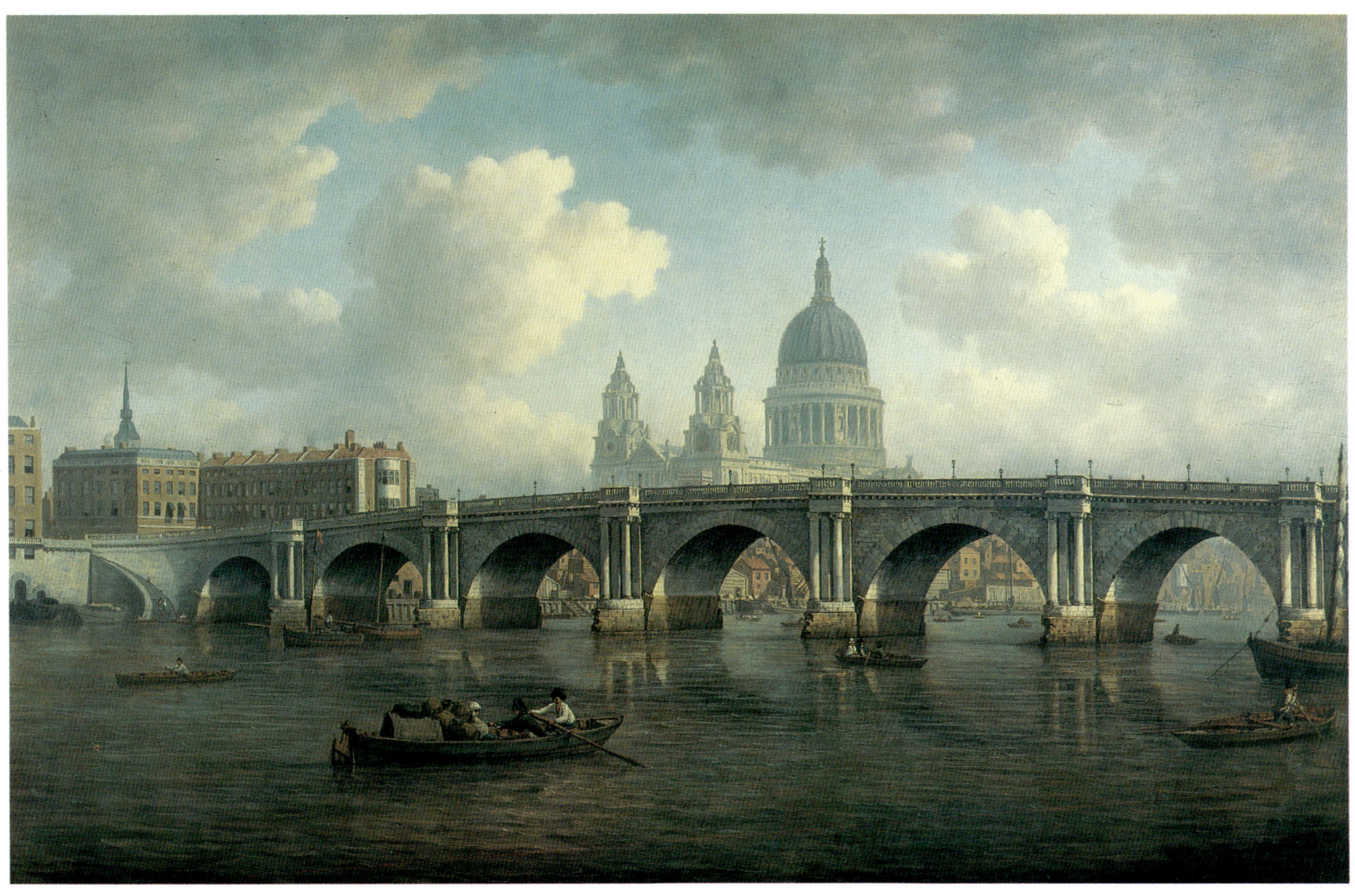

75 William Marlow

Blackfriars Bridge and St Paul's Cathedral, London

Oil on canvas, ca. 1788
42 × 66 ins (106.8 × 167.7 cm)
The Corporation of London, Guildhall Art Gallery

A second, almost identical version of this composition exists which differs only in a few details of the boats on the river (sold at Christie's, 12 April 1991, lot 59). Either painting might be the "View of Blackfriars Bridge" exhibited at the Royal Academy in 1788 (no. 243). Marlow's sensitivity to light and atmosphere could on occasion equal Samuel Scott's in subtlety, and in this view he achieves a particularly fine balance between topographical precision in rendering the details of the architecture of the bridge, crisply defined by the play of light and shade, and the delicately nuanced reflections in the water and atmosphere which softens the waterside buildings seen through the arches and the imposing mass of St Paul's. Like Canaletto and Scott, Marlow was also an attentive observer of the life and activity of London's river. ML

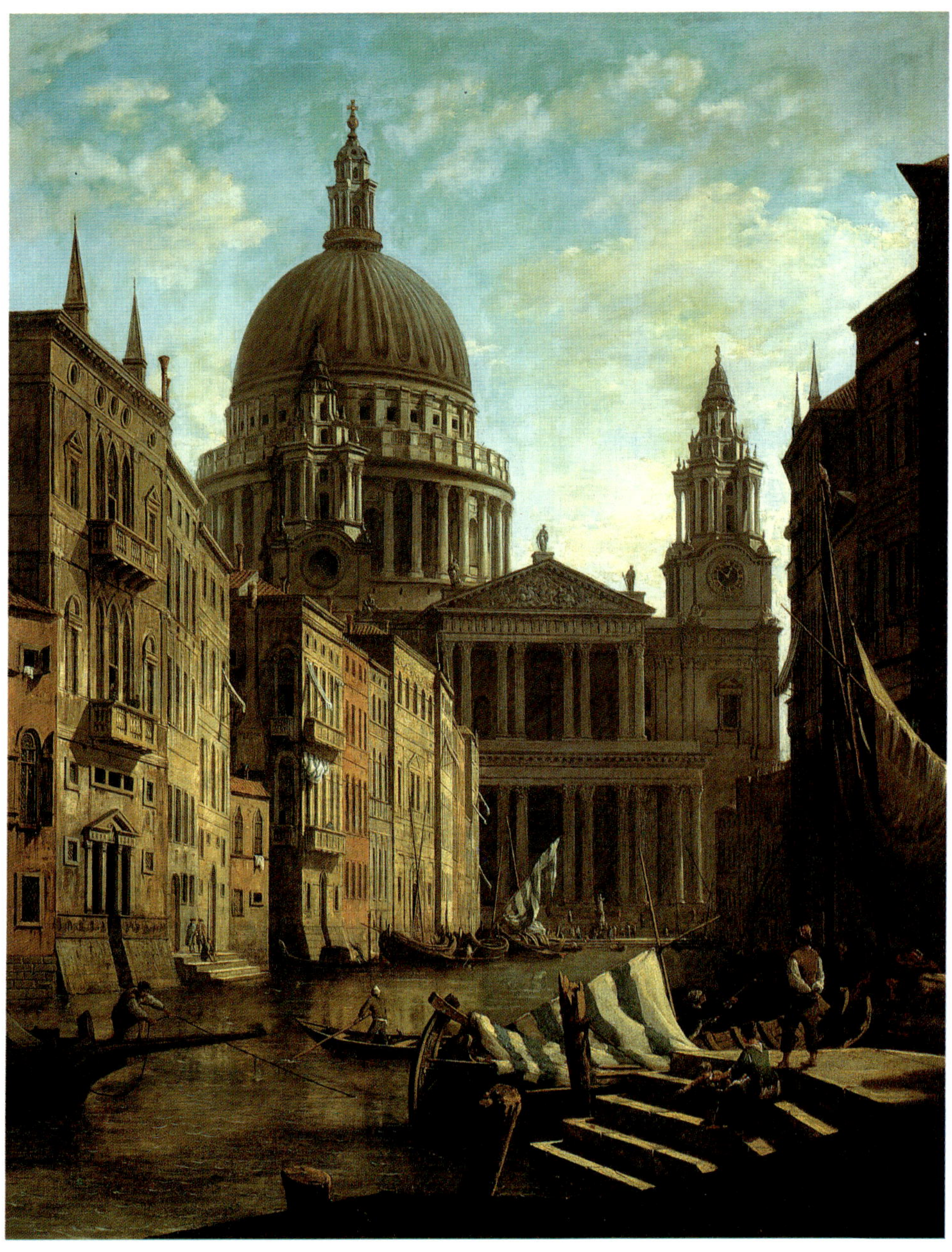

76 William Marlow

Capriccio of St Paul's Cathedral on the Grand Canal

Oil on canvas, ca. 1797
51 × 41 ins (129 × 104 cm)
Signed lower right: W. Marlow
The Trustees of the Tate Gallery, London

Although Marlow must have been aware of *capricci* painted by Canaletto and other artists, English as well as Italian, this appears to be unique in his œuvre and arouses curiosity as to its function and meaning. Normally the picture is dated to around 1795 which certainly fits well enough with its style. The view of St Paul's west front corresponds very closely to the angle from which it is viewed in the engraving of his *View of Ludgate Street with the west front of St Paul's* which was published in 1795 and of which there are two painted versions. In this work, however, part of the west front is obscured by the tower of St Martin Ludgate. The view of the Grand Canal has been shown to be a copy taken from an engraving after Canaletto.[1] Marlow twice exhibited the St Paul's from Ludgate Street view at the Royal Academy, in 1795 and 1796 — on the second occasion a critic took him to task for repeating himself.[2] Marlow's apparently inexplicable venture into *capriccio* painting might be explained, however, if it is considered in the context of the events which occurred on the Continent in 1797. On 16 May in that year the French entered Venice and proclaimed the end of the Republic; in October by the Treaty of Campo Formio Venice was ceded to Austria. The suppression of the ancient Republic was seen in Britain, herself at war with France, as a symbol of the threat to liberty with which Venice had been identified by earlier eighteenth-century writers. Venice, like London, was a commercial centre and capital of an empire (though it had mostly been lost long before 1797). Possibly William Marlow may have painted this otherwise extraordinary picture to express sentiments similar to those which William Wordsworth condensed into his sonnet *On the Extinction of the Venetian Republic*:

Once did she hold the gorgeous east in fee;
And was the safeguard of the west: the worth
Of Venice did not fall below her birth,
Venice, the eldest child of Liberty

. . .

Men are we, and must grieve when even the
    Shade
Of that which once was great, is passed
    away.

Placing St Paul's on the Grand Canal would have had a powerful resonance in the closing years of the eighteenth century. ML

1. F.J.B. Watson, 'Baudin, Canaletto and Marlow', *Burlington Magazine* XCVII, 1955, p.391.
2. *The London Packet*, 1796, Royal Academy review.

77 John Donowell
fl. 1753–86

A view of the Grand Walk, Marylebone Gardens

Watercolour and pen over pencil, ca. 1761
$10\frac{1}{8} \times 16\frac{1}{8}$ ins (25.4 × 40.8 cm)

Signed bottom right: Jn.º Donowell d.; inscribed verso: FIA / Nath.ˡ Smith / A View of Marebone [*sic*] Gardens as seen from the Head of the Grand Walk / with its beautiful Orchistra [*sic*] & Pavilion &c.

Birmingham Museums and Art Gallery

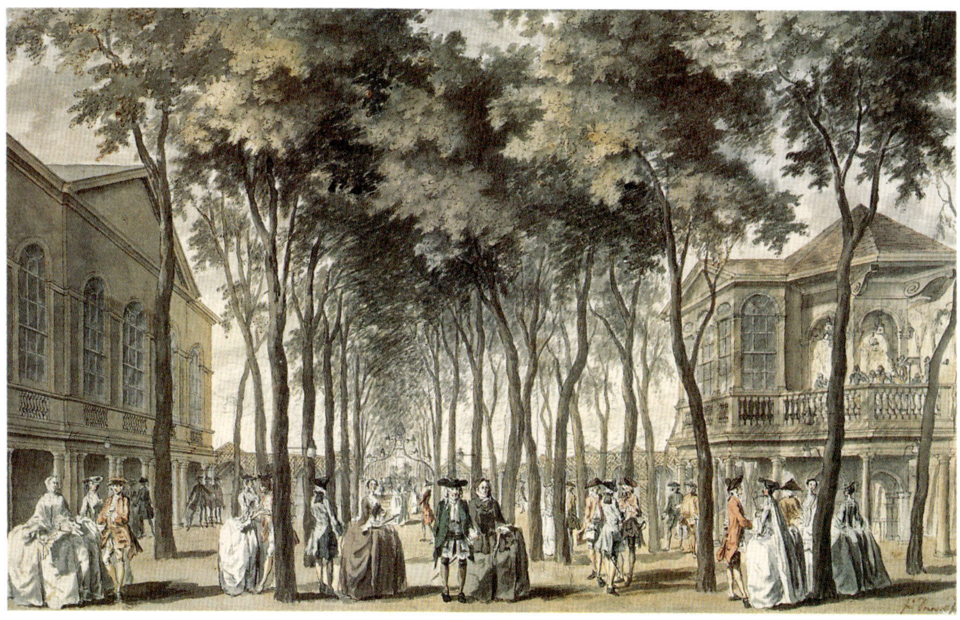

In many ways comparable with Canaletto's views of Vauxhall and Ranelagh Gardens [cat. nos. 28 and 29], this is the most important surviving drawing by Donowell. Although less well known, he stands beside Thomas Sandby [see cat. no. 59] and Thomas Malton [see cat. no. 91] as one of the leading architect-draughtsmen in the third quarter of the century. An exhibitor at the Free Society (1761), the Society of Artists (1762–70) and the Royal Academy (1778–86), he had a number of his drawings engraved, one of the earliest being of this view, published in 1761.

The gardens, on the east side of Marylebone High Street, were open to the public as early as 1688, when Samuel Pepys recorded a visit in his diary. Greatly improved from 1738, when the first orchestra building was erected, they had become one of London's most fashionable pleasure gardens by 1760; the music of Handel (also a visitor) was often played, under the direction of Thomas Arne. Despite the attraction of balloon ascents and firework displays, the popularity of Marylebone declined rapidly, and the gardens were closed at the end of the season of 1777–78.

Donowell's drawing rivals the work of the brothers Sandby in its lively combination of line and colour, with some of the figures having the character both of portraits (like the elderly couple in the foreground) and caricature (especially the dandified young men). Its original owner may have been the sculptor Nathaniel Smith (fl. 1755–1800), assistant to Joseph Wilton and Joseph Nollekens. sw

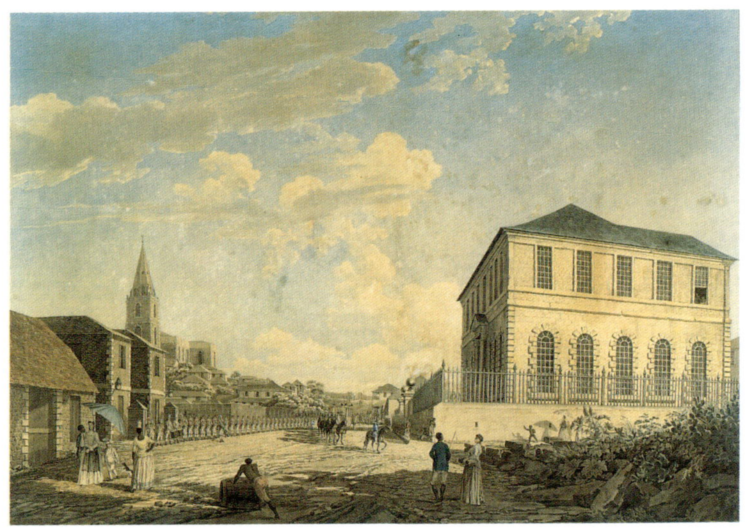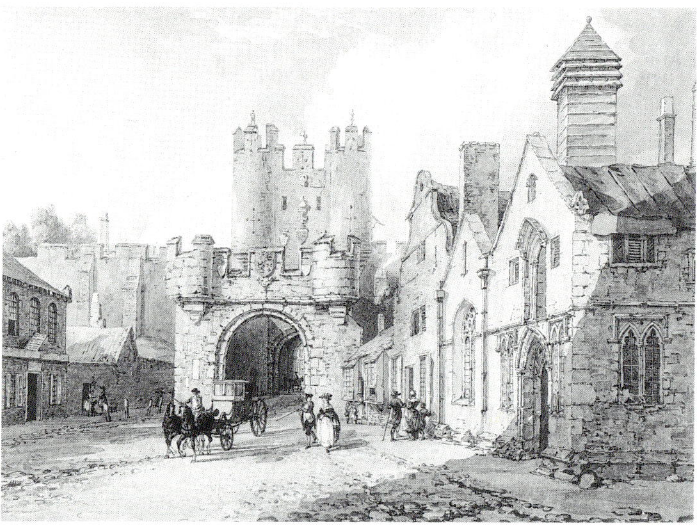

78 Thomas Hearne 1744–1813

The Court House and Guard House in the town of St John's, Antigua

Pen and ink with watercolour, ca. 1771–77
$20\frac{1}{8} \times 29$ ins (51.1×73.6 cm)
The Trustees of the Victoria and Albert Museum, London

Topographical draughtsmen from England could be found in the eighteenth century not only on the Continent accompanying Grand Tourists or working in centres like Rome for English visitors but also attached to voyages of exploration, to embassies, and on trips to different parts of Britain's expanding empire. Thomas Hearne spent over three years based in Antigua working for the governor of the Leeward Islands between 1771 and 1775. Before that he had trained under William Woollett (1735–1785), the most accomplished engraver of landscapes in London in the 1760s. The exacting art of engraving taught Hearne to attend meticulously to detail in his work, and through Woollett he

was introduced to the arts of landscape and topographical drawing. His view of the Antigua Court House and Guard House with the governor arriving is an early example of Hearne's characteristic combination of very precise drawing with a rendering of light which articulates the architectural particulars and plays on surfaces to reveal their textures. The clarifying brilliance of the illumination is appropriate to the Caribbean setting, but it is also a feature of English topographical painting and drawing that had been given a new emphasis by the example of Canaletto and his followers. ML

79 Thomas Hearne

Micklegate Bar and the Hospital of St Thomas, York

Pen and ink with watercolour, 1777
$7\frac{1}{4} \times 10\frac{1}{8}$ ins (18.4×25.7 cm)
The Whitworth Art Gallery, University of Manchester

After returning to England from the West Indies in 1775 Hearne devoted himself to making watercolour drawings of architectural antiquities and picturesque buildings often set in landscapes. Many of his watercolours of ancient gothic remains appeared as plates in the two volumes of *The Antiquities of Great Britain* which he published in collaboration with the engraver William Byrne and which did much to establish Hearne's reputation and influence as one of the leading topographical draughtsmen of the later eighteenth century. In *Micklegate Bar*, used for one of the plates in the first volume and published in 1782, his interest in the picturesque potential of gothic architecture and the intricate details of mouldings and the weathered surfaces of old stonework is fully developed and shows clear signs of Paul Sandby's influence. This drawing derives from a tour of the north of England Hearne made in 1777 in the company of Sir George Beaumont, an important collector, patron of landscape artists and amateur painter who had previously toured the Lake District with Joseph Farington. Hearne would have known Farington's

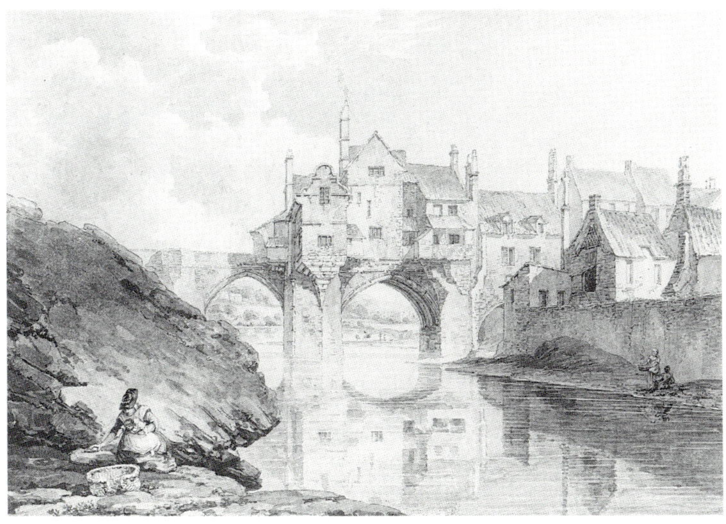 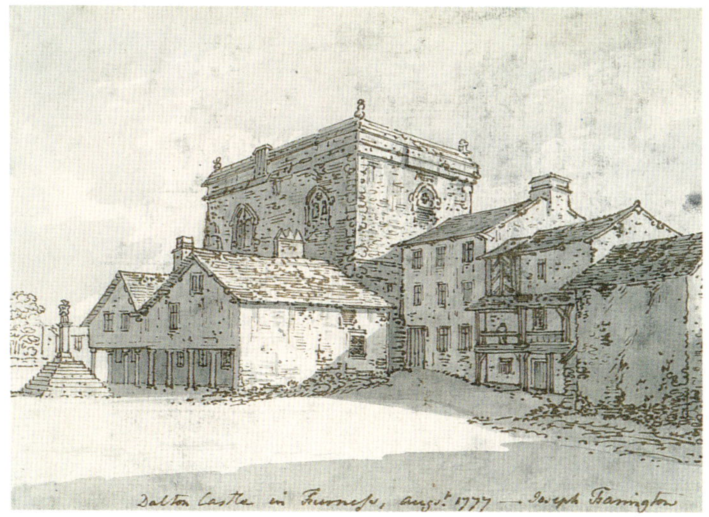

drawings by this date, and from him could have developed the technique of drawing the details of masonry using his pen in a manner that loosely reflects Canaletto's draughtsmanship. ML

80 Thomas Hearne

Elvet Bridge, Durham

Pencil and touches of pen and ink with watercolour, 1781
$7\frac{1}{4} \times 10\frac{1}{2}$ ins (18.4 × 26.6 cm)
The Visitors of the Ashmolean Museum, Oxford

In the way that light plays over the stonework of the medieval bridge and on the gabled houses built at one end of it Hearne's view suggests comparisons with other English painters more immediately influenced by Canaletto such as William Marlow and Paul Sandby. The compositional device of framing the view between the arches and the reflections of the bridge might also go back to precedents in Canaletto and Samuel Scott, although

by the time this watercolour was painted it is unlikely that any direct reference to a specific source was intended. Hearne's picturesque scenes were among the works which influenced younger painters of the next generation, most notably Turner and Girtin in the mid–1790s when they were regular visitors to Dr Monro's house in The Adelphi. Monro was an avid collector of Hearne's watercolours and it was in part at least from drawings like this that Girtin and Turner among others developed and perfected their understanding of topographical painting at the beginning of their careers. ML

81 Joseph Farington
1747–1821

Dalton Castle, Cumbria

Pencil and brown ink, with ink wash, 1777
$7\frac{1}{2} \times 10\frac{5}{8}$ ins (19.0 × 27.0 cm)
Inscribed bottom: Dalton Castle in Furness, Augs.^{t} 1777 – Joseph Farington
Birmingham Museums and Art Gallery

Joseph Farington is rightly cited as one of the first of a younger generation of artists to have been influenced by Canaletto's drawing style. Indeed, he owned four drawings by Canaletto, which he sold in 1820 to his friend Dr Thomas Monro. This study is a good example of the wiry 'line and dot' technique, using a reed pen with brown ink to delineate ancient masonry and hard-edged ink wash to give crisp effects of light and shade, which derives directly from Canaletto.

The second son of a clergyman from Lancashire, Farington was sent to London in 1763, at the age of sixteen, to become a pupil of Richard Wilson. He accompanied his teacher on several sketching tours, and exhibited at the Incorporated Society of Artists from 1765 until 1773; in 1769 he enrolled as a student in the newly founded Schools of the Royal Academy of Arts, of which he was to become an Associate in 1783 and a full member in 1785. From 1776 to 1781 he lived in Keswick, making many topographical drawings in and around the Lake District. SW

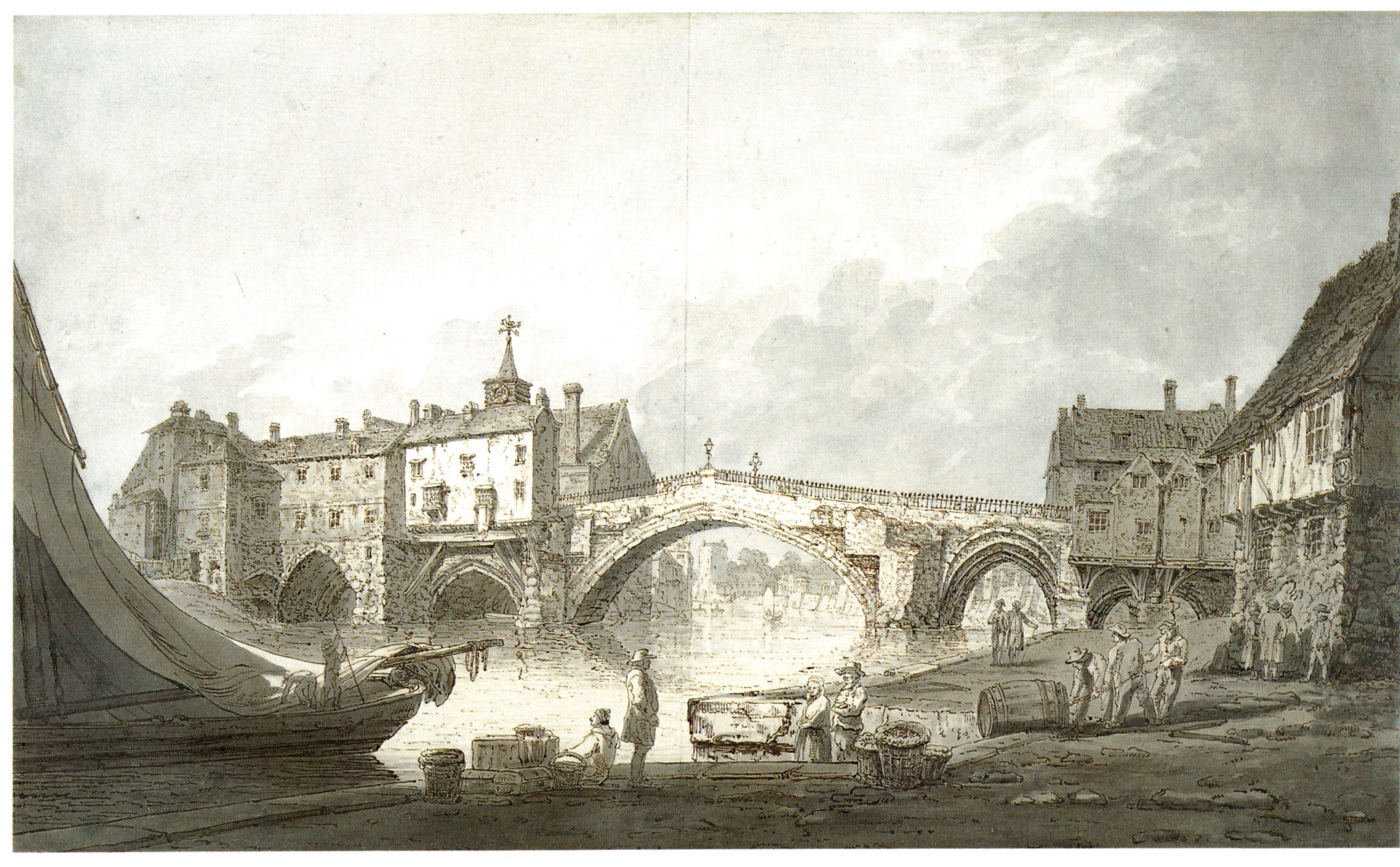

82 Joseph Farington

The Old Ouse Bridge at York

Pen and brown ink with ink wash, ca. 1783
$17\frac{3}{4} \times 30\frac{1}{8}$ ins (45.1 × 76.5 cm)
Birmingham Museums and Art Gallery

Remarkably, this is one of two identical drawings: the other, signed and dated 1783, is in York City Art Gallery. Both predate a huge oil painting (40 × 60 ins), now in the Hall of the Merchant Adventurers' Company, York; oddly, this has different figures. Exhibited at the Royal Academy in 1784, the oil was bought by a shipping agent, Charles Offley, and at his sale in 1809 was described as "a most correct view and capital performance, in which is combined the colouring of Wilson and the masterly spirit of Canaletti".[1]

As so often with Farington's work, however, the drawing remains livelier and more interesting than the painting. It is a *tour de force*, not only in scale but in variety of effect, in a style of pen draughtsmanship directly emulating Canaletto. This proved perfect for the rendering of picturesque details of old timber and crumbling masonry, and Farington has simply but cleverly given the boat and figures exactly the same treatment in order that they should blend into the overall composition. The dark left corner caused by a broad sweep of sail is used in contrast with the sunlit river and bridge, very much echoing Canaletto's use of such chiaroscuro.

The Ouse Bridge was a popular subject for late eighteenth-century draughtsmen, including Thomas Girtin, whose large watercolour of 1800 (made after the demolition of the medieval shops on the bridge) is in the Yale Center for British Art, New Haven. sw

1. Quoted by Michael Clarke, 'Farington's "Ouse Bridge" Rediscovered', *Leeds Art Calendar* LXXVIII, 1976.

83 Joseph Farington

Seathwaite, near Staveley, Cumbria

Pen and brown ink with ink wash, 1786?
$7\frac{3}{4} \times 11\frac{1}{8}$ ins (19.7 × 28.4 cm)

Inscribed bottom left: Seethwaite near
Stavely/ August 6th; signed bottom right:
Joseph Farington

City of Nottingham Museums, Castle
Museum and Art Gallery

Farington found no hindrance in main-
taining the same drawing style for landscape. Here he combines a highly effective
rendering of interlocking stone walls with
the softer sinuous lines of grass, trees and
distant hills.

Staveley is a small village at the foot of
Lake Windermere, beneath Cartmel Fell. A
date of 1786 has been suggested, as there
are drawings of Lancaster (Fitzwilliam
Museum, Cambridge) dated from August
of that year. sw

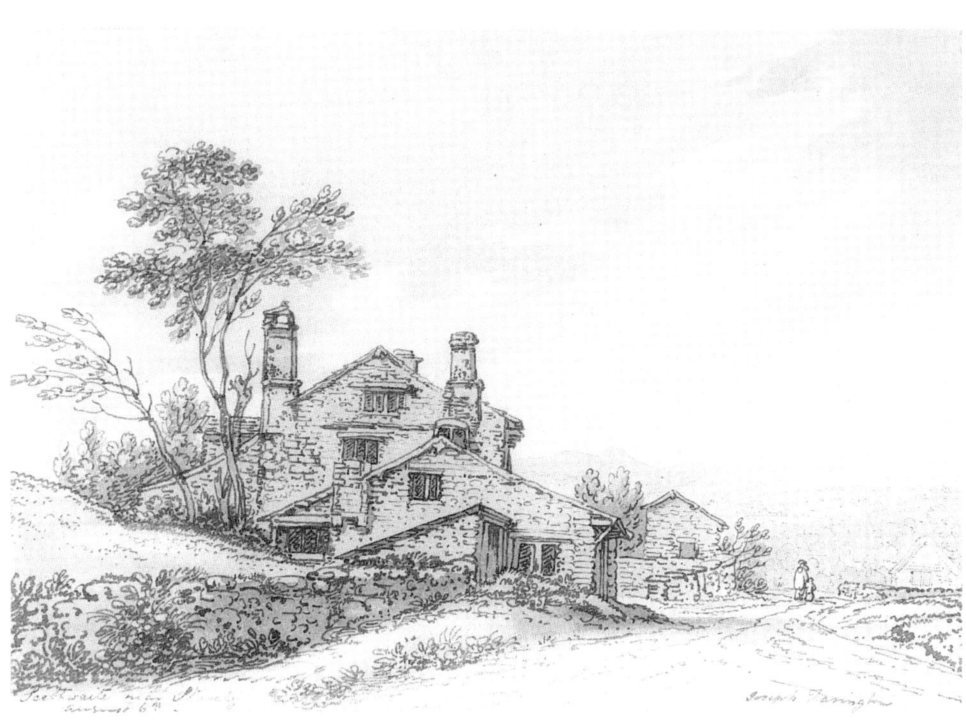

84 Joseph Farington

Westgate Bridge, Gloucester

Pen and ink with ink wash, 1789
$8\frac{7}{8} \times 14\frac{7}{8}$ ins (22.5 × 37.9 cm)
Gloucester City Museums

This simple but tranquil scene was possibly intended for engraving, but the
drawing is clearly unfinished at the left
side. A study in the sketchbook now in
the Victoria and Albert Museum, used
during Farington's tour of the West Midlands in 1789, carries copious notes detail-
ing the building materials of this ancient
bridge. There is a separate study of the

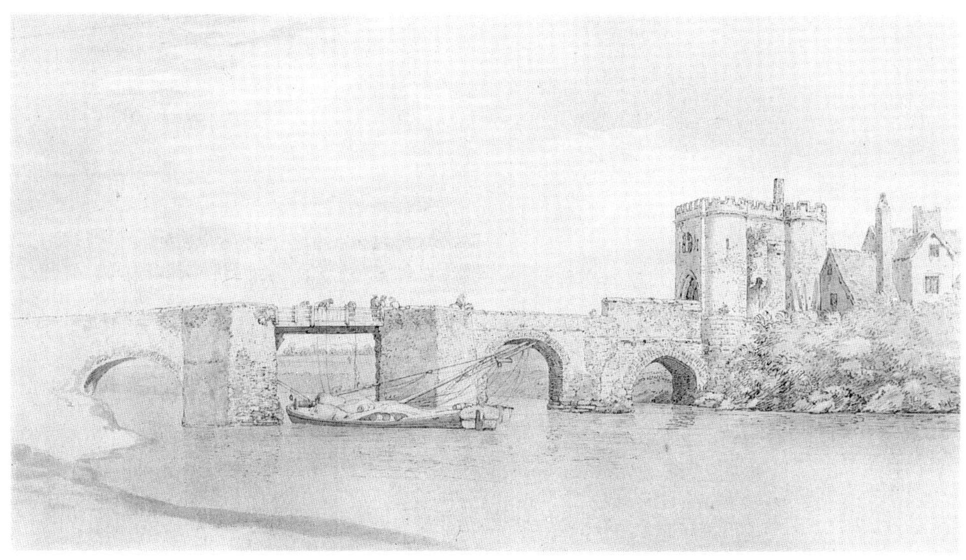

boat, with its mast being lowered to pass
beneath the footbridge — a charming vignette of working life that recalls Canaletto's fascination for such details. sw

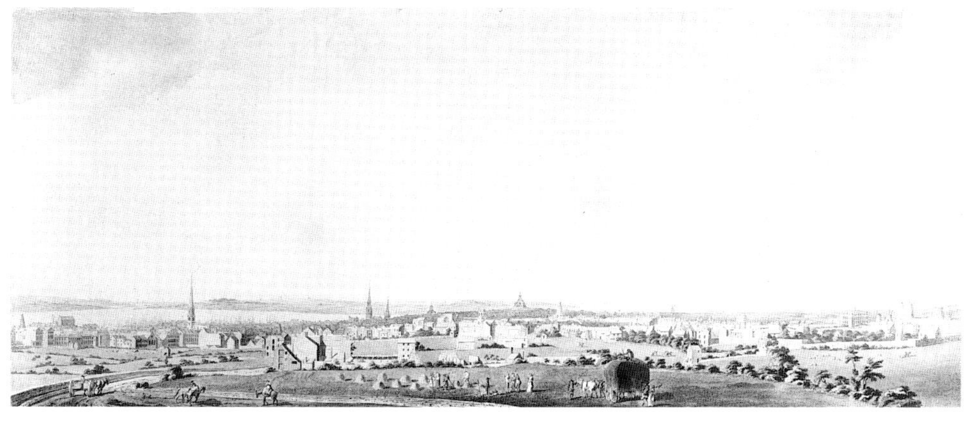

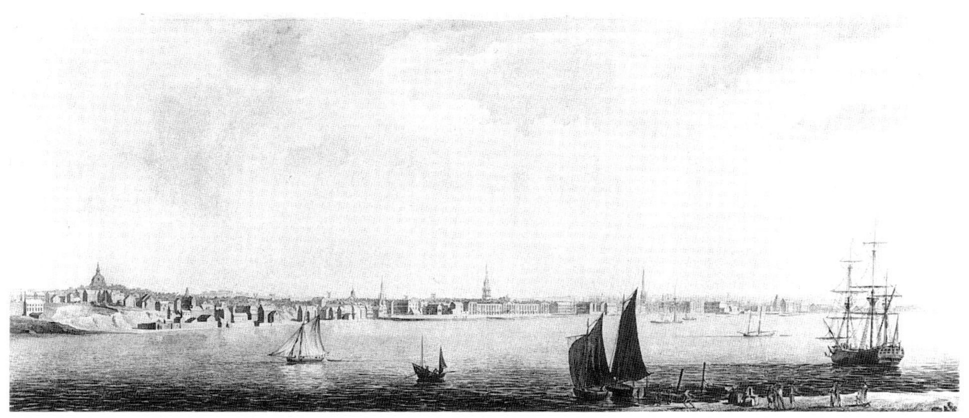

85 Michael 'Angelo' Rooker
1747–1801

Liverpool from the Bowling Green

Pen and ink with watercolour, 1769
12½ × 30 ins (31.4 × 76 cm)

The Board of Trustees of the National
Museums and Galleries on Merseyside,
Walker Art Gallery, Liverpool

86 Michael 'Angelo' Rooker

Liverpool from Seacombe Boat-house

Pen and ink with watercolour, 1769
12 × 30 ins (30.5 × 76 cm)

The Board of Trustees of the National
Museums and Galleries on Merseyside,
Walker Art Gallery, Liverpool

Michael 'Angelo' Rooker's artistic origins
lie firmly within the tradition of English
topographical drawing as it had
developed in the 1740s and 1750s. His
father, Edward Rooker, was a prolific
engraver of views as well as an accomplished draughtsman and designer in his
own right; Canaletto was one of the artists
whose work he reproduced for the print
publishers. He was also a close friend of
Paul Sandby. Michael 'Angelo' Rooker was
initially trained to draw views by his father
and was then placed with Sandby for a
time in the 1760s, learning from him the
sensitive handling of watercolour washes
and the lively style of drawing figures
which contribute so much local character
to his work. These two panoramic drawings of Liverpool were his first Royal
Academy exhibits: they were shown in
1769 (the first exhibition of the new
Academy which had been founded in
1768) and are described in the catalogue as
"stained drawings", the term normally used
at that time for topographical watercolours
consisting of a careful outline drawing with
the tones laid in with evenly applied grey
washes before colour was added in delicate
pale tints. When these views were made
Liverpool was still at the beginning of the
rapid growth of commerce and industry
which was to propel the city to the fore-
front of the Industrial Revolution by 1800.
Both views have a breadth and uniformity
of treatment across the whole extent of the
scene which can be compared to Canaletto's approach in paintings like his *Chelsea
Hospital and Ranelagh Gardens* or his Greenwich views [cat. no. 30]. ML

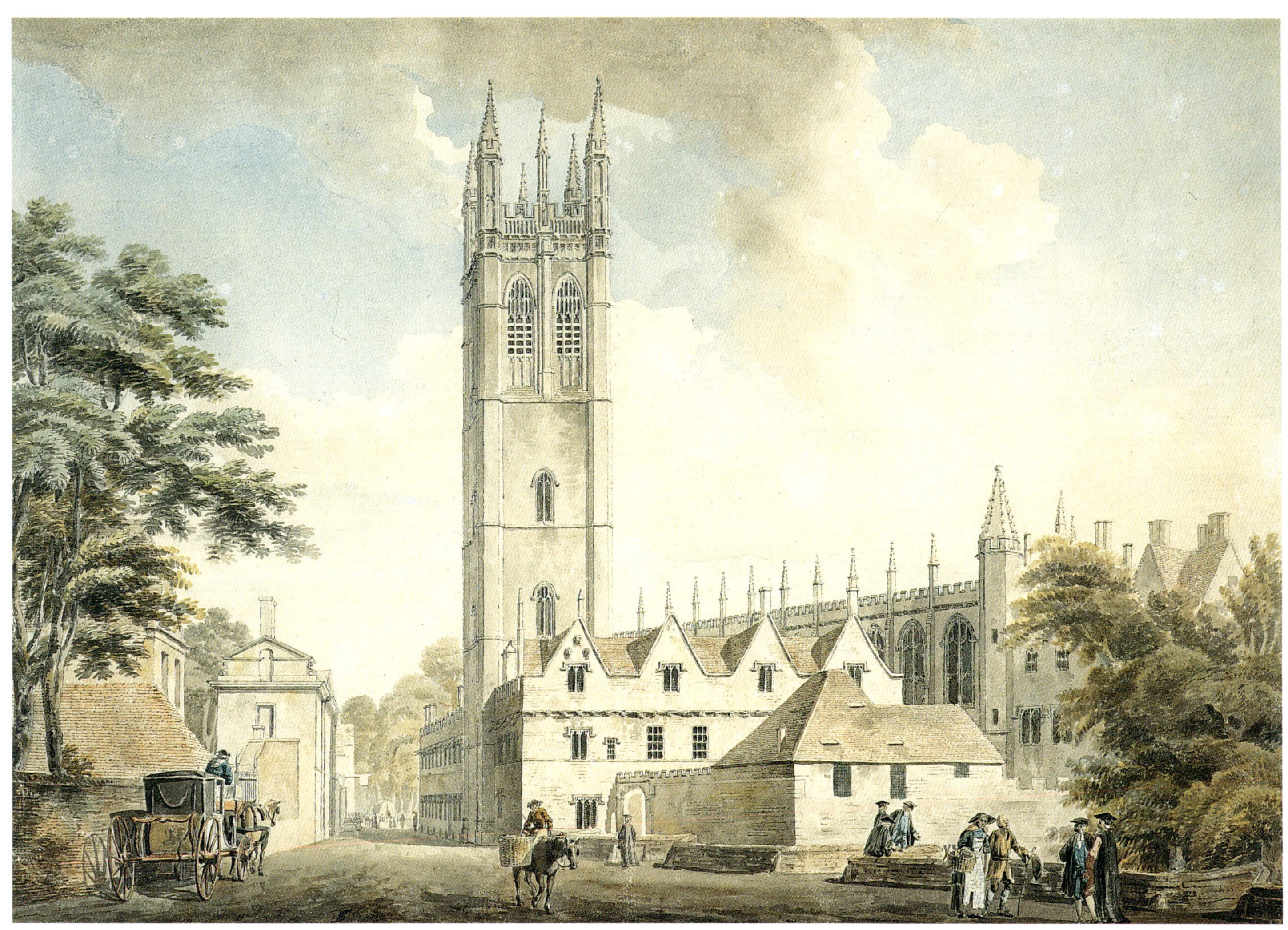

87 Michael 'Angelo' Rooker

Magdalen Bridge and Tower, Oxford

Pen and ink and watercolour over pencil, ca. 1770

$7\frac{7}{8} \times 12\frac{3}{8}$ ins (31.3 × 45.2 cm)

Inscribed on former mount (in a later hand): Part of Magdalen Bridge taken down A.D. 1771 with Old Buildings of Physic Garden and "Noah's Ark" on the left

Birmingham Museums and Art Gallery

This is a crisp early drawing, reflecting the period in Rooker's career when he was working both as a draughtsman and as an engraver in the studio of his father Edward. The subject was engraved for *The Oxford Almanack* of 1771. First issued in 1674, the *Almanack* began bearing topographical headpieces in 1766, the Rookers being responsible for every plate from 1769 to 1788 (Edward died in 1774). Suc-ceeding artists included Malton, Nattes, Turner, J.C. Buckler and A.C. Pugin.

The artist "evidently wanted to record the view before it was altered. In 1770 one of the arches of the old bridge gave way, and an Act of Parliament was passed to allow the bridge to be removed. By 1779 a new bridge was in place, designed by John Gwynne, Edward Rooker's former associate."[1] sw

1. Patrick Conner, *Michael Angelo Rooker*, London, 1984, p.9.

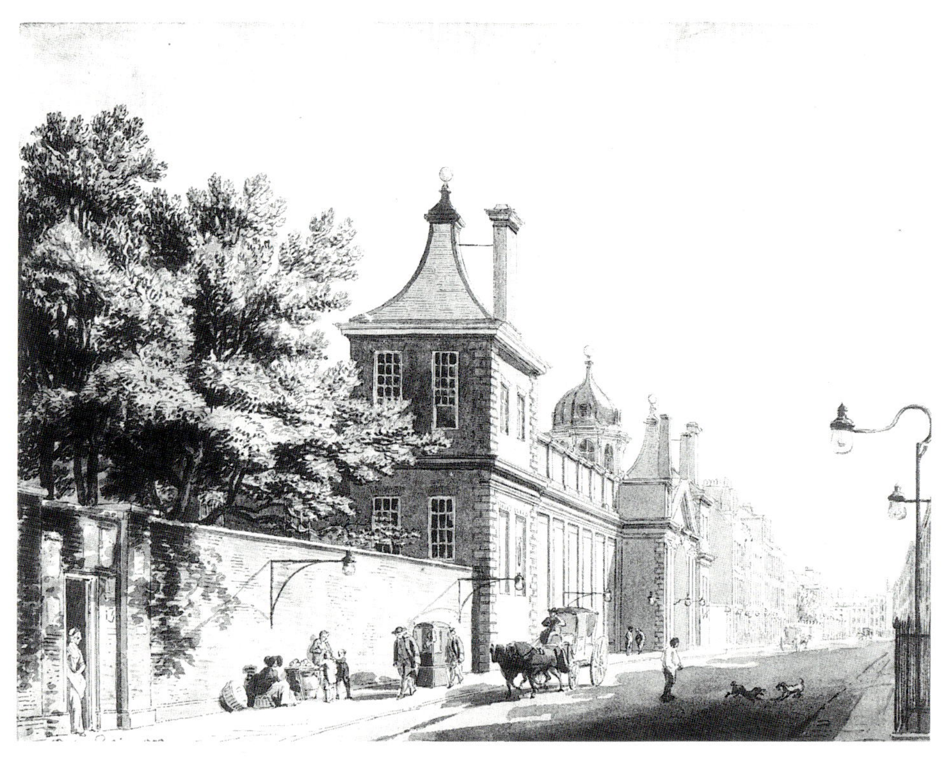

88 Michael 'Angelo' Rooker

The porch of Montagu House, London

Pen and ink and watercolour, 1778
$6\frac{1}{8} \times 8\frac{1}{16}$ ins (15.6 × 20.4 cm)
Signed and dated lower left: MA Rooker
Delin 1778
The Trustees of the British Museum, London

In this London street scene the principal subject is Montagu House which in 1759 had been opened as the newly founded British Museum. It was later demolished and the present Greek Revival museum building fronting on to Great Russell Street was built on the site of the old house and its gardens. Rooker's precise drawing and his use of light to sharpen the detail and render the textures of brick and stone clearly show how he had acquired through Paul Sandby an understanding of Canaletto's method of articulating an architectural prospect. Rooker's attention to detail combined with the sophisticated refinement of his drawing style and distribution of accents make him one of the most attractive and informative of topographers working in England in the later eighteenth century. These qualities are particularly evident in the series of views he did for the *Oxford Almanack* [see cat. no. 87], which were to have an important influence on J.M.W. Turner in the late 1780s and early 1790s. They provide a link between the generation of artists who carried topographical painting forward into the nineteenth century and their predecessors who adapted Canalettesque values to English picturesque views. ML

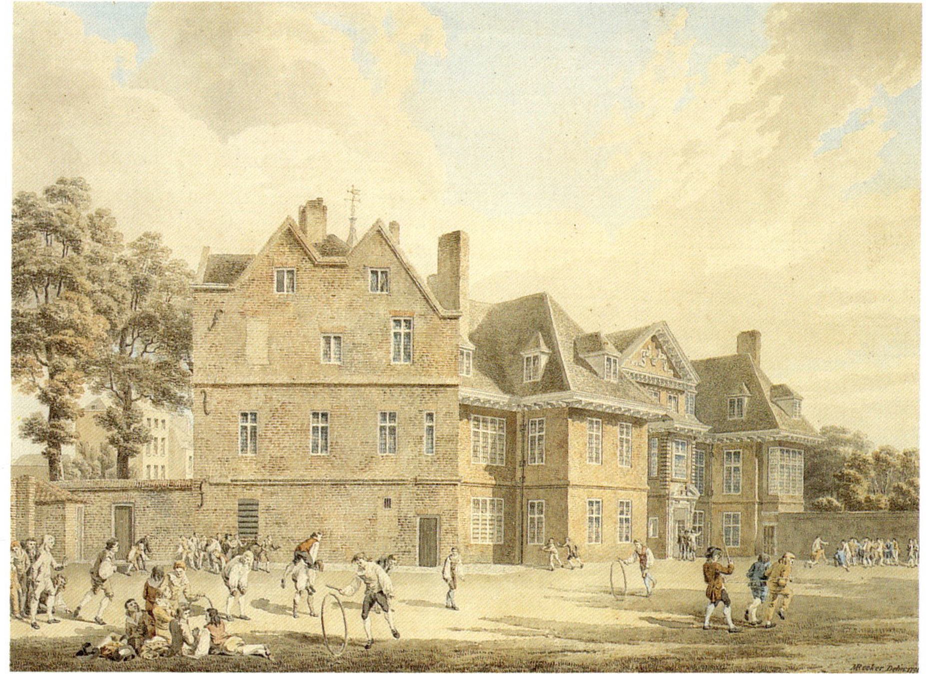

89 Michael 'Angelo' Rooker

The Manor of Marylebone as a school

Pencil and watercolour, 1790
$10\frac{11}{16} \times 14\frac{1}{8}$ ins (27.1 × 35.7 cm)
The Syndics of the Fitzwilliam Museum, Cambridge

Rooker painted this watercolour and a companion view of the garden front of the old manor house one year before it was destroyed in a fire. At the time it was a school run by the Reverend and Mrs Fountayne who operated a successful private academy for the sons of the socially respectable. As the drawing shows, the old house was a fascinating architectural mixture of styles, with an Elizabethan gabled wing on to which a classically ornamented seventeenth-century extension had been added. In this watercolour Rooker's later manner is fully developed: the minute discrimination of detail and texture in rendering the brickwork and the emphasis on the picturesqueness of the building's configuration are characteristic of his finest work, as are the marvellously lively figures of the pupils playing in the school yard. The contrast between the venerable pile and youthful exuberance gives the scene an animating vitality of a kind which often occurs in Rooker's work and which Turner seems to have learned from his example. ML

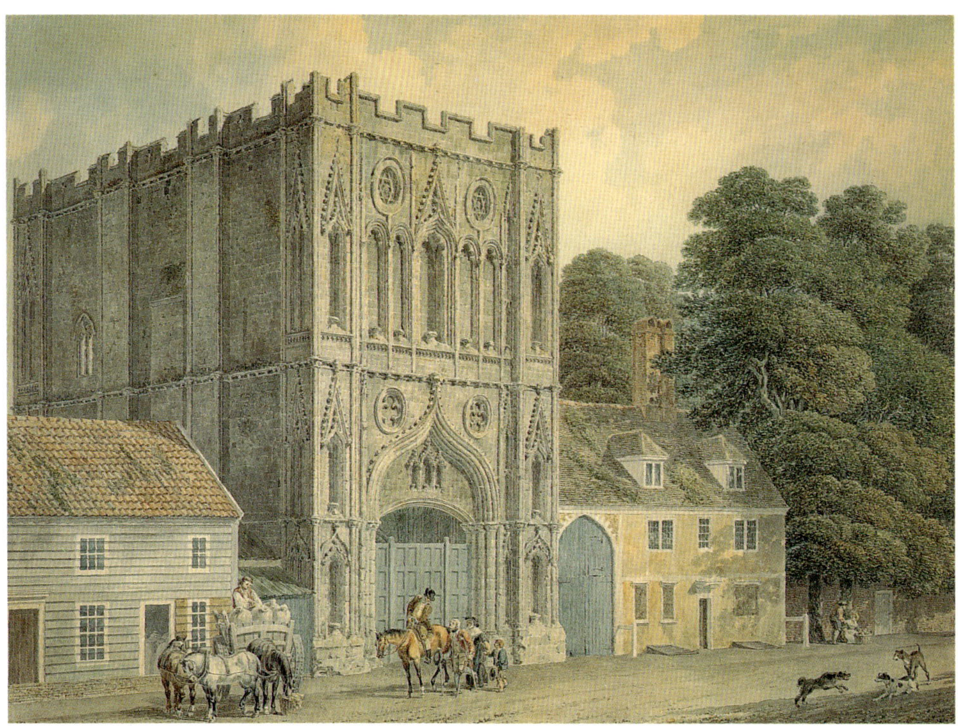

90 Michael 'Angelo' Rooker

The west front of the Abbey Gate, Bury St Edmunds

Watercolour over pencil, 1797
$15\frac{1}{4} \times 20\frac{1}{4}$ ins (38.0 × 53.3 cm)
Signed bottom left: M A Rooker [initials in monogram]
Birmingham Museums and Art Gallery

Typical of Rooker's more sophisticated later work, this watercolour has figures appropriate to each element of the street scene – a carter outside the storehouse, a gentleman offering help to a crippled serviceman (perhaps symbolizing the charity also offered by the Church), and the domestic group with dogs beneath a fine stand of trees.

Together with this in the Birmingham Museums collection is a similar view of the other (east) side of the Gate, showing its rather more ruinous condition, but with a gardener tending the Abbey grounds. Dating from the fourteenth century, the gateway has niches which are said to have held statues of the martyred St Edmund and the two archers who killed him. These watercolours can be identified with exhibits at the Royal Academy exhibition of 1797. SW

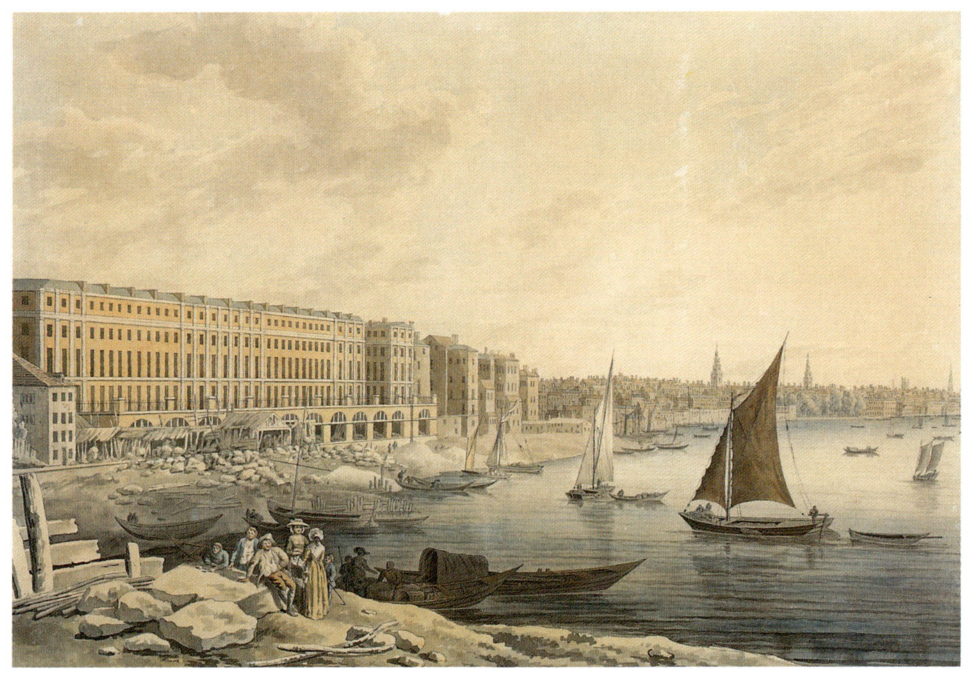

91 Thomas Malton the Younger 1748–1804

Royal Terrace, The Adelphi, London

Watercolour, 1774
$19\frac{3}{4} \times 28\frac{3}{4}$ ins (49.2 × 73 cm)
Yale Center for British Art (Paul Mellon Collection), New Haven

As a topographical draughtsman Thomas Malton the Younger excelled in the accurate perspective and minutely precise detail of his architectural views. His father, Thomas Malton the Elder (1726–1801), also drew architectural subjects and in 1775 published a *Complete Treatise on Perspective*. The younger Malton ran an evening school teaching perspective and drawing in the 1780s which Turner and Girtin attended. He regularly exhibited architectural views at the Royal Academy between 1773 and 1803, but because topography was regarded as an inferior activity his nomination for election as an Associate was defeated as he was "only a draughtsman of buildings". His drawings are meticulously exact and mathematically correct. This example is a characteristic specimen of Malton's precision. Exhibited at the Royal Academy in 1774, it shows the main terrace overlooking the Thames of the Adelphi development by Robert and James Adam. This part of the scheme had recently been completed, but as the deliveries of stone and building supplies on the embankment show work was still proceeding with the development behind Royal Terrace. Very little of The Adelphi survives today, most of it having been demolished in the 1930s. ML

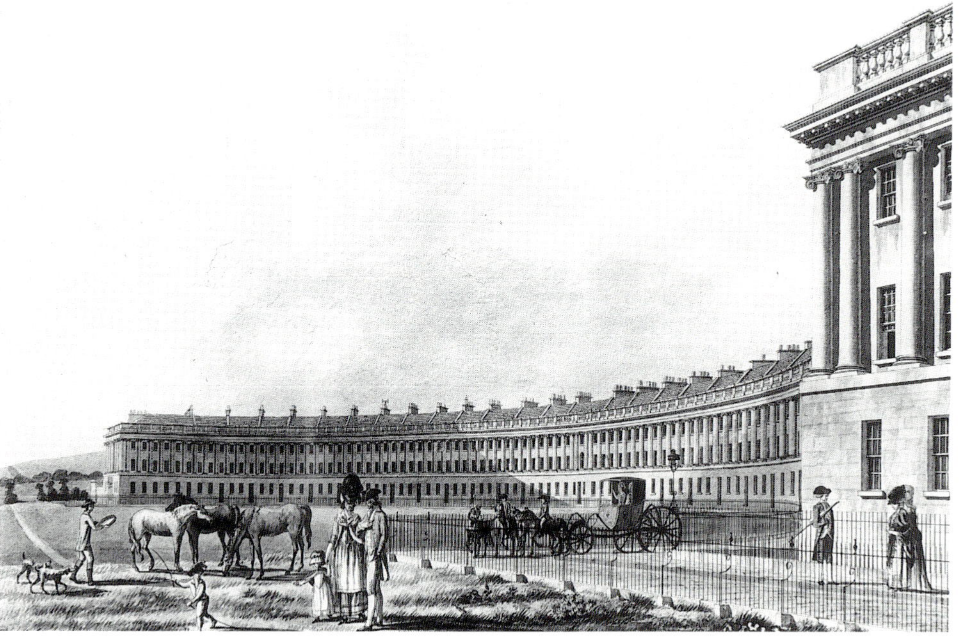

92 Thomas Malton the Younger

The Royal Crescent, Bath

Pencil with watercolour and ink, 1777
$12\frac{15}{16} \times 19$ ins (32.9×48.3 cm)

93 Thomas Malton the Younger

Queen Square, Bath

Pencil with watercolour and ink, 1784
$13\frac{1}{16} \times 18\frac{7}{8}$ ins (33.2×48 cm)

94 Thomas Malton the Younger

The Circus, Bath

Pencil with watercolour and ink, 1784
$12\frac{7}{8} \times 18\frac{7}{8}$ ins (32.7×48.1 cm)
Bath City Council, Victoria Art Gallery

Malton mainly concentrated on London scenes, but he also made a series of drawings of Bath from which aquatint engravings were made. With their immaculately precise outlines, carefully applied washes to define light and shade, and delicate tints of colour these are typical of Malton's restrained and very literal approach to recording appearances. However, his Bath subjects are not only of interest for the views they give of the city's architecture, since their figurative content offers an informative account of the elegant and fashionable society that frequented the season as well as those who served their needs. These examples show three of the principal features of the Georgian

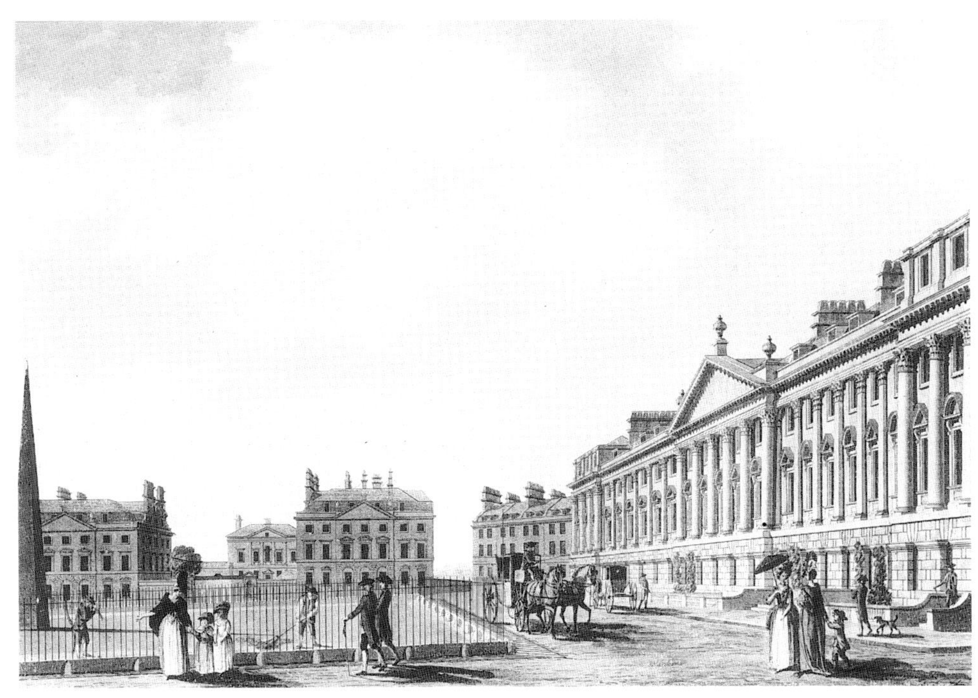

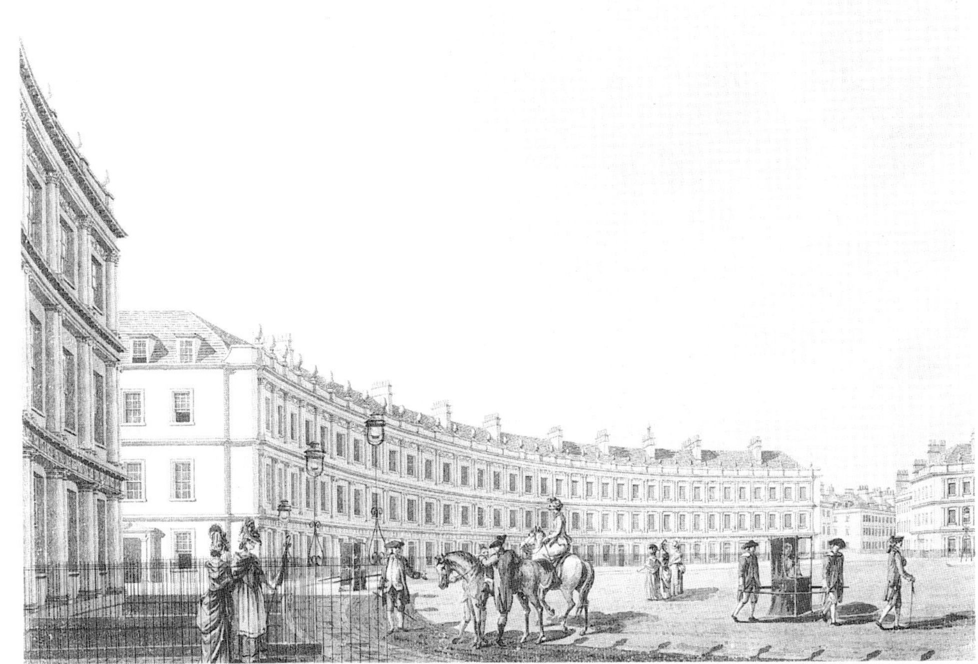

development of Bath as a social resort:
Queen Square laid out 1728–34, the Circus
of 1754–67, both designed by John Wood
the Elder, and the Royal Crescent built
1767–76 to the designs of John Wood the
Younger. The two later drawings were
done on Malton's third visit to Bath in
1784; he was also there in 1769 and 1775.
ML

95 Thomas Malton the Younger

The Strand with Somerset House, London

Watercolour over pencil, ca. 1792
13 × 19 ins (33 × 48.3 cm)
The Trustees of the Victoria and Albert
Museum, London

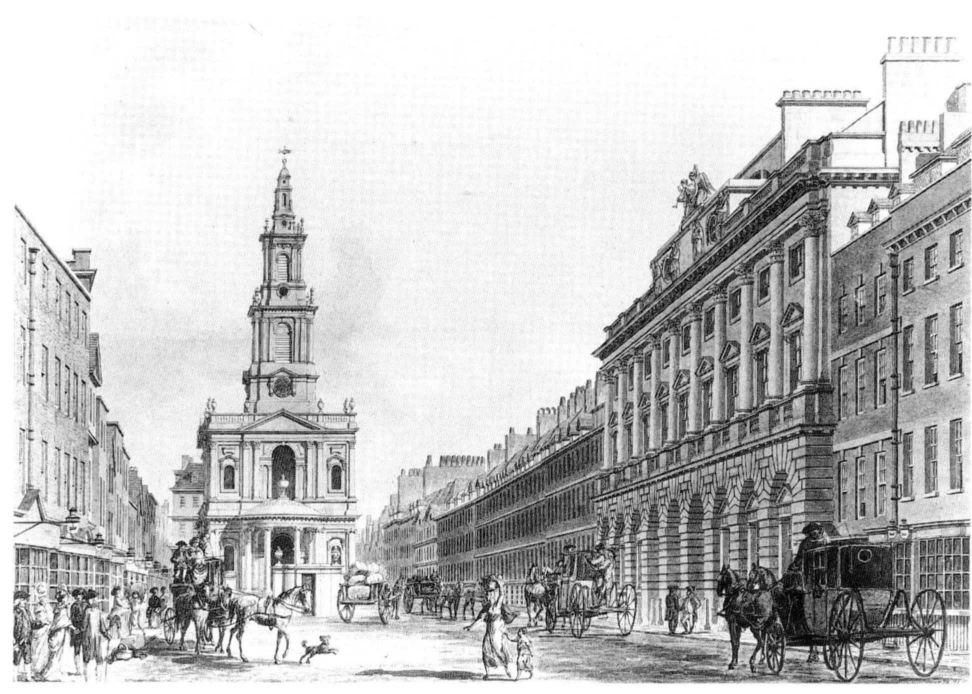

In 1792 Malton published his major contribution to London's topography, *A Picturesque Tour through the Cities of London and
Westminster*, for which he had prepared a
series of drawings which were reproduced
in aquatint engravings for the volume. The
original watercolours for these are Malton's finest achievement as a recorder of
London's architecture and the life on its
streets and are among the most sophisticated examples of the eighteenth-century
tradition of objectively recorded urban
topography which had developed out of
precedents set in the 1740s and 1750s.
Artistically they definitively exemplify the
topographer's skill, but they also demonstrate the limitations which led critics like
the Royal Academy's Professor of Painting
Henry Fuseli to regard what he disparag-
ingly called "views" as nothing more than
"the tame delineation of a given spot"
which, although they may delight "perhaps
the antiquary or the traveller … to every
other eye they are little more than top-

ography".[1] In this meticulously precise
drawing Malton shows two of London's
eighteenth-century architectural masterpieces, the church of St Mary le Strand
designed by James Gibbs and on the right
the neoclassical entrance façade to the new
Somerset House by Sir William Chambers,
replacing the earlier buildings on the site
extending from the Strand to the River
Thames. Until it moved to Burlington
House on Piccadilly in the nineteenth century the Royal Academy was housed in
the part of Somerset House shown in the
drawing. ML

1. J. Knowles, *The Life and Writings of Henry
Fuseli*, London 1831, II, p.217.

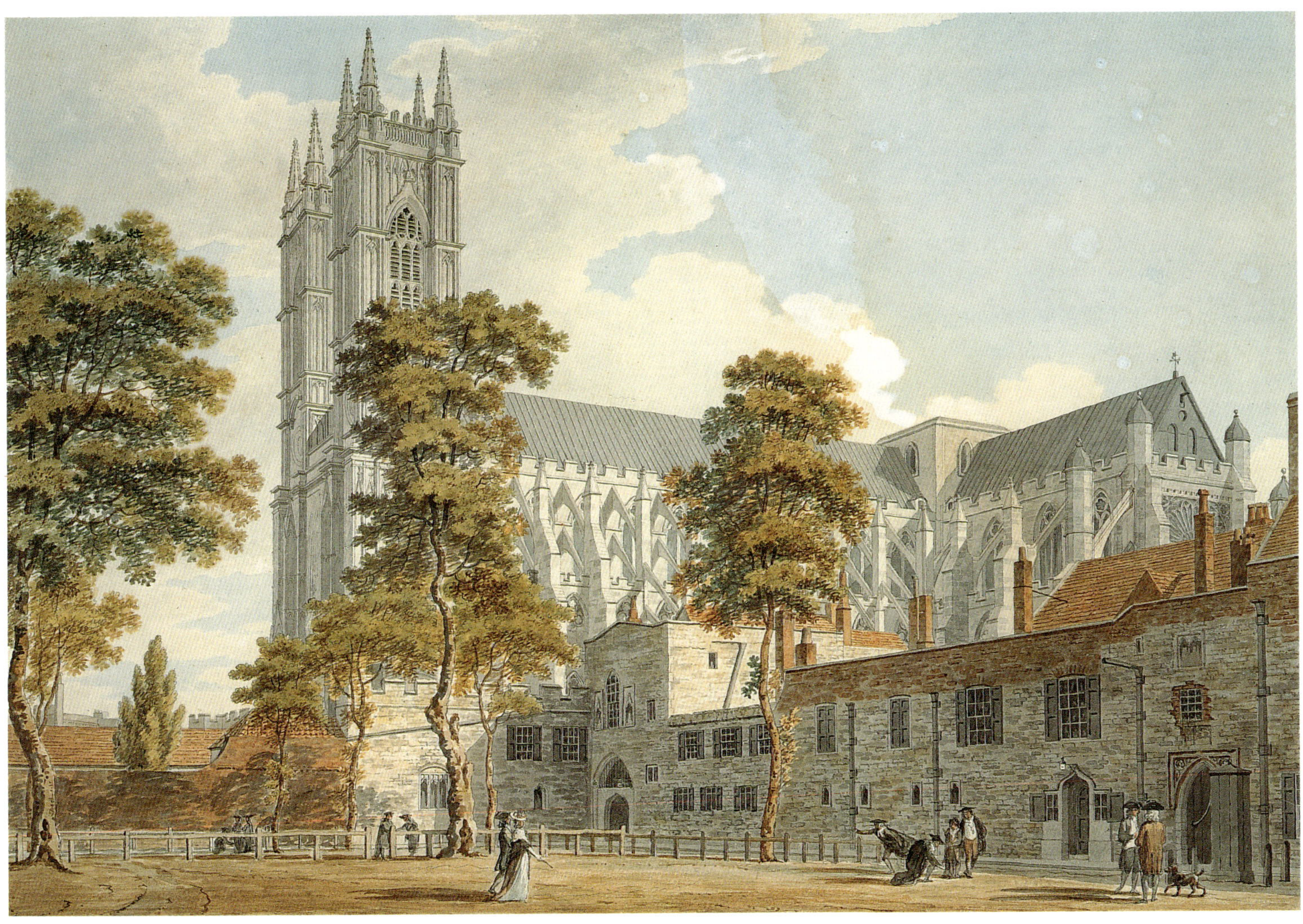

96 Thomas Malton the Younger

Westminster Abbey from the Schools

Watercolour over pencil, ca. 1792
$12\frac{7}{8} \times 18\frac{7}{8}$ ins (32.9 × 48.0 cm)
Birmingham Museums and Art Gallery

This was one of the first subjects to be engraved in aquatint for *A Picturesque Tour through the Cities of London and Westminster*: plate 6 of volume I, the print bears a publication date of 21 August 1792. The view depicts a corner of the ancient Westminster School buildings picturesquely contrasted with the great bulk of the Abbey, not long enhanced by Nicholas Hawksmoor's west towers of 1735–40.

The engraving omits several of the foreground figures (and the dog), which are among Malton's most delightful and Canalettesque groups of staffage. The bright contrast and long shadows are consistent with the idea of representing a morning scene. sw

97 Thomas Rowlandson
1756–1827

A view of Windsor Castle from Eton

Pen and blue grey wash, ca. 1790
$10\frac{3}{4} \times 17\frac{1}{8}$ ins (27.3 × 43.5 cm)
The Royal Institution of Cornwall, The
Royal Cornwall Museum, Truro

While there is no clear evidence, it seems
likely that Rowlandson would have
known of Canaletto's ability as a
draughtsman, and Canaletto's etchings
must have been easily available to him.
As a caricaturist, he would also have been
familiar with the work of Italian artists
such as Pier Leone Ghezzi (1674–1755),
whose humorous drawings and etchings
were brought back from Rome as souvenirs of the Grand Tour.

Within Rowlandson's less frivolous
work, some of his most impressive drawings are those which combine architecture
and figure groups in a way that invites
comparison with Canaletto's English drawings. The use of strong shadows, and the
strengthening of the foreground buildings,
are particularly evident in this subject. In a
larger version (Royal Collection) the street
becomes animated with a royal hunting
party, reducing all the architecture to a
rather flattened backdrop. The Round
Tower of the Castle is shown in the squat
form it presented before Sir Jeffry Wyat-
ville's romantic alterations which began in
1824. sw

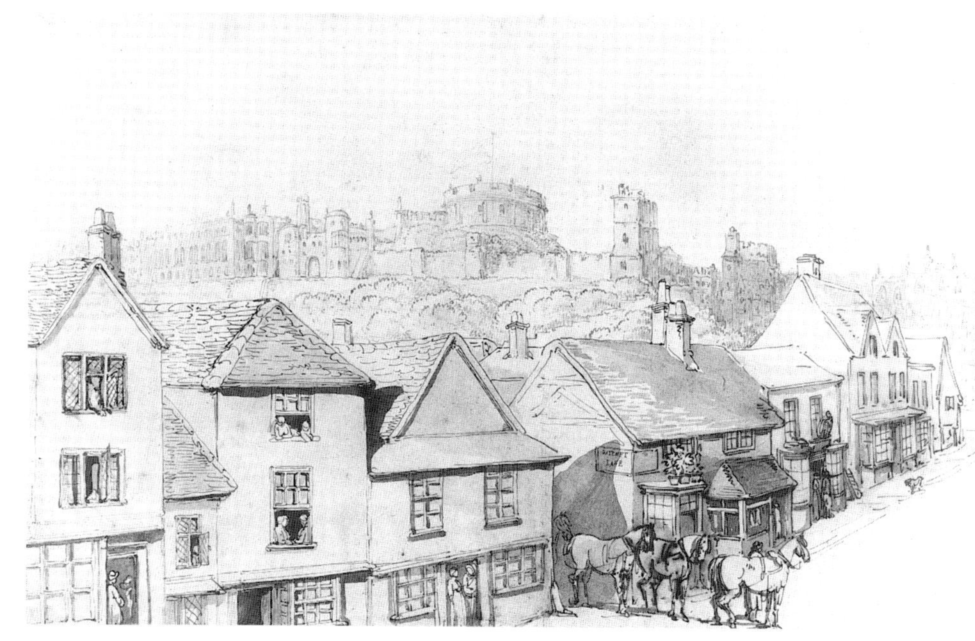

98 Thomas Rowlandson

Feyge Dam and part of the Fish Market at Amsterdam

Pen and ink and watercolour over pencil,
ca. 1794
$16\frac{5}{8} \times 21\frac{5}{8}$ ins (42.3 × 54.9 cm)
Bolton Museum and Art Gallery

Ironically, just as Canaletto made some of
his finest drawings in England, so Rowlandson's grandest and most panoramic
townscapes were the product of travel on
the Continent. The exact date of his tour
of Germany and the Low Countries is
unclear, but there are surviving drawings
of Cologne, Düsseldorf and Juliers in
Westphalia which bear the date 1791, and
in the Birmingham Museums collection is
an evident on-the-spot sketch inscribed
"drawn at Amsterdam 1792". In view of
the outbreak of war with France, it is
unlikely that the artist could have travelled

abroad much later than this. On the same
scale as this sheet are a view of the Place
de Mer in Antwerp and another of the
Stadhuis in Amsterdam: all were probably
worked up from sketches in about 1794,
being subsequently etched for publication
by Rudolph Ackermann in 1797. Many of
Rowlandson's finest Continental views,
including this one, were probably originally owned by his frequent travelling
companion, the banker Matthew Michell.

Following the example of Canaletto,
Rowlandson achieves a serene balance
between the bustle of street (and here,
quayside) life and the *gravitas* of public
buildings – the vertical emphases of Dutch
architecture aiding the contrast with the
horizontal foreground elements of boats,
jetty and water. Rowlandson's wiry pen
line brilliantly enlivens all manner of individual figures, from the (probably illicit)
gamblers in the boat on the extreme left to
the fishermen and their customers who
provide the central focus of attention. sw

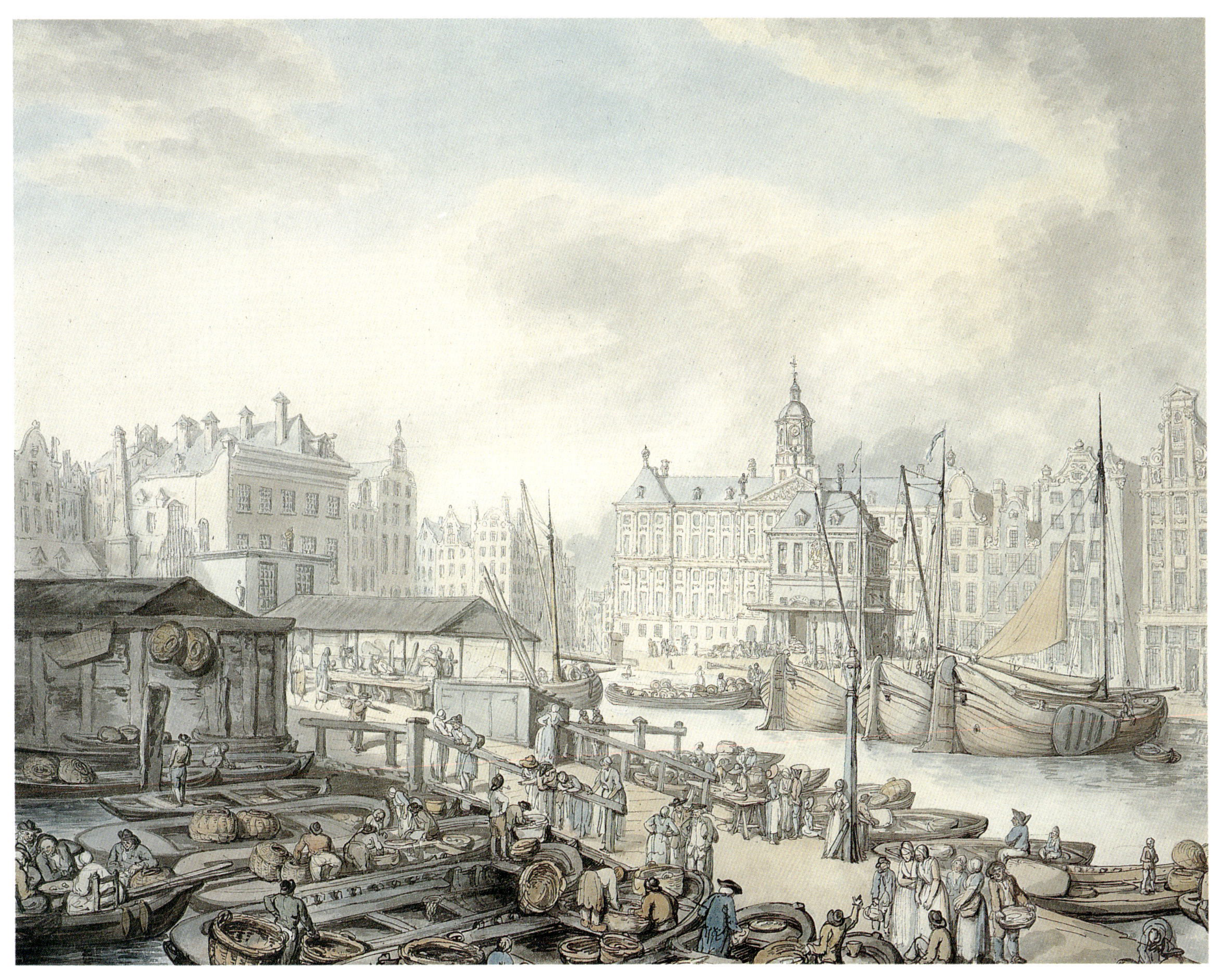

99 William Alexander
1767–1816

Chinese barges of Lord Macartney's Embassy preparing to pass under a bridge

Pencil and watercolour, ca. 1795
11 × 17 ins (27.9 × 43.2 cm)
Signed bottom right: W. Alexander del[t]
The Trustees of the Cecil Higgins Art Gallery, Bedford

Having shown modest talent as a top-ographical watercolourist in England, Alexander achieved celebrity by joining, as its official draughtsman, the first British embassy to reach China, led by Lord Macartney. He was away for two years, from September 1792 to September 1794, and on his return converted a mass of sketches into scores of finished water-colours. Many of these were engraved as illustrations to Sir George Staunton's *An Authentic Account of an Embassy from the King of Great Britain to the Emperor of China*, published in 1797.

Six versions are known of this, one of the most elaborate scenes, possibly repre-senting Soochow, which the Embassy reached on 7 November 1793. The artist has included himself in the composition, sketching on the big barge in the centre. The combination of boats and bustling figures struck an immediate chord in Alex-ander's mind, as noted in his journal: "At 2 p.m. arrived at the famous and flourishing city of Sou-tcheou, passing through but a portion of it where the canal is close under the walls of the city... many houses pro-ject over the canal reminding me of Canaletti's views in Venice".[1] sw

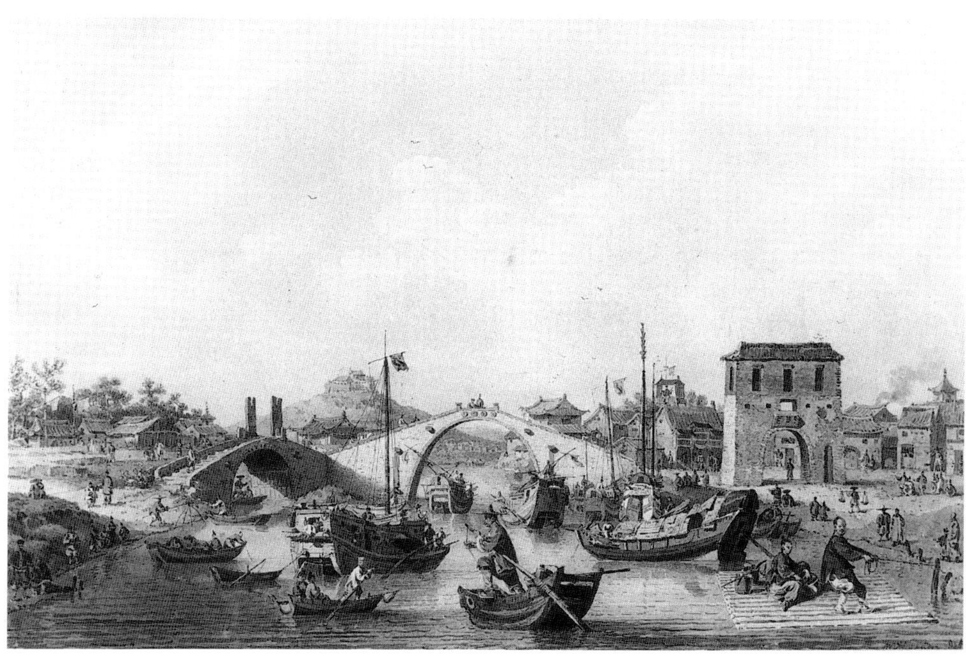

1. Quoted by Patrick Conner and Susan Legouix Sloman, *William Alexander: An English Artist in Imperial China*, exhibition catalogue, Brighton and Nottingham 1981.

100 William Alexander

Stern view of a boat descending an inclined plane or glacis near Ning Po

Pencil and watercolour, 1793
$10\frac{5}{8} \times 14\frac{3}{4}$ ins (27.0 × 37.6 cm)
Inscribed bottom right: WA; verso: Stern view of a boat going down one of the Glacies [*sic*] – November 1793
Birmingham Museums and Art Gallery

Equally redolent of a bustling Venetian canal scene, this is one of two depictions (the other is in the Whitworth Art Gal-lery, University of Manchester) of the system of inclined planes used on the waterway between Hangchow and Chusan to transfer barges from one level to another. The artist travelled from Chusan to Canton in November 1793, ahead of Macartney and the greater part of the Embassy [see cat. no. 99]. Although there are rather more figures in this subject, their faces are barely delineated, giving an increased sense of a large crowd. sw

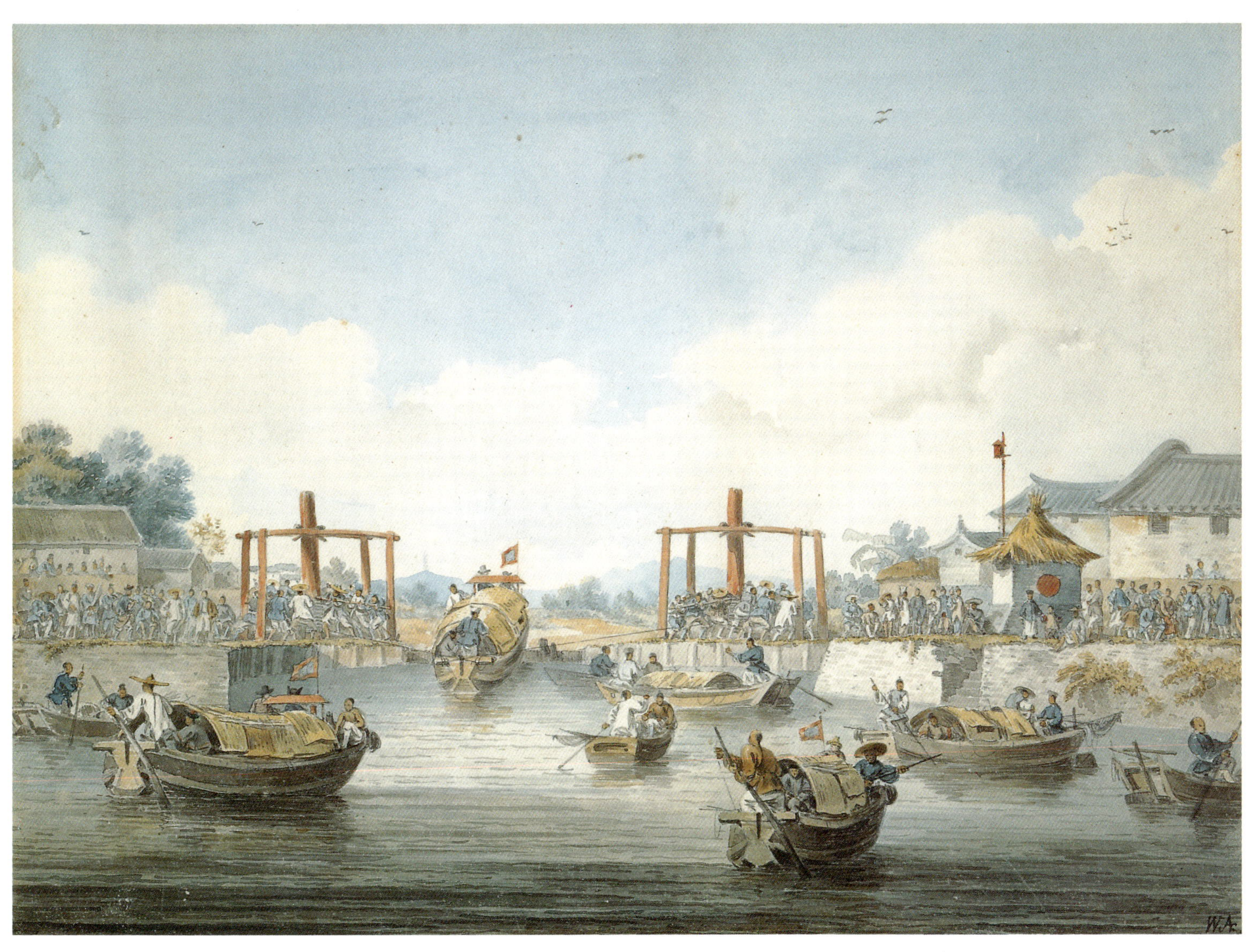

101 James Miller fl. 1773–91

St Paul's Church, Covent Garden, London, from the Piazza

Watercolour over pencil, ca. 1775?
$19\frac{3}{4} \times 16$ ins (50.2 × 40.5 cm)
Yale Center for British Art (Paul Mellon Collection), New Haven

This striking drawing has been quite reasonably attributed to the interesting but elusive topographical watercolourist James Miller. The figures are much more in his style than in that of Thomas Sandby, to whom a larger but otherwise identical watercolour (sold at Christie's, 14 March 1978, lot 126) has been attributed, on the evidence of similarity with other views of the Piazza. Miller seems to have been one of several artist sons (along with John Frederick and Richard) of the German engraver Johann Sebastian Müller (born ca. 1715, died 1792), who had anglicised his name and settled at Dorset Court, London, by 1768. James's best works are large watercolours of London street scenes, somewhat in the manner of Thomas Malton but with equal attention to street life as to architecture.

The compositional device of a view seen through an arcade was used many times by Canaletto, especially in the later *capricci* [cat. no. 40]. Here, the artist exploits to the full the dramatic potential for chiaroscuro, while still offering the spectator plenty of salient architectural detail. Planned by Inigo Jones in 1631 for the fourth Earl of Bedford, Covent Garden was London's first real square, but only the north and east sides – soon known as the Piazza – were fully developed. Although this vista of St Paul's Church (also by Jones, 1631–38) from the north-east corner of the Piazza can still be obtained today, it is from beneath arcades rebuilt in 1880. sw

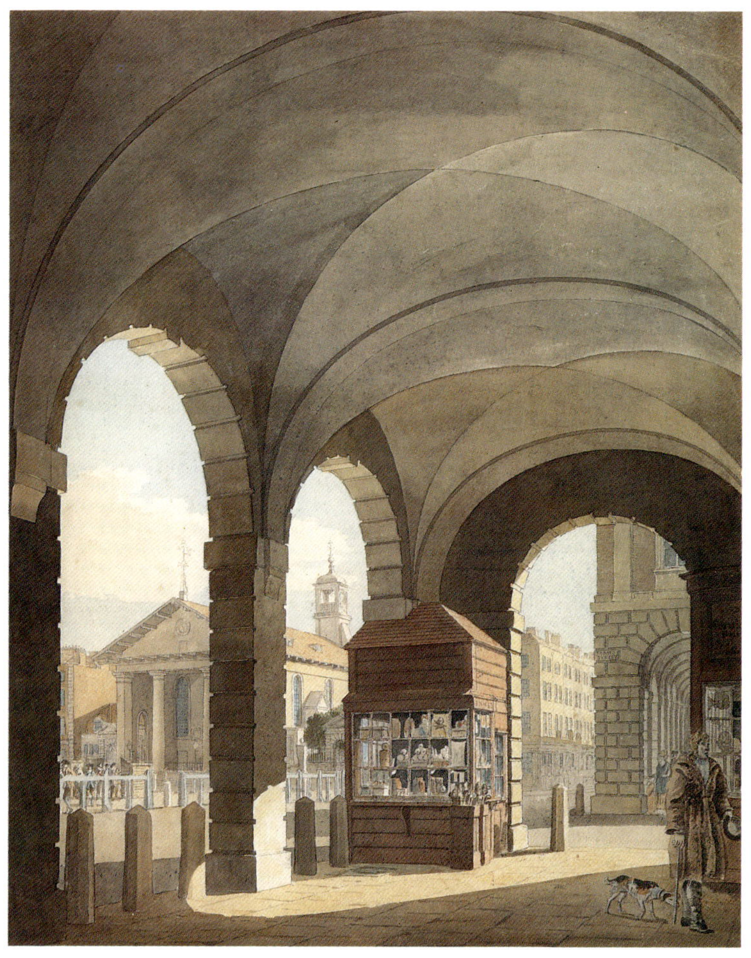

102 James Miller

A view towards Hanover Square, London, from Holles Street

Pen and ink, watercolour and bodycolour over pencil, ca. 1775
$18\frac{7}{8} \times 26\frac{3}{8}$ ins (48.0 × 67.0 cm)
Birmingham Museums and Art Gallery

This is the most delightful of all the watercolours attributed to Miller. It can be dated to about 1775, being doubtless similar to works such as *A view near Lord Grosvenor's House*, a watercolour exhibited at the Society of Artists in 1776. After taking pains to reproduce in great detail all the signs and street furniture which clearly fascinated him, the artist has then conjured up a mighty wind to buffet every hawker, resident and passer-by – a human but rather frivolous touch in which one cannot imagine Sandby, Malton or even Rooker indulging.

The view is from the short street joining Cavendish Square with Oxford Street, looking beyond to Hanover Square, with the portico and tower of St George's Church (by John James, 1720–25) as the

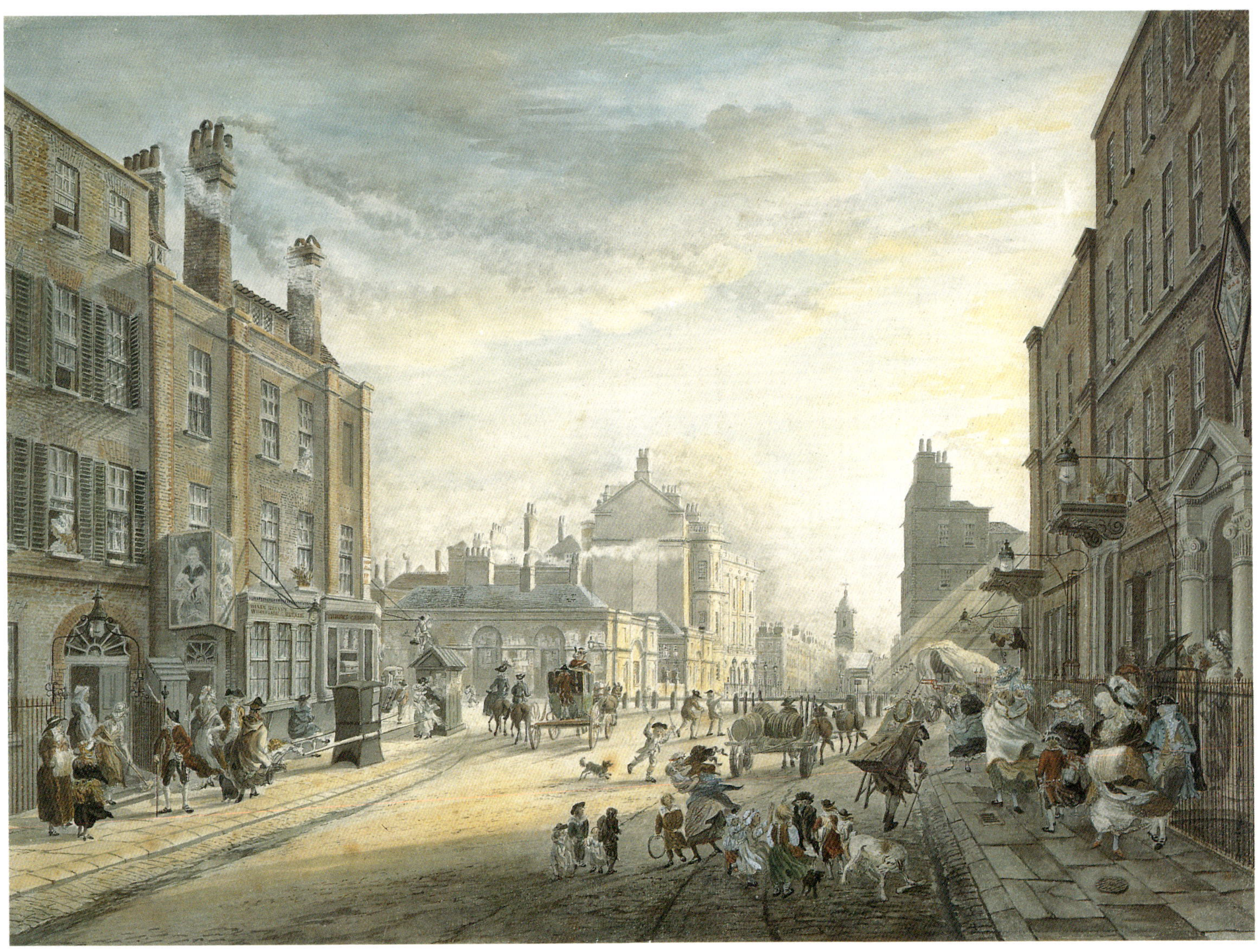

focal point. This was the Cavendish-Harley estate, planned in 1719–20 by John Prince (the self-styled 'Prince of Builders'), who held the leases of the houses shown on the left. On the right is the town house of an aristocrat (of the Tory party, the development south of Oxford Street being Whig ground). Writing about the Cavendish Square area, a contemporary commentator noted how "many a nobleman whose proud seat in the country is adorned with all the riches of architecture, porticoes, and columns . . . is here [in London] content with a simple dwelling, convenient within, and unornamental without".[1] sw

1 J. Stuart, *Critical Observations on the Building and Improvements in London, 1771*; quoted by John Summerson, *Georgian London*, new edition, 1988.

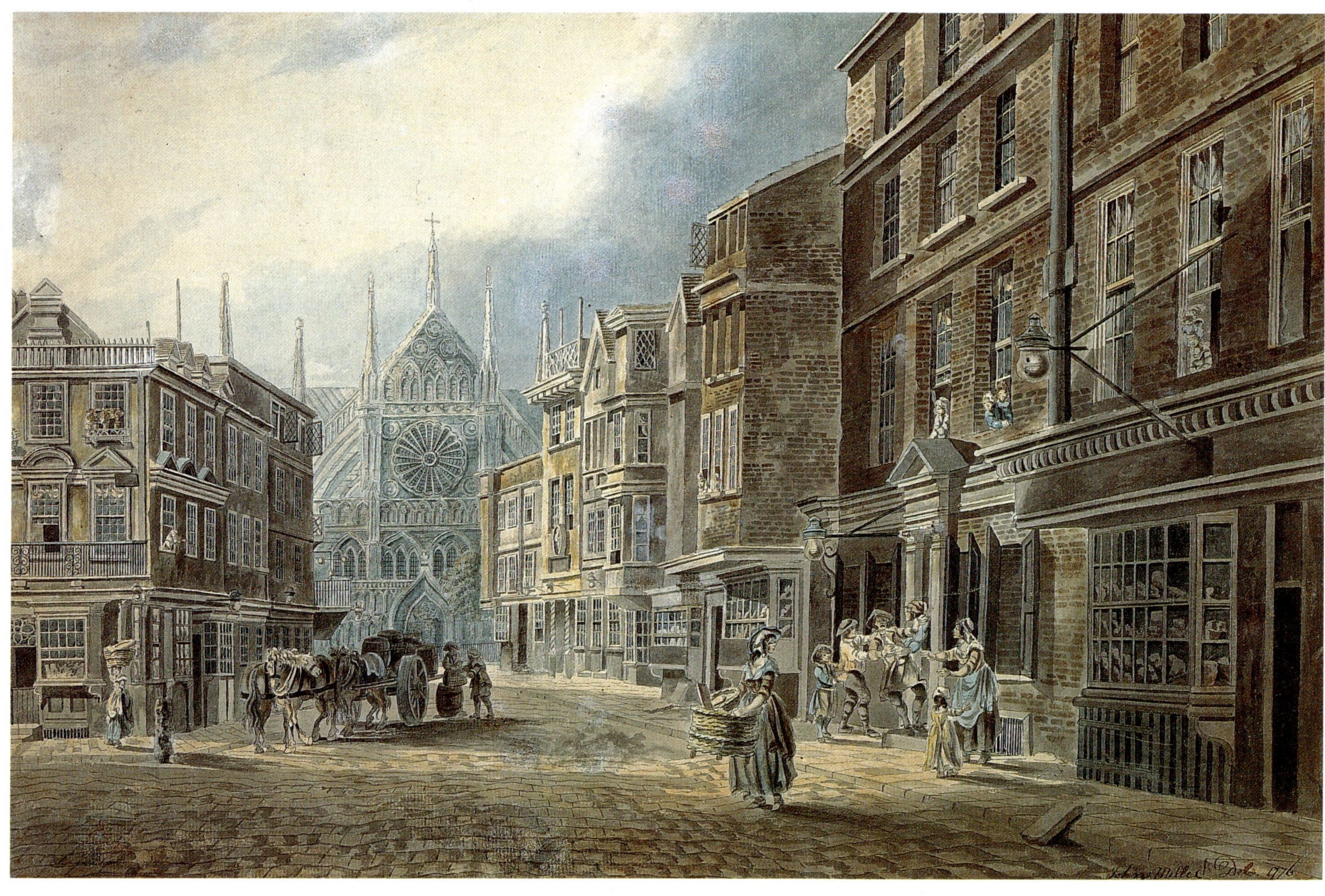

103 James Miller

Old Tothill Street, London, leading to Westminster Abbey

Pen and ink and watercolour over pencil, 1776
$12\frac{1}{4} \times 19\frac{3}{8}$ ins (31.0 × 49.3 cm)

Signed and dated bottom right: James [altered, in a later hand, to John] Miller Del. 1776

Birmingham Museums and Art Gallery

Lively figures are again the focus of attention in this view of a now vanished part of London. The area north of Westminster Abbey contained a warren of ancient streets which gathered an increasingly insalubrious reputation: the fracas taking place on the right of the scene may reflect this. The writer George Augustus Sala remembered it as "a cloaca of narrow, tortuous, shabby, stifling streets".[1] The fire which destroyed the Palace of Westminster in 1834 offered an opportunity to clear the site for an open public space, which is now Parliament Square.

This watercolour is possibly *A North East View of Westminster Abbey* exhibited at the Society of Artists in 1777 with a companion picture, *A South East View of Westminster Abbey, with Old Palace Yard*. sw

1. Quoted by Nikolaus Pevsner, *The Buildings of England, London I: The Cities of London and Westminster*, 3rd edition, 1973.

104 Thomas Girtin 1775–1802

Westminster from Adelphi Terrace

Pen and brown ink with grey washes,
ca. 1795
$11\frac{1}{2} \times 8\frac{1}{2}$ ins (29.5 × 21.7 cm)
A.H. Baldwin & Sons Ltd, London

Thomas Girtin was apprenticed to the
topographical draughtsman and watercolourist Edward Dayes in 1788. His early
training was in the conventional tradition
of picturesque and antiquarian topography
and he followed his teacher's manner of
making tinted drawings with pen outlines
washed in with pale grey and blue watercolours. By 1795 Girtin had made the
acquaintance of Dr Thomas Monro and
together with Turner and other young
watercolour artists frequented his house in
The Adelphi where they made copies of
drawings by various artists in the collection of Monro and his neighbour John
Henderson. Both owned works by
Canaletto, and this drawing taken from a
first-floor window in The Adelphi clearly
shows the Venetian's influence in the use
of the pen combined with grey washes to
lay in the tones and describe the effects of
light and shade playing on masonry. The
view shows the railings of Adelphi Terrace
in the foreground with the River Thames
looking towards Westminster Bridge in the
distance; at the right is the tower of the
York Buildings Waterworks. Beyond it are
the towers and roof of Westminster
Abbey, and in the distance the four corner
towers of St John Smith Square appear
over the rooftops. The whole is handled in
a very Canalettesque manner. The drawing
may have belonged to Dr Monro and is
possibly the Girtin sold by his executors in
1833 (lot 50, "The Thames from Adelphi").
ML

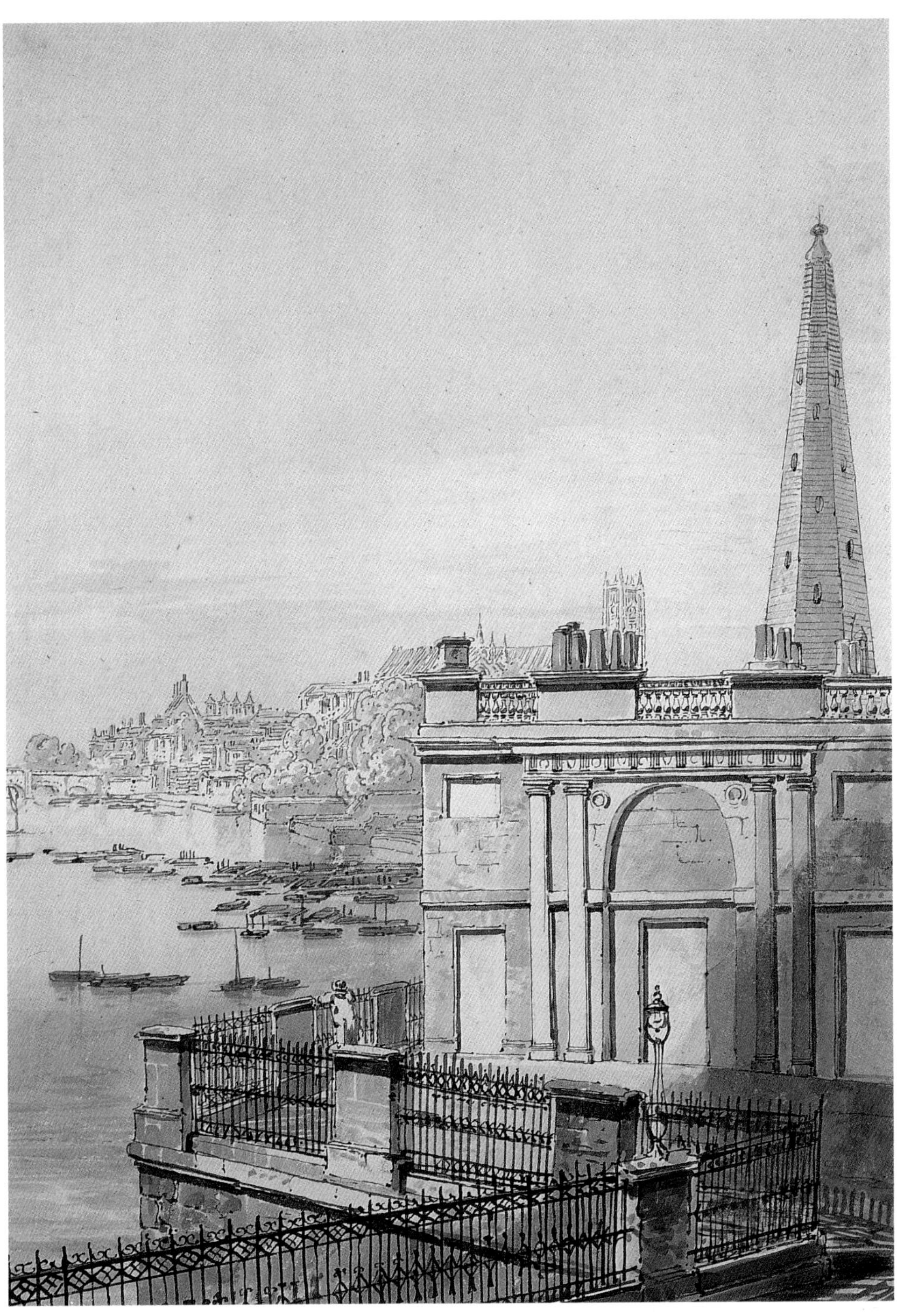

105 Thomas Girtin

Durham Cathedral

Pen and ink with grey wash, 1796
$7 \times 9\frac{1}{2}$ ins (17.8 × 24.1 cm)
Inscribed lower left: Girtin
Private collection

In this drawing Girtin demonstrates his
mastery of the English picturesque topographical tradition as it had evolved
during the last quarter of the eighteenth
century in the hands of watercolourists
like Paul Sandby, Michael 'Angelo'
Rooker, Thomas Hearne and his teacher
Edward Dayes for depicting ancient
monuments and illustrating antiquarian
studies. In 1796 he made a tour to the
north of England and Scotland, and this
drawing is probably a worked up compositional study made from a sketch done at
the time. It was used for two finished
watercolours, one now in the Birmingham
Museums collection [cat. no. 106] and
another at the Victoria and Albert
Museum, London. The drawing technique
employed for the architecture is strongly
suggestive of Canaletto's draughtsmanship,
and the handling of wash to create an
interplay of light and shade as well as to
organize the complex shapes of the houses
clustered below Durham Castle shows how
much he had learned from studying the
earlier artist's views. The drawing style is
also quite similar technically to pen and
wash compositional studies of views made
by William Marlow, who is known to have
attended *conversazioni* at Dr Monro's house
and whose work Girtin certainly knew. ML

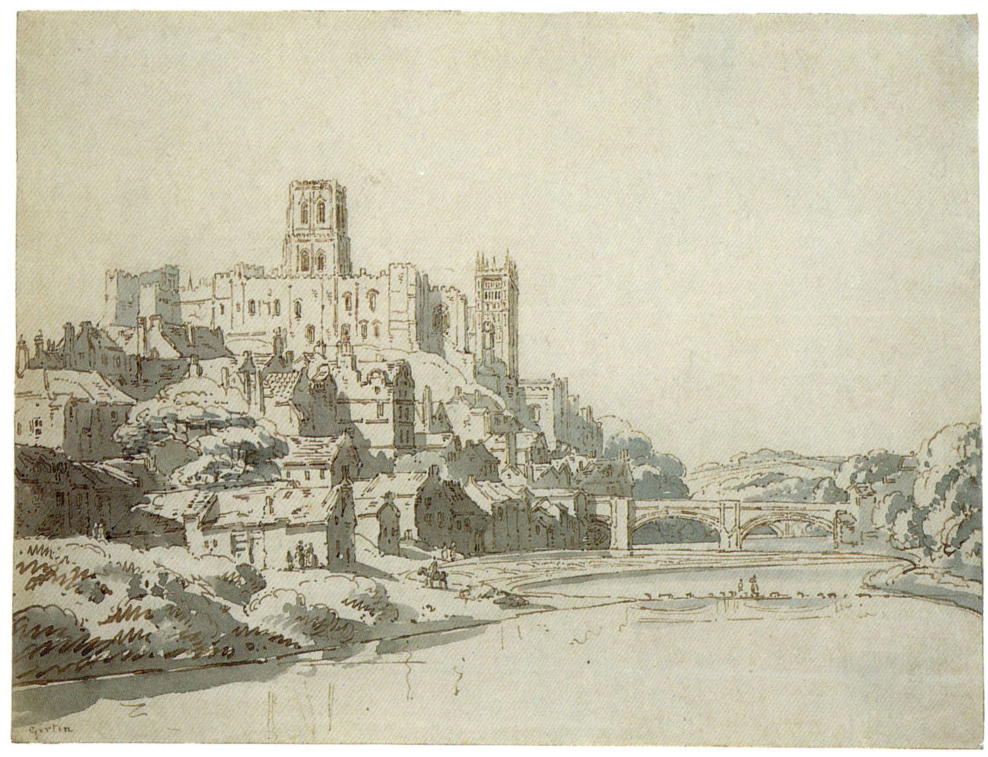

106 Thomas Girtin

Durham Cathedral and Bridge

Watercolour over pencil on coarse cream
paper, ca. 1797–98
$10\frac{1}{8} \times 14\frac{3}{8}$ ins (25.8 × 36.6 cm)
Verso: *Hilly landscape*, in watercolour over
pencil
Birmingham Museums and Art Gallery

From the two on-the-spot drawings of
Durham Cathedral and Bridge made
during the 1796 tour, Girtin produced finished watercolours of dramatically different
effect. A pencil study, now in the Museum
of Fine Arts, Boston, formed the basis of
the large (16 × 21 ins) and elaborate work
in the Whitworth Art Gallery, University
of Manchester, while the pen drawing [cat.
no. 105] was used for the present watercolour and for a larger version now in the
Victoria and Albert Museum.

The Whitworth subject, signed and
dated 1799, is the more powerful composition, the view being from river level
beyond the broad arches of the Bridge
towards the dominating Castle walls and
Cathedral towers. If this recalls the
Canaletto of large, formal canvases, then
the Birmingham watercolour is more redolent of the Venetian master's soft and
subtle draughtsmanship, with Girtin laying
his muted but wonderfully effective earth
colours over a scaffolding of typically
crumbly lines and dots (which themselves
complement the flecks in a rather coarse
paper). SW

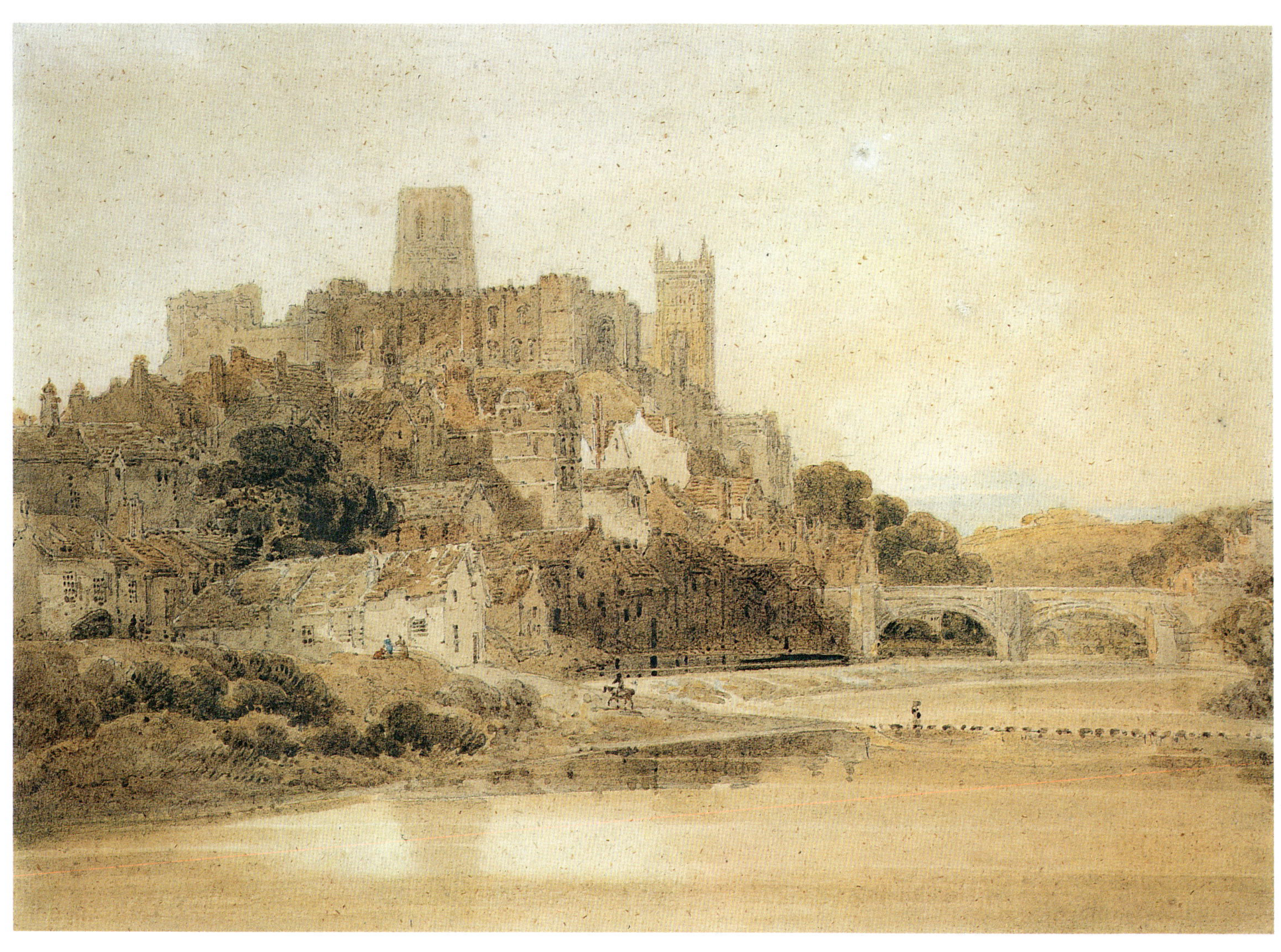

107 Thomas Girtin

Ruins of the Savoy Palace, London

Pen and brown ink with grey wash,
1795–96
$8\frac{1}{4} \times 12\frac{1}{4}$ ins (20.9 × 31.1 cm)
Yale Center for British Art (Paul Mellon
Collection), New Haven

The Savoy Palace, originally built in 1245
and restored by Henry VII, stood beside
the River Thames between York Stairs and
Old Somerset House. In the eighteenth
century the Palace had become dilapidated,
but parts of it were renovated and used for
various purposes – as a barracks, as a military prison, to house the King's Printing
Press, to provide chapels for different
foreign denominations and dissenting
faiths, and for commercial uses. As Girtin's
drawing shows, it was also in parts a ruin
which provided artists with an attractively
picturesque subject for antiquarian topography. It was eventually cleared away in
the nineteenth century to open up the
northern approach to Waterloo Bridge.[1]

In Girtin's drawing the river with part of
Westminster Bridge just visible can be seen
behind the architectural remains and workmen. The treatment is obviously inspired
by Canaletto in its use of a suggestive,
broken line and the animating accents contributed by the grey wash. The choice and
presentation of subject is typical of the
contemporary English taste for picturesque
antiquities. It is, however, a drawing which
has been compared in its decorative com-
pilation of attractively lit stonework and
old gothic structures to some of Canaletto's *capriccio* drawings of which there were
examples in John Henderson's collection in
The Adelphi and which Girtin certainly
knew.[2] The penmanship is also reminiscent
of Canaletto's etching style. ML

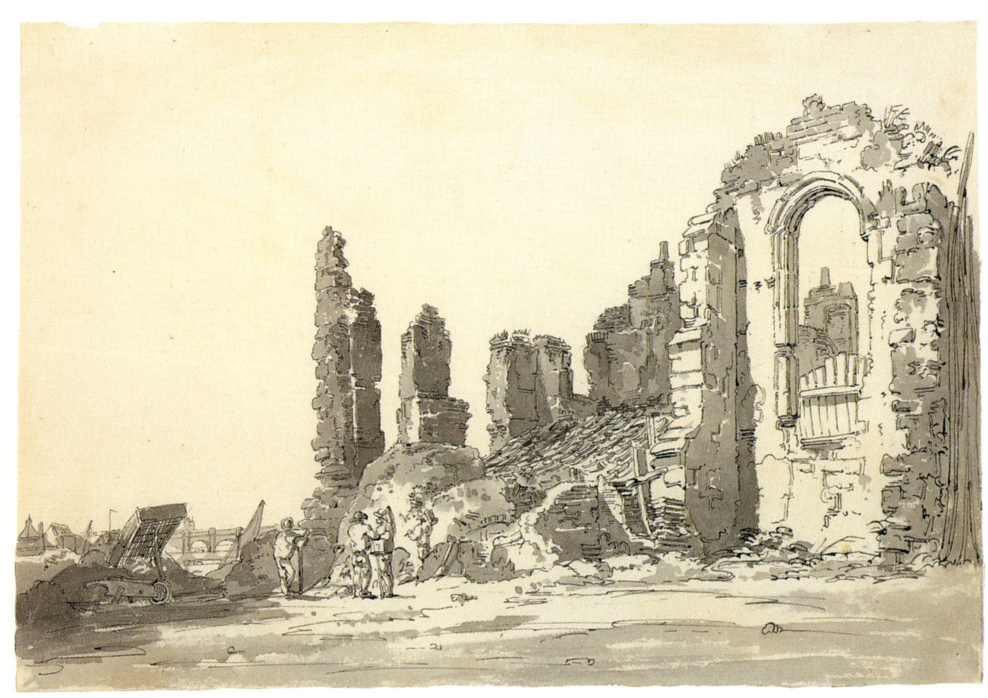

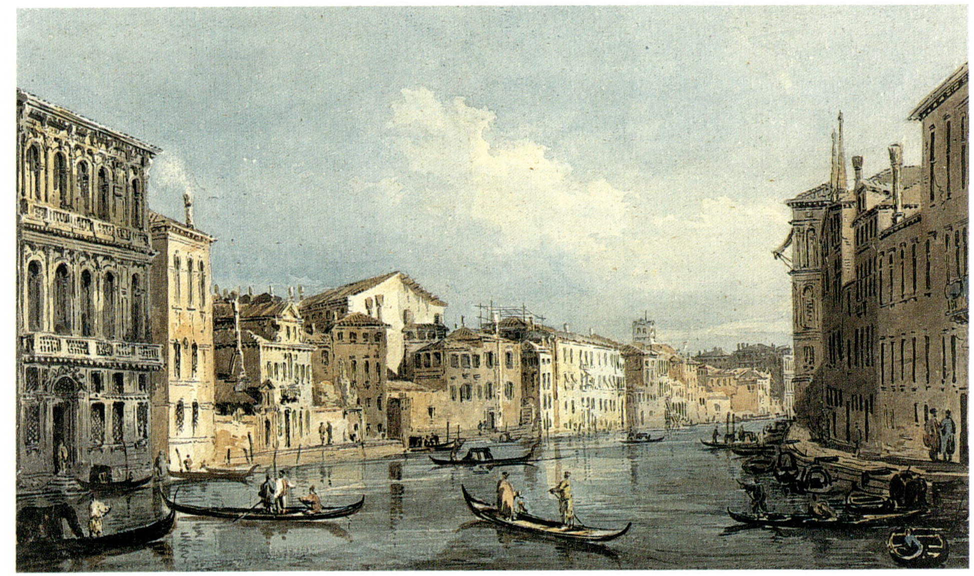

1. For the Savoy, see Hugh Phillips, *The
Thames about 1750*, London 1951, p.106.
2. Thomas Girtin and David Loshak, *The Art of
Thomas Girtin*, London 1954, p.61.

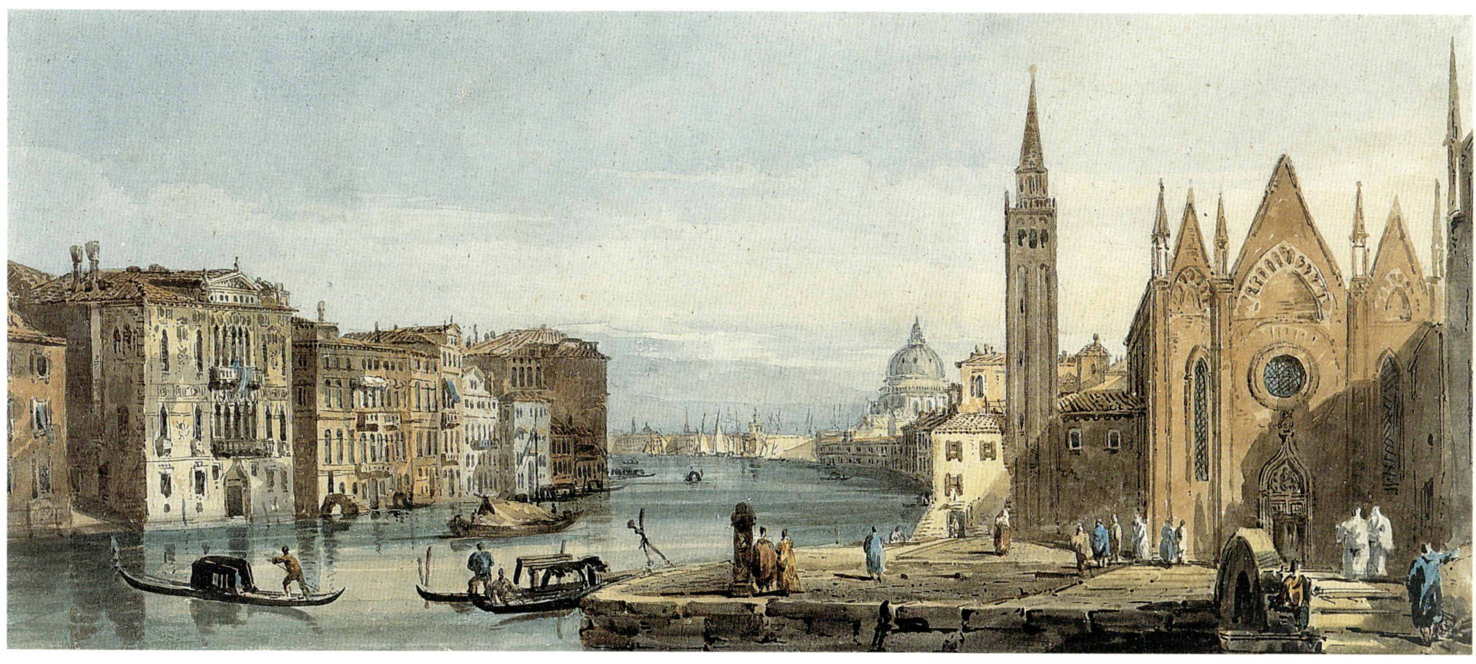

108 Thomas Girtin

After Canaletto: The Grand Canal, Venice, from Santa Maria della Carità to the Bacino di San Marco

Watercolour, 1797
$8\frac{1}{4} \times 19\frac{1}{4}$ ins (20.6 × 48.9 cm)
The Trustees of the British Museum, London

109 Thomas Girtin

After Canaletto: The Grand Canal, Venice, looking east from the Palazzo Flangini to San Marcuola

Watercolour, 1797
$9\frac{3}{4} \times 15\frac{3}{4}$ ins (24.8 × 40 cm)
The Trustees of the British Museum, London

Both these watercolours, together with two more similar copies after Canaletto also in the British Museum, have a provenance that goes back to John Henderson whose collection in The Adelphi which Girtin knew well included a number of works by Canaletto, paintings as well as drawings. These and the other two related watercolours, however, are done from prints and reproduce engravings in the second, enlarged 1742 edition of the set by Antonio Visentini published under the title *Prospectus Magni Canalis Venetiarum.*

The original painting of the Grand Canal with the gothic church of Santa Maria della Carità on the right is in the Royal Collection, and was one of the pictures belonging to Consul Joseph Smith which he included in the first set of fourteen Visentini prints issued in 1735. The other watercolour is based on a print of a painting done after 1735 which must have passed through Smith's hands: no picture exactly corresponding to Visentini's engraving is known, but there is a very similar view with a different arrangement of figures and gondolas.[1] Girtin has precisely followed the composition of the print he has copied in each case, but added his own colours. Since Turner was another regular visitor to The Adelphi between 1795 and 1798 he must also have seen the same Canaletto sources.
ML

1. W.G. Constable (revised J.G. Links), *Canaletto*, 1976, II, nos. 196, 257.

110 Thomas Girtin

All Saints Pavement, York

Watercolour, 1800
$10\frac{3}{4} \times 14\frac{3}{4}$ ins (27.3 × 37.5 cm)
Private collection

Girtin visited Yorkshire in 1800, staying at
Harewood with his patron Edward (later
Viscount) Lascelles. At this time his style
was undergoing a major change from the
picturesque topography of his earlier work
to a much richer and more expressive
treatment of landscape and architectural
subjects. In the latter especially he displays
a more powerfully evocative and suggestive sense of atmosphere as well as a more
pronounced monumentality and drama
that owe something to his having copied
etchings by Giovanni Battista Piranesi, the
eighteenth-century Italian artist originally
from Venice who was widely admired for
his imaginatively inspired views of Rome
and Roman antiquities. In this street scene
looking towards the tower and gothic lantern of All Saints Pavement, Girtin's newly
invigorated style is fully developed, but
there are still features which reflect his earlier debt to Canalettesque properties. There
are hints of Canaletto's drawing style in
the treatment of the stonework of the
window tracery and buttresses of the foreground church, and the handling of the
brush with its free use of abbreviated
dashes and accents may be traced to the
same source. Contemporary with this
watercolour is another of *Wetherby Bridge,
Yorkshire* (British Museum),[1] which shows a
view of village houses seen through two
arches of a bridge in a composition which
makes specific reference to the Canaletto-
Scott-Marlow tradition and indicates the
extent to which Girtin had incorporated
their formal vocabulary into his own repertoire. ML

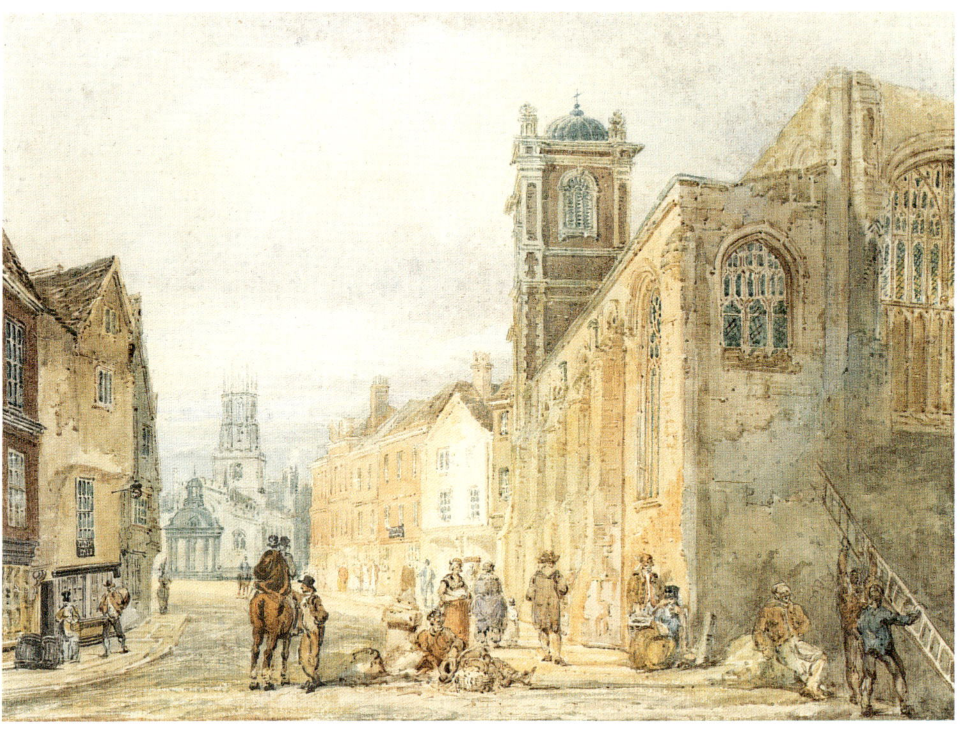

1. *Watercolours by Thomas Girtin*, catalogue by
Francis W. Hawcroft, Manchester, Whitworth
Art Gallery, 1975, no. 75.

111 Joseph Mallord William Turner 1775–1851

Warwick Castle and Bridge

Pencil and watercolour, with gum, 1794
$16\frac{3}{4} \times 20\frac{3}{4}$ ins (42.5 × 52.7 cm)
The Whitworth Art Gallery, University of
Manchester

Turner's earliest signed and dated drawings, from 1787, include a copy of an
engraving of Oxford after Michael
'Angelo' Rooker; by the end of 1789,
when he was fourteen, he was working
with Thomas Malton whose exacting and
precise topographical drawing style he
quickly learned to emulate. Other very
early works by Turner include copies made
after Paul Sandby and watercolour drawings which clearly reveal that he looked
carefully at Thomas Hearne and Edward
Dayes. Thus, from the very beginning of
his career, Turner's artistic origins are
located within the English topographical
tradition. He showed his first watercolour
at the Royal Academy in 1790. Probably
from 1792 he knew both Dr Thomas
Monro and Thomas Girtin, and in 1793
the tour he made taking in Worcester,
Hereford, Tewkesbury and Tintern may
have been to work on commissions for
John Henderson. He was, therefore, drawn
into the circle of Monro, Henderson and
their artist friends: by these means he was
exposed to a wide variety of artistic

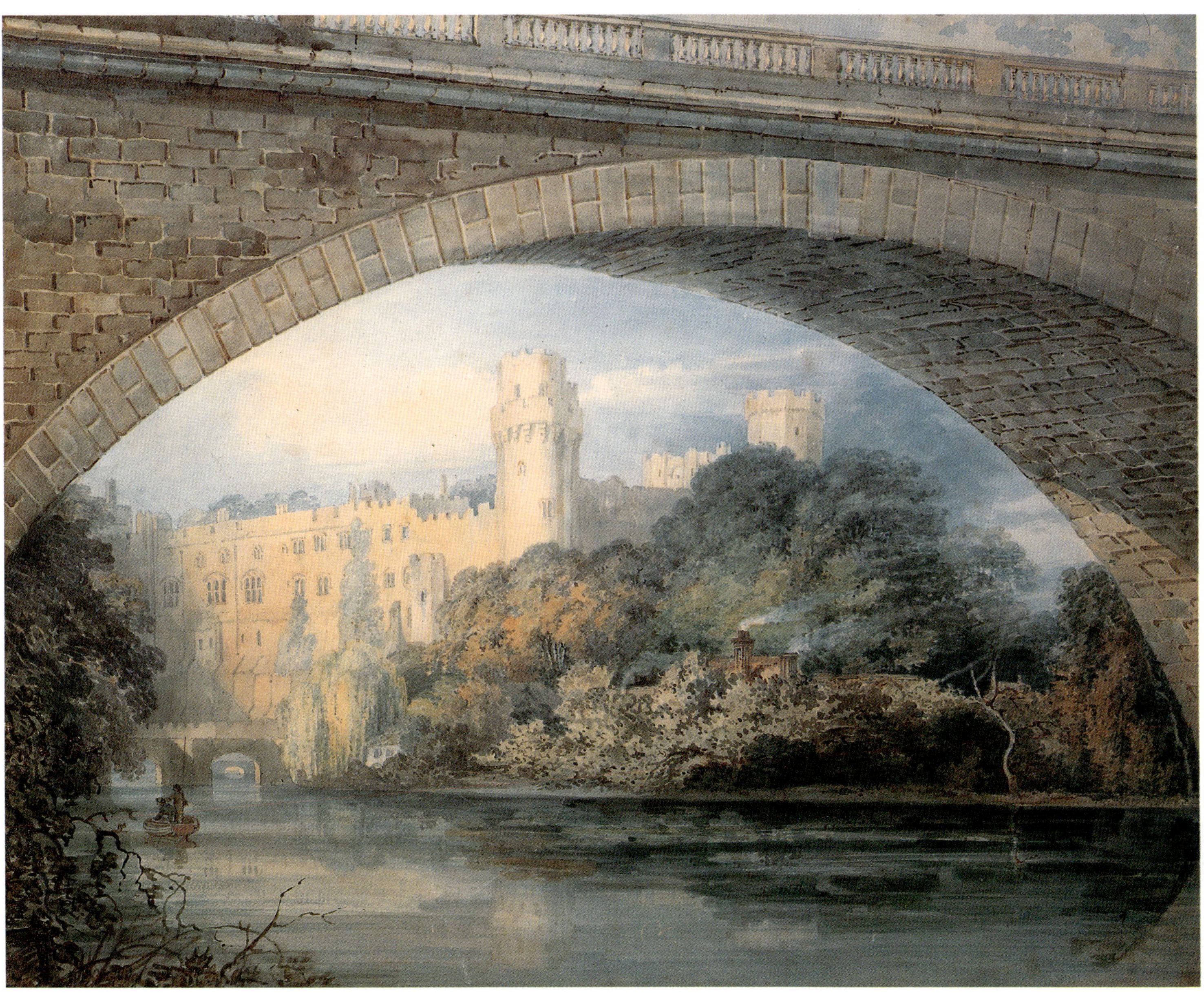

experiences which embraced the whole range of English landscape and topographical painting and certainly included works by Canaletto and his English followers and successors. Turner was always an artist who responded imaginatively and creatively to the visual stimulus of others' work, and in his own watercolours and paintings the originality with which he continually reinterpreted earlier or contemporary artists' ideas is constantly apparent. In this 1794 view of Warwick Castle seen through the arch of the bridge there are recollections not only of Canaletto's classic device of framing a view but also of the picturesque styles of watercolourists such as Hearne, Sandby and Dayes. The drawing may have belonged to Dr Monro who encouraged young painters to copy works by Canaletto. ML

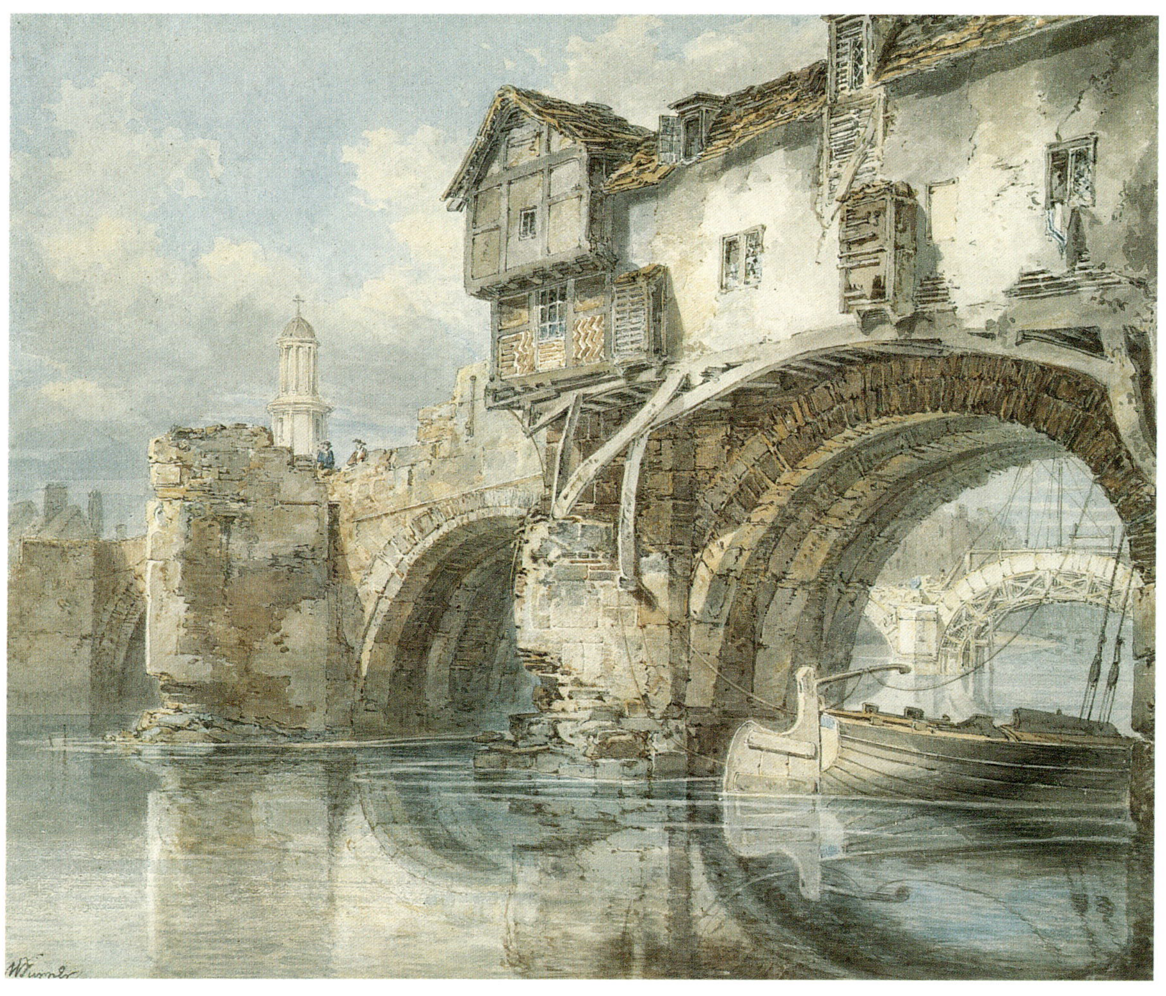

112 J.M.W. Turner

The Old Bridge, Shrewsbury

Pencil and watercolour, 1794
$9 \times 10\frac{13}{16}$ ins (22.9 × 27.5 cm)
Signed and dated lower left: W. Turner 1794
The Whitworth Art Gallery, University of
Manchester

Turner exhibited this watercolour at the
Royal Academy in 1795 as "Welsh Bridge
at Shrewsbury" (no. 593). In his 1794–95
drawings Turner achieved a complete mastery of the vocabulary of picturesque topography combined with a subtle
comprehension of tonal effect and atmospheric suggestion. As Andrew Wilton has
observed, in the work of this period
"Turner's understanding of architecture
seems to attain a new pitch of insight,
marked not only by the firmness and precision of drawing, but by a fresh sense of
artistic licence".[1] The composition of this
watercolour and its use of the arch motif
are adaptations of pictorial formulations
that Canaletto had been the first to use in
England in the 1740s. Turner's interest in
the construction of the new bridge seen
through the near arch recalls the 1746
Canaletto of the arch of Westminster
Bridge with its wooden centring [cat.
no. 6]. Here Turner is also concerned to
contrast the medieval bridge with its
modern replacement, the new structure
rising beyond the old serving as a symbol
of progress in the industrial age which was
transforming Shrewsbury, one of the early

centres where rapid changes were overtaking the old world of pre-industrial England. The picturesquely decaying antiquity in the foreground should be read as an emblem of the past confronted by the challenge of the new order. ML

1. Andrew Wilton, *The Life and Work of J.M.W. Turner*, London 1979, p.38.

113 J.M.W. Turner

Blackfriars Bridge, London

Pencil and watercolour with scratching out, ca. 1795
$10\frac{1}{4} \times 6\frac{3}{4}$ ins (26 × 17.2 cm)
The Whitworth Art Gallery, University of Manchester

This watercolour illustrates particularly dramatically Turner's ability to borrow a motif from other artists and use it inventively to enrich and enhance the impact of his treatment of a familiar motif in British topographical painting. The acute perspective and dominating mass of Robert Mylne's neoclassical bridge built between 1760 and 1769 creates a boldly foreshortened composition which is redolent of the eighteenth century's concept of sublimity in its emphatic grandeur of scale and strong contrasts of light and shade, bringing to mind Piranesi's prints of monumental Roman structures. It also adapts the sharply foreshortened composition of Canaletto's *Westminster Bridge under construction* painted in 1746–47 for Sir Hugh Smithson [fig. 2], a composition which was reused by William Marlow and others; Turner himself adapted it for another early watercolour of *Westminster Bridge* (1796–97, University College of Wales, Aberystwyth).[1] In his *Blackfriars Bridge*, however, he has brought the viewpoint

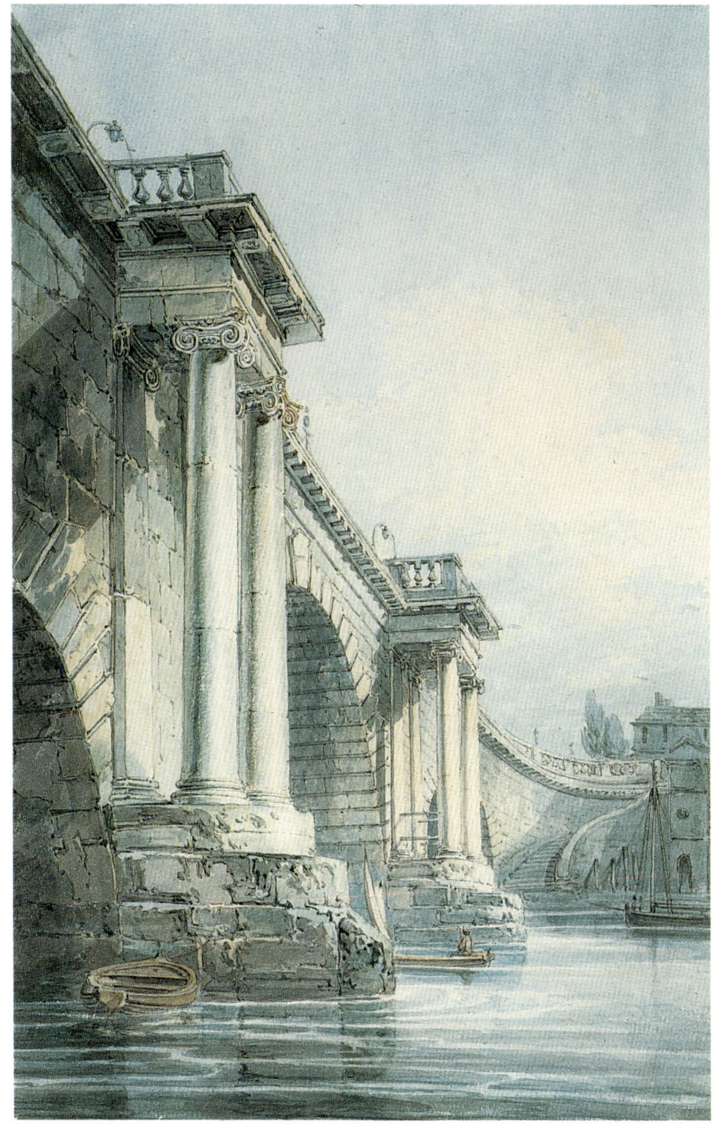

closer to the base of one of the piers and concentrated the view on a short section rather than the whole length of the bridge, thereby achieving a much more visually dramatic result. The play of light on the stonework suggested by his application of washes, and his use of the brush to delineate the masonry and details recollect Canaletto's draughtsmanship and almost

certainly reflects what he learned from drawings belonging to Dr Monro and John Henderson. ML

1. Andrew Wilton, *The Life and Work of J.M.W. Turner*, London 1979, cat. no. 96.

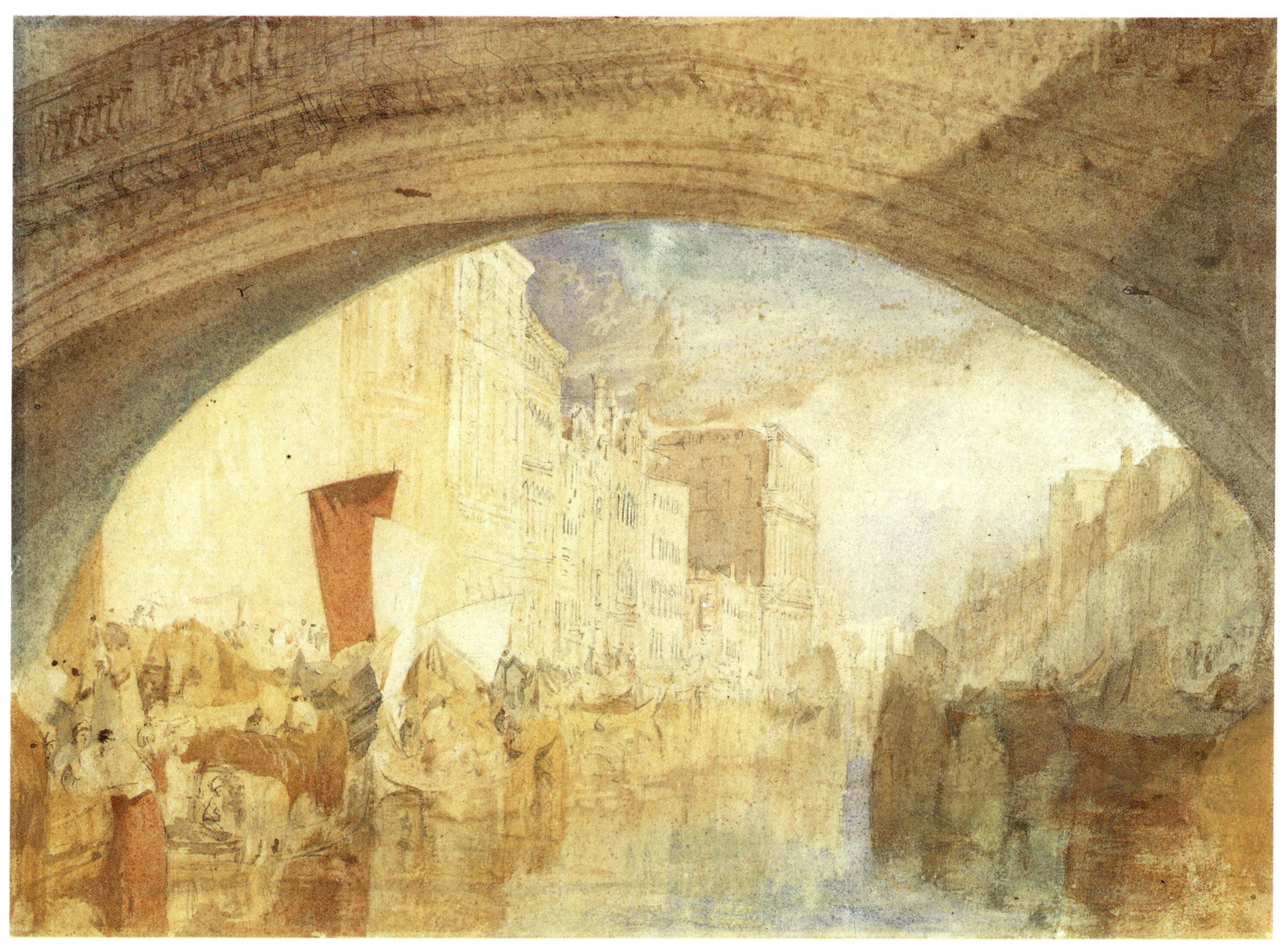

114 J.M.W. Turner

The Grand Canal, Venice, from below the Rialto Bridge

Pencil and watercolour, ca. 1820
$11\frac{5}{16} \times 16$ ins (28.7 × 40.7 cm)
The National Gallery of Ireland, Dublin

Turner first visited Venice in 1819; he went there on two subsequent occasions, in 1833 (the more probable date, rather than 1835 as some authorities state) and 1840. After the end of the Napoleonic Wars in 1815 Continental travel was possible once again, and in the years that followed English artists responded to the popular demand for pictures of European scenery which was stimulated by the growth of tourism across a wider social spectrum than had been the case in the eighteenth century. The vision of Venice cultivated in the imaginations and experience of nineteenth-century British visitors was conditioned in part by their familiarity with the works of the eighteenth-century *vedutisti*, especially Canaletto whose pictures were known to many in the originals as well as through copies and engraved reproductions, but in part also through the writings of romantic poets such as Byron

and Shelley. In 1819 Turner was captivated
by the colour and spectacle of Venice; the
watercolours he made during his visit are
among the most evanescent and atmospherically suggestive he ever did. His studies made in Venice and the later oils and
watercolours which resulted from this and
subsequent visits display a vividly sensational as well as romantically charged
poetic vision in which reality and sensibility are combined in a series of brilliant
evocations of the place and its associations.
In this unfinished watercolour the initial
spontaneous response of a sketch is pre-
served together with the beginnings of a
more elaborated development – it offers a
vivid insight into the way Turner's transfiguring imagination was inspired by his
experience of the city. Turner often relates
the reality he experienced to the work of
earlier artists, and here the framing arch
and festively crowded Grand Canal may
have been suggested by recollections of
Canaletto. ML

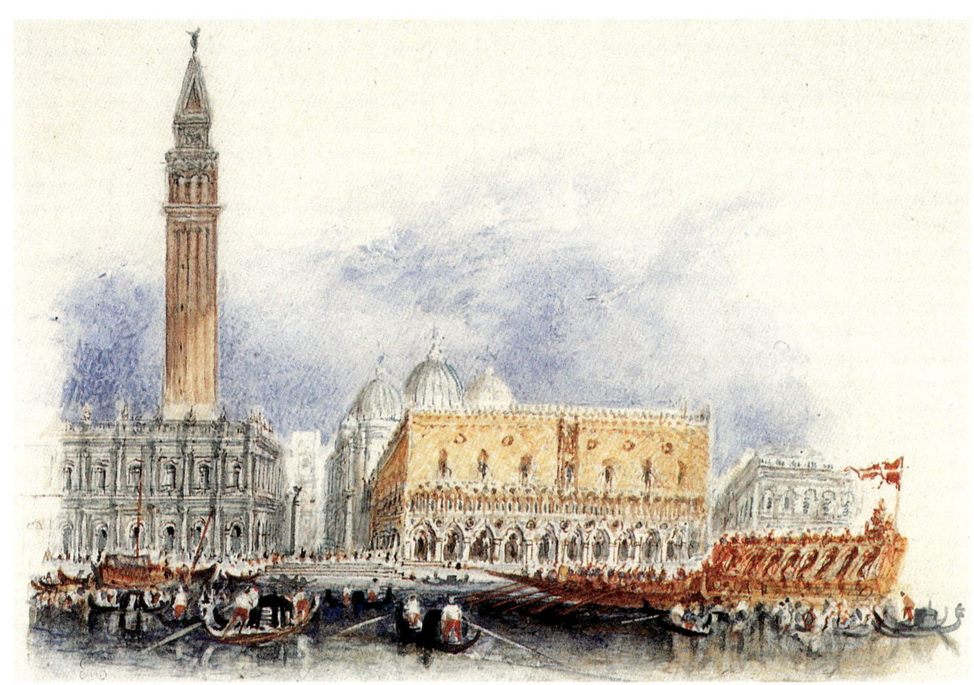

115 J.M.W. Turner

The Doge's Palace, Venice

Pencil and watercolour with scratching out,
ca. 1827
$4\frac{7}{8} \times 7\frac{3}{16}$ ins (12.3 × 18.3 cm) vignette image
The Trustees of the Tate Gallery, London

This watercolour was one of a series of
vignettes made to illustrate *Italy*, a poem
in two parts by Samuel Rogers. Its separate
parts had first appeared in 1822 and 1828
respectively. In 1826 Rogers approached
Turner to design illustrations for another
edition which was eventually published in
1830 and became a great popular success
because of the finely engraved vignette
views. John Ruskin later recalled that it was
this book which first introduced him to
Turner's work and so inspired his passion-
ate interest in art. Turner had sketched the
view of the Campanile and Doge's Palace

in 1819, but when he came to make the
vignette for Rogers he turned as well to
Canaletto, introducing the Ducal barge Il
Bucintoro and animated flotillas of gondolas. The source he consulted was one of
Visentini's engravings from the 1742 collection of plates, *Prospectus Magni Canalis
Venetiarum*. There are, however, considerable differences in the architecture, and
Turner has taken major liberties with San-
sovino's Library on the left of the Piazzetta. His vignette is an evocation of the
splendours of Venice's past before the
Republic was suppressed by the French in
1797, and the vivid intensity of the colour
communicates the feeling of nostalgia for
what had been lost which so often informs
the romantic vision of Venice in the nineteenth century. ML

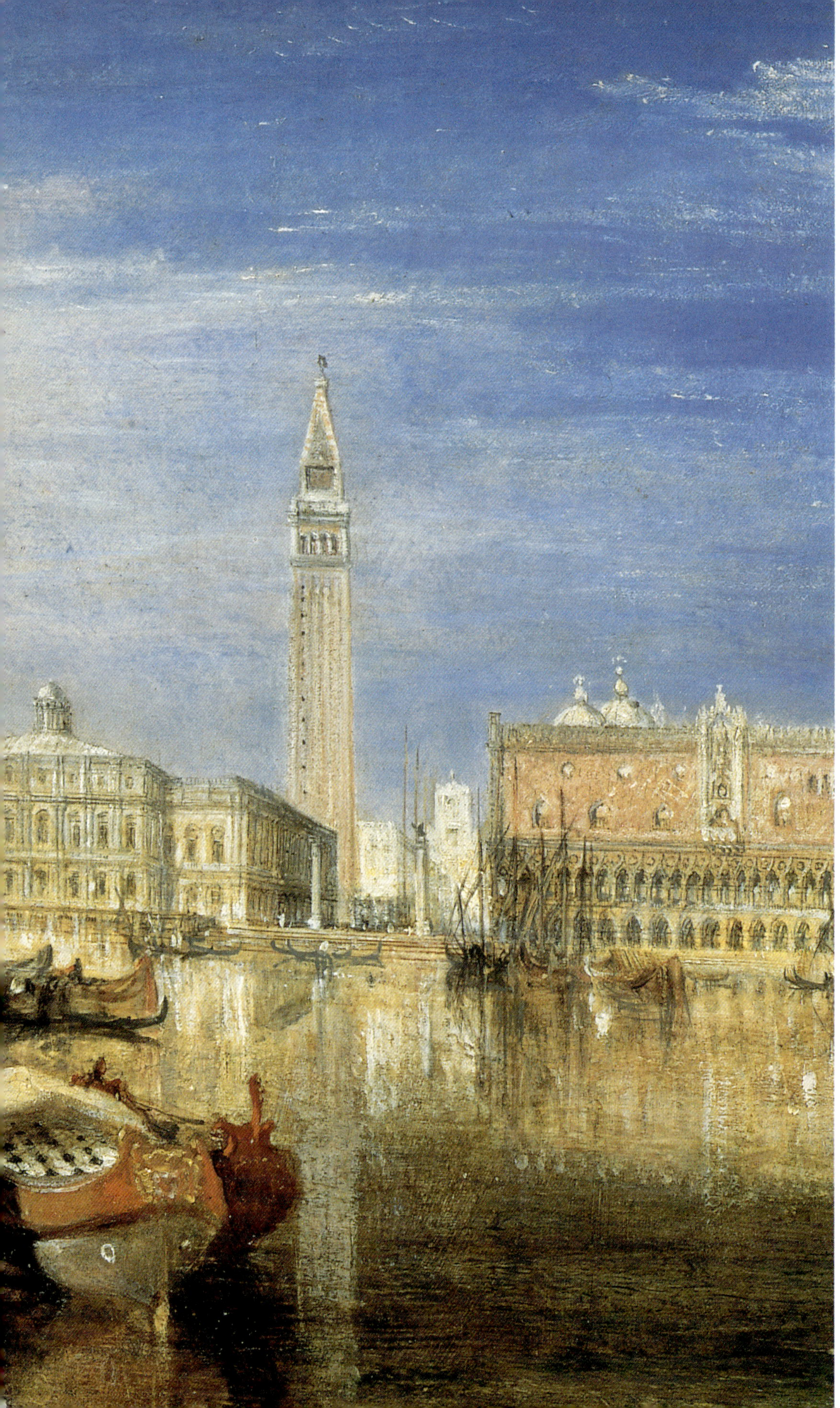

116 J.M.W. Turner

The Bridge of Sighs, Doge's Palace and Customs House, Venice: Canaletto painting

Oil on mahogany panel, 1833
$20\frac{1}{8} \times 32\frac{1}{2}$ ins (51×82.5 cm)
The Trustees of the Tate Gallery, London

Turner showed this painting (entitled *Bridge of Sighs, Ducal Palace and Custom House, Venice: Canaletti Painting*) at the Royal Academy in 1833. According to a report in the *Morning Chronicle* (6 June 1833) it was painted just before the summer show opened to get the better of a rather "flashy" Venetian piece by a younger, rising artist who was attracting a great deal of critical attention. Such stories about Turner abound, and are probably often apocryphal. On this occasion Turner supposedly intended to put Clarkson Stanfield's effort in the shade by painting the picture, "it is said, in two or three days, on learning that Mr Stanfield was employed on a similar subject – not in the way of rivalry, of course, for he is the last to admit to anything of the kind, but generously we will suppose, to give him a lesson in atmosphere and poetry". The painting is clearly conceived as a tribute to Canaletto as the most celebrated of all the Venetian *vedute* painters. Turner painted other pictures in which historically famous artists are represented (Raphael and Watteau), and often he refers to the great masters of the past stylistically in his own work to signify his relationship to tradition. In this he does both: Canaletto's presence in the picture (at the left, standing before his easel and apparently working on a picture in an elaborate gilded frame) gives the painting an elevating historical meaning, while as a view it is invested with an imaginative

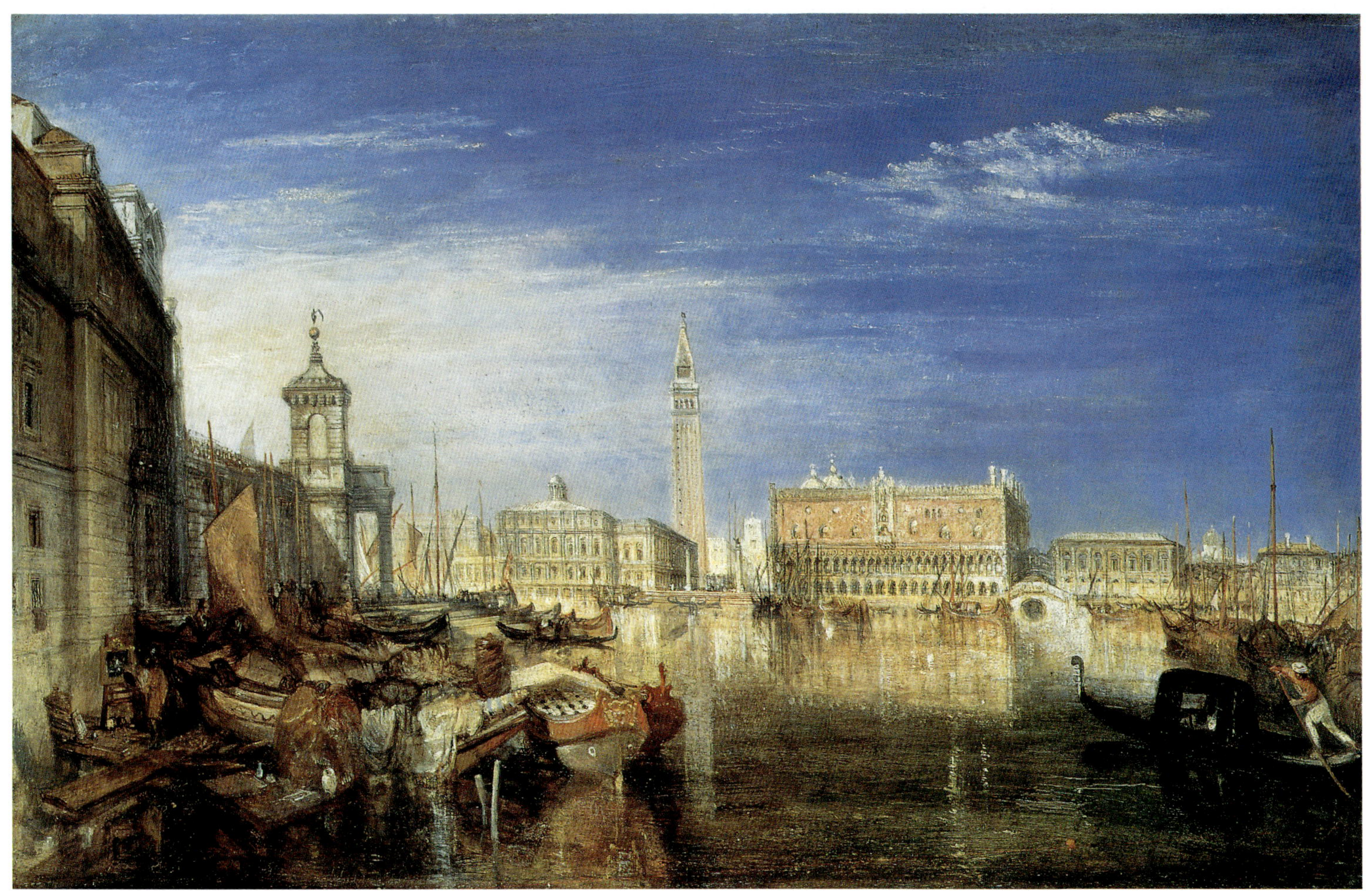

impulse that goes far beyond traditional topography. It was this kind of picture Ruskin had in mind when he wrote how Venice liberated Turner's genius: "There he found freedom of space, brilliancy of light, variety of colour … and to Venice we owe many of the motives in which his highest powers of colour have been displayed …".[1] ML

1. John Ruskin, *Modern Painters*, I, 1843 (*Complete Works* Library Edition, London 1903–12, III, p.244).

117 John Sell Cotman
1782–1842

View on the River Sarthe at Alençon

Pencil, 1823
$9\frac{3}{16} \times 13$ ins (23.3 × 33.2 cm)
Inscribed with title lower left, signed and
dated: J.S. Cotman Decr 24th 1823;
numbered lower right: 1863
The Trustees of the British Museum, London

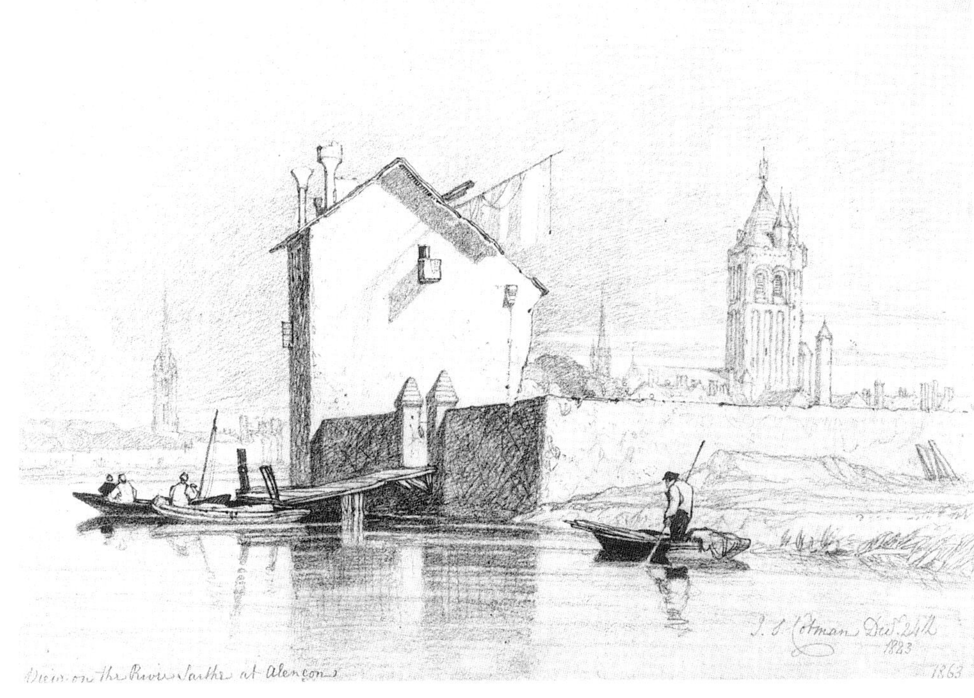

Despite its title specifically identifying the
location as a scene in Normandy this
drawing is in fact based freely on a composition by Canaletto.[1] Cotman must
have known the original from an etching
published by Josef Wagner in Venice
between 1760 and 1765 as one of a set of
six entitled *Sei Villaggi Campestri* each reproducing a drawing by Canaletto. Different versions of Canaletto's drawing are
known, but the one that is likeliest to have
been used for Wagner's print is the example in the Ashmolean Museum, Oxford
[cat. no. 39]. The same scene with some
variations was adapted for one of the six
capricci Canaletto painted in England in
1754–55 for Baron King [cat. nos. 37 and
38]. Cotman has taken the essentials of
Canaletto's design and by replacing the
campanili in the distance far left and on the
right with the towers and spires of two of
Alençon's churches, and adding a third
where Canaletto has a tree, he has transformed the subject into a scene in Normandy. Cotman visited Normandy three
times in 1817, 1818 and 1820, making
drawings to illustrate a book on *The Architectural Antiquities of Normandy* by his
patron Dawson Turner who had a large
print collection. In 1823 Cotman moved
from Yarmouth where he had been working for Dawson Turner to Norwich. There

he earned his living as a drawing master,
and the number 1863 inscribed here lower
right indicates that this is one of his large
lending library of drawings he had made
for pupils to learn from copying. Cotman's
interest in Canaletto must go back to the
late 1790s when, as a student in London,
he used to attend evening sessions for
young artists at Dr Monro's Adelphi house
and there would have seen (and possibly
copied) examples of his work. ML

1. Catherine Whistler, 'A Canaletto source for
Cotman', *The Ashmolean* XX, Summer/Autumn
1991, pp.11–13.

118 Samuel Prout 1783–1852

Domodossola, Piedmont

Pen and ink, watercolour and bodycolour
with gum, ca. 1825–30
18 × 23¾ ins (45.5 × 60.4 cm)
The Trustees of the Victoria and Albert
Museum, London

Samuel Prout was born in Plymouth
where he received his initial training in
watercolour painting and in drawing picturesque scenery. His first important
patron was the antiquary John Britton
who employed him to make drawings of
archaeological and architectural subjects
from 1801. He also copied sketches by
artists such as William Alexander, Thomas
Hearne, Turner and others whose work
Britton admired and used to illustrate his
books. Since Britton was a prolific writer
on antiquities who commissioned and collected large numbers of drawings to illustrate his various publications, Prout quickly
became proficient in the conventions of
picturesque topography and in precisely
recording architectural subjects. He was in
London working for Britton from late
1801, and over the next twenty years he
became a regular exhibitor at the Royal
Academy and the watercolour societies; he
also established a reputation as a teacher
and produced a series of sketching manuals
for two of the leading London fine art
dealers, Thomas Palser and Rudolph
Ackermann. In 1819 he visited France for
the first time, and thereafter travelled
extensively on the Continent in the 1820s
and 1830s. From these visits he produced
many lithographs of picturesque subjects
abroad, and engravings after his work
appeared in publications such as *The Landscape Annual* and *The Continental Tourist*.

From early on Prout admired Canaletto's
draughtsmanship, and there are echoes of it

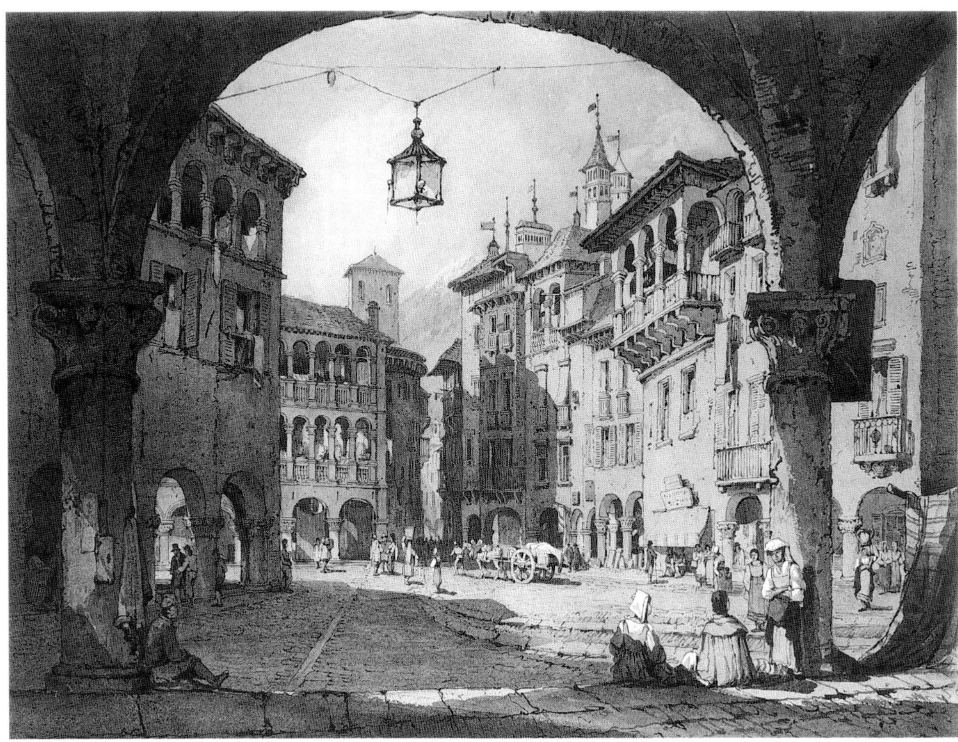

in the way he uses a broken-line technique
and sometimes employs pen and ink to
reinforce and enliven the architectural
details in his watercolours. In this view of a
piazza in Domodossola in northern Italy he
also adapts a Canalettesque motif in framing the scene through an arch and sus-
pending a lantern against the sky – a
recollection perhaps of Canaletto's *capriccio*
etching of a *Portico with a lantern* [cat. no.
40]. Prout first visited Italy in 1824, and
this watercolour probably dates from
1825–30. Prout's interest in Canaletto

around the middle of his career is documented in some of his letters, for example
in one he wrote to Sir William Knighton
describing a visit to Windsor where he
"…was especially delighted in a hasty look
at His Majesty's superb, & invaluable collection of Canalettis" and expressing the
wish that "…I shall, at a future day, be
indulged in spending an hour for the
express purpose of studying them, as pictures more connected with my pursuit than
any other collection in the world". ML

119 David Roberts 1796–1864

Santa Maria della Salute, Venice

Oil on canvas, 1862
28 × 45 ins (71.1 × 114.3 cm)
Signed and dated lower right: David Roberts
RA/ 1862
Sheffield City Art Galleries

The son of a poor Edinburgh cobbler, David Roberts became an artist having first been apprenticed to a house painter, then graduating from scene-painting for a travelling circus to stage sets in various theatres before ending up at the Drury Lane Theatre in London in 1822. He developed his drawing and painting style for finer work by teaching himself using manuals, copying, and through his contacts with other painters such as Clarkson Stanfield whom he worked alongside at Drury Lane. Roberts was one of the artists who exploited most effectively the nineteenth-century British fashion for travel and the popularity of printed collections of views of picturesque and exotic places. His most celebrated publications were the series of coloured lithographs of *Picturesque Sketches in Spain during the years 1822 and 1823* and his *Views in the Holy Land, Syria, Idumea, Arabia, Egypt and Nubia* (1842–49). He became a regular and prolific exhibitor at the Royal Academy and was elected a Royal Academician in 1841. His paintings and watercolours of Venice are very characteristic of the kind of conventional topographical work in which artists like Bonington and Turner far excelled him. Where their paintings of Venetian subjects have a vivid brilliance and evocative splendour, Roberts produced competently drawn and technically proficient views which are more decorative than inspirationally expressive. They are, though, typical of the continuing British fascination with Venice which

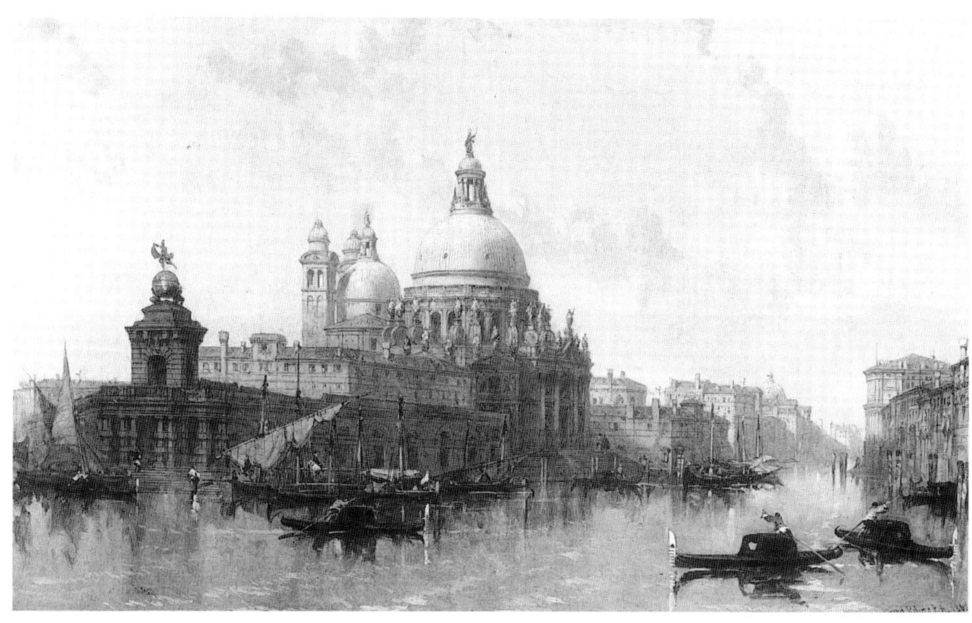

enjoyed such an intense revival in the middle decades of the nineteenth century. Roberts is perhaps closer to Canaletto in intention than Turner, though his paintings are not at all like his eighteenth-century predecessor's except in subject matter: his paintings record rather than interpret Venice. Where Turner's vision is sometimes almost pure poetry, Roberts's is finely crafted prose. ML

120 James Holland 1800–1870

The Grand Canal, Venice

Watercolour and bodycolour over charcoal, 1844
$14\frac{1}{8} \times 18\frac{3}{4}$ ins (36.0 × 47.8 cm)
Signed and dated on sail of boat, left:
JH/1844
Birmingham Museums and Art Gallery

In 1842 Holland resigned from the Old Water Colour Society in the hope of gaining election to the Royal Academy; like several others who trod this path, he was unsuccessful, and returned to the fold in 1856. This watercolour, one of many Venetian subjects produced in these interim years, was probably an exhibit at the Society of British Artists, an institution rather more sympathetic to aspiring draughtsmen-painters than the Academy.

Holland tended to stick to expansive views of the city's main arteries rather than

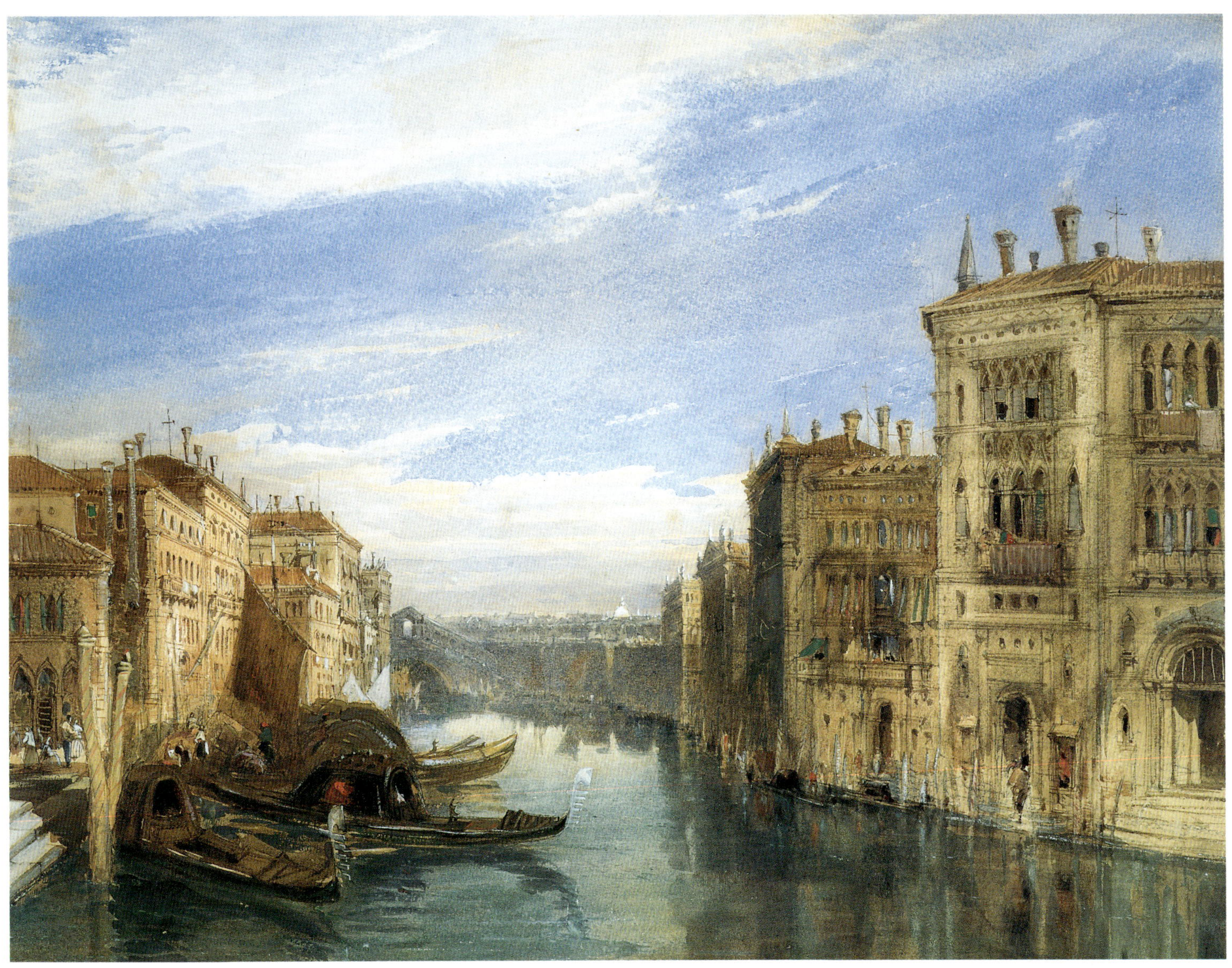

diving into the more picturesque side canals. In this respect he perhaps provided the last fading link between the Victorian era and that of Canaletto, although his vision was a thoroughly romantic one. Hugh Stokes recognised that "his Venice is the Venice of Byron rather than of Goldoni", and that while "he had not the unfatigued and fresh observation or the delicacy of Bonington, the calculated unimaginative method of Canaletto, or the elusive, flickering light and shade of Guardi . . . he gives us a very personal point of view, and in many cases a very beautiful one."[1]

sw

1 'James Holland', *Walker's Quarterly*, no.23, n.d. [1926], pp.35–36.

121 James Holland

The Doge's Palace and Customs House, Venice

Watercolour and bodycolour over pencil,
1851 or 1857?
$12\frac{1}{2} \times 20\frac{3}{4}$ ins (31.8×55.2 cm)
Inscribed verso: James Holland / Venice
The Provost and Fellows of Eton College

Holland's first visit to Venice had been in
1835; John James Ruskin, father of the
critic, was a purchaser of one of the four
Venetian subjects shown at the Old Water
Colour Society in the following year.
Although his imagination was fired for
many years thereafter [cat. nos. 122 and
123], Holland paid further visits to
replenish his stock of ideas in 1845, 1851
and 1857.

   This expansive sketch – presumably
made from a gondola – has the feel of a
more mature work, either in preparation
for an oil suitable for the Royal Academy
or Society of British Artists or for a late
exhibition watercolour. Though architectural form and detail begin to dissolve, Holland's image – even down to the detail of
huddled figures by the Customs House at
the left – remains essentially one in the
spirit of the eighteenth-century *vedutisti*. SW

122 James Holland

The Grand Canal and Santa Maria della Salute, Venice

Watercolour and bodycolour over pencil,
1857
$14 \times 20\frac{1}{4}$ ins (35.5×51.5 cm)
Signed and inscribed bottom right: JH
Venezia Octr. 1857 E. 4 p.m.
The Provost and Fellows of Eton College

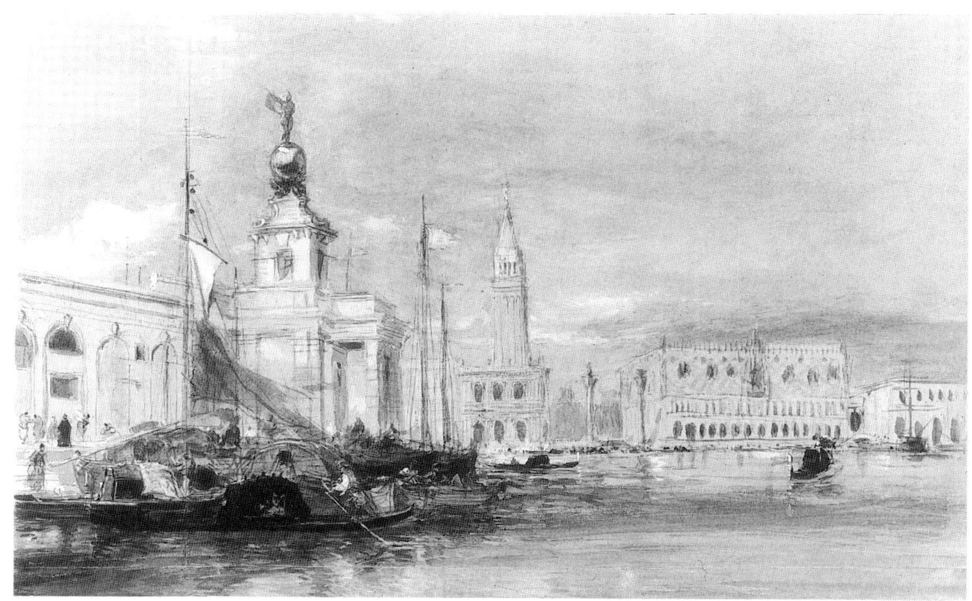

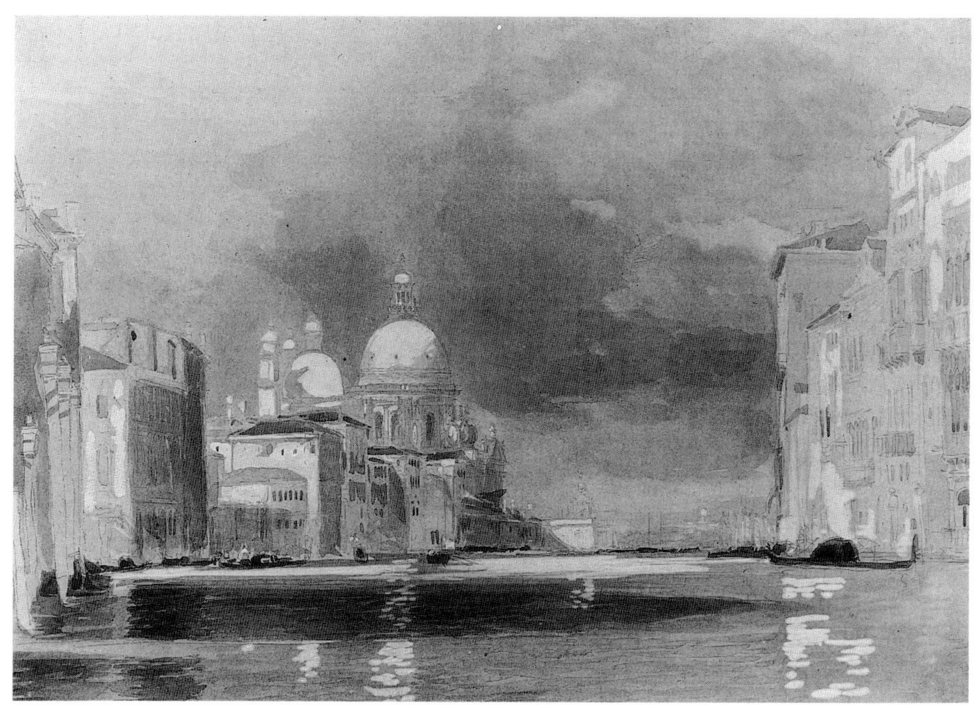

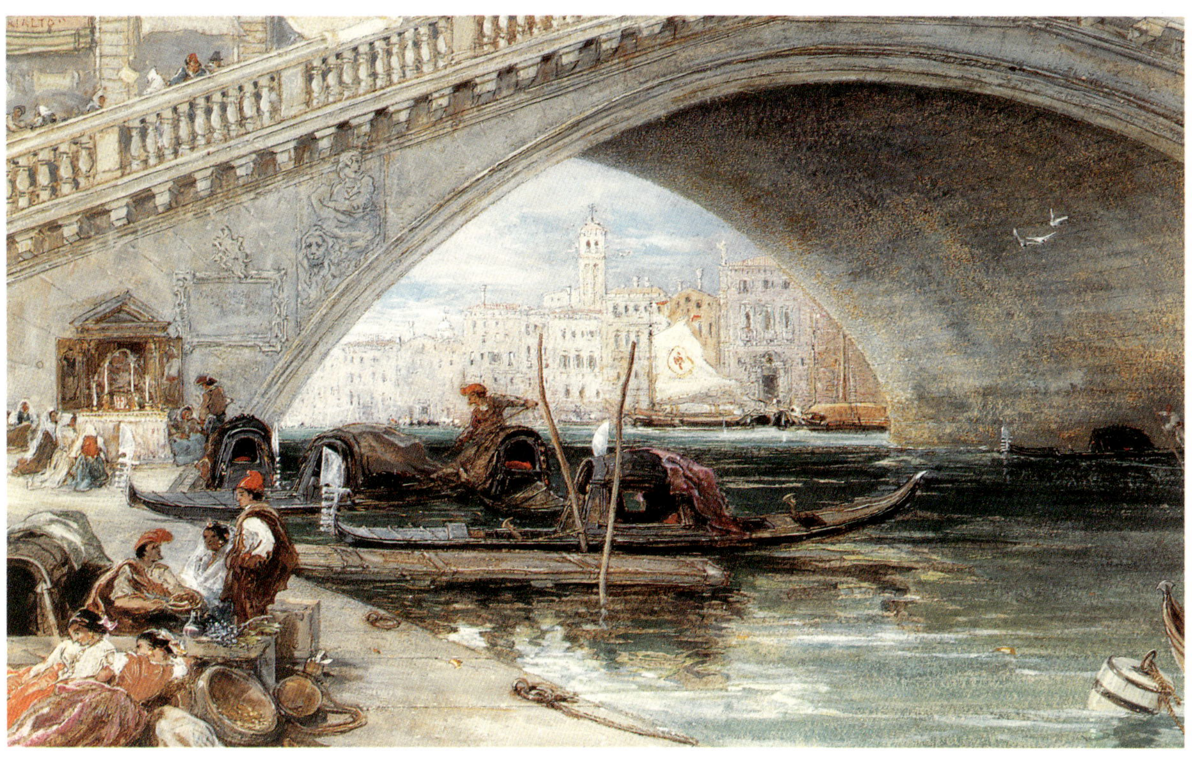

From Holland's visit in 1857 there survives an exceptional body of drawings annotated with the hour of day as well as the date. Like Bonington's freer watercolours [cat. no. 125], they have a sparkling freshness, responding directly to the light and colour of Venice. Watercolours painted with calculated deliberation in the studio could not be expected to match this, as Holland recognised when making his celebrated remark: "Parting with a sketch is like parting with a tooth. Once sold it cannot be replaced." sw

123 James Holland

Gondoliers beneath the Rialto Bridge, Venice

Watercolour and bodycolour over pencil, 1863
$12\frac{1}{2} \times 21\frac{1}{4}$ ins (32.0 × 54.0 cm)
Signed and dated on box, left: JH / 63
Private collection

This splendid late watercolour, which once belonged to the watercolourist Myles Birket Foster, shows Holland still ringing the changes of Venetian subject matter. It is probably identifiable as *The Rialto*, exhibited at the Old Water Colour Society in 1863.

By mid century, both Ruskin and Thackeray were expressing their dissatisfaction with the hackneyed views of Venice to be seen year after year on exhibition walls. In 1850, the latter wrote: "How long are we to go on with Venice, Verona, Lago di So-and-So, and Ponte di What d'ye-call-em? I am weary of gondolas, striped awnings, sailors with red night (or rather day) caps, cobalt distances and posts in water."[1]

However, the *Art Journal*'s critic in 1863 recognised Holland's ingenuity of composition, which offers a distant echo of Canaletto's use of the device of a framing bridge: "Mr. Holland with his rapturous love of colour makes *The Rialto* span, with its single arch of grey, the emerald green of the canal beneath, set off by the red caps of Venetian boatmen".[1] sw

1 Quoted by Martin Hardie, *Water-colour Painting in Britain, III: The Victorian Period*, London 1968, pp.35, 34.

124 Richard Parkes Bonington 1802–1828

The Doge's Palace, Venice, with a religious procession

Oil on canvas, 1827
45 × 64 ins (114.5 × 162.5 cm)
Signed bottom right: R P Bonington
The Trustees of the Tate Gallery, London

Shortly after moving into his own studio in Paris, Bonington set off on 4 April 1826 for his first (and only) trip to Italy, in the company of his friend Charles Rivet. They spent a little less than a month in Venice, leaving on 19 May for Padua and then Florence. As well as sketching in oil and watercolour, Bonington made numerous drawings which he was to turn into finished works in both media.

A pencil drawing now at Bowood served as the basis for a watercolour (Wallace Collection) and small oil (Louvre, Paris), as well as this, one of Bonington's largest and most ambitious paintings. It can be identified as the *Vue du palais ducal à Venise* shown at the Paris Salon in November 1827 and subsequently exhibited at the British Institution in February 1828. In his account of the Salon, the critic Auguste Jal wrote that 'Bonington is a clever fellow … His view of the Ducal Palace in Venice is a masterpiece. I do love what the Canaletti so justly extoll. Vivacity, firmness, effect, colour, breadth of touch, all are in this painting.'[1]

Such a composition offers conscious acknowledgement of Canaletto's work (the artist's father owned a set of the etchings), and as Bonington was one of the first British painters to exhibit large-scale views of Venice, contemporary criticism could hardly resist the comparison. Mostly this was in Bonington's favour: writing in 1832,

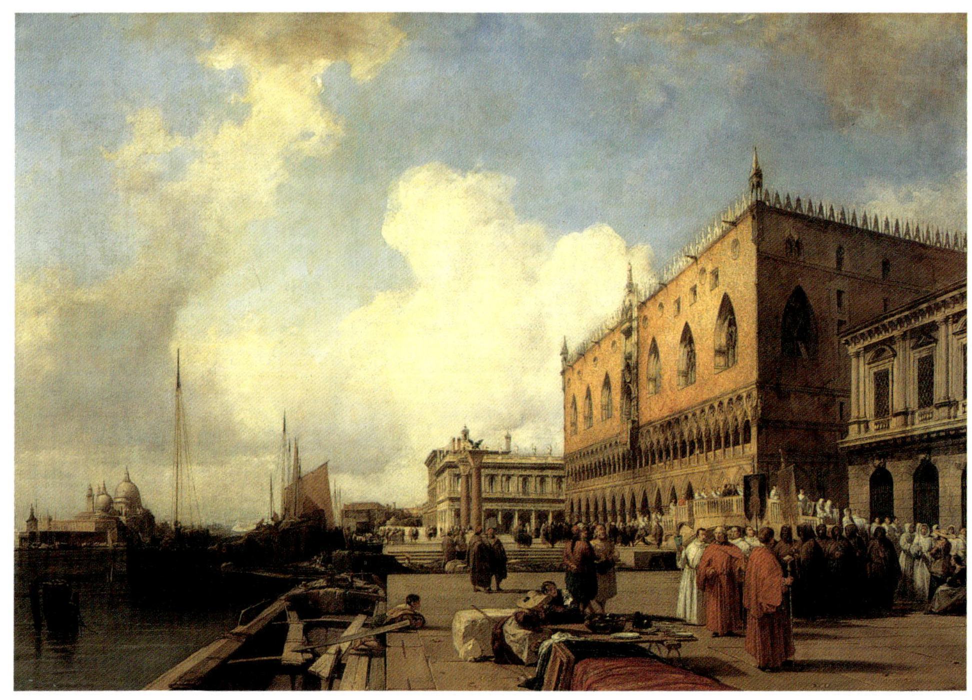

Allan Cunningham found "a painful precision about Canaletto – a disagreeable slavishness of fidelity… [whereas] Bonington had not half of his minute precision, and yet he had too much; but his brilliant and poetical colouring threw a lustre over these mechanical over-accuracies".[2] sw

1 Quoted by Patrick Noon in *Richard Parkes Bonington: 'On the Pleasure of Painting'*, New Haven, Yale Center for British Art, 1991, p.72.
2 *The Lives of the Most Eminent British Painters and Sculptors*, 1832 (revised edition, London 1879, II, p.336).

125 Richard Parkes Bonington

Church of the Gesuati, Venice

Watercolour over pencil, ca. 1827
11 × 7¾ ins (28.0 × 19.7 cm)
Signed lower right: RPB
City of Nottingham Museums, Castle Museum and Art Gallery

Having met the challenge of freshly rendering the great set-pieces of Venice's architecture, Bonington discovered in her side streets and minor canals the infinite picturesque compositions that were to prove bread and butter for a generation of topographical painters.

This superb bravura sketch is far removed from Canaletto's vision of Venice, but its innate romanticism may serve to explain the impression made on many early nineteenth-century visitors familiar with the city chiefly through Canaletto's images. One writer, Antoine Valéry, used the two artists' work to express a typical reaction: "The paintings of Canaletto have so familiarised us with the harbour, the squares, and monuments of Venice that when we penetrate into the city itself, it appears as if already known to us. Bonington, an English artist of melancholy cast, has painted some new views of Venice, in which is most perfectly sketched its present state of desolation; these, compared with those of the Venetian painter, resemble the picture of a woman still beautiful, but worn down by age and misfortune."[1] sw

1 *Voyages historiques et littéraires en Italie*, Paris 1831 (translated 1839); quoted by Patrick Noon in *Richard Parkes Bonington: 'On the Pleasure of Painting'*, New Haven, Yale Center for British Art, 1991.

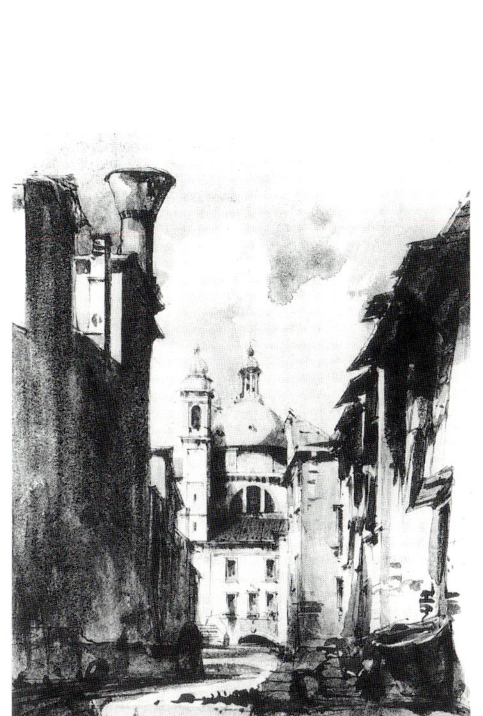

126 Richard Parkes Bonington

The Pont des Arts and Ile de la Cité, Paris, from the Quai du Louvre

Black, red and brown chalk with bodycolour on blue-grey paper, ca. 1828
14 × 20 ins (35.5 × 50.7 cm)
Inscribed, on an old label: Bonington / Paris – the last production of Bonington
Birmingham Museums and Art Gallery

Although not quite the last drawing from Bonington's hand, this expansive study is certainly very late, and has been mooted as the possible first step towards a series of Paris views perhaps commissioned for engraving.

His consummate skill in capturing local colour and atmosphere, as well as architectural detail, in such sketches of Paris was sadly destined never to be transformed into major works that would rival the brilliant Venetian subjects of 1826–27. Nevertheless, this panoramic view dominated by the sweeping curve of the bridge falls into a tradition of urban view-painting invigorated by Canaletto's first views of the new Westminster Bridge. sw

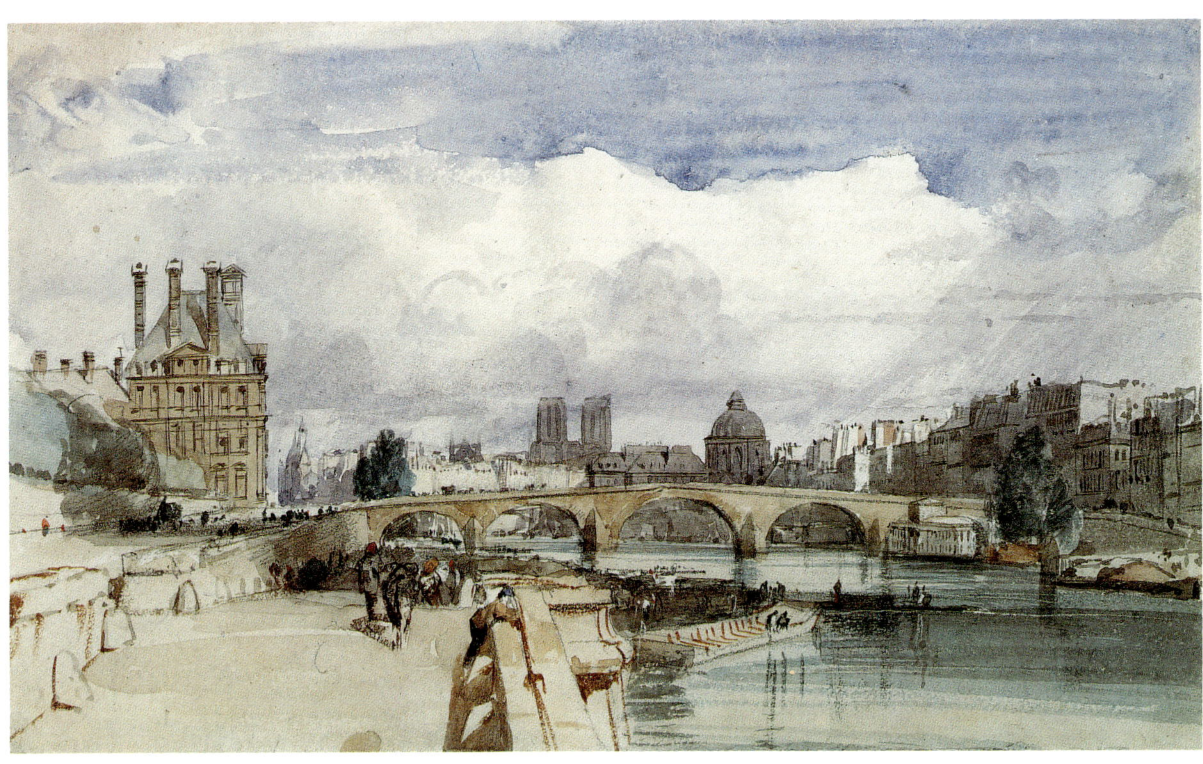

127 Thomas Shotter Boys
1803–1874

Le Pont Royal, Paris

Watercolour, 1830
$5\frac{5}{16} \times 9\frac{1}{2}$ ins (14.3 × 24.1 cm)
Yale Center for British Art (Paul Mellon
Collection), New Haven

Boys produced two of the finest sets of
topographical prints done by a British
artist in the nineteenth century, a series of
coloured lithographs entitled *Picturesque
Architecture in Paris, Ghent, Antwerp, Rouen*
issued in 1839 and another consisting of
twenty-six lithographs coloured by hand
of *Original Views of London as It Is* which
appeared in 1842. In both series Boys por-
trays his subjects with an immediacy of
effect and visual acuity which convey an
especially vivid and fresh impression of the
places he depicts. Like his watercolours
they combine a sensitive eye for the topographical particularities of a place with
specific qualities of light and atmosphere
that give each scene a visually spontaneous
impact. In his prints as well as his watercolours Boys successfully reconciles the
requirements of traditional topography
with the more sensational values the nineteenth century introduced. The accuracy of
his drawing and observation owed much
to his initial training as an engraver (he
was apprenticed in 1817 to George Cooke
who produced some notable plates reproducing paintings and watercolours by
Turner, among others), while his watercolour technique was learned from Richard
Parkes Bonington whom he knew in Paris
where he lived from the mid–1820s until
1837. Watercolours like *Le Pont Royal, Paris*
clearly reveal an awareness of the earlier
views of the city Thomas Girtin had done
(especially a series of etched outlines in
which the influence of the eighteenth-
century topographical tradition is most
strongly present) as well as of Bonington's
vivid technique. His works of the 1830s
show how nineteenth-century painters
extended and reinvigorated the art of topography. Here, the general composition of
the view and the suggestion of detail on
the buildings drawn in with a deftly handled brush-point look back by way of Bonington (to whom this watercolour was
previously ascribed) and Girtin ultimately
to the kind of topography that had
developed in the eighteenth century. ML

SELECTED BIBLIOGRAPHY

Canaletto

Katherine Baetjer and J.G. Links, *Canaletto*, exhibition catalogue, New York, The Metropolitan Museum of Art, 1989

Alessandro Bettagno *et al.*, *Canaletto: Disegni, dipinti, incisioni*, exhibition catalogue, Venice, Fondazione Giorgio Cini, 1982

Ruth Bromberg, *Canaletto's Etchings*, revised edition San Francisco 1993

David Buttery, 'Canaletto at Warwick', *Burlington Magazine* CXXIX, July 1987, pp.437–45

David Buttery, *Canaletto and Warwick Castle*, Chichester 1992

W.G. Constable (revised J.G. Links), *Canaletto*, 2 vols, Oxford 1976; 3rd edition with supplement by J.G. Links, Oxford 1989

Jane Dacey, 'A note on Canaletto's views of Greenwich', *Burlington Magazine* CXXIII, August 1981, pp.485–87

Elizabeth Einberg, *Manners and Morals. Hogarth and British Painting 1700–1760*, exhibition catalogue, London, Tate Gallery, 1987

Elizabeth Einberg, *Canaletto: The Old Horse Guards from St. James's Park c. 1749*, Tate Gallery Publications 1992

Hilda F. Finberg, 'Canaletto in England', *Walpole Society* IX, pp.21–76; X, Supplement

Francis Haskell, *Patrons and Painters: A Study in the Relations Between Italian Art and Society in the Age of the Baroque*, London 1963; revised edition, New Haven and London 1980

John Hayes, 'Parliament Street and Canaletto's Views of Whitehall', *Burlington Magazine* C, October 1958, pp.341–49

Gervase Jackson-Stops (ed.), *The Treasure Houses of Britain. Five Hundred Years of Private Patronage and Art Collecting*, exhibition catalogue, Washington, National Gallery of Art, 1986

Michael Levey, *The Eighteenth Century Italian Schools*, National Gallery Catalogues, London, 1956; revised edition, London 1971

Michael Levey, *Canaletto: Paintings in the Collection of Her Majesty the Queen*, London 1964

J.G. Links, *Canaletto and his patrons*, London 1977

J.G. Links, 'Canaletto and Old Westminster. A city in the making', *Apollo*, May 1992, pp.280–87

L. Lippincott, *Selling Art in Georgian London: The Rise of Arthur Pond*, London 1983

Christopher Lloyd, *A King's Purchase. King George III and the Collection of Consul Smith*, exhibition catalogue, London, The Queen's Gallery (Buckingham Palace), 1993

Oliver Millar and Charlotte Millar, *Canaletto. Paintings & Drawings*, exhibition catalogue, London, The Queen's Gallery (Buckingham Palace), 1980

Hugh Phillips, *The Thames about 1750*, London 1951

Harley Preston, *London and the Thames. Paintings of Three Centuries*, exhibition catalogue, London,

National Maritime Museum (at Somerset House), 1977

Nicholas Ross, *Canaletto*, London 1993

R.J.B. Walker, *Old Westminster Bridge: The Bridge of Fools*, 1979

Malcolm Warner (ed.), *The Image of London: Views by Travellers and Emigrés 1550–1920*, exhibition catalogue, London, Barbican Art Gallery, 1987

English Painters

Martin Hardie, *Watercolour Painting in Britain*, 3 vols, London 1966–68

Louis Hawes, *Presences of Nature. British Landscape 1780–1830*, New Haven, Yale Center for British Art, 1982

Luke Herrmann, *British Landscape Painting of the Eighteenth Century*, London 1973

Lindsay Stainton, *British Landscape Watercolours 1600–1860*, exhibition catalogue, London, British Museum, 1985

Christopher White, *English Landscape 1630–1850*, exhibition catalogue, New Haven, Yale Center for British Art, 1977

William T. Whitley, *Artists and their Friends in England 1700–1799*, 2 vols, London 1928

Ellis Waterhouse, *Painting in Britain 1550–1790*, 4th edition, Harmondsworth 1978

Ellis Waterhouse, *Dictionary of British 18th Century Painters*, Woodbridge 1981

See also citations in the notes to individual catalogue entries

INDEX OF ARTISTS AND PATRONS

Page nos. in *italics* indicate an illustration; page nos. in **bold** indicate a catalogue entry

Ackermann, Rudolph 160, 181
Adam, William 132
Alexander, William 108, **161–62**, 181
Amigoni, Carlotta 34
Amigoni, Jacopo 10–11, 34–5, 44, 57, *102*
Arne, Thomas 147

Banks, Sir Joseph 135, 138
Barnard, Bishop William 72
Bartolozzi, Francesco 43
Baudin, Joseph 37, 39–40, 60
Beaufort, Duke of 18
Beaumont, Sir George 148
Bedford, John Russell 4th Duke of 15, 38
Bellotto, Bernardo 29n, 56, 112, 139
Bellucci, Antonio 11, 33
Berardi, Fabio 44
Bickham, George 105, 106
Blackford, John 72
Boitard, Louis-Philippe 39–40
Bonington, Richard Parkes 115, 182–83, 185, **186–87**, 188
Bowles, John 42–43
Bowles, Thomas 44, 106, 131
Boydell, John 40, 44–45, 138
Boys, Thomas Shotter **188**
Brand, Thomas 96
Brindley, John 41–42, 50, 64, 110
Britton, John 181
Brooke, Lord see Warwick
Brown, Lancelot 'Capability' 82, 85
Buck, Samuel and Nathaniel 36, 40, 43
Buckler, John Chessell 153
Burdett, Peter 138

Burlington, Richard Boyle 3rd Earl of 33, 133
Busiri, Giambattista 40
Byrne, William 43, 148
Byron, George Gordon 6th Baron 115, 176, 183

Canal, Antonio or Canaletto *passim*
Canal, Bernardo 11–12, 56–57
Canot, J.S. 44
Carlevaris, Luca 12, 31, *31*, 38, 56
Carlisle, Earl of 31, 38
Cavendish, Lord James 40
Chandos, James Brydges 1st Duke of 33
Chesterfield, Earl of 57
Cimaroli, Giovanni Battista 11, *58*, 58
Clowes, B. 44
Conduitt, John 13
Constable, John 115–16, *116*
Conti, Stefano 28n, 56
Cooke, George 188
Cotman, John Sell 108, **180**
Crewe, John 22, 57
Cumberland, Duke of 132, 134
Cunningham, Allan 182

Dayes, Edward 22, 167–68, 172–73
de la Warr, Lord 88
Dicker, Samuel 25, 44, 96
Donowell, John **147**

Edelinck, Nicolas 34
Edwards, Edward 111, 131
Egerton, Samuel 63
Essex, Countess of 15
Etheridge, William 50

Faber, John II 39

Farington, Joseph 108–09, 148, **149–51**
Fisher, Bishop John 116
Fletcher, Henry 40
Foster, Myles Birket 185
Fountayne, Rev. and Mrs 155
Fourdrinier, Pierre *51*
Fuseli, Henry 158

Gainsborough, Thomas 36, *36*, 110
Garrick, David 142
George I, King 33
George II, King 34, 70
George III, King 14, 16, 24, 57
Ghezzi, Pier Leone 160
Gilpin, Sawrey 126
Girtin, Thomas 22, 106–09, 112, 149–50, 156, **167–72**, 188
Goldoni, Carlo 15
Goldsmiths' Company 21, 72, 74, 77
Grenville, George 15
Greville, Charles 24, 106, 138–39
Greville, Francis see Warwick
Guardi, Francesco 32, 183
Gwynne, John 153

Hamilton, Sir William 102
Handel, George Frederic 33, 147
Harding, Francis 37, 111
Harris, James 105
Hayman, Francis 35
Haytley, Edward 36, 110, *110*
Hearne, Thomas 108, **148–49**, 168, 172–73, 181
Henderson, John 107–09, 167, 170–72, 175
Herbert, William 44
Hill, Samuel 15, 38, 56, 62–63
Hill, Thomas 16, 68
Hincliffe, John 57
Hoare, Sir Richard 94

Hogarth, William 20–21, 28, 33–35, 39–40, 106, 110, 125
Holland, James **182–85**
Hollar, Wenceslaus 36
Hollis, Thomas 25, 57, 91, 96
Hulett, James 95
Hunt, William Henry 109

Jal, Auguste 186
James, William (W.) 106, 111–12, **130–31**
Jarvis, J. 44
Joli, Antonio 11, 33, 48–49, 51, 57, **102–03**, 111, 128
Jure, John 51

King, James 51
King, 4th Baron 26, 99, 100, 180
Knapton, John and Paul 40
Knighton, Sir William 181
Knights of the Order of the Bath 57, 88
Knyff, Leendert 36

Labelye, Charles 47, 94
Lambert, George 36, 44–45
Lascelles, Edward 172
Laurie & Whittle 106
Lediard, Thomas 47
Leeds, 4th Duke of 15
Leicester, Earl of 60
Lincoln, Lord 39
Lobkowicz, Prince 18, 57, 103

Macartney, George 1st Earl 162
McSwiney, Owen 11–16, 56–58, 60, 68
Malton, Thomas the Elder 156
Malton, Thomas the Younger 22, 43, 147, 153, **156–59**, 164, 172
Manchester, Charles Montagu 4th Earl and 1st Duke of 30–32
Mann, Sir Horace 112, 139

INDEX OF PLACES DEPICTED